THE GOD WHO JUSTIFIES

THE GOD WHO JUSTIFIES

JAMES R. WHITE

Cover design by Eric Walljasper

Scripture credits are located on page 395.

Published by Bethany House Publishers
A Ministry of Bethany Fellowship International
11400 Hampshire Avenue South
Bloomington, Minnesota 55438
www.bethanyhouse.com

Printed in the United States of America

Library of Congress Cataloging-in-Publication Data

White, James R. (James Robert), 1962–
The God who justifies : a comprehensive study of the doctrine of justification / by James R. White.
p. cm.
Includes bibliographical references and index.
ISBN 0-7642-2288-0 (alk. paper)
1. Justification. 2. Justification—Biblical teaching. 3. Bible. N.T. Epistles—Criticism, interpretation, etc. I. Title.
BT764.3 .W47 2001
234'.7—dc21

2001001255

This work is dedicated with Christian love and honor to some of my closest brothers in the Lord who have been so instrumental in encouraging me in the path of righteousness. Christian brothers are a gift from God, so with heartfelt thanks I dedicate this work to:

Brick Darrow,
a brother whose constancy in faith challenges and encourages me;

George Soto,
my truly powerful brother in Christ;

Michael Porter,
to whom I am often the student;

Warren Smith,
my long lost younger brother and dear friend;

Michael O'Fallon,
whose dedication and selfless service to Christ inspire all who know him;

David King,
my dear fellow minister in the gospel;

Colin Smith,
my British brother, Phil Keaggy fan, and everyday encourager;

&

My fellow elders Don Cross and Don Fry,
with whom I share the call of the gospel at the Phoenix Reformed Baptist Church.

BHP Books by James R. White

The Forgotten Trinity
The God Who Justifies
Grieving: Our Path Back to Peace
Is the Mormon My Brother?
The King James Only Controversy
Letters to a Mormon Elder
Mary—Another Redeemer?
The Roman Catholic Controversy
*What's With the Dudes at the Door?**
*What's With the Mutant in the Microscope?**

Do you have comments? Please address them to:

Alpha and Omega Ministries
P.O. Box 37106
Phoenix, AZ 85069

Visit our Web page at http://www.aomin.org
for information about Mormonism, Jehovah's Witnesses,
Roman Catholicism, and General Apologetics, and
listings of debates, tapes, tracts, etc.

*with Kevin Johnson

JAMES WHITE is the author of several acclaimed books, including *The King James Only Controversy* and *The Forgotten Trinity*. He is an elder of the Phoenix Reformed Baptist Church, director of Alpha and Omega Ministries—a Christian apologetics organization, an adjunct professor with Golden Gate Baptist Theological Seminary, and professor of apologetics with Columbia Evangelical Seminary. He and his family live in Phoenix.

Contents

INTRODUCTION

A Neglected Yet Vital Issue

Throughout the history of what is called the Christian church there has been a constant desire on the part of some to "return to the simplicity and purity of the apostolic era." Many today seek to rid themselves of the trappings of the modern church and return to what they seem to believe was a "golden age" of the church, a time when apostles walked the earth and proclaimed with authority the truth of God in Jesus Christ.

Yet when we take time to consider the writings of those apostles, we discover that their ministry was hardly one of ease and simplicity. In fact, the letters they wrote, primarily preserved for us in the writings of Paul, reveal a situation that is hauntingly like what we experience today. They struggled with difficulties in the church that ran the gamut from personal bickering, gossiping, and slander, to sin in the camp, strife between parties, and jealousy among church leaders (what we would call today "church politics"). But most telling is the constant struggle the apostles themselves faced with false teachers. Heresy, a word that seemingly has fallen out of the modern church lexicon, was a constant concern for John, Peter, Luke, and Paul.

Immediately the Christian with a finger on the pulse of most of contemporary Christendom senses a "disconnect" at this point. Heresy, false teaching, false doctrine—such seem so "out of touch" with the modern day, for they assume the one thing our culture has been so adamant on denying: objective standards of morality and truth. No one can be seeker-friendly while clashing openly and directly with the main pillar of cultural orthodoxy: subjectivism ("My truth is cool, yours is too '-ism' "). The church that unashamedly tells people "This is truth, what you embrace is error. Repent and believe the gospel" is immediately consigned to the trash heap of the old ways that no longer work. Such a fellowship might as well hang a sign out front: "Proud Member of the Church Shrinkage Movement."

But the disconnect only widens when one considers the topics that occupied the minds of the early Christian leaders. When you simply look at the amount of text produced by Paul and Peter and John and James, and divide it up by topic, what seemed most important to them? The dreaded *t* word, theology, appears immediately, along with the *d* word, doctrine. Doctrines like the deity of Christ, the Resurrection, and most importantly, the gospel, along with the attendant beliefs in sin, repentance, justification, and adoption into the family of God, are what form the backbone of the apostolic message. From these truths come the exhortations to godly living, honoring God in our behavior, actions, and thoughts, and loving our fellow believers in the fellowship of the Spirit. Conspicuous by their absence are passages about self-fulfillment and all other such modern buzzwords and phrases that pack seminars and sell videos.

The apostle Paul's constant emphasis on foundational truths that are not, in and of themselves, attractive to the seeker has caused many a theologian to question Paul's balance and, hence, his authority. And this comes out with the strongest clarity when considering the combined testimony of his letters to the church in Rome and to the churches of Galatia. In these two letters Paul emphasizes the doctrine of justification with such frequency and regularity that no one can miss his point. He believes this doctrine is at the very heart of the gospel and that when one denies or compromises on this vital point, the gospel itself is lost! So "narrow" is his view that he insists that those who disagree with him on this topic are not truly Christians! Such strident speaking is surely out of step with today's politically correct way of thinking.

There was a time not so long ago when most in the church believed it was necessary for Christians to be as "narrow" as the apostle Paul. They shared with him the belief that there is one divine truth, revealed by God, and that people are subject to that truth regardless of their own personal feelings about the subject. Of course some believed God had revealed this truth in ways outside Scripture alone; this precipitated the great battle of the Reformation. But even then, the battle lines drawn on both sides were created by those who believed the issues truly were important. Those who still agree today find themselves in a vast minority. This book is for that minority.

THOSE WHO FORGET THE PAST . . .

We stand on the shoulders of giants. Modern Christians owe so much to those loyal men and women who sacrificed to give us a wonderful heritage and whose lives are such a testimony to God's faithfulness to His people. Sadly, for many in the church today, church history extends back twenty, fifty, maybe a hundred years. The idea that God has been slowly, patiently building His church through many centuries is encouraging to the believer, especially when it is coupled with the recognition that God uses very flawed people—like us! But so many today miss out on the benefit of knowing about God's faithfulness over time because they simply ignore the study of church history altogether.

Frequently this situation results in the contemporary church making the same mistakes over again—not learning from history tends to cause us to reinvent the wheel on a nearly generational basis. There are historical issues that are *directly* related to the purity of the church and to the gospel of Jesus Christ that have been addressed in the past by godly believers with great insight and understanding. The Reformation showed quite clearly what those matters were. The most basic was that of *sola scriptura,* the doctrine that the Bible, and the Bible alone, is the sole infallible rule of faith for the church. What we believe must be founded on the Bible alone, *and all of the Bible,* or it is not truly Christian.

Not only this, but the traditions of the church, no matter how important we may feel them to be, are *not* equal in authority with the inspired words of Scripture. Christians look to the Bible as their single infallible source of authority and truth. From this principle of *sola scriptura* came what might be called the central *material* doctrine of the Reformation: justification by faith. When Scripture was allowed to speak with its full voice, the doctrine of God's free and gracious justification of sinful men based upon the completed work of Jesus Christ upon the cross of Calvary stood in stark contrast to the teaching of mediaeval Catholicism, a doctrine based upon human action, meritorious works, indulgences, and penance. J. I. Packer, in his fine introductory essay to James Buchanan's work *The Doctrine of Justification,* wrote,

> Martin Luther described the doctrine of justification by faith as *articulus stantis vel cadentis ecclesiae*—the article of faith that decides whether the church is standing or falling. By this he meant that when this doctrine is understood, believed, and preached, as it was in New Testament times, the church stands in the grace of God and is alive; but where it is neglected, overlaid, or denied, as it was in mediaeval Catholicism, the church falls from grace and its life drains away, leaving it in a state of darkness and death. The reason why the Reformation happened, and Protestant churches came into being, was that Luther and his fellow Reformers believed completely in this respect that no faithful Christian could with a good conscience continue within her ranks.[1]

If the health of the church can be measured by how often and with what devotion and gratitude she speaks of justification, then

---

[1]J. I. Packer in James Buchanan, *The Doctrine of Justification* (Banner of Truth Trust, 1984), vii.

it would seem that not all is well in our day. How often we talk of prophecy, how we receive the "blessings of God" in a material sense, end-times speculations, and what new political topic or movement we are supposed to be involved in tells us nothing positive about the church. But when Christians are continually thankful for and amazed at the grace of God that has brought them into a state where they stand righteous before God, clothed in the righteousness of Jesus Christ, then it can be safely said that those Christians, and therefore the church, are thinking properly and are concentrating on the important issues.

What happens when the doctrine of justification is ignored or downplayed? Here again the modern disinterest in matters historical rears its head, for history gives clear answer to this question. One need only look to the Roman Catholic system in the year 1517 to see what happens when the gospel itself, as expressed in Paul's clear and unambiguous doctrine of justification by faith, is smothered under layer after layer of tradition and error. People are enslaved to a system of penances and works, and the blessed peace that God promised to the believer is nowhere to be found.

Nothing has changed over time. Today the very same question of justification must be dealt with. To ignore it is not an option, for even to attempt to do so is in itself a decision against the biblical position. The guiding principles of the Reformation are again under attack, and the de-protestantization of Protestantism continues at a fast pace. Many today are honestly asking the question "Why should there be a split in the church? Why not go back to Rome?" And many are doing just that, for the "Protestant" denominations in which they find themselves are no longer truly Protestant—that is, they have jettisoned *sola scriptura*, and it is sure that justification by faith will inevitably follow behind.

The God Who Justifies is meant to call believers to a fresh appreciation of, understanding of, and dedication to the great doctrine of justification. It is my thesis that there is no understanding (let alone proclaiming!) the gospel of Jesus Christ without a firm understanding of this divine declaration whereby God the Father declares us right with Him by virtue of what Christ has done for us and our faith in Him. The weaker our knowledge of justification, the less clear and powerful will be our gospel preaching.

This work does not seek to impress anyone other than the believer who desires to know what God has said in His Word. The first eight chapters are meant to explain, exhort, and at times preach with passion the truth of justification. The remaining chapters present the exegetical basis for the proclamation already given. The depth of exegesis will depend directly upon the relevance of the passage being examined and how central it is in the battle over justification. Therefore, Romans 3–4 have lengthy exegetical chapters with more detailed discussion of issues relating to grammar, lexical information, syntax, etc., for these topics are necessary in establishing the truth. The same is true for the chapter on James 2:14–26. Other passages that are not as central receive less in-depth examination. The goal throughout is to provide the believer with a solid basis upon which to trust in the divine work of justification in his or her own life, and then to give bold confidence in the proclamation of this truth in the face of the many religious systems that deny it.

CHAPTER 1

The Heart of the Gospel

God is wise; His wisdom appears on every page of the sacred Scriptures. The Bible's balance, insight, compelling truthfulness in describing the human condition—all these speak to the redeemed heart as weighty evidence of its divine origin. But even though all Scripture is God-breathed and profitable, still we find certain sections, sometimes chapters or paragraphs or verses, that capture the imagination in an uncommon fashion. These are special treasures of the Spirit, hidden away to satisfy the souls of God's people throughout the ages. One such pearl of great price is found in the prophecy of Isaiah 6:

> **6:1** In the year of King Uzziah's death, I [Isaiah] saw the sovereign master seated on a high, elevated throne. The hem of his robe filled the temple. **6:2** Seraphs stood over him; each one had six wings. With two wings they covered their faces, with two they covered their feet, and they used the remaining two to fly. **6:3** They called out to one another, "The Lord who

> leads armies has absolute sovereign authority! His majestic splendor fills the entire earth!" **6:4** The sound of their voices shook the door frames, and the temple was filled with smoke.

The vision of the mighty Yahweh sitting upon His throne cannot help but stop the ever-wandering mind of the reader and focus one's attention. The person who believes heaven to be his destiny cannot help but wonder what it is like, and but a scarce few times Scripture draws aside the curtain of eternity and allows us a scintillating glimpse. Here Isaiah sees, hears, and feels the awesome power of worship at the very throne itself. The created angels, enveloped in worship, cry out to one another in ceaseless recognition of the wondrous power of God. Creatures in no danger of forgetfulness remind one another of God's majestic splendor, for His grandeur is so overwhelming it can only be stated, not described. Their words are so powerful they shake the firmest portions of the temple, and the vision is obscured by smoke.

> **6:5** I said, "Too bad for me! I am destroyed, for my lips are contaminated by sin, and I live among people whose lips are contaminated by sin. My eyes have seen the king, the Lord who leads armies." **6:6** But then one of the seraphs flew toward me. In his hand was a hot coal he had taken from the altar with tongs. **6:7** He touched my mouth with it and said, "Look, this coal has touched your lips. Your evil is removed; your sin is forgiven."

The prophet is overwhelmed by the vision. The holiest man in Israel sees his unholiness in the light of a holiness not of this earth. He is unclean, contaminated by sin, unfit to stand, kneel, lie, or grovel before the throne of Him who defines holiness. Isaiah says he is destroyed, undone, because he senses his sinfulness in his speech as well as in his association with a sinful people, Israel. He knows that only perfect eyes can look upon the King, the Lord of Hosts. He never thinks of how he is relatively "better" than others. He makes no excuses. No alibi exists in the presence of perfect holiness. He knows his sin, and he knows he is vile in God's sight.

The gospel of Jesus Christ speaks *only* yet *fully* to the heart that understands Isaiah's cry. Just as God provided cleansing for Isaiah through the ministration of one of the seraphs and a burning, cleansing coal from off the holy altar, so God has provided through the work of Jesus Christ the perfect solution to the heart that aches and cries "I am destroyed! I am sinful! I am undone!" The deepest longing of the sin-burdened heart is found in the message of the cross of Christ.

Yet there were in the days of Isaiah so many in his land who had no understanding at all of what he experienced when he saw the Lord. Hardened, cold hearts do not cry out upon seeing the Holy God. Self-righteous ones, untouched by the presence of their own sin, only look with disdain upon those under conviction. Indeed, they may well reproach such people, finding them to be overly sensitive or simply lacking in discernment and sense. Or, as is so often the case, the religiously calloused merely point you to their rites or ordinances, for by them they have salved their own consciences into a comatose silence. "Just have faith in this observance, apply this remedy by engaging in this act of self-denial, and all will be well." They cannot understand how the truth of a person's sin, when it is (by grace) recognized, is like a razor-sharp sword that cuts through all the manmade barriers of religiosity, piercing directly to the heart, the soul, the mind. All the pious acts of humanity cannot rescue Isaiah and all who like him cry "I am undone!" from the conviction of sin. Isaiah found no solace in the offerings he had brought to the altar or in his standing as a child of Abraham. No, he found cleansing *solely* in the act of God.

By God's grace, Isaiah was neither the first nor the last to be offered the chance of seeing himself in the light of God's glorious holiness and thereby to experience true repentance and loathing of his sin. Yes, such is a gracious opportunity extended to men by God. God could justly allow people to continue in their self-delusion and self-righteousness. And it is true that seeing one's sin as it truly is can be a self-shattering experience. But *to be healed one must first be shattered*, and Isaiah, along with godly men and women before and after, experienced this, to his benefit. Scripture records this occurrence in the lives of prophets, kings, and apostles, and outside of Scripture we find eloquent testimony to the continuing work of God's Spirit in opening blind eyes to see the true condition of the human heart. One cannot help but see the results of this ongoing blessing of God upon His people in the words of the unnamed early Christian writer, sometimes called "Mathetes," who wrote to Diognetius:

> But when our wickedness had reached its height, and it had been clearly shown that its reward, punishment and death, was impending over us; and when the time had come which God had before appointed for manifesting His own kindness and power, how the one love of God, through exceeding regard for men, did not regard us with hatred, nor thrust us away, nor remember our iniquity against us, but showed great long-suffering, and bore with us. He Himself took on Him the burden of our iniquities, He gave His own Son as a ransom for us, the holy One for transgressors, the blameless One for the wicked, the righteous One for the unrighteous, the incorruptible One for the corruptible, the immortal One for them that are mortal. For what other thing was capable of covering our sins than His righteousness? By what other one was it possible that we, the wicked and ungodly, could be justified, than by the only Son of God? O sweet exchange! O unsearchable operation! O benefits surpassing all expectation! that the wickedness of many should be hid in a single righteous One, and that the righteousness of One should justify many transgressors! Having therefore convinced us in the former time that our nature was unable to attain to life, and having now revealed the Savior who is able to save even those things which it was [formerly] impossible to save, by both these facts He desired to lead us to trust in His kindness, to esteem Him our Nourisher, Father, Teacher, Counselor, Healer, our Wisdom, Light, Honor, Glory, Power, and Life.[1]

One finds similar sentiments in Augustine's searching of his own soul, not only in his *Confessions* but in his letters as well. Yet in our modern era another name has been connected with that shattering recognition of God's holiness and human guilt, a name

[1]Mathetes to Diognetius, 9.

that speaks good or evil depending on one's religious affiliations. One man's struggle with sin, within the context of the predominant religious structure of his time, led to a veritable revolution, one that continues to this day despite the opposition of most of contemporary culture. The monk of Wittenberg, the professor of theology who enjoyed discussing spiritual topics over beer and pretzels, was forced into his life of Reformer by an Isaiah-like conviction of his own sinfulness in the light of an unshakable conviction of the utter holiness of God. R. C. Sproul has described it as Luther's insanity,[2] his soul-shaking, heart-wrenching knowledge that the God who punishes does so justly and rightly and that he, Luther, is the proper object of God's wrath. The story is well known to students of history, but not so well known anymore as to preclude its repetition.

Luther's first problem was that he was a lawyer. Such study convinced him of the necessity and intrinsic rightness of law. God's law, then, by definition would be the highest and greatest standard, binding upon every human being, relentless in its pursuit of any lawbreaker. Unlike a human judge, God, the divine Judge, could not in any way fudge on the holy standard. The law had to be applied to perfection, for God himself is perfect. Luther's training imprinted his thinking with the awesome *weight* of law and of guilt when that law is spurned, and it forged in him an unbreakable link between the holiness and power of the Lawgiver and the law itself.

Luther's second problem was that he was foolish enough to go outside during a terrifying thunderstorm. When lightning struck close to him during a downpour in July of 1505, he fell to his face and, convinced his life was about to end, cried out to the patron saint of miners (his father's trade), "Help me, St. Anne, I'll become a monk!" Of course, Luther did not die, but he did feel he had made a vow he could not break. He took oaths seriously, and he feared the judgment of God (even more than the wrath of his parents) if he were to renege on his promise.

And so Luther entered upon monastic life as an Augustinian.

---

[2]R. C. Sproul, *The Holiness of God* (Tyndale, 1986), 99ff.

He chose a strict order, one whose rules reflected the overpowering force of the law of God in miniature. And here the revolution began, for the walls of the monastery only reminded the young monk of the walls that bound him in his sin. As he sought God's favor through confession, penance, and sacrifice, he found his condition worsened, not bettered. The more he chanted and prayed and fasted, the more he was convinced of the holiness of God and of his own sinfulness. His own words speak of his inward suffering:

> I was indeed a pious monk and kept the rules of my order so strictly that I can say: If ever a monk gained heaven through monkery, it should have been I. All my monastic brethren who knew me will testify to this. I would have martyred myself to death with fasting, praying, reading, and other good works had I remained a monk much longer.[3]
>
> As a monk I lived an irreproachable life. Nevertheless I felt that I was a sinner before God. My conscience was restless, and I could not depend on God being propitiated by my satisfactions. Not only did I not love, but I actually hated the righteous God who punishes sinners.[4]

Luther's legally oriented mind could not escape the relentless necessity of *punishment.* The power and might of God demanded punishment for sin, and there seemed no escape.

> Do you not know that God dwells in light inaccessible? We weak and ignorant creatures want to probe and understand the incomprehensible majesty of the unfathomable light of the wonder of God. We approach; we prepare ourselves to approach. What wonder then that his majesty overpowers us and shatters![5]

This led to one of the most famous incidents in church history. Scholars differ on the details, but all are agreed that it took place when Luther attempted to offer his first Mass. Schooled in

---

[3]As cited by Hans Hillerbrand, *The Reformation* (Baker, 1987), 24.
[4]Ibid., 27.
[5]As cited by Roland Bainton, *Here I Stand* (Abingdon Press, 1978), 43.

mediaeval Roman Catholic theology, unaware of the relative newness of the concept of transubstantiation,[6] even Brother Luther believed firmly that he was about to perform a miracle and stand in the very presence of God. When he came to a particular point in the liturgy, he froze. As he later recounted the experience,

> At these words I was utterly stupefied and terror-stricken. I thought to myself, "With what tongue shall I address such Majesty, seeing that all men ought to tremble in the presence of even an earthly prince? Who am I, that I should lift up mine eyes or raise my hands to the divine Majesty. The angels surround him. At his nod the earth trembles. And shall I, a miserable little pygmy, say 'I want this, I ask for that'? For I am dust and ashes and full of sin and I am speaking to the living, eternal and true God."[7]

It was this deep sense of the holiness and power of God that compelled Luther into his reluctant role as Reformer. In our complex era it may seem almost simplistic, but to his mind the problem was clear: God is holy. Man is sinful. God must, *and will*, punish sin. Luther was sinful. Luther must be punished. All the sacraments and penances he performed were as imperfect as he was: even when he did what the church taught him was "good" he could see the marks of sin upon it. When he fasted, was he not proud? When he confessed, did he not fear and withhold love from God? Could not God *smell* his fear of judgment? How could any of the religious works avail before a perfectly holy God? He felt trapped, hopeless.

But God did not leave the monk of Wittenberg in his state of despair. The very phrase that struck fear in his heart, "the righteousness of God," became the key to his dungeon, for he learned that there is a righteousness of God that is imputed to the sinner by faith, and *faith alone.* The word that had once tormented his soul became the sweet avenue of escape. He could trust not in

---

[6]The early church spoke much of the "real presence" of Christ, but this did not imply or establish the complex, philosophically based idea of transubstantiation, which did not become prevalent until after the turn of the millennium and which was not made a dogma until the Fourth Lateran Council in A.D. 1215.

[7]Bainton, 30.

his own righteousness, which he knew would never avail before God, but in the righteousness of Christ, imputed to him freely by grace. As he would later express it:

> I, Dr. Martin Luther, the unworthy evangelist of the Lord Jesus Christ, thus think and thus affirm:—That this article,—namely, that faith alone, without works, justifies us before God,—can never be overthrown, for . . . Christ alone, the Son of God, died for our sins; but if He alone takes away our sins, then men, with all their works, are to be excluded from all concurrence in procuring the pardon of sin and justification. Nor can I embrace Christ otherwise than by faith *alone*; He cannot be apprehended by works. But if faith, before works follow, apprehends the Redeemer, it is undoubtedly true, that faith *alone*, before works, and without works, appropriates the benefit of redemption, which is no other than justification, or deliverance from sin. This is our doctrine; so the Holy Spirit teaches, and the whole Christian Church. In this, by the grace of God, will we stand fast, Amen![8]

Why did Luther stand so firmly for the truth of justification by faith *alone* without the addition of human merits against the combined force of Rome and State? He knew what every soul that has been freed from the prison of despair knows: Only one key opens that lock; there is only one way out. The soul that continues to cling to works, no matter how penitential or self-effacing, is a soul that has not yet seen its true state. Such a person needs an Isaiah-like experience to confess, "I am undone, a man of unclean lips." Oh, that God would grant such visions to many this day!

BUT WITTENBERG WAS LONG AGO

There are few Luthers today. Isaiah seems passé. Now we medicate and analyze. Luther would be counseled to stop being so hard on himself. Isaiah would not find a wide audience for his message and his confession that he lived among a people of "un-

---

[8]James Buchanan, *Justification* (Banner of Truth, 1984), 129.

clean lips," for such would be contra-indicated by the most current and up-to-date research and polling data. And both would be warned that their views would not be seeker-friendly, since they would involve the discussion of such turn-off subjects as sin, judgment, justice, wrath, and repentance.

Those blessed to experience the crushing recognition of God's holiness and their own sinful state may be tempted to feel more than just a little alone in a modern Western culture where Valium is as likely a refuge for the feeling as is prayerful repentance and the heartfelt seeking of the Savior. Society's constant emphasis upon self-worth coupled with its fervent proclamation of moral relativism ("Sinner? Are you kidding? You're the best you could be!") has resulted in a cultural inoculation against conviction of sin.

The church, reflecting the deep inroads society has made upon it, has adopted new ways of thinking about the gospel that, in reality, are *other* gospels. John Murray saw this process taking place years ago:

> And we all are all wrong with him because we have all sinned and come short of the glory of God. Far too frequently we fail to entertain the gravity of this fact. Hence the reality of our sin and the reality of the wrath of God upon us for our sin do not come into our reckoning. This is the reason why the grand article of justification does not ring the bells in the innermost depths of our spirit. And this is the reason why the gospel of justification is to such an extent a meaningless sound in the world and in the church of the twentieth century. We are not imbued with the profound sense of the reality of God, of his majesty and holiness. And sin, if reckoned with at all, is little more than a misfortune or maladjustment.[9]

Naturalistic materialism (the de facto religion of Western culture, maintaining that all that exists can be seen, smelled, weighed, or measured, and the supernatural is a fairy tale with no existence) has no place for majesty or grandeur in the spiritual realm, let alone absolute moral standards. Transcendent law and

---

[9]John Murray, *Redemption Accomplished and Applied* (Eerdmans, 1955), 117.

duty are ideas abandoned on the superhighway of modernism. We have simply outgrown such ideas, or so we think.

In any case, a large portion of what is called Protestantism no longer has any way of understanding the very impulses that gave rise to the upheaval known as the Reformation. The children no longer recognize their ancestors, yet they continue to use the same *words* their forefathers used to speak of that defining experience of conviction of sin, repentance, and abandonment to the only One who can save, Jesus Christ. The result is a possibly fatal case of theological schizophrenia: saying one thing, meaning something completely different. Many have pondered the strange spectacle of today's evangelical Protestantism: paying homage to Luther while placating the sin-sick soul with psychological explanations of Spirit-induced melancholy; printing copies of the confessions that came from the Reformation and putting them in the pews while replacing their *content* in the sermon with man-centered teaching that dares not utter the word "repent."

It is my firm conviction that "Protestant" means absolutely, positively *nothing* unless the one wearing the term believes, breathes, lives, and loves the uncompromised, offensive-to-the-natural-man message of justification by God's free grace by faith in Jesus Christ *alone.* As the term has become institutionalized, it has lost its meaning. In the vast majority of instances today a Protestant has no idea what the word itself denotes, what the historical background behind it was, nor why he should really care. And a label that has been divorced from its significance no longer functions in a meaningful fashion. We need a Reformation in our day that will again draw the line clearly between those who embrace the gospel of God's grace in Christ and those who do not. And how one answers the question "How is a man made right with God?" determines whether one embraces that gospel or not.

One of the greatest works on the doctrine of justification came from the pen of the British divine James Buchanan. It first appeared in 1867 and has withstood the test of time since then as a classic volume on the subject. As with every other man of God who has addressed this central topic, Buchanan intimately knew the necessity of spiritual preparation for the proper understanding of justification. His words deserve to be heard once again:

> The best preparation for the study of this doctrine is—neither great intellectual ability, nor much scholastic learning,—but a conscience impressed with a sense of our actual condition as sinners in the sight of God. A deep conviction of sin is the one thing needful in such an inquiry,—a conviction of the fact of sin, as an awful reality in our own personal experience,—of the power of sin, as an inveterate evil cleaving to us continually, and having its roots deep in the innermost recesses of our hearts,—and of the guilt of sin, past as well as present, as an offence against God, which, once committed, can never cease to be true of us individually, and which, however He may be pleased to deal with it, has deserved His wrath and righteous condemnation. Without some such conviction of sin, we may speculate on this, as on any other, part of divine truth, and bring all the resources of our intellect and learning to bear upon it, but can have no suitable sense of our actual danger, and no serious desire for deliverance from it. To study the subject with advantage, we must have a heartfelt interest in it, as one that bears directly on the salvation of our own souls; and this interest can only be felt in proportion as we realize our guilt, and misery, and danger, as transgressors of God's Law. The Law is still, as it was to the Jewish Church, "a schoolmaster to bring us to Christ, that we may be justified by faith"; and the Law must be applied to the conscience, so as to quicken and arouse it, before we can feel our need of salvation, or make any serious effort to attain it. It is the convinced, and not the careless, sinner, who alone will lay to heart, with some sense of its real meaning and momentous importance, the solemn question—"How shall a man be just with God?"
>
> But more than this. As, without some heartfelt conviction of sin, we could have no feeling of personal interest in the doctrine of Justification, such as is necessary to command our serious attention in the study of it, so we should be scarcely capable of understanding, in their full scriptural meaning, the terms in which it is proposed to us, or the testimonies by which alone it can be established. The doctrine of Salvation, which is taught by the Gospel, presupposes the doctrine of

> Sin, which is taught by the Law; and the two together constitute the sum and substance of God's revealed truth. They are distinct, and even different, from each other; but they are so related that, while there may be some knowledge of sin without any knowledge of salvation, there can be no knowledge of salvation without some knowledge of sin. As this is true of the general doctrine of Salvation, which includes deliverance from the power, as well as from the punishment, of sin, so it is equally true of each of its constituent parts,—the special doctrines of Justification and Sanctification,—with this only difference, that, in the one case, we must have some knowledge of sin, in its legal aspect, as guilt already incurred, in the other, of sin, in its spiritual aspect, as an inveterate inherent depravity.[10]

The fact that the above quote from Buchanan is lengthy must not interfere with the tremendous importance of the truth he pronounces, for it is central to the entire thesis of this work. Justification will only hold the place it deserves in the heart of believers when it is placed at the head of the list of divine truths *both* because we are convinced by the weight of Scripture that it rightly holds this position *and* when this conviction is joined by *the personal, intimate, spiritual knowledge of the sinfulness of sin and the tremendous blessing of free and gracious justification.* Without the scriptural testimony we are left with nothing but subjective desires that lack any meaningful answer; without the conviction of sin we are left with cold, doctrinal orthodoxy that leaves the heart untouched and apathetic.

NO CONTROLLING LEGAL AUTHORITY

There is no question that justification sounds a hollow note in the ear of the person who does not experience the convicting work of the Spirit. But why is it that even believers today—those who *have* experienced that work—shy away from speaking to this

[10]Buchanan, *Justification*, 222–23.

fundamental truth of the gravity and weight of sin? Is it merely a matter of laziness or cowardice on the part of professing believers?

Western civilization has undergone a radical alteration in its view of the world, and of man, over the past few centuries. The change has been faster than almost any that has taken place in the past. The religion of naturalistic materialism has so penetrated our culture that few fully realize the extent of its impact upon our thinking, and this includes the thinking of Christians in the church. Evolutionary theory, the heart and soul of the non-Christian worldview, seeks to present man as the complex (yet random) result of a process of chance that has but one guiding principle: natural selection. And while many become lost in the plethora of arguments over the scientific data, one fact must be understood regarding the impact on Christian theology of such a worldview: without a Creator, man is not God's creature. Without a Creator, there is no Lawgiver, and no law. Without a Creator, there is no *sin.* Hence, those who think in accordance with the "traditions of men" in our day (Colossians 2:8) find a fundamental contradiction between the most basic thrust of the gospel (sin separates from God, Christ's death atones for sin) and the most basic affirmation of their worldview: the nonexistence of a purposeful Creator and divine law, and the denial that man is a creature made in the image of God.

The Christian is to seek actively to think in a manner that is pleasing to God. Believers are described as having the mind of Christ (1 Corinthians 2:16), not a mind that is conformed to the world (Romans 12:2). So there is a clash between the way the Word would lead us to think—with Christ as the sum and substance of God's wisdom, the centerpiece of all our thought and action (Colossians 2:3–9)—and the constant pressure of the world to place ourselves at the center of all things. The more we expose ourselves to the influence of the Spirit of God through worship, prayer, and study, the more our thinking is conformed to standards of godliness. But many Christians today will admit that the time they spend in such pursuits is miniscule in comparison with the time spent under the influence of the world. The result is not surprising: the influence of the world overpowers the influence of Scripture, and the gospel is transformed into a message that does not challenge or convict but instead affirms.

We might take an example from the ever-pervasive technology that has become such a part of our lives. Today everything is recorded digitally. When you have a recording of someone speaking you can load it onto an editing program and alter the speed at which the person is speaking, or you can apply any number of filters to remove elements of the soundtrack you don't like. You can enhance the person's voice, add background effects, change all sorts of things. The *filters* determine the outcome. In the same way, the Scriptures teach that the mind set on the flesh has only one possible outcome—death—while the mind set on the Spirit results in life and peace (Romans 8:5–6). There is a fundamental difference between a redeemed, regenerate, Christ-centered mind and a rebellious, spiritually dead, man-centered mind. Both may encounter the same set of facts, but the filtered outcome will vary greatly.

Paul warned Christians against "arguments that sound reasonable" (Colossians 2:4) and those always-present teachers in the church who seek to "captivate you through an empty, deceitful philosophy" that is *not* in harmony with Christ's lordship (Colossians 2:8). Warnings exist for a purpose. Apostles do not waste our time with irrelevancies. In fact, Paul spoke of the "great struggle" he had for Christians in this regard, his large-scale, consuming concern that believers would know the truth. *Thinking clearly and properly is a trait of the solidly grounded believer, and Paul felt it was something every Christian should experience.* We have the mind of Christ, and we are to think in a way that honors Him. This includes working *hard* at resisting the influence of the world's way of thinking.

What happens when Christians who have been deeply influenced by the world attempt to proclaim the gospel in a society bent upon denying God His place as Sovereign, Creator, and Judge? In many instances the specter of pragmatism arises: "Let's find something that *works* and not worry about the details." And so a truncated gospel replaces the biblical one. This new gospel *fits* with the culture: it does not speak of sin, since that implies a law against which man has sinned, and *that* leads inevitably to a lawgiver. It does not speak of repentance for the same reasons. Instead, it seeks out the felt needs of the culture and seeks to tailor a message that adapts. Wrath and anger do not blend, so they are jettisoned. Love becomes preeminent, but not the love of the Bible, which involves holiness, obedience, self-sacrifice, and the like. No, the mantra is that God loves everyone just as they are, no strings attached. Unlike a good parent whose love will seek the best for the child, God's love is reduced to that of a grandparent who rarely even has contact with his grandchild but only showers him with gifts without any thought of his true and lasting welfare. Therefore it can hardly be surprising that justification, a doctrine that speaks of God as Judge and explains sin, wrath, propitiation, faith, forgiveness, and pardon, would become a theological novelty in such a context.

THE HEART OF THE GOSPEL

Justification. The word *should* bring to mind "the gracious act of God the Father through the perfect work of Jesus Christ whereby *I have been pardoned and made right before God!*" It should be a *personal* word, a *thrilling* word, a word filled with rich meaning. For many, by God's grace, it is. And by that same grace, it always will be.

But if we can lay some of the blame for the decline in attention to the very heart of the gospel on an unwillingness to deal honestly with God's holiness and our own sin, is this the *only* reason the doctrine has fallen from its rightful place in the church's proclamation? No, there is another reason we must examine before we can launch into the proclamation of justification on the basis of Scripture: the role of Christian scholarship in removing power and confidence from the pulpit.

CHAPTER 2

The Centrality of God's Word

The influence of the world on the church extends far beyond the prevalent hesitation to speak about sin and wrath and judgment. In a more destructive way, the world has invaded the church through a channel that, if the name means anything, should be the last and strongest bastion of truth and dedication to the gospel. Christian scholarship, by definition, *should be* descriptive of a body of believing, godly scholars whose first and foremost dedication is to Christian truth and the gospel that proclaims the message of Christ to the world. Christian scholarship *should* start with Christ, "in whom are hidden all the treasures of wisdom and knowledge," and, as a result, should unashamedly bear the reproach of "worldly wisdom" for its dedication to that which is, at its heart, foolish in the eyes of the world (1 Corinthians 1:18ff.). That is, the term "Christian scholarship" should be defined front-to-back: "Christian" should determine the meaning of "scholarship," not the other way around.

Western culture worships scholarship. Scholars are the high priests of technology and science. The media quotes scholarship the same way the apostles quoted the Old Testament. "Thus sayeth the Lord" has become "Thus sayeth the scholars." For many, as soon as the words "scholars say" are uttered, the sure sign of truth has been given. Who can possibly argue with scholarship?

Yet anyone who engages in serious study of any issue soon learns to demythologize scholarship. Scholars are people who are more or less influenced by their traditions and presuppositions, just like everyone else. Allegedly, their training *should* allow them to filter out undue influences. Their wider knowledge should give them a firmer footing for making sound conclusions. They should be able to do in-depth research and use sources in a fair and accurate manner. But all this is assuming that knowledge of facts and research techniques can in some way change the heart of man. The Christian knows better. Those who love God with all their *heart* and *mind* and *strength* know that you cannot isolate the *mind* from the rest of the man. We are a singular whole, a package deal so to speak, and the fundamental assertion of the Christian faith is that man is either operating in harmony with his Creator, thinking as he was designed, or is in rebellion and, to use a modern term, is malfunctioning. All the scholarship in the world cannot change this fact. An unregenerate scholar may have great knowledge of the world in which he lives, but until he sees himself as the creature of God and is brought into submission to the lordship of Christ the Creator, his scholarship will inevitably be used for his own purposes and not for the glory of God.

When we speak of Christian scholarship, we *should* be speaking of something that differs, at its most basic level, from what the world means when it speaks of scholarship. Why? Because Christianity proclaims the radical truth that man is not the sum and substance of all things. Man, as a creature, is dependent upon God for not only his existence but also for his meaning and his knowledge of the universe around him. Christian scholarship, if it is consistently Christian, will differ from the world's scholarship in its starting point. Unlike secular scholarship, it will not begin with the creature. It will begin with Christ, to whom every thought is to be taken captive in obedience (2 Corinthians 10:5). Its results will be predictably different than those of secular scholars when dealing with the same data, since the starting presupposition is different: the Christian begins with the acknowledgment of his createdness, and the secularist with the positive assertion of his naturalistic materialism.

Christian scholarship should also *look* and *behave* differently than secular scholarship. Its goals and methodologies are different. Christian scholars are to pursue their task for the glory of God, never for themselves (Colossians 3:23). They do what they do as *servants*, not as *masters*. Knowledge of the truth is, in their thinking, a gift of grace, not a right to be handled without thankfulness. They serve Christ and, by inevitable extension, His church. They never lord over anyone, never see themselves as the wise and beneficent tutors of the unwashed laity. Instead, they ply their trade to serve, strengthen, and aid in the ministry of the church. *There is no purpose for Christian scholarship outside the purpose of God that He is accomplishing in the church.*

CHRISTIAN SCHOLARSHIP, THE GOSPEL, AND SCRIPTURE

Christian scholarship not only begins in a philosophically different way than does secular scholarship, but it likewise has a completely different *source* of truth from which to work. Secular scholarship sees itself capable of establishing truth based upon its observations and experimentation. Christian scholars know that only God is the ultimate source of all truth, natural or spiritual. And they likewise start with the recognition that God has revealed His truth, both in creation (Romans 1:20ff.) and in His written Word. At this point the Christian scholar and the non-Christian scholar are in sharp contrast with each other.

But of course I speak of the ideal Christian scholar here, of Christian scholarship as it would be consistently expressed in light of biblical truth. Yet it is just here that we encounter the second major reason justification is no longer the centerpiece of Christian proclamation, why the Trinity is so rarely taught or believed, and why Christian theology in general has become a mere add-on rather than the structure that gives substance and meaning to the entire faith. Large numbers of Christian scholars, with few and precious exceptions, have chosen to walk the path of scholarship in general, choosing acceptance by the world as their highest priority.

This may seem a sweeping generalization, but the assertion is all too easily proven. Without referring to theological liberalism (that spectrum of formal Christianity that denies the central truths of the faith and is Christian in name only), even conservative Christian scholars have adopted the methodologies of secularism. Most importantly, even conservative Christian scholars have adopted a view of the foundation of the Christian faith (Scripture) that is not derived from a Christian worldview but from a secular paradigm. This is especially true in Old Testament studies, but the New Testament likewise suffers at the hands of those who embrace a worldview that is thoroughly contradictory to that of the writers of Scripture.

Why is this vital to our present topic? It is the tradition in Western Christianity to train men for the ministry in Bible colleges and seminaries. Without going into the propriety of sending men *out* of the local church to train them (contrary to 2 Timothy 2:2), this methodology has resulted in a Christian educational system that has particular traits and characteristics. And in general, with a few exceptions, this system today promotes a view of Scripture that falls far short of that which was clearly and inarguably held by the apostles and the Lord Jesus Christ himself. The inherent contradiction of believing in Christ for salvation but not believing His own view of Scripture aside, this fact accounts for the diminishment of the emphasis upon justification as a divine truth that is elemental to the church's proclamation within the context of the Christian ministry.

The power of the gospel of grace and the message of justification that changed the face of Europe in the Reformation has, to a great extent, disappeared from that continent. Why? Many factors have contributed to the decline of biblical faith in those lands, but the conjunction of the rise of humanism (with its naturalistic materialism) and the concomitant decline in the view of Scripture as God's inspired revelation in Christian schools and seminaries is undoubtedly a major factor. This process has been slower in America, but it is nonetheless very evident. The preaching of justification—the reality of sin, punishment, and the need of a Savior who is available to the repentant sinner on no other grounds but the empty hand of faith—can only come from one foundation: that the Christian Scriptures, Old and New Testament inclusively, are θεόπνευστος (*theopneustos*, "God-breathed") revelation, the very speaking of God, and are, as a given whole, consistent with themselves, transcending the mere human plane, partaking of the divine in content and coherence. When that foundation is removed, the message must, of necessity, change and acquiesce to the new environment created by a less-than-divine source of authority.

The great men of God who have so strongly trumpeted this truth did so without the first hint of doubt in the divine character of Scripture. Theirs was not a confused, hesitant proclamation, muted by all sorts of caveats like "If Paul really wrote this . . ." or "In this section we encounter a merely cultural teaching without direct relevance today," or "Surely here we see a viewpoint on the part of the Lord that would no longer be applicable." The message came with power not because it was *unscholarly* but because it did not confuse man's definition of scholarship with the truth.

In the simplest of terms, justification is a message based upon the authority of Scripture. Remove that authority, and the message loses its ability to command the hearts and souls of men. A belief in Scripture as merely a useful guide or a monument of human achievement does not provide a sufficient basis for the preaching of the gospel. Only when one is convinced that the message preached comes from God and bears *His* authority will one receive the call to repentance and faith in Christ.

PUZZLES AND CATS

If you have ever attempted to mix fifteen-hundred-piece jigsaw puzzles with a cat, you know the unavoidable result. You work and work for hours on end, only to discover that the final piece is missing. Where could it be? You search and search but never find it. Was it the manufacturer? Or your cuddly feline who constantly ignores your command to stay off of the table? In the end, it doesn't matter, since the result will always be marred, always flawed, for it is missing that last critical part.

Christian truth is a whole—a unified, consistent revelation from God. However, the majority of what is identified as Christian scholarship has jettisoned this very foundational belief. The result of this abdication is not merely a puzzle with a piece or two missing. It is a patchwork of disparate clumps of pieces separated by huge gaping holes. Many have decided there is no such thing as truth and are content instead to do their best in applying whatever scraps of relative belief they are able to gather from this source or that.

But if indeed Christian truth is a whole, from whence does it come? Early Christians seemed to know the answer, and they gave it with great consistency. Augustine put it this way:

> All things that are read from the Holy Scriptures in order to our instruction and salvation, it behooves us to hear with earnest heed. . . . And yet even in regard of them (a thing which ye ought especially to observe, and to commit to your memory, because that which shall make us strong against insidious errors, God has been pleased to put in the Scriptures, against which no man dares to speak, who in any sort wishes to seem a Christian), when He had given Himself to be handled by them, that did not suffice Him, but He would also confirm by means of the Scriptures the heart of them that believe: for He looked forward to us who should be afterwards; seeing that in Him we have nothing that we can handle, but have that which we may read.[1]

Gregory of Nyssa likewise said,

> We make the Holy Scriptures the canon and the rule of every dogma; we of necessity look upon that, and receive alone that

[1]Augustine, *Homilies on the First Epistle of John,* 2:1.

> which may be made conformable to the intention of those writings.[2]

And Cyril of Jerusalem, instructing new converts to the faith, gave them these sound words of advice:

> In regard to the divine and holy mysteries of the faith, not the least part may be handed on without the Holy Scriptures. Do not be led astray by winning words and clever arguments. Even to me, who tell you these things, do not give ready belief, unless you receive from the Holy Scriptures the proof of the things which I announce. The salvation in which we believe is not proved from clever reasoning, but from the Holy Scriptures.[3]

Christians have long believed Scripture is sufficient to function as the rule of faith because of its nature as divine revelation. That is, one can determine an overall teaching regarding a doctrine due to the *necessary corollary of the consistency of that which is inspired by God.* If God is the God of truth, then what He inspired will be consistent with itself. Again, this seems axiomatic, and for centuries it was. But with the coming of "enlightenment" thinking and humanism and a denial of *all* objective truth (including that found in Scripture), what was once axiomatic came under attack and for many became a dinosaur of a long-past age. Once the foundation was gone, the preaching of doctrines *composed*

---

[2]Gregory of Nyssa, *On the Soul and Resurrection*, TLG 46.49.42. The Greek is highly expressive: ἡμεῖς δὲ τῆς ἐξουσίας ἄμοιροι ταύτης ἐσμὲν,τῆς λέγειν φημὶ ἅπερ βουλόμεθα, κανόνι παντὸς δόγματος καὶ νόμῳ κεχρημένοι τῇ ἁγίᾳ Γραφῇ ἀναγκαίως πρὸς ταύτην βλέποντες, τοῦτο δεχόμεθα μόνον, ὅ, τι περ ἂν ᾖ συμφωνουν τῷ τῶν γεγραμμένων σκοπῷ. Gregory uses specific terminology: "canon and the rule of every dogma" clearly refers to a rule of faith in Scripture that supercedes any others.

[3]Cyril of Jerusalem, *Catechetical Lectures* 4:17. Like the quotation above, the Greek of Cyril's comment is striking. He says that "not the least part may be handed on without the Holy Scriptures," μηδὲ τὸ τυχὸν ἄνευ τῶν θείων παραδίδοσθαι γραφῶν, using *paradidōmi*, "tradition" in the verbal form (i.e., "handed on"). Literally, "not the least part of Christian truth can be *traditioned* apart from Scripture." And then, directly relevant to our subject, Cyril says that the "salvation" (σωτηρία), which is "our faith," is "proved" (a strong term used by the apostles to speak of how God has "proved" Jesus was the Messiah, Acts 2:22) from (ἐξ) the holy Scriptures. The Scriptures are the ground and source of the proof of the gospel according to Cyril of Jerusalem, and this was echoed by Athanasius of Alexandria when he wrote, "The holy Scriptures are sufficient for the proclamation of the truth" (αὐτάρκεις μὲν γάρ εἰσιν αἱ ἅγιαι καὶ θεόπνευστοι γραφαὶ πρὸς τὴν τῆς ἀληθείας ἀπαγγελίαν) (Contra Gentes 1:1).

primarily of objective revelation found solely in Scripture of necessity waned. Doctrinal authority, rather than standing upon a consistent ground, became a matter of predilection and taste. And justification, which points so clearly to the sin and depravity we know is in our own hearts, will hardly flourish in such a context.

CALL ME A DINOSAUR

This work is purposefully and proudly out of step with the times. The rejection of modernistic theories that undercut the revelatory nature of Scripture and reduce it to the work of mere human beings is no mere backwoods, knee-jerk reaction. I find modernism and its children bankrupt, both historically and philosophically. I find naturalistic materialism a dead worldview that offers hope to no one. It does not explain man or his experience in this world.

Precious few books have been written on justification since Buchanan wrote his monumental work in Britain after the middle of the nineteenth century. Yes, there have been volumes on the subject. Sadly, though, without a firm belief in the same foundation of authority upon which the apostles stood and upon which the Reformers thundered the truth of justification, a majority of these have lacked the one element that, biblically speaking, is utterly necessary: passion. Passion for the truth of the doctrine. Passion for the God who justifies. Passion for the gospel that has given me life. There is no need for another survey of the history of the doctrine that does not lead to the passionate proclamation of it. Nor is there any need for another compilation of this man's opinion or that man's concerns about the topic. Justification should and must again be a word that thrills the heart of believers, that is often on their tongues, always the object of their thanksgiving, the subject of their singing. This is my goal. I truly desire to see this awesome life-giving truth revived in the hearts of God's people again.

To do so I propose to present the doctrine not as the uncertain conclusion of a torturous process of guesswork and conjecture but as the certain revelation of God's work in Christ Jesus. I will first proclaim the work of the God who justifies by presenting this teaching as it is found in the key passages of Scripture. I shall seek to honor God by carefully presenting justification by grace through faith alone as the only hope for a lost and sinful mankind.

Upon accomplishing this task, I will then present a lengthy section of exegesis of the key texts relating to justification. This is not to pander to scholarship but rather an endeavor to demonstrate that the truths already proclaimed *flow from the living words of inspired Scripture.* We do not desire to engage in eisegesis, the reading *into* the text of Scripture that which it does not actually teach. Instead, this section will provide the basis for the confident and powerful proclamation of the gospel of God's grace. Justification by faith *does* flow from the careful, consistent exegesis of the text. It is only the presupposition that denies the harmony of Scripture's teaching that leads to any other conclusion. And I reject that presupposition.

LOVING THE TRUTH, GLORIFYING GOD

In 1998 I wrote a book titled *The Forgotten Trinity.* In this work I encouraged my fellow believers to learn what it means to love the Trinity, and I have been greatly encouraged by those who have written to me and said, "I do love the Trinity. Thank you for reminding me."

In that very same spirit I long to hear believers speaking the word "justification" with the same passion with which they speak such words as "the cross," "heaven," and even "the Lord." Jesus connected faithfulness to himself with faithfulness to His words, His gospel (Mark 8:38). And Paul surely knew the passion of which I speak when he wrote,

> But I do not consider my life of any account as dear to myself, so that I may finish my course and the ministry which I received from the Lord Jesus, to testify solemnly of the gospel of the grace of God. (Acts 20:24 NASB)

Christians are lovers of truth. Justification by grace through faith is the truth about how God glorifies himself in the salvation of sinners. Surely it is our *duty* to love God's truth, but is it not also our great *privilege,* our great *pleasure,* to be free to love that which the world despises? Surely it is.

Yet just as the Trinity must be *understood* to be loved, so too this doctrine, while so clearly revealed in Scripture, must likewise be explained so that it can be loved. It must be explained because it is the bent of man to corrupt it, twist it, hide it, deny it. So to this task we now turn.

CHAPTER 3

Sinners in the Hands of an Angry God

Jonathan Edwards would undoubtedly be very disappointed if he knew that the vast majority of people who even recognized his name would remember him solely for one sermon he gave, reading from a handwritten manuscript in a less than scintillating voice in Enfield, Connecticut, on July 8, 1741. He preached on a passage few ever hear today, Deuteronomy 32:35: "Their foot shall slide in due time" (KJV). He brought in other texts to emphasize his point, such as Psalm 73:18: "Surely thou didst set them in slippery places: thou castedst them down into destruction" (KJV).

Edwards made his point clear, and he drove it home with relentless logic: "There is nothing that keeps wicked men at any one moment out of hell, but the mere pleasure of God." He spared none in his call to recognize the desperate danger of sin in the face of an infinitely offended God:

> They are now the objects of that very same anger and wrath of God, that is expressed in the torments of hell. And the reason why they do not go down to hell at each moment, is not because God, in whose power they are, is not then very angry with them; as he is with many miserable creatures now tormented in hell, who there feel and bear the fierceness of his wrath. Yea, God is a great deal more angry with great numbers that are now on earth: yea, doubtless, with many that are now in this congregation, who it may be are at ease, than he is with many of those who are now in the flames of hell.

With the precision of a surgeon Edwards closed every door of escape and forced every hearer to deal with the reality of impending judgment and the vaporous nature of man's life. In one of the more famous sections of the sermon he observed,

> It is no security to wicked men for one moment, that there are no visible means of death at hand. It is no security to a natural man, that he is now in health, and that he does not see which way he should now immediately go out of the world by any accident, and that there is no visible danger in any respect in his circumstances. The manifold and continual experience of the world in all ages, shows this is no evidence, that a man is not on the very brink of eternity, and that the next step will not be into another world. The unseen, unthought of ways and means of persons going suddenly out of the world are innumerable and inconceivable. Unconverted men walk over the pit of hell on a rotten covering, and there are innumerable places in this covering so weak that they will not bear their weight, and these places are not seen. The arrows of death fly unseen at noon-day; the sharpest sight cannot discern them. God has so many different unsearchable ways of taking wicked men out of the world and sending them to hell, that there is nothing to make it appear, that God had need to be at the expense of a miracle, or go out of the ordinary course of his providence, to destroy any wicked man, at any moment.

Edwards did not enjoy preaching on this matter, but he felt compelled to address it as a pastor. As he explained,

> The use of this awful subject may be for awakening unconverted persons in this congregation. This that you have heard is the case of every one of you that are out of Christ.—That world of misery, that lake of burning brimstone, is extended abroad under you.

After establishing ten points of theological truth regarding the wrath of God against sinners, Edwards "applied" these truths, as he always did, and it is here that we encounter the two most famous, or for many today, infamous, passages from his pen:

> The bow of God's wrath is bent, and the arrow made ready on the string, and justice bends the arrow at your heart, and strains the bow, and it is nothing but the mere pleasure of God, and that of an angry God, without any promise or obligation at all, that keeps the arrow one moment from being made drunk with your blood. Thus all you that never passed under a great change of heart, by the mighty power of the Spirit of God upon your souls; all you that were never born again, and made new creatures, and raised from being dead in sin, to a state of new, and before altogether unexperienced light and life, are in the hands of an angry God. However you may have reformed your life in many things, and may have had religious affections, and may keep up a form of religion in your families and closets, and in the house of God, it is nothing but his mere pleasure that keeps you from being this moment swallowed up in everlasting destruction. However unconvinced you may now be of the truth of what you hear, by and by you will be fully convinced of it.

And then the paragraph you find quoted most often in English textbooks:

> The God that holds you over the pit of hell, much as one holds a spider, or some loathsome insect over the fire, abhors you, and is dreadfully provoked: his wrath towards you burns like fire; he looks upon you as worthy of nothing else, but to be cast into the fire; he is of purer eyes than to bear to have you in his sight; you are ten thousand times more abominable in his eyes, than the most hateful venomous serpent is in ours.

> You have offended him infinitely more than ever a stubborn rebel did his prince; and yet it is nothing but his hand that holds you from falling into the fire every moment. It is to be ascribed to nothing else, that you did not go to hell the last night; that you were suffered to awake again in this world, after you closed your eyes to sleep. And there is no other reason to be given, why you have not dropped into hell since you arose in the morning, but that God's hand has held you up. There is no other reason to be given why you have not gone to hell, since you have sat here in the house of God, provoking his pure eyes by your sinful wicked manner of attending his solemn worship. Yea, there is nothing else that is to be given as a reason why you do not this very moment drop down into hell.

Without a context such words can be used to make Edwards look like a maddened character from a Poe novel, and this is surely the purpose of many today as they seek to make any kind of preaching of God's judgment on sin a sick novelty of past, unenlightened generations. But this is to distort grossly the truth about Edwards and all who, like him, preached the judgment of God with trembling heart and soul. A fair reading of Edwards's works shows him mild and compassionate, often dwelling upon the "sweetness of Christ." He is taken with God's love, His grace and mercy. Yet Edwards was a man of the Word. He knew what must be preached again today: God's love shines with its full and proper glory *only* when it is seen in its biblical context—against the backdrop of God's holiness and hatred of sin.

The depth of man's sin is not a pleasant subject, and those accustomed to avoiding anything unpleasant will hardly find its discussion attractive. But it is necessary to strip man of his self-righteousness before he can ever understand the perfect righteousness of Christ, let alone understand why this righteousness must be a gift of grace, never the result of works or merit.

GOOD ENOUGH

"I'm not as bad as that guy over there!" So goes the constant behavior of man: we compare ourselves with ourselves and, not surprisingly, we do pretty well. You can always come up with someone who has done more evil than you so that, relatively speaking, you are "better." But even as we pat ourselves on the back, we have a nagging realization that there is a higher standard that we know we can't attain. Our self-boasting is hollow and empty. It does not satisfy.

This is not to say we don't work hard at propping up our self-deception. Some go through life doing little more than making sure they maintain a slight moral edge on someone else, as if this could somehow assuage the conscience. They may even give of themselves so as to obtain, in some manner, "moral merit" by their actions. They may even be religious after a fashion (as long as this does not bring them face-to-face with the holiness of God). But relative morality can never fully satisfy the heart that knows there is a higher law to which we must all answer.

The foolishness of comparing ourselves with ourselves was brought out with force by one of the Reformers:

> Again, it is certain that man never achieves a clear knowledge of himself unless he has first looked upon God's face, and then descends from contemplating him to scrutinize himself. For we always seem to ourselves righteous and upright and wise and holy—this pride is innate in all of us—unless by clear proofs we stand convinced of our own unrighteousness, foulness, folly, and impurity. Moreover, we are not thus convinced if we look merely to ourselves and not also to the Lord, who is the sole standard by which this judgment must be measured. For, because all of us are inclined by nature to hypocrisy, a kind of empty image of righteousness in place of righteousness itself abundantly satisfies us. And because nothing appears within or around us that has not been contaminated by great immorality, what is a little less vile pleases us as a thing most pure—so long as we confine our minds within the limits of human corruption. Just so, an eye to which nothing is shown but black objects judges something dirty white or even rather darkly mottled to be whiteness itself. Indeed, we can discern still more clearly from the bodily senses how much we are deluded in estimating the powers of the soul. For if in broad daylight we either look down upon the ground or

> survey whatever meets our view round about, we seem to ourselves endowed with the strongest and keenest sight; yet when we look up to the sun and gaze straight at it, that power of sight which was particularly strong on earth is at once blunted and confused by a great brilliance, and thus we are compelled to admit that our keenness in looking upon things earthly is sheer dullness when it comes to the sun. So it happens in estimating our spiritual goods. As long as we do not look beyond the earth, being quite content with our own righteousness, wisdom, and virtue, we flatter ourselves most sweetly, and fancy ourselves all but demigods. Suppose we but once begin to raise our thoughts to God, and to ponder his nature, and how completely perfect are his righteousness, wisdom, and power—the straightedge to which we must be shaped. Then, what masquerading earlier as righteousness was pleasing in us will soon grow filthy in its consummate wickedness. What wonderfully impressed us under the name of wisdom will stink in its very foolishness. What wore the face of power will prove itself the most miserable weakness. That is, what in us seems perfection itself corresponds ill to the purity of God.[1]

NO JUSTIFICATION WITHOUT A KNOWLEDGE OF SIN

There truly is no salvation where there is no recognition of sin and a confession of the righteousness of God in the just punishment of it. There may be great religious fervor and a lot of "Christian talk," but unless a person confesses that God is right to punish sin, and that he or she is a guilty sinner, completely deserving of eternal death, there is no true faith, no true repentance, no true salvation.

Self-righteousness is a gross sin in God's eyes. It was the self-righteous attitude of the Pharisees that brought the strongest denunciations from the lips of the Lord Jesus. One of the most striking parables He told goes like this:

> Two men went up to the temple to pray, one a Pharisee and the other a tax collector. The Pharisee stood and prayed about

[1]John Calvin, *Institutes of the Christian Religion*, Book I, 1:2.

> himself like this, "God, I thank you that I am not like other people: extortionists, unrighteous people, adulterers, or even like this tax collector. I fast twice a week; I give a tenth of everything I get." The tax collector, however, stood far off and would not even look up to heaven, but beat his breast and said, "God, be merciful to me, sinner that I am!" I tell you that this man went down to his home justified rather than the Pharisee. For everyone who exalts himself will be humbled, but he who humbles himself will be exalted. (Luke 18:10–14)

One only need read a few verses of Matthew 23 to get the idea that self-righteousness is repugnant to the Son of God. Yet every time a person questions God's right to judge, and the justice of the sentence of condemnation that hangs over *every* person, this is what is causing it: self-righteousness.

Why is it utterly necessary for self-righteousness to be removed before the gospel can work its life-giving miracle? The apostle Paul explained this in Romans 3:19. After spending nearly three chapters demonstrating the universal sinfulness of man, Paul transitions into preaching the gospel, and in so doing he says, "Now we know that whatever the law says, it says to those who are under the law, so that every mouth may be silenced and the whole world may be held accountable to God."

This often-ignored passage actually teaches a vital truth. Before a gospel that is to be preached to every creature can be understood and applied, the *universal need* of all must be established. Self-righteous people do not see their need, or they posit a less vital need than is really the case. In either instance, their mouth is still open, that is, they are continuing to make excuses for themselves. They continue to present self-defenses, no matter how much relative guilt they might admit. As long as the mouth is left open, the gospel cannot be proclaimed, for it only has meaning for those whose mouth has been closed in utter and complete agreement with God on the matter of sin and its judgment.

The terms Paul uses go to the courtroom and portray a defendant who, upon hearing all the testimony against him, is left speechless. No more protestations of innocence. No more excuses. Only silent affirmation of the truth of the charges.

No person has an excuse to offer to God, Paul says. The result is that the entire world is "liable to prosecution," "held accountable." The only person who longs to hear the good news of a way of *forgiveness* is a person who *knows he is justly condemned and helpless.*

The importance of this truth cannot be overstated. Jesus encountered those who thought themselves righteous and who viewed everyone else a sinner. The Pharisees could not understand Jesus' ministry because they did not see themselves to be in need of a savior.

"Jesus answered and said to them, 'Those who are well have no need of a physician, but those who are sick; I have not come to call the righteous, but sinners, to repentance' " (Luke 5:31–32 NKJV). The Pharisees thought they were well. Though in reality they suffered the most serious spiritual sickness, they had already pronounced themselves healthy.

We know that there are people going about their business this very day who are in fact seriously ill but do not know it. Their *physical* disease will surface with a vengeance in the near future, and there may be little hope in treatment.

As it is on the physical plane, so it is on the spiritual. The greatest danger is to be ignorant of one's spiritual condition. Like so many middle-aged men who, to their detriment, feel that ache or pain but ignore it, so the large portion of Adam's posterity works hard at ignoring the voice of conscience that informs them of their sinful condition. They do not seek the only remedy to their disease, for they blissfully think themselves healthy. They perceive no *need,* so they seek no *remedy.*

Jesus says He did not come to call the righteous. His words, "Come to Me," fall upon deaf ears for those who are not weak nor weary (Matthew 11:28). The person who does not hunger and thirst for righteousness (Matthew 5:6), being satiated with the empty substitute of self-righteousness, will not seek something more in Christ. To these Jesus says, "I did not come to call you." What words of despair! The gospel has nothing to say to the sinner who is not broken and contrite, silent in agreement with the sentence passed upon him. Jesus does not offer to come alongside and add to a person's standing. His message is not an accessory to what a person already has. The physician heals only those who first know their desperate and *mortal* condition.

The same words that are so harsh to the self-righteous are the very marrow of hope for the hurting, for the Lamb of God has come to call *sinners* to repentance. Those who refuse to be called sinners hear no words of hope, but those who know and admit their true condition hear the gracious words of the Savior; they are addressed, in grace, to them! What a glorious Redeemer!

Why emphasize this so strongly in a work on justification? Because it is the root, the ground, the very foundation upon which the doctrine stands. Err here, and the rest of the doctrine will be materially and fundamentally altered. Change the biblical teaching of man's need, and you will of necessity have to change the nature of the salvation God provides. *Every fundamental error regarding the doctrine of justification that man has ever invented flows from a denial of the nature and impact of sin in man's life.* Indeed, when one allows man to make *any* kind of response to God, to cling to *any* shred of self-righteousness, the result will *always* be an addition to faith alone as the means of justification. Justification becomes a process, a cooperative effort, as soon as the defendant is allowed to make excuses for himself. The *sola* in the great Reformation credo *sola fide* ("faith alone")—faith without the addition of any meritorious human actions—dies the death of a thousand qualifications whenever man's deadness in sin is compromised.

Since every other "gospel" regarding justification begins with a nonbiblical view of man in sin, we *must* close off every avenue of compromise. So we look to Scripture now to show that what we have seen in the words of Jesus Christ and His apostle Paul are consistent with the rest of the biblical revelation concerning man. We will first hear again Paul's testimony to the sinfulness of mankind from Romans 1, but in so doing we will focus our attention on an oft-neglected aspect of his teaching, the fact that *man willfully suppresses the knowledge of God.* Next, the *inabilities of man* that come from his condition as a sinner will be seen in Romans 3. Finally, what it means for man to be "dead in sin" will bring us to the end of the bad news that prepares the way for the good news of salvation in Christ Jesus.

I KNOW, BUT I REFUSE TO ADMIT IT

> For the wrath of God is revealed from heaven against all ungodliness and unrighteousness of people who suppress the truth by their unrighteousness, because what can be known about God is plain to them, because God has made it plain to them. For since the creation of the world his invisible attributes—his eternal power and divine nature—have been clearly seen, because they are understood through what has been made. So people are without excuse. For although they knew God, they did not glorify him as God or give him thanks, but they became futile in their thoughts and their senseless hearts were darkened. Although they claimed to be wise, they became fools and exchanged the glory of the immortal God for an image resembling mortal human beings or birds or four-footed animals or reptiles. (Romans 1:18–23)

He who seeks to be just in God's sight is no longer suppressing the knowledge of God, no longer arguing with his Creator. As Paul began his presentation of the gospel of grace in his epistle to the Romans, he began at the only place you can: the state of man, which explains both man's need and God's provision. God's wrath is being revealed from heaven. It is not something that will only come in the future—God's wrath is a present reality in the world *today.* Edwards was right. Yet upon whom does this wrath come? It is not an arbitrary wrath, but instead comes upon men for specific reasons. Scripture teaches that men "suppress the truth by their unrighteousness" or better, "*in* unrighteousness." This is something men *do.* It isn't an accident. It isn't done out of ignorance. There is a purposeful, rebellious act of suppression on the part of men (mankind—women are just as guilty as men). And the wrath of God descends with divine regularity upon those who act in this way.

God has revealed that He exists. The world around us, and our own constitution, speak so clearly, so inarguably of God's existence that God can hold all men accountable to give thanks to Him and to glorify Him. Those who refuse to do so are without excuse, without a defense. This is not to say that they do not, and will not, offer excuses. But a defense is different than an excuse. Men are good at excuses, but they cannot construct any meaningful defense for their rejection of what is plainly revealed all around them. From God's perspective, the many excuses of men are not defenses but only smoke and mirrors.

How this relates to justification is clear: If indeed man is a purposeful rebel, suppressing the knowledge of God, and yet without excuse for this rebellion in the sight of God, can we expect this wanton rebel to convert *himself*? It is not as if man is a neutral moral agent here: there is an activity to his rebellion, one of unrighteous suppression. How can one who is running *away* from God be turned again? Does the answer lie within the rebel or the Savior? The truth is that the nature of man as sinner and the nature of Christ as redeemer will both point to the utter necessity of salvation by God's grace through the empty hand of faith. Yet it is just this truth that we are very quick to dismiss, for it speaks to *what fills our own hearts.* It is all too easily forgotten—expunged from the record, so to speak. And there is more:

> Therefore God gave them over in the desires of their hearts to impurity, to dishonor their bodies among themselves. They exchanged the truth of God for a lie and worshiped and served the creation rather than the Creator, who is blessed forever! Amen. (Romans 1:24–25)

The apostle says that rebel sinners twist the relationship between God as Creator and man as creation. What rightfully belongs to God and God alone, man gives to himself or to the created order. This is known as idolatry. While many limit the scope of this ominous word to the gross worshiping of hideous idols in the jungles of some far-off land, in reality idolatry is one of the most common sins of mankind. Men exchange the truth of God for a lie, and they are more than happy to offer worship and service to the creation when they *know* it is to be given to God alone.

Sin always has consequences. God is not mocked. God "gives men over" in their sin. This is a judgment on His part. But God is under no obligation to restrain men in their sin (He surely does this constantly, but it is a free act of grace, not something He can be *constrained* to do), and He can, and does, judicially give them over to the result of their sins. This hardening of the sinner's heart leads to another important truth about man in sin: "Although they fully know God's righteous decree that those who practice such things deserve to die, they not only do them but also approve of those who practice them" (Romans 1:32).

It is perfectly right to describe this as "the insanity of sin," and a moment's reflection will show this to be the case. What kind of a person, knowing that it is just and righteous for God to punish *with death* those who willfully practice the impudent acts of rebellion Paul had cataloged in the previous verses, would not only continue on in this kind of behavior but also give open approval to others who likewise engage in such behavior? Don't miss the impact of Paul's assertion: They *fully know* that God's law is righteous and just and proper. They *fully know* that God is just and righteous to place under the very penalty of death those who rebel against Him and spit in His face, trampling His majesty and flouting His power and sovereign kingship.

Surely the majority of men and women today would argue against Paul's teaching. They would say it is not fair that God would punish with death those who commit adultery or engage in homosexual behavior (sins listed in the preceding verses). But this deception is more of the insanity of sin: to know the truth fully and yet to argue against it. This fits perfectly with the self-destructive behavior of sinful man: Denial of what you know to be true results in a feverish proclamation of what you *wish* was the truth. And while such a sinner screams loudly in God's face that He does not exist and His law is irrelevant, he likewise does all in his power to stir up others to join in his capital crime against the King of Creation. Sin is truly insane.

SHUT UP, JUST SHUT UP

We have all experienced it. Maybe it was a childhood acquaintance who simply could not take responsibility for his misdeeds. Maybe a fellow high school student who constantly made excuses for his actions. Maybe a co-worker who can't stop blaming everyone else for his failures and errors. Possibly a public figure caught red-handed but always ready with an excuse, a dodge, a ploy to escape condemnation. We all know what it is like to hear a person make excuse after excuse after excuse when he has clearly been shown to be guilty of an infraction, guilty of sin.

Likewise, we have seen what happens when a person stands before a judge silent, condemned, convicted. The eyes fall to the ground. No more excuses, no more denials. Silent submission as the person acquiesces to the truth of the charges. Admission of guilt, acceptance of punishment. It is the opposite posture to the one before. The mouth is closed. No more defenses.

The apostle Paul knew that for the gospel to be properly understood every excuse had to be ripped from the hand of the penitent sinner. The person who will find mercy before the throne of God is not the one who comes with a flapping jaw, making excuses for his sin. Instead, the person who has given up on finding any excuse at all is the one who is ready to hear the words of pardon and forgiveness. And to get to this point, Paul pulls out all the stops and calls as witness the entire span of the ancient Hebrew Scriptures. Drawing from many portions of the Old Testament, but especially from the psalms, Paul creates a catena of passages meant to drive every last bastion of self-righteousness from the breast of any person who would hear his message of justification by faith. His words are like hammer blows:

> What then? Are we better off? Certainly not, for we have already charged that Jews and Greeks alike are all under sin, just as it is written:
>
> > *"There is no one righteous, not even one,*
> > *there is no one who understands,*
> > *there is no one who seeks God.*

All have turned away,
together they have become worthless;
there is no one who shows kindness, not even one."
"Their throats are open graves,
they deceive with their tongues,
the poison of asps is under their lips."
"Their mouths are full of cursing and bitterness."
"Their feet are swift to shed blood,
ruin and misery are in their paths,
and the way of peace they have not known."
"There is no fear of God before their eyes."
(Romans 3:9–18)

We are given an apostolic interpretation of exactly what Paul wants us to hear in these words, for he offers them as support of a charge he says he has already made, that "Jews and Greeks alike are all under sin." The words that follow are not new to him: these truths are spread throughout the Scriptures. But when they are concentrated in one place their impact is greatly increased. To the self-righteous, Paul says, "There are none righteous." To the wise one, he says, "You do not understand." To the person who thinks he is seeking God, he says, "No, there is no God-seeker, all are walking in rebellion outside of God's grace." To the one who says, "I'm not far from God," he says, "You have turned away." To the person who points to his accomplishments and deeds, Paul says, "You have become worthless." To the one who boasts in his deeds and works, he says, "You have done no true deeds of kindness and goodness."

Just as Isaiah did, Paul accuses all men of having unclean lips. He points to their anger, their hatred, and their bloodshed. He accuses mankind of not knowing the way of peace. And he concludes with the summary indictment of the entire human race: "There is no fear of God before their eyes." They are creatures who have no respect, awe, or fear of their very Creator. They disdain His law and set themselves up as the final arbiter of truth and goodness.

In our modern day we must be reminded frequently of the necessity of these truths. The person who will balk at Paul's accusations is the person who is not yet ready to hear the gospel of grace about to be announced. The "I still have a few problems with this idea of sin" person is not yet ready to hear about the perfect Savior. And the message of faith—how that faith must be a complete abandonment to Christ, trusting nothing in itself, but all in the Savior—makes no sense to the person who has yet to confess God's righteous judgment upon his sin.

DEAD IN SIN

Two divine truths necessitate the doctrine of justification by grace through faith alone. First is the solitary and sovereign grace of God. The second is the state of man in sin, specifically, the biblically revealed truth that man is *dead in sin*, separated from God, outside the realm of spiritual life, incapable of doing good in and of himself. And it is just this truth that is so reprehensible to the person who continues to trust, in any fashion, in his own goodness.

Paul emphasized the incapacity of man through the use of the phrase "dead in sin." Note his words to the Ephesians:

> And although you were dead in your transgressions and sins, in which you formerly lived according to this world's present path, according to the ruler of the kingdom of the air, the ruler of the spirit that is now energizing the sons of disobedience, among whom all of us also formerly lived out our lives in the cravings of our flesh, indulging the desires of the flesh and the mind, and were by nature children of wrath even as the rest . . . (Ephesians 2:1–3)

Here the apostle describes the desperate and hopeless condition of *everyone*, including Christians prior to the gracious act of regeneration (Ephesians 2:5). We all share this state: deadness in trespasses and sins, enslavement to the "ruler of the kingdom of the air," sonship to disobedience, servitude to the cravings and desires of the flesh, the terror-filled description "children of wrath." Paul leaves man no quarter when he says that we were these things *by nature*. It is the state into which we are born, the children of Adam—fallen, corrupt, depraved (Romans 5:12ff.).

Every "gospel" that departs from the apostolic gospel will in some fashion weaken this proclamation and will make room for some level of boasting on the part of man, refusing to say man is dead in sin but instead seeing him as weakened, sick, but still in some fashion capable of doing good and contributing to his own salvation. It is all a matter of degree; some religions give much to man, others less, but man's religions share this one thing: they refuse to see man as dead in sin.

The fact that we *must* see this truth is brought out in another passage:

> And even though you were dead in your transgressions and in the uncircumcision of your flesh, he nevertheless made you alive with him, having forgiven all your transgressions. (Colossians 2:13)

In both Ephesians 2 and Colossians 2 the truth of our deadness in sin is stated as the basis for the glorious proclamation of God's gracious work of *raising dead sinners to spiritual life.* The resurrection that believers have experienced (being born again, made a new creature, however else one describes it) is left to a mere "reformation" or "improvement of life" if the radical truth of the *deadness of man in sin* is muted or abandoned.

So why do men fight so against the Bible's teaching that man is dead in sin? Because it removes all possibility of works-salvation. That is, man's merit, man's work, man's action is destroyed by the recognition of the truth of our state outside of Christ. All pride, all boasting, is excluded, and man is left, as we have seen, with a closed mouth.

The act of saving man brings God glory (Ephesians 1:5–6). The saved heart longs to see the Savior glorified, so that the more we grow in grace and knowledge of Christ, the more we desire to see Him and Him alone glorified in our own salvation. As a result, the more we contemplate the gospel, the more clearly we are able to see both the full extent of our own incapacity and His perfect ability. It is a long process: our pride is strong, our ego resilient.

But as we die more and more to self and live in the light of His truth, we come to truly appreciate the resurrection power of Christ that saved us and made us new.

HATRED AND ENMITY

"Dead in sin" refers to our incapacity to do what is spiritually good and pleasing in God's sight. But some seem to think that "dead in sin" means that man is inactive, even passive. This is not the Bible's teaching. In fact, as unpopular as it is, the Bible is clear that there are two classes of people in the world: God-haters and God-lovers. One either loves God, is the friend of God, is submitted to Him, and is in obedience to His revealed will, or one hates Him, is His enemy, and is in rebellion against Him and His revealed will. The myth of neutrality is so prevalent in our society that the following passages of Scripture are rarely the topic of exegetical preaching or teaching. Yet their message is unmistakable:

> You shall not bow down to them or serve them, for I, the Lord, your God, am a jealous God, visiting the iniquity of the fathers on the children to the third and fourth generations to those who hate me, but showing faithful love to thousands belonging to those who love me and to those who keep my commandments. (Exodus 20:5–6)

Both groups, the God-haters and the God-lovers, are seen here in the Ten Commandments. Conspicuous by its absence is the "God-neutral" group. God's judgment falls upon God-haters:

> It is not because you were more numerous than all the other peoples that the Lord considered and chose you—for in fact you were the smallest of all peoples—but because of his love for you and his faithfulness to the oath he swore to your ancestors the Lord brought you out with great power, redeeming you from the place of slavery, from the power of Pharaoh king of Egypt. Therefore, take note that it is the Lord your God who is God, the faithful God who keeps covenant faithfully with those who love him and keep his commandments, to a

> thousand generations, but who pays back those who hate him as they deserve and destroys them. He will not ignore those who hate him but will repay them as they deserve. (Deuteronomy 7:7–10)

Another term that is used often is God's "enemies."

> And when the ark journeyed, Moses would say, "Rise up, Lord, and may your enemies be scattered and those who hate you flee before you." (Numbers 10:35)

Often the two terms are used in tandem in the Old Testament:

> O God, do not be silent!
> Do not ignore us! Do not be inactive, O God!
> For look, your enemies are making a commotion;
> those who hate you are hostile. (Psalm 83:1–2)

The "wicked" are enemies of God by nature. In Psalm 68 the terms "enemies," "adversaries," and "the wicked" are paralleled with one another:

> God springs into action!
> His enemies scatter;
> his adversaries run from him.
> As smoke is driven away by the wind, so you drive them away.
> As wax melts before fire,
> so the wicked are destroyed before God. (Psalm 68:1–2)

The godly desire the vindication of God and the destruction of His enemies:

> May those who hate the Lord cower in fear before him!
> May they be permanently humiliated! (Psalm 81:15)
>
> But evil men will die;
> the Lord's enemies will be incinerated—
> they will go up in smoke. (Psalm 37:20)
>
> Say to God:
> How awesome are your deeds!

> Because of your great power your enemies cower in fear before you. (Psalm 66:3)

> Our God is a God who delivers;
> the Lord, the sovereign Master, can rescue from death.
> Indeed God strikes the heads of his enemies,
> the hairy foreheads of those who persist in rebellion. (Psalm 68:20–21)

> Indeed, look at your enemies, O Lord!
> Indeed, look at how your enemies perish!
> All the evildoers are scattered! (Psalm 92:9)

Do these passages seem harsh or unloving? If so, is it possible that you have been infected by an unbiblical view of God and God's truth? Many respond to these verses by saying, "But that's the God of the Old Testament. The God of the New Testament is loving." *There is only one God, and the God of the Old Testament is identical in every way to the God of the New.* Consider what Paul said in a passage that is well known to many:

> For if while we were enemies we were reconciled to God through the death of his son, how much more, since we have been reconciled, will we be saved by his life? (Romans 5:10)

Right in the middle of speaking of reconciliation and salvation, Paul takes it as *a commonly accepted truth among all Christians* that before our conversion we were enemies who had to experience reconciliation to God. In fact, Paul insists that an attitude of enmity toward God is part and parcel of the unredeemed man:

> The outlook of the flesh is hostile to God, for it does not submit to the law of God, nor is it able to do so. Those who are in the flesh cannot please God. (Romans 8:7–8)

The person who thinks himself neutral with reference to God is deceived. There is no such thing as putting God on hold. There is no gray area when it comes to one's relationship to the Creator. Many would say, "Oh, well, I'm undecided about that. Maybe God is there, maybe not—I don't know." Is this something different from being the enemy of God? In no way. Can you imagine a child saying, "Well, I don't know if I accept the idea that I have parents or not. I'm still considering the possibilities." We saw above that men *know God exists* and yet suppress that knowledge. Claiming to be neutral is just as much an act of rebellion as directly denying His existence and His right to impose boundaries upon our behavior (i.e., His law). The rebel is open about suppressing the knowledge of God; the hypocrite says, "Who, me, suppressing the knowledge of God? Gracious sakes no, I'm just a skeptic. I'm no enemy of God. I'm not even sure there is a God!" If God exists, then speaking in this fashion is just as much an act of rebellion as joining the American Atheists.

THE BAD NEWS CONCLUDED

So what kind of salvation does one offer to the person described as actively and in blatant unrighteousness suppressing the knowledge of the existence of God, as one who does not seek God but instead seeks after every opportunity to banish the fear of God from before his eyes? What is there for one who is dead in sin, enslaved to its power, entombed in the very grasp of spiritual death itself, an enemy of God who hates Him? Offering a gospel that says "Do this" to such a person would be a mockery. Saying "I'll do most of the work; you just add a small part" would likewise result in utter failure. The biblical teaching on the nature of man in sin demands a God-centered salvation and a Savior who is powerful and able to accomplish the task entrusted to Him by the Father. The Reformers understood this and said, *Soli Deo Gloria*, "to God alone be the glory," for salvation is, *and must be*, solely a divine act.

CHAPTER 4

What Is Justification by Faith?

We have now seen the desperation of man's condition. Sin holds man in slavery (John 8:33–34), resulting in spiritual death and separation from God. If man, then, is so desperately incapable of saving himself, what is to be done?

The Christian answer is found in the gospel of Jesus Christ. Christians believe the gospel is the *only* answer for all people, anywhere. The only answer for sin is what God has done in Christ Jesus.

Men have died for it. They have suffered the loss of family and friends, possessions and position. It has divided husbands and wives, parents and children. Yet, almost ironically, it is called the "good news," the gospel. It is good news to those who believe the bad news about their sin and who desire, by God's grace, to be at peace with Him; for everyone else, it is foolishness (1 Corinthians 1:18ff.). The apostle Paul boldly proclaimed, "I am not ashamed of the gospel" (Romans 1:16).

You cannot speak of the gospel without addressing its central aspect, justification. Anyone who takes the time to read through the great passages of the Bible that address the question of salvation, such as Paul's epistle to the Romans or his strong letter to the churches of Galatia, quickly discovers the centrality of the concept of justification to the entire gospel of Christ. Those who have been justified have peace with God (Romans 5:1) and are no longer under His wrath. How does this take place? How does one go from being the enemy of God to being at peace with God? This is what justification is about.

And yet there are many "doctrines" of justification proclaimed in our world today. There are as many different doctrines as there are denominations and religious groups. So is this vital issue just a matter of opinion? Is it not true that good men have differed on the issue and that no one can truly know what justification teaches? Or are the Scriptures sufficient to define the gospel that we so confidently believe and proclaim? *Without hesitation* we say the Bible is more than sufficient to give us a consistent teaching on this vital truth.

Before looking closely at each of the elements of the doctrine (imputation, faith, etc.), it would be good to review justification itself.

JUSTIFICATION BY FAITH DEFINED

The doctrine of justification was at the center of the conflict that was the Reformation. The 1689 *London Confession* (also known as the *Baptist Confession*) defined justification as seen below. Anyone familiar with the *Westminster Confession of Faith* will recognize that this is almost exactly what is to be found in that great document as well.

> (1) Those whom God effectually calleth, he also freely justifieth, not by infusing righteousness into them, but by pardoning their sins, and by accounting and accepting their persons as righteous; not for anything wrought in them, or done

by them, but for Christ's sake alone; not by imputing faith itself, the act of believing, or any other evangelical obedience to them, as their righteousness; but by imputing Christ's active obedience unto the whole law, and passive obedience in his death for their whole and sole righteousness, they receiving and resting on him and his righteousness by faith, which faith they have not of themselves; it is the gift of God.

(2) Faith thus receiving and resting on Christ and his righteousness, is the alone instrument of justification; yet it is not alone in the person justified, but is ever accompanied with all other saving graces, and is no dead faith, but worketh by love.

(3) Christ, by his obedience and death, did fully discharge the debt of all those that are justified; and did, by the sacrifice of himself in the blood of his cross, undergoing in their stead the penalty due unto them, make a proper, real, and full satisfaction to God's justice in their behalf; yet, inasmuch as he was given by the Father for them, and his obedience and satisfaction accepted in their stead, and both freely, not for anything in them, their justification is only of free grace, that both the exact justice and right grace of God might be glorified in the justification of sinners.

(4) God did from all eternity decree to justify all the elect, and Christ did in the fulness of time die for their sins, and rise again for their justification; nevertheless, they are not justified personally, until the Holy Spirit doth in due time actually apply Christ unto them.

(5) God doth continue to forgive the sins of those that are justified, and although they can never fall from the state of justification, yet they may, by their sins, fall under God's fatherly displeasure; and in that condition they have not usually the light of his countenance restored unto them, until they humble themselves, confess their sins, beg pardon, and renew their faith and repentance.

(6) The justification of believers under the Old Testament was, in all these respects, one and the same with the justification of believers under the New Testament.

First, the Protestant doctrine denies, repeatedly, that justification involves an infusion of righteousness. Justification does not change the person but instead changes the person's *status*. This is foundationally important: Justification involves the forgiveness of the sins of those who are called, as well as "accounting and accepting their persons as righteous." Therefore, the Protestant position presented here teaches that justification is a declaration on the part of God relevant to the believer. It is a *judicial* (or *forensic*) proclamation about the person's relationship to God.

Second, this act of justification is undertaken by God (God is the One who justifies) and is not based in any way upon anything wrought in believers or done by them. Rather, the action is undertaken "for Christ's sake alone." Justification, then, is a free act of God's grace and is in no way dependent upon human actions, works, merits, or dispositions. As the Bible puts it, God is the Justifier. It is a divine act, not a human accomplishment!

Next, the framers of this definition of justification carefully avoided asserting that any "act of evangelical obedience" can possibly be the grounds of justification. Instead, they specifically denied that faith itself, the act of believing, or anything else is imputed as our righteousness. Why were they so concerned about this? The next section answers this question by asserting that it is Christ's *obedience*, both active and passive, that is *imputed* to the believer.[1] To make any action of man (including the action of faith) the basis of justification is to take away from the righteousness of Christ, which is the true basis of Christian justification.

If it is by the imputation of Christ's righteousness that the believer is justified, what is the instrument of this action? The instrument is said to be faith, but this is no bare intellectual assent to the facts of the gospel. This is a faith that results in the person "believing and resting on him and his righteousness." This faith is supernatural in origin, for it is "not of themselves, it is the gift of God." This is a living faith, one that looks to Christ alone for

---

[1]Protestant theologians have identified a twofold nature to justification. John Murray used the terms "constitutive" and "declarative" to describe this: "Justification is therefore a constitutive act whereby the righteousness of Christ is imputed to our account and we are accordingly accepted as righteous in God's sight. . . . Justification is both a declarative and a constitutive act of God's free grace." (*Redemption Accomplished and Applied*, 124.) The constitutive element is the positive *imputation* of Christ's righteousness to the believer, and this is the grounds, then, of the "declarative" element, that being the declaration of the righteousness of the believer. It should be noted that the imputation of Christ's righteousness is taken in the same sense as it is in the New Testament—as a legal imputation, not a subjective one.

salvation. The second section expands upon this view, asserting that faith is the "alone instrument of justification." No works of human merit can bring about this justification. No religious rites or activities can justify.

Note, however, that faith is but the *instrument* and, as was said earlier, not the *basis* of justification. We are not justified because we believe, but we are justified *through* faith, faith being the "appropriating organ" by which justification comes. This kind of faith, the *Confession* asserts, is "not alone" but is "ever accompanied with all other saving graces, and is no dead faith, but worketh by love." As has been said many times, faith alone saves, but a saving faith is never alone.

How, then, can God justify, or declare righteous, a sinful man or woman? Is this act of justification merely a fiction, an assertion with no reality? How can a holy God call a sinful man "just"? He can do so because of the work of Jesus Christ as the substitute for His people. The *Confession* asserts that Christ "did fully discharge the debt of all those that are justified, and did, by the sacrifice of himself in the blood of his cross, undergoing in their stead the penalty due unto them, make a proper, real, and full satisfaction to God's justice in their behalf."

The penalty of the transgression of God's law by sinners, then, is laid upon their substitute, Jesus Christ. The Father can accept the work of Christ (His "obedience and satisfaction") on behalf of His people and can, on that basis, justify them and declare them righteous, for the whole penalty and burden of sin has been removed by Christ for all those who are in union with Him. Since the work of Christ is complete in and of itself without the addition of human actions, God receives all the glory for the justification of sinners.

Further, the *Confession* links the doctrine of justification with the sovereign decree of God, acknowledging that justification proceeded out of God's eternal decree to justify "all the elect." While this was God's eternal purpose, men themselves have not been justified from eternity;[2] rather, they are justified upon the exercise

[2]Some Reformed theologians did develop a doctrine of "eternal justification," but this view has never commanded a large following, as it does not conform to biblical teaching on the nature of faith or to the order in which God applies the perfect salvation He has provided in Christ.

of the divine gift of faith or, as the *Confession* said, when the "Holy Spirit doth in due time actually apply Christ unto them."

Finally, the Protestant position asserts that justification is a *once-for-all* action on the part of God. One who is justified cannot become "unjustified," for all of the believer's sins have been forgiven on the basis of the work of Christ. Yet the sins of the believer can bring him into a position of existing under the "fatherly displeasure" of God.

The great Princeton theologian Charles Hodge provided a brief and concise (for him, anyway) definition of justification.

1. [Justification is] an act, and not, as sanctification, a continued and progressive work.
2. It is an act of grace to the sinner. In himself he deserves condemnation when God justifies him.
3. As to the nature of the act, it is, in the first place, not an efficient act, or an act of power. It does not produce any subjective change in the person justified. It does not effect a change of character, making those good who were bad, those holy who were unholy. That is done in regeneration and sanctification. In the second place, it is not a mere executive act, as when a sovereign pardons a criminal, and thereby restores him to his civil rights, or to his former status in the commonwealth. In the third place, it is a forensic, or judicial act, the act of a judge, not of a sovereign. That is, in the case of the sinner, or, *in foro Dei,* it is an act of God not in his character of sovereign, but in his character of judge. It is a declarative act in which God pronounces the sinner just or righteous, that is, declares that the claims of justice, so far as he is concerned, are satisfied, so that he cannot be justly condemned, but is in justice entitled to the reward promised or due to perfect righteousness.
4. The meritorious ground of justification is not faith; we are not justified on account of our faith, considered as a virtuous or holy act or state of mind. Nor are our works of any kind the ground of justification. Nothing done by us or wrought in us satisfies the demands of justice, or can be the ground or reason of the declaration that justice as far as it concerns us is satisfied. The ground of justification is the

righteousness of Christ, active and passive, *i.e.*, including his perfect obedience to the law as a covenant, and his enduring the penalty of the law in our stead and on our behalf.

5. The righteousness of Christ is in justification imputed to the believer. That is, is set to his account, so that he is entitled to plead it at the bar of God, as though it were personally and inherently his own.
6. Faith is the condition of justification. That is, so far as adults are concerned, God does not impute the righteousness of Christ to the sinner, until and unless, he (through grace) receives and rests on Christ alone for his salvation.[3]

Protestants believe that their confessions, while useful for the definition of faith and doctrine, have no divine authority. Unless scriptural basis can be found, no authority can be claimed.

DO WE HAVE TO BE SO SPECIFIC?

Justification is a doctrine based upon the very heart of Scripture, flowing from numerous passages that fully address the issue (such as Romans 3–5; Galatians 1–3, etc.). The fine distinctions theologians make in discussing justification are necessary and fully understandable in light of the conflict that has raged over the topic through the centuries.

The gospel has been the target of attack since the Lord Jesus walked into Galilee and said, "Repent and believe the gospel!" (Mark 1:15). It was under attack throughout His ministry. It was under attack as soon as He ascended into heaven. God had to perform miracles to make sure men like Peter and Paul understood it. The church gathered for its first council in Acts 15 because men were insisting upon adding to God's grace. Paul fought his entire life to defend the truth of the gospel. A constant refrain of his preaching and teaching, recorded in both Acts 20:24–35 and 2 Timothy 3:10–17, is that false teachers would always be attacking the faith. Jude, toward the end of the apostolic

[3]Charles Hodge, *Systematic Theology* (Eerdmans, 1986), III:117–18.

period, exhorts Christians to "contend earnestly for the faith" that was once for all delivered to the saints (3–4).

Because of this ongoing controversy, Christians must invest considerable energy in the defense of the gospel *as a labor of love for God.* It is not an act of love to allow the truth of His gospel to be trampled underfoot. Also, to successfully respond to the attacks upon the gospel we must know it intimately. We learn from Galatians and Romans that many of the attempts to undercut the gospel are based upon "twisting" the Scriptures (see also 2 Peter 3:16). This twisting can involve blatant denial of scriptural truths (as when members of the LDS Church proclaim there are many gods) or much more subtle redefinitions (as when we are told that grace is *necessary* but is not *sufficient* to bring about salvation). Yet in either case, we need to have a solid understanding of the truth so as to be able to detect the error.

Therefore we must be very specific when we speak of the gospel as a whole and justification in particular. We must dig deeply into the words of the text of Scripture itself, and we must listen carefully to what is preached even by those in our own fellowship to make sure that what is being said is in accordance with the truth. It is a never-ending challenge, but it is a task to which we bend ourselves as a labor of grateful reverence and love to God.

Genesis 15:6 says, "Then [Abram] believed in the LORD; and He reckoned [imputed] it to him as righteousness" (NASB). This tremendous passage gives us the outline of how we will proclaim the truth of God's work as the "Justifier" in the next few chapters. First, we must define, very carefully and very closely, the meaning of the words "justify," "justification," and "righteousness." We must be aware of the historical fact that the translation of the word "justify" and its derivatives has *greatly influenced* how it has been understood (and that mainly to the detriment of the truth).

Then, the significance of the word "faith" must be considered. Yes, even the meaning of a word so taken for granted is necessary, for what does it truly mean to "believe in Christ"? Is this merely to believe certain facts about Him and His work? What is the nature of saving faith? How does it differ from belief that does not result in salvation?

Next, how can a holy God declare any sinful man "righteous"? Upon what grounds can such a declaration be made?

Finally, what does it mean for God to "reckon" or "impute" righteousness? Each word in Genesis 15:6 is used to its fullest by the New Testament to explain and pronounce the wonder of God's work of salvation, and it is truly our *privilege* to have the freedom and opportunity to consider this work of our gracious God.

CHAPTER 5

Justified: The Bible's Meaning

You are justified only when God the Father, based upon the meritorious work of Jesus Christ in your place, *declares* you to be so upon the exercise of the gift of faith. This faith is directed solely to the God who "justifies the ungodly" (NASB). To be justified means to be declared right with God by virtue of the remission of sins accomplished by Jesus: Christ's righteousness is imputed to the believer, and the believer's sins are imputed to Christ, who bears them in His body on the tree. Justification is from beginning to end a divine action, based upon the mercy of God the Father and the work of Jesus Christ the Son.

Such is the proclamation of the faith. But there are so many who deny this divine truth that we must look very carefully at its meaning. Often we are told that the word simply does not bear the narrow, confined meaning we ascribe to it when we speak of the action of God the Father as He "justifies" the one who believes in Jesus Christ. We are told that justification involves *changing the sinner* so that he is now just and therefore acceptable, in his own person, before God.

Does this really matter? Does it matter whether justification is a divine *declaration* based solely on the work of Christ in the place of a sinner or a divine *action* that makes the sinner subjectively pleasing to God?

THE PROBLEM OF THE ENGLISH LANGUAGE

The predominance of the English language has had a profound impact upon theology. Many in English-speaking lands believe that their theology is firmly based upon the Bible when, in fact, it is firmly based upon their reading into the Bible meanings based upon English usage rather than the intention of the original authors. Combine this with the fact that the richness of the original languages often defies the wording of the less-exact English, and we can see why we must be very, very careful to define terms in their original context and language rather than as we might automatically understand them in English. In other words, we must avoid the excess baggage that frequently comes with the limitations of our language and make sure that what we *think* the text is saying is what it really *is* saying.

I have often asked classes and Bible study groups, "What is the difference between the words 'justification' and 'righteousness' as used in the Bible?" In nearly every instance the answers follow the lines of the meanings of the English terms themselves. We seem to believe naturally that "righteousness" has a *moral* character about it. For us, to be righteous speaks of being morally upright, sinless, pure, and it is often defined as a state in which one lives. On the other hand, in common opinion "justification" speaks of something *legal* in character. Justification, it is often said, is something done *for* us, while righteousness is something done *in* us. Righteousness is moral, justification legal. Or so the English usage commonly goes.

While these ideas certainly are understandable, English meaning does not indicate the correct *biblical* meaning. The fact of the matter is, there are not two different terms used in the Bible (the New Testament, primarily) that are translated as "righteousness" and "justification." There is only one term or, perhaps better, one family of terms, *dikaios* (the adjective), *dikaiosune* (the noun), and *dikaioō* (the verb).[1] It is the translator's decision whether to render *dikaiosune* as "righteousness" or as "justification." Normally, the choice is made upon the basis of context—it would be rather awkward to use one or the other term in certain situations. For example, it is easier to say "Therefore, having been justified . . ." than it is to say "Therefore, having been made righteous . . ." Similarly, it flows better to speak of receiving righteousness than it does receiving justification.

Why are two different English terms used to translate the one Greek term (or the one Hebrew term in the Old Testament, *zedekah*)?[2] In this situation, we discover that the biblical term does carry within it the subtleties of both the English words "righteousness" and "justification." That is, *there are obviously instances in which the biblical term speaks of a moral or ethical quality when it speaks of someone being righteous.* Protestants do not by any stretch of the imagination assert that the words "righteousness" and "justification" always, and in every instance, refer solely and completely to a divine act of God whereby He makes a legal declaration regarding the relationship of the believer to himself.[3] Every word, including "justification," has to be defined *as it is used by an author in its own context.* And remember, an author may use a word one way in one context, and with another nuance or meaning in a different context. This is why one cannot sit down with *Strong's Concordance,* assign a single meaning to a word, and then read that meaning into every passage from Genesis to Revelation. Serious study of the text defies this type of simplistic methodology, and the doctrine of justification by faith is not based upon such thinking.

It is easy to demonstrate that the term "righteous" can refer

[1]δίκαιος, δικαιοσύνη, δικαιόω

[2]צְדָקָה

[3]One must keep in mind the different fine points expressed by a substantive (noun or adjective) and a verb. The verbal form δικαιόω does, by its nature, carry a range of meaning that is more narrow than the substantive forms.

to a state of being in right relationship to God in the sense of being morally upright. Joseph was righteous (Matthew 1:19), and Zachariah and Elizabeth were just also (Luke 1:6). The Old Testament is filled with similar passages referring to the moral uprightness of men and women.

However, there are many times when the term is used in a legal sense only, especially when speaking of the verbal form. In these instances it speaks of the person's relationship to a standard or law. The question we must ask, then, is which is the primary meaning? When we come to the actual doctrine of justification in the New Testament, *which meaning predominates*? This is a most important inquiry, for the Protestant position teaches that it is the judicial or legal sense that is in view in the doctrine of justification by faith, *not* the moral or ethical one.

Many other religions depend upon identifying righteousness as an ethical or moral issue, reflective not of an action on the part of God but instead focusing upon what man is in himself. And if, in fact, justification involves a *subjective change* in man (focusing justification upon man rather than upon God) where man is made intrinsically pleasing to God so that he is acceptable, it follows inevitably that the entire work of salvation will become dependent upon man's actions. Is this what we find in Scripture?

JUSTIFICATION IN THE OLD TESTAMENT

The reason we must look closely at the Old Testament text is easily understood when we keep in mind that what we call the Old Testament today was merely the Scriptures of the early church. And the most often used form of those Scriptures was the Greek translation thereof, the *Septuagint*.[4] The New Testament authors quote frequently from the Septuagint, so the meaning and use of

---

[4]Alister McGrath provides a summary of the issues involved in correctly understanding and also translating the relevant Hebrew terms into Greek, and from there into the context of the New Testament, and then into our modern languages. This is found in his monumental work *Iustitia Dei: A History of the Christian Doctrine of Justification* (Cambridge University Press, 1998), 4–16.

words in that translation of the Bible has a great impact on understanding how the word is being used in New Testament writings.

In the Old Testament, the term "to justify" is often used in the *judicial* sense, that is, in the context of the court of law. Given the parallels that exist between Paul's use of the same words to describe justification by faith *in the very contexts that define the doctrine we are examining*, we should look carefully at some of the key passages. We'll examine both the NET and the NASB.

EXODUS 23:7

> Keep your distance from a false charge—do not kill the innocent and the righteous, for I do not justify the wicked. (NET)

> Keep far from a false charge, and do not kill the innocent or the righteous, for I will not acquit the guilty. (NASB)

Clearly the context of Exodus 23 is legal. The preceding verses include instructions on lawsuits and general exhortations to justice and honesty. In this one verse we have judicial terms such as "false charge," "acquit," and "guilty." We also see the key word used twice—once as a substantive ("righteous" or "just" in the phrase "do not kill the innocent and the *righteous*")[5] and once as a verb ("justify" or "acquit" in the phrase "*justify* the wicked").[6]

In the first phrase God's law says that the innocent or the righteous are not to be killed. Obviously, this does not mean "those who are sinlessly perfect" but rather those who are innocent or righteous *in the eyes of the law.* This is a legal, not a moral, description.

But even more important is the second phrase, "I do not justify the wicked." Some might think this is contradictory to Paul's description of God as the one who *does* justify the ungodly (Romans 4:5), yet such would involve ignoring the context of the two statements. God, in His justice, does not "justify the wicked." He

[5]In Hebrew, צַדִּיק, and very importantly in the Greek translation of the Old Testament (which was the Bible of the New Testament church), known as the *Septuagint* (often abbreviated LXX), δίκαιον.

[6]אַצְדִּיק, and in the LXX, δικαιώσεις.

justifies the ungodly in His mercy and grace, and only on the basis of the work of Christ that satisfies the demands of His absolute holiness and justice. In this passage, God is stating simple justice: He will not justify the wicked.

But what does this mean? It's obvious that God is not saying He does not internally change the nature of wicked men into that which is objectively pleasing to Him—this He does. The context in this passage is forensic, that is, legal. God *is* saying He will not declare a wicked man to be righteous, for such would be a perversion of justice. God does not do this in justification by faith, either: Christ's substitutionary death is the sole basis of his declaration. This use of the verb "justify" is clearly a forensic, legal declaration regarding an individual's standing before God and His law.

DEUTERONOMY 25:1

Again in Deuteronomy 25:1, the context is the court of law. In this case (as we'll find as well in the New Testament) "to justify" is used in contrast with "condemn."

> If controversy arises between people and they go to court for judgment and the judges hear the case, they shall exonerate the just but condemn the guilty. (NET)

> If there is a dispute between men and they go to court, and the judges decide their case, and they justify the righteous and condemn the wicked . . . (NASB)

Here the English language hides a bit of the thrust of the original. The Hebrew says "justify the just," which is rendered most literally by the NASB. The Hebrew uses the verbal form and the substantive form of the same root *(zedek)*, and the Greek Septuagint literally renders the phrase using the all-important term *dikaios*, the same word that comes into our New Testament and is translated "justify." The passage speaks both of "justifying the just" and of "condemning the condemned," for the same Hebrew words are used in the same forms for those who are guilty.

When a judge, upon examination of a case, pronounces his

judgment upon the disputants, his verdict does not in some way *change* those who have been judged. His statement, "This person is in the right and that person is in the wrong" does not alter those who are being judged. It is a *forensic* statement, a pronouncement of a judicial decision. The just or innocent man was already just and innocent, just as the guilty man walked into the courtroom guilty. The judge announces a verdict; it does not change the person about whom it is made.

Why is all of this important? Because the doctrine of justification by faith says justification is something God does based upon the work of Christ: it is a forensic declaration, not something that involves a subjective change of the believer. Justification is about our status, while sanctification is about the work of God whereby we are changed and conformed to His image. Confusing the two utterly undoes the glorious nature of justification.

PROVERBS 17:15

> The one who acquits the guilty and condemns the innocent—
> both of them are an abomination to the Lord. (NET)
>
> He who justifies the wicked and he who condemns the righteous, Both of them alike are an abomination to the Lord. (NASB)

Here again, "justify" and "condemn" are placed in contrast. Now, if "justify" meant "to change a person inwardly so as to make him holy or good," this passage would make no sense at all. What could possibly be wrong with changing an evil man and making him good? In fact, God is doing that in all those who are being sanctified, as the New Testament teaches. But this is not what Proverbs 17:15 is talking about. It is not viewing this act of justifying as changing the person; instead, the writer is clearly speaking of the sinfulness of declaring a person who is evil to be just, as well as the outrage of declaring an innocent person to be guilty. Both are abhorrent to God, and both are clearly *declarations* relative to law.

ISAIAH 5:23

The fifth chapter of Isaiah includes a series of woes pronounced upon the unrighteous Israelites. One of these woes speaks to the perversion of justice that was rampant among them:

> They pronounce the guilty innocent for a payoff,
> they ignore the just cause of the innocent. (NET)

> Who justify the wicked for a bribe,
> And take away the rights of the ones who are in the right! (NASB)

By this point we see a clear pattern. The NET renders the important term as "pronounce innocent," and the NASB uses "justify the wicked." Again the context is legal: the depravity of the nation has extended into the courtroom itself. For a bribe a corrupt judge will pronounce guilty those who are not. One can again see how the term is forensic in nature: the statement of the judge does not actually change the innocent person into a guilty person; the guilty person is still innocent. This is a proclamation, a verdict, albeit a corrupt one.

ISAIAH 53: THE SUFFERING SERVANT JUSTIFIES MANY

Surely when we think of the Old Testament, however, the key passage that strikes us is the great messianic "gospel" found in Isaiah 53. Here we find all the key words piling upon one another, leading to the prophetic proclamation of the justifying work of the Savior. We read of a substitutionary work, for the Messiah bears our griefs (v. 4); He is pierced and crushed for our transgressions and iniquities; Yahweh causes the iniquity of us all to "fall on Him" (v. 6). He is cut off for the transgression of the people (v. 8), though no deceit is found in His mouth (v. 9). He offers himself as a "guilt offering" (v. 10). And so we read,

> As a result of the anguish of His soul,
> He will see it and be satisfied;
> By His knowledge the Righteous One,
> My Servant, will justify the many,
> As He will bear their iniquities.

Therefore, I will allot Him a portion with the great,
And He will divide the booty with the strong;
Because He poured out Himself to death,
And was numbered with the transgressors;
Yet He Himself bore the sin of many,
And interceded for the transgressors.
(Isaiah 53:11–12 NASB)

If one did not know this comes from Isaiah one might locate its origin in Romans or Galatians, so explicit is the passage in speaking to the work of God in salvation. The suffering servant "will justify the many," and He will do so by bearing their iniquities, a clear reference to substitutionary atonement.

The next verse expresses the same thought in the context of bearing sin and interceding for transgressors, both vital aspects of the Messiah's ministry. But our primary concern here is the meaning of "justify" as seen in these prophetic words. The Messiah justifies (it is always a divine work), and He does so by bearing the iniquities of those justified. This is the very basis of the Protestant doctrine of justification: Sinners are declared righteous before God solely because of the sin-bearing work of the Messiah in their place. The act of justifying them is seen to be consistent with what has come before; it is a declaration, based upon the work of another.

THE SOURCE OF PAUL'S UNDERSTANDING OF JUSTIFICATION

The impact of the Septuagint on the vocabulary and teaching of the New Testament is well known. The apostles communicated the gospel to an audience that primarily used and read only the Septuagint. If, then, we find that the verb "to justify" was used in legal, forensic contexts in the Septuagint, it would speak clearly to the background from which Paul derived his use of the term.

And so we come to one of the most vital aspects of this inquiry: *Are* Protestants warranted in limiting the meaning of "justification" in the key Pauline passages (Romans 3–5; 8:29–34; Galatians 1–5) that specifically address how sinful men and women are made right with God to a forensic, legal declaration?[7]

The answer depends very much upon whether we believe that Paul is consistent with himself in his teaching and theology (i.e., that his writings are supernatural in their origin and substance, an assumption not shared by many who comment upon the subject today). If so, then it follows that we can in fact identify a consistent usage of the term *in the specific contexts that teach justification by grace through faith.* In Romans and Galatians we have entire discourses on justification, and a consistent use of the term "justify" by the apostle can be traced directly to the same spectrum of Old Testament verses we have just examined. That is, it is the Protestant assertion that since Paul places the words "righteousness," "justify," "just," etc., in the context of the court of law (as we shall see), the verses we just examined provide the background and hence support the forensic, legal use of these terms that is so plainly present therein. In fact, the prime passage Paul uses in his teaching, Genesis 15:6, bears this out.

GENESIS 15:6

> Then he believed in the Lord; and He reckoned it to him as righteousness.[8]

Genesis 15:6 is cited four times in the New Testament,[9] and it forms the basis of Paul's lengthy argument in the fourth chapter of Romans concerning justification by faith. Paul even imported the language of the Septuagint directly into his own presentation of the doctrine. When Abraham believed God, God counted (or reckoned) it to him as righteousness. This imputation (or reckoning) of righteousness obviously had nothing to do with a sub-

---

[7]The forensic context of these passages is established in the exegetical chapters later in this work.

[8]NASB rendering. The NET rendering is so dynamic that it is not really usable to discuss its citation in the New Testament, as it translates the last phrase, "and the Lord considered his response of faith worthy of a reward." This differs so greatly from the Pauline use as to cause significant confusion.

[9]Romans 4:3, 9; Galatians 3:6; James 2:23.

jective change made in Abraham; instead, it referred to Abraham's relationship to or standing with God. The key issue for Paul is that God's reckoning Abraham as righteous was due solely and completely to faith, not to anything Abraham did.

Genesis 15:6 is not, in its original setting, placed in a forensic or legal context. But keeping in mind the consistency of Paul's presentation and the centrality of this passage to his own understanding and preaching, it follows inevitably that if Paul places "righteousness" in contexts that are inarguably legal without giving any indication that he is making a shift from the meaning in Genesis 15:6, then this is his understanding here as well. That this is the case is borne out in reference to two passages.

First, Romans 4:1–8 provides believers with an extended apostolic interpretation of Genesis 15:6. It's obvious that Paul used this passage as his chief proof text in his disputes with the Jews over the nature of salvation itself. The entirety of Romans 4 is really an extended commentary on the significance of Abraham's justification. But the primary weight of his understanding is found in verses three through ten:

> **4:3** For what does the scripture say? "*Abraham believed God, and it was credited to him as righteousness.*" **4:4** Now to the one who works, his pay is not credited due to grace but due to obligation. **4:5** But to the one who does not work, but believes in the one who declares the ungodly righteous, his faith is credited as righteousness.
>
> **4:6** So even David himself speaks regarding the blessedness of the man to whom God credits righteousness apart from works:
>
> **4:7** "*Blessed are those whose lawless deeds are forgiven, and whose sins are covered;*
>
> **4:8** *Blessed is the one against whom the Lord will never count sin.*"
>
> **4:9** Is this blessedness then for the circumcision or also for the uncircumcision? For we say, "faith *was credited to* Abraham *as righteousness.*" **4:10** How then was it credited to him? Was he circumcised at the time, or not? No, he was not circumcised but uncircumcised!

This passage is thoroughly examined elsewhere, but for our purposes the use of the term "righteousness" as drawn from Genesis 15:6 (cited twice) captures our interest. Does it make sense to interpret this word as "God *declared* Abraham to be in right relationship with Him when he believed God's promises" or "God *changed* Abraham into a righteous man because he had faith in Him"? The difference is not semantic, but definitional.

We will look closely at the meaning of "imputation" at a later point, but for now it is vital to recognize that the consistent meaning in the key passages of Scripture that define justification refers to something God *declares* about one who has *faith* in His promises. Paul emphasizes that the faith Abraham had was a *meritless* faith, i.e., a faith making no demands, seeking no reward from God (4:4–5). This empty hand of faith that brings no bribe, no work, no merit, as in the case of Abraham, results in the imputation of righteousness apart from works.

The righteousness that is imputed to the believer comes from outside himself: it is something *given to him*, not something *done within him.* The free character of this justification is further demonstrated by pointing out that Abraham was justified *before* he received the sign of circumcision: no acts of obedience to God figured in the imputation to him of righteousness based on free and nondemanding faith.

But no passage in the New Testament testifies more clearly to the forensic/legal character of Paul's doctrine of justification than these words to the church at Rome:

> **8:30** And those [God] predestined, he also called; and those he called, he also justified; and those he justified, he also glorified. **8:31** What then shall we say about these things? If God is for us, who can be against us? **8:32** Indeed, he who did not spare his own Son, but gave him up for us all—how will he not also, along with him, freely give us all things? **8:33** Who will bring any charge against God's elect? It is God who justifies. **8:34** Who is the one who will condemn? Christ is the one who died (and more than that he was raised), who is at the right hand of God, and who also is interceding for us.

While we will be thoroughly examining these verses later, for now we use them to establish, beyond controversy, that the apostle placed "justifies" directly into the context of the court of law. Paul asks, "Who will bring any charge against God's elect?" (verse 33), and the term for "charge" has been widely documented in secular Greek texts regarding the bringing of accusations in legal proceedings. Any person sitting in the congregation in Rome, hearing this letter read, would immediately think of the Roman legal system and formal charges in a court.

If all of the passages we saw from the Old Testament were not enough, the answer given to the rhetorical question surely establishes the Protestant use of the verb "to justify." The impossibility of a charge being successfully brought against one of God's elect[10] is found in the stark assertion "It is God who justifies." The charge would have to be presented before the judge in the courtroom. *God* is, by nature, the Judge of all, yet, it is *God* who "justifies." God declares His elect to be just on the basis of the work of Christ performed on their behalf. Surely this position would make no sense if it meant God is the one who infuses grace and makes someone inwardly pleasing in His sight. Such a person once justified could, by his actions, undo this inward change, overthrowing the entire point Paul has made.

This reasoning comes out in verse 34 as well. "Who is the one who will condemn?" Again the word comes directly from the courtroom, used in Greek documents to speak of condemnation in legal proceedings. It is clear that God will not bring charges against His elect, for He declares them righteous. Who then can utter the sentence of condemnation over them? None, for the One who intercedes for them is none other than Christ Jesus, who has died and risen again in their place.

It is not surprising to learn that the word translated "interceding" comes directly from the courtroom also. It refers to making an appeal, and here, to appealing for another, interceding for another. No one in Rome listening to Paul's words for the first time would think of any other context than the legal one.

---

[10]I say it is impossible because of what was said in verse 30: God glorifies *all* whom He justifies. If one is justified (a work of God), one will likewise be glorified (a work of God that infallibly follows upon all those who are justified).

So the Protestant has firm ground upon which to state that Paul uses the verb "to justify" in a forensic, legal context here in Romans 8, and that this is perfectly in harmony with his use in Romans 3–5, Galatians, and elsewhere.

"SCHOLARSHIP" AGREES

There is general agreement today across a wide spectrum of "scholarship" that what we have seen so far does indeed accurately represent both the meaning of the Hebrew and Greek terms involved *and* Paul's use of them in the New Testament. Scholarly works emphasize that the term refers to relationship, and hence the declaratory element of "justify" is in the forefront, for the idea of actually changing someone by justifying them would not refer at all to relationship. Even when God is referred to as righteous, the underlying concept is connected with His unchanging nature and that He will always be true to His own law, for He is the Lawgiver. A comment in the *Theological Dictionary of the New Testament* states,

> That God posits law, and that He is bound to it as a just God, is a fundamental tenet in the OT knowledge of faith in all its variations. . . . God's action is a perfect whole which stands because all His ways are right. . . . Yahweh's law is righteous because He is righteous. . . . One may rely upon it because it is nor [*sic*: not] crooked or devious; the mind of Yahweh is upright as that of one who is righteous.[11]

The term "to justify" in the Septuagint conveys the same judicial meaning that is to be found in the New Testament[12] and

---

[11]Gottfried Quell, *The Theological Dictionary of the New Testament*, ed. Gerhard Kittel, III:176. See as well the discussion by Schrenk, III:195–96.

[12]"In the LXX δικαιοῦν (corresponding to צדק) is a forensic term. Yet it does not have a predominant negative connotation ('to condemn') as in Gk., but is constantly used in the positive sense of 'to pronounce righteous,' 'to justify,' 'to vindicate.' . . . The forensic element is even stronger in the LXX than the Mas. Thus in Is. 45:25 the Mas. בַּיהוָה יִצְדְּקוּ means that they find righteousness in Yahweh, whereas the LXX ἀπο κυριου δικαιωθησονται . . . means that they are declared righteous by Him." (Gottlob Schrenk, TDNT, II:212)

that is so clearly propounded in Paul's theology. The great scholar and theologian John Murray has likewise affirmed this "forensic" aspect of Paul's use of "justify,"[13] and John Calvin added,

> As to the word *righteousness,* we must attend to the phraseology of Moses. When he says, that "he believed in the Lord, and he counted it to him for righteousness," he intimates that that person is righteous who is reckoned as such in the sight of God. Now, since men have not righteousness dwelling within themselves, they obtain this by imputation; because God holds their faith as accounted for righteousness. We are therefore said to be "justified by faith," (Rom. iii.28; v. 1,) not because faith infuses into us a habit or quality, but because we are accepted by God.[14]

Louis Berkhof also emphasized the important distinction between subjectively changing someone and declaring them righteous on the basis of the work of another:

> Our word *Justification* (from the Latin *jusificare,* composed of *justus* and *facare,* and therefore meaning "to make righteous") . . . is apt to give the impression that justification denotes a change that is brought about in man, which is not the case. In the use of the English word the danger is not so great, because the people in general do not understand its derivation. . . . "To justify" in the Scriptural sense of the word, is to effect an objective relation, the state of righteousness, by a judicial sentence. This can be done in a two fold way: (a) by bringing into account the actual subjective condition of a

[13]"*Forensic.* This meaning corresponds to that of our English term 'justify'. It is the declarative force that appears in sharp distinction from the causative. In the Hiphil this is explicit in Exod. 23:7; Deut. 25:1; I Kings 8:32; II Chron. 6:23; Job 27:5; Prov. 17:15; Isa. 5:23. In the Piel this meaning is not less apparent in Job 32:2; 33:32 and, in the Hithpael, Gen. 44:16 may not be essentially different. The instances in the Hiphil and Piel are so clear that there is no need to discuss them; no other connotation would be feasible'. The expiatory character of the context of Isa. 53:11 would point definitely in the same direction and, as will be observed later on, the forensic signification in the Hiphil and Piel stems is so pervasive that no other force suggests itself unless there is an obvious consideration to the contrary'. We see, therefore, that there is a pervasive use of the forensic signification of the root צדק in the Qal, Hiphil, and Piel stems and the one instance of the Hithpael (Gen. 44:16) is not essentially different. With respect to the Hiphil and Piel the usage is such that no other signification would suggest itself unless there were some obvious considerations requiring another." (John Murray, *Romans,* 338–39).

[14]John Calvin, *Commentary on Galatians* (3:6), Ages Library CD-ROM.

> person (to justify the just or the righteous), Jas. 2:21; or (b) by imputing to a person the righteousness of another, that is, by accounting him righteous though he is inwardly unrighteous. The latter is the usual sense of justification in the New Testament.[15]

Therefore, we see that "righteousness" or "justification" refers to one's relationship to a standard, most often the law of God, and that the action of declaring righteous or just does not involve a subjective change in the person so described, but is instead a declaration, a pronouncement, concerning that person's status relative to the law. When we read of our being "justified by his grace" (Titus 3:7), we see that this is a pronouncement of our proper relationship to the law of God that is undertaken solely on the basis of God's grace.

When a man is justified, he himself is not changed *(the change takes place in regeneration and sanctification).* Instead, God declares that he is no longer under the penalty or curse of the law. How can this be when the man is still a sinner? The *Baptist Confession* was correct in seeing that the righteousness of Jesus Christ is imputed to those who have faith in Christ, and it is on this basis that they are declared just or righteous.

JUSTIFICATION AND SANCTIFICATION

Many errors about the work of God in salvation could be avoided if everyone would recognize one fact: Justification, while intimately connected to sanctification (both are actions of God's free grace), is a separate divine act, with a differing time frame of operation. That is, while it is completely true that everyone who is justified will also be sanctified (made experientially holy—conformed to the image of Christ, made more like Him through growth in grace and the knowledge of Christ), it is likewise just as true that justification must be distinguished from sanctification. If it is not, tremendous errors result, for inevitably this wrong view

---

[15]Louis Berkhof, *Systematic Theology* (Eerdmans, 1982), 511.

results in a confusion of the *experience* of sanctification with the *grounds* upon which all of the work of God rests, the perfect sacrificial work of Christ on Calvary.

Surely both justification and sanctification are spoken of in Scripture as part and parcel of the singular work of God in saving His people. Both are gracious works (even sanctification, which may make use of all sorts of means, including suffering, sickness, pain, turmoil, and even failure, is a work of grace). Both are only "in Christ" (no one is justified, or made like Him, outside of His work), and so some confuse the two, mainly drawing from passages that do not, again, use specific terminology to address the doctrines in dispute. For example, Paul makes reference to both doctrines as flowing from the one and only Savior, Jesus Christ, in 1 Corinthians 1:30: "He is the reason you have a relationship with Christ Jesus, who became for us wisdom from God, and righteousness and sanctification and redemption."

Paul does not here enter into the temporal relationship between justification and sanctification, but instead teaches that all of salvation, every treasure of the Christian heart, is found solely in Christ. He distinguishes between righteousness and sanctification just as he does between righteousness and redemption.

Another way the Bible distinguishes between the two is in teaching that justification takes place in the past, while sanctification is ongoing. This comes out in one of the key passages in Paul's writings, Romans 5:1: "Therefore, since we have been declared righteous by faith, we have peace with God through our Lord Jesus Christ."

As the exegesis offered later will show, this passage makes our justification the grounds and basis of our peace with God. Hence, it is clearly a past action, one that precedes and determines our relationship with God. And unlike sanctification, it is not something that is being worked out over time. It is a declaration made by God upon the exercise of saving faith, which then inevitably and infallibly begins the experience of sanctification in the life of the believer.

Louis Berkhof summarized the differences between justification and sanctification:

1. Justification removes the guilt of sin and restores the sinner to all the filial rights involved in his state as a child of God, including an eternal inheritance. Sanctification removes the pollution of sin and renews the sinner ever-increasingly in conformity with the image of God.
2. Justification takes place outside the sinner in the tribunal of God, and does not change his inner life, though the sentence is brought home to him subjectively. Sanctification, on the other hand, takes place in the inner life of man and gradually affects his whole being.
3. Justification takes place once for all. It is not repeated, neither is it a process; it is complete at once and for all time. There is no more or less in justification; man is either fully justified, or he is not justified at all. In distinction from it sanctification is a continuous process, which is never completed in this life.
4. While the meritorious cause of both lies in the merits of Christ, there is a difference in the efficient cause. Speaking economically, God the Father declares the sinner righteous, and God the Holy Spirit sanctifies him.[16]

William Hendriksen similarly expressed the important differences between justification and sanctification in these words:

> Justification is a matter of *imputation* (reckoning, charging): the sinner's guilt is imputed to Christ; the latter's righteousness is imputed to the sinner (Gen. 15:6; Ps. 32:1; Isa. 53:4–6; Jer. 23:6; Rom. 5:18, 19). Sanctification is a matter of *transformation* (II Cor. 3:17, 18). In justification the Father takes the lead (Rom. 8:33); in sanctification the Holy Spirit does (II Thess. 2:13). The first is a "once for all" verdict, the second a life-long process. Nevertheless, although the two should never be identified, neither should they be separated. They are distinct but not separate. In justifying the sinner, God may be viewed as the Judge who presides over a law court. The prisoner is standing in the dock. The Judge acquits the prisoner, pronouncing him "not guilty but righteous." The former prisoner is now a free man. But the story does not end here. The

[16]Ibid., 513–14.

Judge now turns to that free man and adopts him as his son, and even imparts his own Spirit to him (Rom. 8:15; Gal. 4:5, 6). Here justification and sanctification touch each other, as it were; for, out of gratitude, this justified person, through the enabling power of the Spirit, begins to fight against his sins and to abound in good works to the glory of his Judge-Father. Good works never justify anyone, but no truly justified person wants to be without them (Eph. 2:8–10).[17]

SO WHAT DOES IT MEAN?

Leon Morris expressed our conclusion with simplicity:

> How can the death of Christ change the verdict on sinners from "Guilty" to "Innocent"? Some have said in effect, "It is by changing the guilty, by transforming them so that they are no longer bad people, but good ones." No one will want to minimize the transformation that takes place in a true conversion or to obscure the fact that this is an important part of being a Christian.
>
> However, such a transformation does not fit the justification terminology. It is sometimes argued that the verb normally translated "to justify" (*dikaioō*) means "to make righteous" rather than "to declare righteous." But this agrees neither with the word's formation nor with its usage. Verbs ending in *-oō* and referring to moral qualities have a declarative sense; they do not mean "to make—." And the usage is never for the transformation of the accused; it always refers to a declaration of his innocence.[18]

And in a similar summary fashion William Hendriksen rightly explained it in these words, emphasizing the fullness of the work of God in salvation.

> Justification is that act of God the Father whereby he counts our sins to be Christ's and Christ's righteousness to be ours

[17]William Hendriksen, *Galatians* (Baker, 1989), 98.

[18]Leon Morris, *New Testament Theology* (Zondervan, 1986), 70. A footnote is included that reads, "Thus, ἀξιόω means 'to deem worthy,' 'to reckon worthy,' not 'to make worthy'; ὁμοιόω means 'to declare to be like.' "

> (II Cor. 5:21). It is the opposite of *condemnation* (Rom. 8:33, 34). It implies deliverance from the curse of God because that curse was placed on Christ (Gal. 3:11–13). It means *forgiveness* full and free (Rom. 4:6–8). It is God's free gift, the fruit of *sovereign grace,* and not in any way the result of human "goodness" or "accomplishment" (Rom 3:24; 5:5, 8, 9). It brings peace to the soul (Rom. 5:1), a peace that passes all understanding. It fills the heart with such thanksgiving that it produces in the life of the believer a rich harvest of good works. Hence, justification and sanctification, though ever distinct, are never separate but stand in the closest possible relation to each other (Rom. 6:2; 8:1, 2).[19]

We have seen that in the Old Testament the term "justify" often carries with it a very clear and forceful forensic/legal meaning that is picked up by the apostle Paul in the New Testament. We have seen that we must recognize this aspect of justification so as to not confuse it with sanctification and overturn the entire work of Christ by making it a cooperative effort that is dependent upon man's actions for completion and success.

But the ultimate proof of the real meaning of justification is found in that when we examine the biblical meaning of "faith" or "belief" and then look at the meaning of "impute" or "reckon," we find that the only consistent meaning of "justification" is, in fact, the legal, forensic one. These terms, then, will be what we examine next.

---

[19]William Hendriksen, *1 & 2 Timothy & Titus* (Baker, 1989), 393.

CHAPTER 6

The Grounds of Justification: The Cross of Christ

> There is no more pointed way of denying that we are justified on account of the state of our own hearts, or the character of our own acts, than by saying that we are justified by a propitiatory sacrifice. This latter declaration places of necessity the ground of acceptance out of ourselves; it is something done for us, not something experienced, or produced in us, or performed by us.[1]

Justification, in the biblical sense, is a declaration concerning the relationship of a man to God and His law. It is a legal statement that a man is no longer under the curse of the law but stands righteous, just, before the bar of God. The Scriptures distinguish between justification and sanctification, teaching that justification is a statement *about* a man, while sanctification is an action that *changes* a man.

[1]Charles Hodge, *Commentary on Romans*, 95.

But for all of this, are we right to say that justification can be limited to the bare declaration of the believer's proper standing before God? Is there not more? Yes, there is. What is "more" is found in what the Bible teaches about *how* God can righteously declare an unjust man to be just—on what basis He does so. As we have already stated, the ground of our justification is the work of Jesus Christ, the righteousness of our Lord, and it is on this incredible truth that the heart of the redeemed loves to dwell. It is the marrow of prayer, the soul of praise.

God does not say something is so when it in fact is not. When God says that the penalty of the law has been fulfilled and that the believer stands positively righteous before the Eternal Judge, then this is the case. It cannot be otherwise. But we have said that the individual man is not changed *subjectively* in justification. Though he is reborn and changed by the work of the Spirit in regeneration, and God continues the process of sanctification throughout his life, justification itself does not change the man. So how can it be said that a man is justified if he is not changed by justification?

The answer is to be found in the imputation of the righteousness of Jesus Christ. What is the righteousness of Christ? Charles Hodge wrote,

> By the righteousness of Christ is meant all he became, did, and suffered to satisfy the demands of divine justice, and merit for his people the forgiveness of sin and the gift of eternal life. The righteousness of Christ is commonly represented as including his active and passive obedience.[2]

The righteousness of Christ includes the entire work of Jesus in redeeming sinners by His substitutionary death (this would be the passive element of His obedience) as well as His perfect and complete obedience to the entire law of God (this would be the active element of His obedience).

Of course, the division of active and passive obedience is not strictly biblical, in that the Bible does not use these exact terms. We are not talking about two different aspects when we speak of

---

[2]Hodge, *Systematic Theology*, III:142.

Christ's righteousness. We are identifying instead a positive and negative aspect of His obedience. In reality, we are struggling to use human language to describe the breadth and depth of the work of the Lord Jesus—no small task indeed!

Christ endured the penalty of the law in our place. "God made the one who did not know sin to be sin for us, so that in him we would become the righteousness of God" (2 Corinthians 5:21). The sinless one was punished as sinner so that sinners could be treated as sinless. He gave His life on behalf of His body, the church, and in so doing provided full and complete forgiveness of sins. It was by His obedience that many are made righteous (Romans 5:19).

But there is another aspect of Christ's righteousness that is often missed. Christ, acting as the head of His people, obeyed the law of God perfectly throughout His life. His was an *active* obedience to the law, resulting in a *positive* aspect to the righteousness that is imputed to the believer. What we are saying is that a person who has been justified through the imputation of the righteousness of Jesus Christ to him is not simply pardoned but has a positive, proper standing before God. The righteousness that is his is not the bare lack of something upon which he can be condemned; it is a positive fulfillment of the commands of God. One is not said to have "fulfilled the law" by simply not doing anything that violates the commandments. One fulfills the law not just by abstaining from murder, but by loving God perfectly and loving one's neighbor as oneself.

If the righteousness that is imputed to the believer were a bare pardon or forgiveness, then he would be left at a neutral point, having no active obedience to the law of God to plead before the holy Judge. But since the elect are joined with Christ, their Head, His active, positive obedience to the Father is imputed to them as part of His righteousness just as His suffering in their stead provides them with redemption and release.

The judicial character of justification is in no way compromised by the recognition of the fullness of the righteousness that is ours in Christ. God constitutes our just position through the work of Christ and then declares it to be so upon the action of faith. The imputation of the righteousness of Christ is the action of the merciful Father, who sees the accomplishment of His Son on behalf of His people as sufficient and complete. John Murray commented,

> When we think of such an act of grace on God's part, we have the answer to our question: how can God justify the ungodly? The righteousness of Christ is the righteousness of his perfect obedience, a righteousness undefiled and undefilable, a righteousness which not only warrants the justification of the ungodly but one that necessarily elicits and constrains such justification. God cannot but accept into his favour those who are invested with the righteousness of his own Son.[3]

And Charles Hodge further asserted,

> So when righteousness is imputed to the believer, he does not thereby become subjectively righteous. If the righteousness be adequate, and if the imputation be made on adequate grounds and by competent authority, the person to whom the imputation is made has the right to be treated as righteous. And, therefore, in the forensic, although not in the moral or subjective sense, the imputation of the righteousness of Christ does make the sinner righteous. That is, it gives him a right to the full pardon of all his sins and a claim in justice to eternal life.[4]

While many accept the imputation of the righteousness of Christ relevant to the remission of sins, they draw back from the idea of Christ's active obedience toward God being imputed as well. Frequently this problem is related to a misunderstanding of the *union with Christ* that is the gracious gift to the elect. This union is important in understanding the true nature of justification, the right standing that is given to everyone who believes in Christ.

---

[3]Murray, *Redemption Accomplished and Applied*, 124.
[4]Hodge, *Systematic Theology*, III:145.

UNITED WITH CHRIST

To understand how the righteousness of Christ in all its fullness can be the possession of the redeemed, it is important to recognize the reality of the union of the elect with Christ. The Lord Jesus taught that they (the elect) had been given to Him by the Father (John 6:37–39). They were chosen in Him "before the foundation of the world" (Ephesians 1:4). So important is the union of Christ with His people that "in Christ" or "in Him" is central to Paul's theology of salvation. He can say that the death of Christ was his death (Galatians 2:20), and the resurrection of Christ his own resurrection (Ephesians 2:6). The relationship between Christ and His people is so close that Paul can use the marriage relationship between man and woman as an example of Christ and His church (Ephesians 5:25–32).

Another symbol used to describe this intimate relationship between the redeemed and their Lord is that of heirship. Believers are said to be "fellow heirs" with Christ (NASB). Christ shares His life with them, and He shares His inheritance with them as well. Surely if the redeemed can be called fellow heirs with Christ, and can even be said to have the mind of Christ (1 Corinthians 2:16), it is not too difficult to see how Christ's righteousness, including His active obedience to the Father, can be imputed to His people for their justification. What Christ did, He did in our stead, in our place. This is true of His death, which brings us forgiveness of sins, and it is also true of His holy, sinless life of obedience to the law of God, which provides to us who are unworthy and ungodly a positive standing before the Father.

Furthermore, we can see the error of reducing the doctrine of justification to merely the pardon of past sins. If justification is something that is an ongoing process or is something that can be lost and gained again, then it is hardly the imputation of the righteousness of Christ! Is the righteousness of Christ something that can be obliterated or destroyed by the action of men? Is it but a temporal thing that has to be propped up and maintained by the feverish activity of creatures? Is one who stands robed in the righteousness of Christ liable to fall repeatedly from this position? Is one forgiven and lost, forgiven and lost, in a seemingly never-ending cycle? Surely not! One who has been justified stands before God uncondemned *and uncondemnable*—not because of what he is in himself, but because of what Christ is in him.

"There is therefore now no condemnation *for those who are in Christ Jesus*" (Romans 8:1). The reason for this is clear: all who are "in Christ" partake of His righteousness and have been declared free from the curse of the law, and therefore there can be no possible grounds of condemnation for them. Have they ever transgressed the law? Christ has borne their penalty. Have they failed to love God as they should? Christ has loved the Father perfectly in their place. The Judge has declared them just. His Son stands in their place perfectly righteous. Who can possibly bring a charge, then, against God's elect (Romans 8:33)?

FORGIVENESS OF ALL SIN

Another area of controversy relates to the *permanence* of the declaration of justification. The truth is, if justification is a one-time declaration by God, intimately connected with the forgiveness of sins through the work of Christ, then it follows that all of the believer's sins have been forgiven him for Christ's sake. This remission of all sins is not limited to past sins only, but to all sins—past, present, and future. If it were not so, then justification would have to be repeated over and over again, and the imputation of the righteousness of Christ would be little more than a fiction, lowered to the level of the animal sacrifices of the old covenant, which had to be offered over and over again as a symbol of the continued presence of sin. Instead of this, all our transgressions were laid upon Christ and were, therefore, nailed to the cross (Colossians 2:13–14).

The problem with accepting this fact is easy to see: how can we speak of sins being forgiven when they haven't even been committed yet? And why do we read that we as believers are to confess our sins (1 John 1:9)? Yet on the other hand, it seems far more difficult to understand how Christ's death is insufficient to bring about full pardon of all sins, instead needing to be reapplied repeatedly.

First, we note that at the time of the death of Christ, *all* the sins of *all* believers for the next two millennia were yet future. So if we believe that *any* of our sins were laid upon Christ, even if we limit this to our past sins, we are asserting that future sins were laid upon Christ in the past. Therefore the idea that future sins can be said to be forgiven in the death of Christ is basic to the whole presentation of the efficacy of His saving work. Our problem lies in the fact that we are caught in the middle, so to speak, knowing all too well our past and present sins but not yet knowledgeable about our future trespasses. If we confess, however, that our past sins were forgiven in the work of Christ long ago, we should not reject that our future sins can be laid upon Him as well.

Second, Paul presents an important truth relevant to this matter in his quotation of David's words from Psalm 31:

> *Blessed are those whose lawless deeds are forgiven, and whose sins are covered; blessed is the one against whom the Lord will never count sin.* (Romans 4:7–8)

As we will see in the exegesis of this passage, the parallel of "forgiven" and "covered" is found in the denial of the future imputation of sin to the believer—the "non-imputation" of sin (the NET uses "count sin" for the more literal "impute sin"). This suggests to us that it is best to think of the forgiveness of future sins in the sense of non-imputation of those sins. Hodge explained:

> The sins which are pardoned in justification include all sins, past, present, and future. It does indeed seem to be a solecism that sins should be forgiven before they are committed. Forgiveness involves remission of penalty. But how can a penalty be remitted before it is incurred? This is only an apparent difficulty arising out of the inadequacy of human language. The righteousness of Christ is a perpetual donation. It is a robe which hides, or as the Bible expresses it, covers from the eye of justice the sin of the believer. They are sins; they deserve

> the wrath and curse of God, but the necessity for the infliction of that curse no longer exists. The believer feels the constant necessity for confession and prayer for pardon, but the ground of pardon is present for him to offer and plead. So that it would perhaps be a more correct statement to say that in justification the believer receives the promise that God will not deal with him according to his transgressions, rather than to say that sins are forgiven before they are committed.[5]

Hodge goes on to develop this idea in the light of Romans 6:14, where believers "are not under law but under grace." That is, God deals with the elect graciously, not imputing their sins to them (2 Corinthians 5:19; Romans 4:8) but instead looking to the death of Christ on Calvary as sufficient grounds upon which to forgive.

Further, those who are no longer under the condemnation of the law, who stand robed in the righteousness of Jesus Christ, are given a title to eternal life. Again, this gift is not based upon anything the redeemed have done or will do. They do nothing to deserve it. Instead, Christ is the one who has merited eternal life, and since His righteousness is imputed to those who are justified, then they too merit eternal life, and they cannot possibly fail to receive it.

The recognition of this truth is in no way a warrant or license to sin. The heart that knows the price paid for its redemption does not seek to add to the cost. Indeed, when God removes our heart of stone and gives us a heart of flesh (Ezekiel 36:26), the result is that we desire to walk in His ways and commandments (Ezekiel 36:27). It is our love for Christ that prompts our new natures to seek Him and walk in paths of righteousness. In Hodge's *Commentary on Romans*, we hear,

> All modes of preaching must be erroneous, which do not lead sinners to feel that the great thing to be done, and done first, is to receive the Lord Jesus Christ, and to turn unto God through him. And all religious experience must be defective, which does not embrace distinctly a sense of the justice of our

[5]Ibid., 163–64.

condemnation, and a conviction of the sufficiency of the work of Christ, and an exclusive reliance upon it as such.[6]

THE WRATH OF GOD AND PROPITIATION

Theologians should be those enraptured by the beauty of the unchanging object of their study: the eternal, immutable God. But theologians are people, and they are influenced, to greater or lesser extents, by the society and era in which they live. The cultural decay of modern times has inspired many a theological denial of biblical truth, most often when that biblical truth speaks to something that is unfashionable.

One such issue that directly impacts the doctrine of justification is the oft-repeated biblical phrase "the wrath of God." While most would think the Old Testament the strongest witness to the wrath of God (Israel's destruction of the corrupt, vile Canaanite peoples is often cited), in reality the phrase appears often in the New Testament in theologically significant passages.

Yet it is surely out of vogue to speak of God's wrath or to admit that God has wrath against sin. Even in conservative circles, the traditional saying "God hates the sin but loves the sinner" has been so often repeated that such passages as Psalm 5:5 ("You hate all who do iniquity," NASB) and Psalm 11:5 ("And the one who loves violence His soul hates," NASB) have been practically decanonized. For many, it is an unfortunate miscalculation of the Holy Spirit that right on the heels of such a passage as John 3:16, we read the words, "The one who rejects the Son will not see life, but God's wrath remains on him" (John 3:36).

The result is a widespread denial in modern theological writings of the existence of any such thing as the wrath of God. And of course, once you no longer have wrath against sin, the related issues of atonement, sacrifice, justice, holiness, and punishment are all removed from their biblical moorings and redefined (or simply done away with). Many today unashamedly confess a God

[6]Hodge, *Commentary on Romans*, 103.

who is less than human. That is, while we know that a man who would not experience wrath against injustice and evil is less than a man, yet we find many preaching a God who can look upon evil and injustice and unholiness and respond with merely a smile and a pat of His less-than-omnipotent hand.

The denial of the wrath of God leads inevitably to a destruction of the doctrine of justification. Why does a person need justification when, in fact, sin is really not that big an issue? If there is no wrath, there need be no forgiveness, no mercy, no grace, no redemption, no sacrifice. And most importantly, there need be no propitiatory sacrifice. A propitiatory sacrifice is one that both takes away wrath and brings forgiveness of sin. This is why many modern theologians prefer the less strident term "expiation," which lacks the element of the removal of wrath.

Leon Morris, upon examining the issue minutely, made note of many such denials of the reality of the wrath of God, indicated that the list of citations could probably be extended indefinitely, and replied:

> Perhaps the difficulty arises because we are making a false antithesis between the divine wrath and the divine love. We are handicapped by the fact that we must necessarily use terms properly applicable to human affairs, and for us it is very difficult to be simultaneously wrathful and loving. But, upon analysis, this seems to be largely because our anger is such a selfish passion, usually involving a large element of irrationality together with a lack of self-control. . . . Those who object to the conception of the wrath of God should realize that what is meant is not some irrational passion bursting forth uncontrollably, but a burning zeal for the right coupled with a perfect hatred for everything that is evil. It may be that wrath is not a perfect word to describe such an attitude, but no better has been suggested, and we must refuse to accept alternatives which do not give expression to the truth in question. . . . We sometimes find among men an affection which is untempered by a sterner side, and this we call sentimentality. It is not such that the Bible thinks of when it speaks of the love of God, but rather of a love which is so jealous for the good of the loved one that it blazes out in fiery wrath against everything that is

> evil. . . . The evidence that the Bible means what it says when it uses this term is so strong that, as we saw earlier, S. R. Driver can speak of propitiation as one of the three main categories used in the New Testament to interpret the death of Christ. From a slightly different point of view Denney says: "If the propitiatory death of Jesus is eliminated from the love of God, it might be unfair to say that the love of God is robbed of all meaning, but it is certainly robbed of its apostolic meaning." The writers of the New Testament know nothing of a love which does not react in the very strongest fashion against every form of sin.[7]

As the exegesis of the relevant passages will show, the only consistent way of viewing propitiation as used in the New Testament is to understand it as the sacrifice that brings forgiveness of sins *and* removes the wrath of a just God against that sin. To view the cross of Christ outside of the wrath of God is to see it in only one dimension, one that is surely not consistent with the biblical revelation.

THE GREAT CONTROVERSY: THE NATURE OF SAVING FAITH

Before looking at the role of faith in justification, there is a major issue that must be raised and examined. Evangelicals will always say "We are saved by grace through faith alone," but what is meant by the word "faith"? And more to the point, is faith something that is completely human, a mixture of human action and divine assistance, or a divine enablement, a gift? The question has divided theologians for centuries, mainly because it speaks to the concepts of free will, the extent of the depravity of man, and the role of man in salvation. Emotions often run very high when anyone suggests that man's capacities and abilities are less than we would like them to be. But it is not possible to avoid addressing this issue.

---

[7]Leon Morris, *The Apostolic Preaching of the Cross* (Eerdmans, 1983), 208–10.

Of the elements that come into play when discussing the nature of saving faith, the impact of sin upon the soul, the meaning of such phrases as "dead in sin," "slaves to sin," "unable to do what is pleasing," "unable to come," etc.—all must be examined for a fair and biblical conclusion to be drawn. It is not our intention to go into each of these here. Instead, the main issue that must be addressed is this: Does the Bible say saving faith is a gift of God, an ability given as part of God's work of regeneration, or is it something that every person, either with the mere assistance of grace or outside of grace, is able to perform? The reason for asking the question is clear: If what we have said thus far is true, and justification is a divine act based upon the work of Christ, is all of this dependent for its success upon a merely human action, or even an action that is partly human, partly derived by grace, and yet fully outside the sovereign decree of God? The issue goes to whether salvation is to God's glory alone or whether it leads to a divided glory.

There is no question that faith is something that man does. Man believes. But does sinful man have the ability to believe *savingly* in and of himself, outside of the miracle of regeneration? The passages we have already examined about man's deadness in sin and the extended study of Romans 1 that will be presented in the exegetical section suggest strongly that viewing saving faith as an ability latent in all men and women *prior to* regeneration is unwarranted. God-haters lack the ability to do what is pleasing to God (Romans 8:7–8).

If this observation is accurate, then it must follow that the Bible would speak of saving faith as a gift—a work of God—and would connect it with the role of the Spirit, who likewise gives all other gifts to the redeemed. And this is exactly what we find. Paul began many of his epistles with thanksgiving to God for the love *and the faith* of the Christians to whom he was writing. For example:

> We always give thanks to God, the father of our Lord Jesus Christ, when we pray for you, since we heard about your faith in Christ Jesus and the love that you have for all the saints. (Colossians 1:3–4)

> We ought to thank God always for you, brothers and sisters, and rightly so, because your faith flourishes more and more and the love of each one of you all for one another is ever greater. (2 Thessalonians 1:3)

Why should thanks be given to God for something that is within the capacity of all men and women everywhere? The giving of thanks indicates that the faith for which the thanks is being given is, in fact, a work of God within them. And that is what we find in these passages:

> But the fruit of the Spirit is love, joy, peace, patience, kindness, goodness, faithfulness [πίστις, "faith"]. (Galatians 5:22)

> Peace to the brothers and sisters, and love with faith, from God the Father and the Lord Jesus Christ. Grace be with all of those who love our Lord Jesus Christ with an undying love. (Ephesians 6:23–24)

> Our Lord's grace was abundant, bringing faith and love in Christ Jesus. (1 Timothy 1:14)

Peter's words are unambiguous and clear:

> From Simeon Peter, a slave and apostle of Jesus Christ, to those who through the righteousness of our God and Savior, Jesus Christ, have been granted a faith just as precious as ours. (2 Peter 1:1)

Probably the most explicit assertion that faith is a gift of God is found in these words to the Philippians:

> For it has been granted to you not only to believe in Christ but also to suffer for him. (Philippians 1:29)

Two things are here "granted" (ἐχαρίσθη) to believers: τὸ ὑπὲρ αὐτοῦ πάσχειν, *"to suffer for him"* and τὸ εἰς αὐτὸν πιστεύειν, *"to believe in Him."* This is the normal term used for saving faith (πιστεύειν). Some might suggest that what is referred to here are opportunities to suffer, and hence opportunities to believe. But this would not explain how it is that the very act of belief can be described as something given to Christians. This theme of faith as a gift is much more widespread than many know:

> And on the basis of faith in Jesus' name, his very name has made this man strong whom you see and know. The faith that is through Jesus has given him this complete health in the presence of you all. (Acts 3:16)

> Through him you now trust in God, who raised him from the dead and gave him glory, so that your faith and hope are in God. (1 Peter 1:21)

In fact, faith is said to have an origin and a finisher in the person of the Lord Jesus Christ:

> Therefore, since we are surrounded by such a great cloud of witnesses, we must get rid of every weight and the sin that clings so closely, and run with endurance the race set out for us, keeping our eyes fixed on Jesus, the pioneer and perfecter of our faith. For the joy set out for him he endured the cross, disregarding its shame, and has taken his seat at the right hand of the throne of God. (Hebrews 12:1–2)

The Greek term *archegon* (ἀρχηγὸν), translated here as "pioneer," refers to the origin, source, beginning, and then by extension, author. *Teleiōten* (τελειωτὴν) refers to one who completes and perfects. Such terms are fitting if indeed faith is the work of the Spirit of God in the redeemed, but not if it is in fact a human capacity that may, or may not, be actuated by grace.

These passages present a clear doctrine of faith as the work of the Spirit, a gracious gift given to those who receive mercy and grace from God. This explains, then, how Romans 8:30 can say that all those who are justified will likewise be glorified, and this without fail: Faith is not a disruption in the divine work of salvation, one that gives man the final say in the matter. It is the result of regeneration, an ability granted by God to those He draws to His Son.

Justified by Faith, Faith Alone, Faith Without Works, *Sola Fide!*

I cannot express this truth any more clearly or beautifully than Robert Reymond in his *New Systematic Theology of the Christian Faith:*

> With a gloriously monotonous regularity Paul pits faith off over against all law-keeping as its diametrical opposite as to referent. Whereas the latter relies on the human effort of the law-keeper *looking to himself* to render satisfaction before God, the former repudiates and *looks entirely away from all human effort* to the cross work of Jesus Christ, who alone by his sacrificial death rendered satisfaction before God for men.[8]

Reymond quotes a number of passages from the apostle Paul (Romans 3:20–22, 28; 4:5, 14; 10:4; Galatians 2:16; 3:11; Philippians 3:9) and passionately concludes,

> From such verses it is plain that Paul taught that justification is by "faith alone" *(sola fide).* The Roman Catholic Church has always objected to the use of this *sola* ("alone") attached to *fide,* contending that nowhere does Paul say "alone" when speaking of the faith that justifies, and that where the Bible does attach *sola* to *fide* when speaking of justification it declares: "You see that a person is justified by what he does and not by faith alone" (James 2:24). All this is true enough, but I would insist, as the above citations indicate, that when Paul declares (1) that a man is justified "by faith apart from [χωρὶς, *chōris*] works of the law," (2) that the man "who works not but believes in him who justifies the ungodly" is the man whom God regards as righteous, (3) that a man is "not justified by works of the law but through faith," and (4) that "by the Law no man is justified before God . . . because the righteous by faith shall live," he is asserting the "aloneness" of faith as the "alone" instrument of justification as surely as if he had used the word "alone," and he is asserting it even more vigorously than if he had simply employed μόνος *monos* ("alone") each time.[9]

---

[8]Robert Reymond, *A New Systematic Theology of the Christian Faith* (Thomas Nelson, 1998), 732.

[9]Ibid.

Reymond then cites this very relevant section from Calvin, who likewise heard the same objections to his proclamation of *sola fide* at the time of the Reformation. Remembering the context of battle and struggle will help explain the language used:

> Now the reader sees how fairly the Sophists today cavil against our doctrine when we say that man is justified by faith alone [Romans 3:28]. They dare not deny that man is justified by faith because it recurs so often in Scripture. But since the word "alone" is nowhere expressed, they do not allow this addition to be made. Is it so? But what will they reply to these words of Paul where he contends that righteousness cannot be of faith unless it be free [Romans 4:2 ff.]? How will a free gift agree with works? With what chicaneries will they elude what he says in another passage, that God's righteousness is revealed in the gospel [Romans 1:17]? If righteousness is revealed in the gospel, surely no mutilated or half righteousness but a full and perfect righteousness is contained there. The law therefore has no place in it. Not only by a false but by an obviously ridiculous shift they insist upon excluding this adjective. Does not he who takes everything from works firmly enough ascribe everything to faith alone? What, I pray, do these expressions mean: "His righteousness has been manifested apart from the law" [Romans 3:21]; and, "Man is freely justified" [Romans 3:24]; and, "Apart from the works of the law" [Romans 3:28]?[10]

How else indeed can we say that we are justified by anything other than faith? *Sola fide* has never, ever meant "justified by a barren, dead faith that is not Spirit-borne nor accompanied by all the rest of the work of God in His redeemed people." The *alone* has always referred to the denial of any *additions* to faith, especially those that speak to merit. Calvin continued,

> I term it salvation of free gift, because it is given us simply of God, so as we bring not anything with us [to the attainment thereof] but only an eager desire to be filled with the thing that we want. Therefore it standeth us on hand to come as

[10]Calvin, *Institutes of the Christian Religion*, III:11:19.

> poor beggars unto God, if we mind to be justified for our Lord Jesus Christ's sake. For if we imagine ever so small a drop of deserving in ourselves, it stoppeth us from coming to our Lord Jesus Christ. And not without cause doth an ancient Doctor say, that we cannot receive the Salvation that is offered us in our Lord Jesus Christ, except we have first dispatched the minding of our own deserts, and acknowledged that there is nothing but utter wretchedness in ourselves.[11]

Faith, then, abandons all claim to any merit or reward. It is a passive instrument. It is not meritorious in itself. Hodge explained it in these words:

> The part assigned to faith in the work of our reconciliation to God is that of an instrument; it apprehends or appropriates the meritorious ground of our acceptance, the work or righteousness of Christ. It is not itself that ground, nor the means of attaining an inherent righteousness acceptable to God. This is obvious, 1. Because our justification would not then be gratuitous, or without works. Paul would then teach the very reverse of the doctrine which he has been labouring to establish, viz, that it is not on account of works of righteousness, i.e. works of the highest order of excellence, that we are accepted, since these works would then be the real ground of our acceptance. 2. Because we are said to be justified by faith, of which Christ is the object, by faith in his blood, by faith in him as a sacrifice.[12]

As B. B. Warfield put it, "The saving power of faith resides thus not in itself, but in the Almighty Saviour on whom it rests. . . . It is not, strictly speaking, even faith in Christ that saves, but Christ that saves through faith."[13]

> But why does faith receive such honour as to be entitled a cause of our justification? First, we must observe, that it is

[11]Calvin, *Sermons on Galatians*, Sermon 3 (*The John Calvin Collection*, Ages Library CD-ROM, 1999).

[12]Hodge, *Commentary on Romans*, 94.

[13]Benjamin B. Warfield, "The Biblical Doctrine of Faith" in *The Works of Benjamin B. Warfield* (Baker, 1981), II:504.

> merely an instrumental cause; for, strictly speaking, our righteousness is nothing else than God's free acceptance of us, on which our salvation is founded. But as the Lord testifies his love and grace in the gospel, by offering to us that righteousness of which I have spoken, so we receive it by faith. And thus, when we ascribe to faith a man's justification, we are not treating of the principal cause, but merely pointing out the way in which men arrive at true righteousness. For this righteousness is not a quality which exists in men, but is the mere gift of God, and is enjoyed by faith only; and not even as a reward justly due to faith, but because we receive by faith what God freely gives.[14]

Consider the last line of this citation well. Righteousness is not a quality in man but a declaration on the part of God based on the cross-work of Christ; justification is free and gracious, "enjoyed" by faith *only* since God has deemed it proper to make the declaration *solely* upon the exercise of the divinely given gift. Justification is not a reward given *to* faith, but instead the empty hand of faith—bringing no plea other than "Christ is sufficient! Be merciful to me, the sinner! I believe!"—is the only hand that will find itself grasped by the hand of God's almighty grace.

---

[14]Calvin, *Commentary on Galatians* (3:6).

CHAPTER 7

Imputation: The Only Hope of the Sinful Soul

Imputation. It sounds so . . . dry, formal, technical. Sort of like saying "File Allocation Table" or "Insurance Rate." So why in the world would anyone suggest that it is the only hope of the sinful soul? How can such a term figure in the hope of the Christian? The following information will make the answers very, very clear.

If the Bible's use of the word "impute" or "reckon" in the key passages we've been studying means something like "change someone inwardly so that he is pleasing to God," then most everything we have seen so far is really irrelevant, since all the work of salvation falls back upon man and his ability to maintain some state into which justification places him. But if "reckon" means "credit to one's account and treat them accordingly," everything is different. The righteousness of Christ then, imputed to a believer, becomes the basis upon which God can and does treat the believer as just, even though the believer well knows that he continues to experience sin and failure in this life.

Said another way, if "impute" means "change inwardly," then man's religions have been right all along, and our relationship with God is an on-again, off-again roller coaster of penances and works. But if "impute" means "credit to one's account and treat accordingly," then the righteousness that is imputed by faith is Christ's perfect righteousness, and the resulting relationship, secured by the work of the Divine Substitute himself, produces the very peace Paul promised (Romans 5:1), and all the praise and glory can go solely to God for His work in Christ *(Soli Deo Gloria).* "Impute" is a small word, but the sin-wearied soul who realizes what it really means finds it to be a true source of hope and constant encouragement.

IMPUTATION IN THE OLD TESTAMENT

The term translated "reckon" or "impute" in the Old Testament often has the bare meaning of "consider" or to "think about." But there are a number of passages in which the term refers to considering the person in a particular light and treating him in accordance with this consideration. And what it surely does *not* mean in these passages is that the person is somehow subjectively changed.

One example of this is Leviticus 17:4:

> . . . and has not brought it to the doorway of the tent of meeting to present it as an offering to the Lord before the tabernacle of the Lord, bloodguiltiness is to be reckoned to that man. He has shed blood and that man shall be cut off from among his people. (NASB)

Here, any man who did not bring an animal he had slaughtered to the door of the tabernacle as an offering to the Lord, as the Scripture says, had bloodguiltiness *reckoned* to him. Surely this guilt was not *infused* into the man, but he was *legally declared guilty* of blood. By this point it should not be overly surprising to note the legal, or forensic, nature of the context.

I suggest that this is the proper background for Paul's understanding of the term in Genesis 15:6 as well. As we saw, Paul cites Genesis 15:6 a number of times as a foundational passage indicating that salvation has *always* been by grace through faith (Romans 4:3, 9, 22; Galatians 3:6). This is especially clear in a legal context, and that is what we have in Romans 3–4.

The Hebrew term for "impute" or "reckon," *hashav*,[1] has some very interesting uses in the Old Testament. We need to discover the background of Paul's use of the term as it is found relative to the imputation of righteousness.

In Genesis 31:14–15 Rachel and Leah, Jacob's wives, speak of their father and the treatment they have received at his hand:

> "Do we still have any portion or inheritance in our father's house? Are we not reckoned [*hashav*] by him as foreigners? For he has sold us, and has also entirely consumed our purchase price." (NASB)

Of course, Rachel and Leah were not foreigners, but they were *reckoned* as such by their father. This imputation did not involve changing their nature as his daughters, but it did involve treating them as if they had a different status than was truly theirs.

One other example: in Leviticus 25:31 the law concerning redemption rights is presented:

> The houses of the villages, however, which have no surrounding wall shall be considered [*hashav*] as open fields; they have redemption rights and revert in the jubilee. (NASB)

The houses in unwalled villages were to be treated as if they were open fields; they were not, of course, open fields, but legally they were treated as if they were. This imputation or reckoning did not involve bulldozing the houses so that they subjectively would become open fields, but instead they would be considered to be open fields for legal purposes.

All of the examples listed above of this use of *hashav* are translated in the Septuagint by the very same term[2] Paul uses in

---

[1]חשב
[2]λογίζομαι

Romans 4 when he speaks of the imputation or reckoning of righteousness to the believer! Why is this significant? Because scholars recognize that Paul used the Septuagint as his main source of biblical citations, and his vocabulary is deeply influenced by it. Just as we saw that the Septuagint's definition of "justify" provides vital background for that term's usage in the New Testament, so too these examples relating to "impute" fit consistently with the idea of "imputing righteousness" in Paul's theology. Hodge examined the biblical evidence and said,

> These and numerous similar passages render the Scriptural idea of imputation perfectly clear. It is laying anything to one's charge, and treating him accordingly. It produces no change in the individual to whom the imputation is made; it simply alters his relation to the law. All those objections, therefore, to the doctrine expressed by this term, which are founded on the assumption that imputation alters the moral character of men; that it implies an infusion of either sin or holiness, rest on a misconception of its nature. It is, so far as the mere force of the term is concerned, a matter of perfect indifference whether the thing imputed belonged antecedently to the person to whom the imputation is made or not. It is just as common and correct to speak of laying to a man's charge what does not belong to him, as what does. That a thing can seldom be justly imputed to a person to whom it does not personally belong, is a matter of course. But that the word itself implies that the thing imputed must belong to the person concerned, is a singular misconception. These remarks have, of course, reference only to the meaning of the word. Whether the Bible actually teaches that there is an imputation of either sin or righteousness, to any to whom it does not personally belong, is another question. . . .
>
> Paul, speaking to Philemon of the debt of Onesimus, says, "put that on my account," i.e., impute it to me. The word used in this case is the same as that which occurs in Rom. 5 v. 13, "Sin is not imputed where there is no law"; and is in its root and usage precisely synonymous with the word employed in the passage before us [Romans 4], when the latter is used in reference to imputation. No less than twice also, in this very

chapter, vers. 6 and 11, Paul speaks of "imputing righteousness," not to those to whom it personally belongs, certainly, but to the ungodly, ver. 5; to those who have no works, ver. 6.[3]

And the inevitable result of seeing this biblical evidence in the entire context of the theology of Scripture is:

> So when righteousness is imputed to the believer, he does not thereby become subjectively righteous. If the righteousness be adequate, and if the imputation be made on adequate grounds and by competent authority, the person to whom the imputation is made has the right to be treated as righteous. And, therefore, in the forensic, although not in the moral or subjective sense, the imputation of the righteousness of Christ does make the sinner righteous. That is, it gives him a right to the full pardon of all his sins and a claim in justice to eternal life.[4]

The imputation of the righteousness of Christ is the action of the merciful Father who sees the accomplishment of His Son in behalf of His people as sufficient and complete. John Murray commented,

> When we think of such an act of grace on God's part, we have the answer to our question: how can God justify the ungodly?

---

[3]Hodge, *Commentary on Romans*, 106–107.

[4]Hodge, *Systematic Theology*, III:145. Likewise he elsewhere added this vital information:

> It never was, as shown above, the doctrine of the Reformation, or of the Lutheran and Reformed divines, that the imputation of righteousness affects the moral character of those concerned. It is true, whom God justifies he also sanctifies; but justification is not sanctification, and the imputation of righteousness is not the infusion of righteousness. These are the first principles of the doctrine of the Reformers. "The fourth grand error of the Papists in the article of justification," says an old divine, "is concerning that which we call the form thereof. For they, denying and deriding the imputation of Christ's righteousness, (without which, notwithstanding, no man can be saved,) do hold that men are justified by infusion, and not by imputation of righteousness; we, on the contrary, do hold, according to the Scriptures, that we are justified before God, only by the imputation of Christ's righteousness, and not by infusion. And our meaning, when we say that God imputeth Christ's righteousness unto us, is nothing else but this: that he graciously accepteth for us, and in our behalf, the righteousness of Christ, that is, both as to his obedience, which, in the days of his flesh, he performed for us; and passive, that is, his sufferings, which he sustained for us, as if we had in our own persons both performed and suffered the same ourselves. Howbeit, we confess that the Lord doth infuse righteousness into the faithful; yet not as he justifieth, but as he sanctifieth them." Bishop Downame on Justification, 261. (Hodge, *Commentary on Romans*, 114).

> The righteousness of Christ is the righteousness of his perfect obedience, a righteousness undefiled and undefilable, a righteousness which not only warrants the justification of the ungodly but one that necessarily elicits and constrains such justification. God cannot but accept into his favour those who are invested with the righteousness of his own Son.[5]

WHY THIS IS VITAL

So why press this point so strongly? Because the only righteousness the Christian has is an *imputed* righteousness, and if that imputation involves a subjective change in the person (i.e., if it means that we are *made* righteous, and hence pleasing to God) rather than the crediting of the righteousness of another (Christ), the entire gospel message takes on a completely different meaning and nature. The focus moves away from the perfection of the work of Christ on behalf of the believer to the maintenance of a state or condition. The glory for salvation itself is divided between the Savior and the saved, for the work of the one only makes it possible for the other to engage in "self-salvation."

What is more, any other understanding of imputation would be inconsistent with the meanings of "justification" and "faith" we have already seen in Scripture. Not only would seeing imputation as infusion or subjective change result in a contradictory meaning of "justify," but it would likewise undercut the freeness of grace and the "empty hand of faith." As we have seen before, it is the consistency and harmony of the various elements of the doctrine with each other that testify to its overall truth. This is the mark of truly biblical belief: consistency through Scripture and with itself.

Why is imputation the only hope of the sinful soul? Because it is the one who knows the stain of his sin who knows that he must have a righteousness that is not his own. Paul knew this personally, for he expressed his desire that he might "be found in Him, not

---

[5]Murray, *Redemption Accomplished and Applied*, 124.

having a righteousness of my own derived from the Law, but that which is through faith in Christ, the righteousness which comes from God on the basis of faith" (Philippians 3:9 NASB).

Paul sought the alien righteousness that comes only from God, only by faith, and only from Christ. He rejected the idea of having a "righteousness of my own derived from the Law," that is, one inherent within him that comes from obeying God's highest revelation of His moral standards. Paul knew that no man could live up to such a standard to begin with. So he looked outside of himself to a righteousness imputed whose origin and source is God. This is why imputation is such a beautiful word to the sinner who feels so keenly his lack of righteousness and the perfection of the righteousness of Christ. Such a gift cannot be purchased, earned, or merited. It must be imputed by grace.

CHAPTER 8

Luther's Dunghill

I doubt Martin Luther any longer cares that he is remembered as a beer-drinking, pretzel-eating theologian whose illustrations were often more earthy than the sensibilities of many modern readers can allow. Hiding behind his gruff exterior was a sharp intellect and a sensitive heart that could express itself in the most surprising ways.

One of Luther's most famous illustrations comes from the rural farms of Germany. Farmers, needing a way to fertilize their fields, would collect the refuse of their farm animals into piles to be spread out on the fields when the weather demanded. These "dunghills" would at times dot the landscape and were, of course, anything but attractive to either see or smell. Drawing on this commonplace occurrence, Luther once attempted to demonstrate the difference between justification and sanctification. He likened our sinful state to a dunghill: ugly and offensive, it has nothing in and of itself that would make it pleasing to anyone, let alone to God.

This is what we are like in our sin. There is nothing that would recommend us to God, nothing that is acceptable, nothing that merits His blessing. We are foul and repulsive in our sin. As I said, Luther's theological illustrations were earthy, brutally honest, and, in this case, perfectly true.

Justification, he went on, is like that first snowfall of the approaching winter, the one that covers everything in a blanket of pure white. Unlike later snowfalls, where man has shoveled and plowed and otherwise worked to clear a path for himself, that first snow is clean, beautiful. Everything is covered in the same uniform blanket—even, Luther points out, those piles of dung. What was once foul is no longer. The smell is gone. The repulsive sight is gone. All is white and clean and pure.

This is how justification differs from sanctification. In justification we receive the pure and spotless righteousness of Christ, a blanket that covers over our sin in the sight of the Father. The dunghill is still, intrinsically and internally, a dunghill—that hasn't changed. What *has* changed is its relationship to an external standard—God's standard.

That first snowfall, the righteousness of Christ, an alien righteousness, the righteousness of *another*, is imputed to us, covering us and removing our offensiveness before God the Father. We do remain sinners inwardly; it is the work of *sanctification* that changes us internally, conforming us ever closer to the image of Christ.

Martin Luther did not deny the renewing work of the Spirit in regeneration—the fact that we are given a new heart, for example. His purpose in this case was solely to show how and why justification differs from sanctification.

Luther has taken his lumps over the years for this illustration. It is common for many to bring up this story and say, "See, Luther and those who follow him in their understanding of justification don't really believe that God changes us. We can just go on sinning and all will be well." Do such objections have merit? Do they carry weight? Is the view of Luther and his followers a legal fairy tale?

I have found the best way to defend Luther on this issue, aside from biblically demonstrating the nature of justification via the imputation of Christ's righteousness and the non-imputation of sin, is to turn the illustration around. How do other religious movements believe that pile of dung can ever hope to be pleasing in God's sight?

The primary teaching of the religions of man is that when a person is "saved," he is made internally and intrinsically pleasing to God. To bring it into Luther's context, when the pile of dung is "saved," it is internally changed from a pile of dung into a pile of . . . gold! A fine, shiny pile of gold that would, of course, be desirable to anyone, including God. God would surely like to have this pile of gold in heaven with Him, so as long as the gold remains what it is—intrinsically pleasing to God—it will enter into His presence.

But man's religions cannot bear a perfect work of salvation that gives no place to man. The very nature of these religious systems requires that salvation be conditional upon continued works on the part of the followers. The idea of failure, falling away, has to be held over the heads of those you wish to control through religious power. So in our illustration, there must be some consequence to failure (sin) on the part of the pile of gold as it goes through life.

Since Roman Catholic apologists are those who most often raise objections to Luther's view (they would be joined by many others, including those involved in Mormonism, the Watchtower Society, and more), let's put the pile of gold into that context. (This is also fair to Luther, who was reacting to the Roman Catholic doctrine to begin with.) In the Roman Catholic system our dunghill would become a pile of gold through the "laver of regeneration," baptism. It would then be internally changed and made pleasing to God.

However, the pile of gold may commit sins during the course of its life on earth. Some sins, it is said, do not destroy the grace of justification that has turned the dunghill into the pile of gold.

These are called venial sins. But there are punishments, temporal punishments, that come with such sins. We would liken these to flecks or globs of dung that appear on the surface of the gold. They are not enough to cause the gold to be rejected by God *en toto*, but some mechanism for cleansing the gold must be envisioned. This leads to the Roman Catholic doctrine of purgatory, the idea of a place of cleansing (or purgation) after death but before entrance into the presence of God.[1]

But what about those serious sins that do, in fact, destroy the grace of justification? These "mortal" sins would instantaneously turn the pile of gold back into a pile of dung. The dunghill must then rely upon other remedies to regain the grace of justification (the sacrament of penance, in this particular case) and again become a pile of gold. Yet there can be temporal punishments for mortal sins as well, so even though the dunghill becomes a gold pile, it's not a perfect gold pile—it still must be concerned about self-purification.

The worst thing with such a system is this: the pile never knows whether it's gold or dung. Since there are requirements that must be fulfilled to obtain justification and maintain it, one can never know if everything that *needs* to be done *has* been done.

And so the real issue of this entire study comes to the fore. Is salvation the work of God? Does God save, perfectly, completely, in accordance with His own purpose and grace? Or is the gospel a "maybe," a "do this and live." Is it a matter of "done in Christ Jesus," or is it "do with help and assistance from God"?

PERFECT SAVIOR, PERFECT SALVATION

Clothed in the righteousness of Christ that is ours by faith and faith alone—*this* is the hope of the believer. Why should God bring you into His presence if you were to die today? So many, when asked this question, respond with talk of works, deeds, or attitudes. Even those who call themselves Christians will speak of

[1]See James White, *The Roman Catholic Controversy* (Bethany House, 1996), 181–96.

things they have done: giving to the church, attending regularly, helping in the nursery.

In reality, there is only one answer to the question that is biblically correct: God will accept me because I am clothed in the perfect righteousness of His Son, a righteousness imputed to me by faith and faith alone. I make no other plea, for none is necessary. I am accepted in the Beloved One, the Son, whose death in my place removes all my sin, and whose perfect righteousness, imputed to me, allows me to hear the words of the Father: "Not guilty. Enter into My presence."

What kind of righteousness is yours? What is the object of your faith? Do you trust in the God who justifies, or do you trust partly in this work, partly in that sacrament, partly in those religious ceremonies? Do you hope that grace will help you to do things that will allow you to merit eternal life? Or do you know, with the assurance of faith, that only Christ and His righteousness can avail for you? There can be no greater treasure in this life than to have the certainty of acceptance with God. Do you have this treasure? Only you can answer that question. None other on earth can truly know. But it is a vital inquiry you cannot afford to ignore.

God has been called many things by man down through the ages. The Bible uses numerous phrases and titles attempting to bring out the grandeur and majesty of Yahweh. But the most precious are those that describe Him as the God who is faithful to His promises, faithful to His covenant of salvation. His Word has given us the most precious title of all—precious, at least, to the one who knows intimately the sin that is his, the guilt, the righteous judgment that hangs over his head—and that title is, "the God who justifies." He is the God who declares righteous by the redemption found only in His Son, Jesus Christ. He is the just and holy Justifier of the one who has faith in Jesus. All glory and honor and thanks go to Him. Let the redeemed of the Lord boast in Him, and in Him alone.

CHAPTER 9

Introduction to Exegetical Defense and Demonstration of Justification by Faith

The following chapters contain a defense of justification based upon exegesis of the text of Scripture itself. The conclusions of the preceding chapters, the proclamation of the gospel made therein, flow from the foundational material we will now examine. As was explained early on, justification by faith is a biblical doctrine in the same sense the Trinity is a biblical doctrine: both flow from the highest view of Scripture as the inspired Word of God, and neither can long stand when that presupposition is abandoned. Both doctrines require one to believe *sola scriptura* (Scripture alone as the infallible revelation of God's truth) and *tota scriptura* (all of Scripture is inspired and profitable). As soon as the historic view of Scripture is replaced with the "new orthodoxy" of liberal criticism, these doctrines, and so many others, become relics of a bygone day, left hanging in midair with no foundation, no ground upon which to stand.

The exegesis offered in the following chapters does not fit in the current paradigm of scholarship that is presented even in many conservative seminaries today. This is not to say that every element of modern scholarship is in error—there are substantive facets of modern exegetical study that are fully in line with biblical truth. But it is the milieu in which these elements are placed that is at issue.

"Believing exegesis" might be the best way to describe what is offered here: exegesis that does not separate itself from the lordship of Christ but sees itself as a servant of the text and of the Lord who gave the text. Instead of approaching it as merely another ancient document that is to be examined on naturalistic grounds, we engage in our task fully accepting the claims of the Lord who walks its every page. One cannot approach the writings of the resurrected Christ (for we believe it is His Spirit that has produced every word of Scripture, both Old and New Testament) as one would approach this morning's newspaper or any document from any era produced by mere men. If the records of the Gospels tell us anything, they tell us that the Lord Jesus (1) rose from the dead and (2) believed the Scriptures to be the very Word of God, *His* speech recorded in written form (Matthew 22:31). If that does not place these writings on a completely different plane than any others, what possibly could?

As a result, the following chapters will not seek to present some kind of consensus of current scholarly opinion. God's truth is not found in the approval of men's beliefs. While one can gather much help from the insights of others, if this does not translate into further confidence in the consistency of Scripture and deeper understanding of God's truth, what good is it? The Jews of Jesus' day did not teach with authority because they merely repeated the opinions of those considered to have special insight (Matthew 7:29).

Even more important than this, the authors and sources cited in *The God Who Justifies* generally will be those that likewise come from a believing perspective. The use of sources that flow out of a fundamentally different worldview and set of presuppositions is limited to the presentation of facts or for the purpose of contrast. Such sources are not used to present conclusions or summaries, as this would be inconsistent at best.

To say it another way: the focus of these chapters is the text of Scripture itself, not the history of how men have argued over various issues raised thereby. As those arguments touch upon the conclusions derived from the text, they will be addressed, but only in such a fashion as to *clarify and augment* the proclamation of divine truth, not to *distract or detract* from it. It is always my intention to distill the best of Christian scholarship into a form that communicates, edifies, and explains.

Because of the thrust of this work, I have chosen to limit my sources to those that are readily available to most Christians today. That is, rather than draw heavily from obscure works, scholarly journals that are not easily obtainable, etc., I have looked to the tried-and-true works of godly Christian scholars. For example, I have often quoted from John Murray's masterful commentary on Romans, for his work most closely approximates the kind of Christian scholarship that I believe honors God and instructs the church. While textually oriented, it is theologically rich, unashamedly confessional, and personally edifying. The work of great men of the past, such as John Calvin and Charles Hodge, still in print and readily available, likewise finds a place in the quotations provided. But the focus never moves to these commentaries: the text is the source of God's truth, and it must always remain central to the discussion of the gospel.

It might seem out of place to include citations of the Greek and Hebrew texts, but the Scriptures were written in languages other than English, and while we have many fine English translations, no in-depth discussion of such a vital topic as justification can avoid dealing with the words that the writers chose to express their inspired message. To limit ourselves to English is to artificially limit the inquiry itself. No one would suggest limiting the discussion of, say, the writings of Blaise Pascal, the great French philosopher and theologian, to English without making reference to his native French. In the same way, when studying Paul's letter to the Galatians or James's letter to Christians from two millennia ago, any serious inquiry will place those works in their own context and their own language.

Beyond these considerations, it is a simple fact that those who oppose the gospel of grace are more than willing to make reference to the original languages in their polemic works. And while this work seeks to be primarily positive in its presentation of the doctrine, one cannot help but touch upon apologetic aspects of the doctrine, for it is presented polemically in the text of the New Testament. For example, in Galatians Paul must defend this doctrine against the most vociferous attack of the Judaizers, and this issue likewise lies behind many of his comments in Romans as well. Scripture warns us that many will be those who seek to "pervert the gospel" (Galatians 1:7). When presenting the truth, then, we must go as deeply into the subject as do those who are opposing the truth and preaching "a different gospel, which is not really another" (Galatians 1:6–7).

Finally, there is a level of confidence that comes from seeing the gospel truth of divine grace in the words chosen by those men who were "carried along by the Holy Spirit [as they] spoke from God" (2 Peter 1:20–21). Many a saint has taken comfort, for instance, from realizing that Jesus used the aorist subjunctive of strong denial when He said, "The one who comes to Me I will certainly not cast out" (John 6:37 NASB), precluding the possibility that He would ever reject one of His own. In the same way, there is joy to be found in realizing that when Paul says, "Therefore, having been justified by faith, we have peace with God" (Romans 5:1 NASB), the act of justification is (1) performed by Another (God, the Justifier) and (2) a past action upon which our peace with God is based and from which that peace flows. Without going into the form of the Greek term chosen by the Holy Spirit and penned by Paul, one always wonders if the English translation is truly communicating something found in the original.

Therefore, we have included entire sections of the Greek text for those who would not otherwise have access to it, so that the discussion can be taken back to the text itself, and the reader can see how the words and phrases fit together. Likewise, in a few places, the textual variations that underlie some of the differences in English translations, or that are theologically relevant, are noted for those with the interest to look into them. The textual basis used in this work is the Nestle-Aland 27th edition *(Novum Testamentum Graece).*

A FINAL REMINDER

"There is no rule of interpretation more obvious and more important than that which requires us to understand the language of a writer in the sense in which he knew he would be understood by the persons to whom he wrote."[1] So said Charles Hodge, and his words remain true today. And yet this basic observation often goes missing in the interpretation of the text of Scripture, mainly due to either (1) an antisupernatural bias on the part of the interpreter or (2) the presence of human traditions that influence and often *determine* the reading of the text. It is our joyous privilege and duty as believers to bend our mind to the task of studying, learning, and obeying God's Word, a lifelong duty from which we are never relieved. It is my hope that the following chapters will not only provide the biblical basis for the proclamation of the gospel that came before, but that the believer who hungers and thirsts for the truth of the Word will find refreshment and edification in these pages.

Before turning to exegesis proper, it might be good to address one issue that has caused some to ignore the actual testimony of the Scriptures, or at least to approach the subject with a prejudice that overthrows the testimony of the inspired authors. The question is, if the early fathers did not believe in *sola fide,* as is alleged, why should anyone today?

SO WHAT ABOUT THE EARLY CHURCH?

There are only a few valid contextual citations—that is, citations that are fair to the context of the author and the author's expressed beliefs and theology—that can be mustered in

[1]Hodge, *Commentary on Romans,* 95.

reference to justification by grace through faith alone in the writings of the early church. Ironically, one is from one of the earliest non-scriptural writings, traditionally identified with Clement, bishop of Rome, around the turn of the first century. The work, more probably produced by the elders of the church at Rome (the monarchical or one-man episcopate did not develop until the middle of the second century, so the church at Rome at that time would have been led by a group of elders, as is the biblical pattern), speaks often of God's work of saving His elect people. In section 32, the epistle makes this bold statement:

> Therefore, all these were glorified and magnified, not because of themselves, or through their own works, or for the righteous deeds they performed, but by His will. And we also, being called by His will in Christ Jesus, are not justified by means of ourselves, nor by our own wisdom or understanding or godliness or works which we have done in holiness of heart; but by that faith through which the Almighty God has justified all those believing from the beginning. To whom be glory for ever and ever, amen.

This statement is surely in harmony with orthodox Protestant understanding of justification, and it can only be made to fit other systems by some imaginative (and anachronistic) redefinition of the terms. In another very orthodox (i.e., biblically based) reference, the anonymous author (sometimes called *Mathetes*, the Greek term for "disciple") writes to Diognetius and explains the leading elements of the Christian faith. In section 9 the author shows the depth of his familiarity with the writings of the apostle Paul:

> This was not that He at all delighted in our sins, but that He simply endured them; nor that He approved the time of working iniquity which then was, but that He sought to form a mind conscious of righteousness, so that being convinced in that time of our unworthiness of attaining life through our own works, it should now, through the kindness of God, be vouchsafed to us; and having made it manifest that in ourselves we were unable to enter into the kingdom of God, we

> might through the power of God be made able. But when our wickedness had reached its height, and it had been clearly shown that its reward, punishment and death, was impending over us; and when the time had come which God had before appointed for manifesting His own kindness and power, how the one love of God, through exceeding regard for men, did not regard us with hatred, nor thrust us away, nor remember our iniquity against us, but showed great long-suffering, and bore with us, He Himself took on Him the burden of our iniquities, He gave His own Son as a ransom for us, the holy One for transgressors, the blameless One for the wicked, the righteous One for the unrighteous, the incorruptible One for the corruptible, the immortal One for them that are mortal. For what other thing was capable of covering our sins than His righteousness? By what other one was it possible that we, the wicked and ungodly, could be justified, than by the only Son of God? O sweet exchange! O unsearchable operation! O benefits surpassing all expectation! that the wickedness of many should be hid in a single righteous One, and that the righteousness of One should justify many transgressors! Having therefore convinced us in the former time that our nature was unable to attain to life, and having now revealed the Savior who is able to save even those things which it was [formerly] impossible to save, by both these facts He desired to lead us to trust in His kindness, to esteem Him our Nourisher, Father, Teacher, Counselor, Healer, our Wisdom, Light, Honor, Glory, Power, and Life.

Aside from these brief glimpses into a period when apostolic teaching continued without philosophical and traditional accretion, most of the discussion one finds of the topic is either based upon considerations far removed from the biblical text or is so shallow and surface-level as to give the reader no real insight into the beliefs of the author.

In *Iustitia Dei* Alister McGrath traces the origins of the ecclesiastical doctrine of justification in the early centuries of the faith. He notes,

> In particular, it can be shown that two major distortions were introduced into the *corpus* of traditional belief within the

eastern church at a very early stage, and were subsequently transferred to the emerging western theological tradition. These are:

1. The introduction of the non-biblical, secular Stoic concept of αὐτεξουσία or *liberum arbitrium* in the articulation of the human response to the divine initiative in justification.
2. The implicit equation of s^ed̲āqâ, δικαιοσύνη and *iustitia,* linked with the particular associations of the Latin term *meritum* . . . inevitably suggested a correlation between human moral effort and justification within the western church.[2]

McGrath goes on to assert that the "*pre*-Augustinian theological tradition . . . may be regarded as having taken a highly questionable path in its articulation of the doctrine of justification in the face of pagan opposition."[3] Indeed, it is questionable whether there was a conscious, focused articulation of the doctrine at all. The period was marked by the Christological and Trinitarian controversies and the all-absorbing fight for survival up until A.D. 313, followed by the Constantinian period of adjustment to the status of a *religio licita.* It was not the period of close reflection upon Paul's letters regarding the meaning of justification, the Old Testament backgrounds, the relationship of such terms as faith, imputation, righteousness, atonement, sanctification, etc. McGrath concludes that the early fathers mentioned justification, but,

> their interest in the concept is . . . minimal, and the term generally occurs in their writings as a direct citation from, or a recognisable allusion to, the epistles of Paul, generally employed for some purpose other than a discussion of the concept of justification itself. . . . Justification was simply not a theological issue in the pre-Augustinian tradition.[4]

McGrath goes on to observe the development of a thoroughly *philosophically* derived definition of free will in the Greek fathers:

---

[2]Alister McGrath, *Iustitia Dei* (Cambridge, 1998), 18.
[3]Ibid., 18–19.
[4]Ibid., 19.

"They taught that man was utterly free in his choice of good or evil."[5] In this they were simply following their predecessors. Theophilus of Antioch had asserted that "God made man free and self-determinate,"[6] so it was hardly a huge leap to Tertullian's introduction of the corresponding Latin term *liberum arbitrium*, "free will," in the West. In all of this the influence of philosophy, as well as the struggle with heretical movements that taught some kind of impersonal fate that left no room for responsibility or judgment, is easily seen. What is conspicuous by its absence is any meaningful exegesis of the Pauline doctrine in the writings of the primitive Christian writers.[7]

The situation changes when Augustine begins to respond to the Pelagian controversy. And while Augustine's insights are often amazingly accurate, he, like anyone, is deeply influenced by the traditions he imbibes as well as the context in which he worked. One of the vital things to remember about Augustine is that he was unable to work with the original language of the Hebrew Old Testament (and hence unable to see the background provided by a study of *zedekah*), being far more influenced by the baggage attached to the Latin that predominated his theological studies. Even the use of *dikaios/dikaiosune* in the Septuagint and the New Testament was overridden in its meaning by the Latin in which he worked.

So broad was Augustine's doctrine of justification that not only

---

[5]Ibid.

[6]Theophilus of Antioch, *Epistula ad Autolycum*, 2:27 (*Thesaurus Linguae Graece*, CD-E, 1999).

[7]One possible exception to this is the unknown author, named Ambrosiaster by Erasmus, who wrote (in Latin) a commentary on the Pauline corpus. Just as Paul's writings have brought men face-to-face with the true gospel throughout history, so too did this author, who wrote somewhere between A.D. 366 and 384. Note these phrases from the *Ancient Commentary on Scripture*, volume VI (InterVarsity Press, 1998) and VII (1999), edited by Gerald Bray. In commenting on Romans 3:24, Ambrosiaster writes, "They are justified freely because they have not done anything nor given anything in return, but by faith alone (Latin: *sola fide*) they have been made holy by the gift of God." Likewise, in commenting on Romans 4:5, "How then can the Jews think that they have been justified by the works of the law in the same way as Abraham, when they see that Abraham was not justified by the works of the law but by faith alone (Latin: *sola fide*)? Therefore there is no need of the law when the ungodly is justified before God by faith alone (Latin: *per solam fidem*)." And regarding 1 Cor. 1:4, "God has decreed that a person who believes in Christ can be saved without works. By faith alone (Latin: *sola fide*) he receives the forgiveness of sins." At the very least, such statements refute clearly the common assertion that Luther coined the phrase "sola fide."

did the meaning of the term *iustificare* ("to make righteous") become established in Western theology (in contradiction to the biblical text), but as McGrath expresses it, "By justification, Augustine comes very close to understanding the restoration of the entire universe to its original order established at creation."[8] A fully biblical reorientation of the term would await the Reformation itself.

It has long been the practice of opponents of *sola fide* to point to the patristic witness and hence preclude the exegetical conclusion of the inspired text itself: "Surely if that is the consistent interpretation of the Scriptures it would have been known from the beginning." But students of church history well know that such an assertion does not follow from the evidence. Many vital biblical topics were not discussed in depth in patristic sources for many centuries. The Atonement, for example, so central and definitional to a Scripture-based understanding of the gospel, did not receive a full treatment until Athanasius's work in the middle of the fourth century. Even then, the history of the church shows the prevalence of wildly unbiblical views of this doctrine despite the depth of teaching found in the book of Hebrews.

Regarding justification, one simply does not find the kind of exegetical study and discussion in the early fathers upon which to base accusations against *sola fide*. It simply was not a subject of debate in their context, so to put great weight upon their default position, when it was a position informed by tradition and not the kind of thoughtful conclusion that comes from conflict that drives one into the text of Scripture, is folly.

Another relevant historical issue is that in many ways a modern exegete is closer to the original writers than interpreters only a few centuries removed. It should be remembered that many of the early fathers lived and worked in a context where they were cut off from extremely important information. The early division that developed between formal Christianity and Judaism resulted in a constantly diminishing knowledge of the Old Testament, the cultural backgrounds of Israel, and even the historical back-

---

[8]McGrath, *Iustitia Dei*, 36.

grounds of the Gospels themselves. The rise of allegorical interpretation likewise increased the mystery of the Old Testament text, and this hermeneutical trend had tremendous impact upon New Testament interpretation as well. The vital facts we have traced from the Old Testament, through the Septuagint, into the context of the apostle Paul, were unknown to the vast majority of writers who lived in the centuries immediately following the apostolic period. To invest nearly infallible authority in their opinions on a subject that was not central to their thinking and that they were not even prepared to address with as much insight and information as later generations is surely unwise.

In conclusion, patristic testimony must be weighed based upon the obvious consideration as to (1) whether the cited fathers were prepared to deal with the issue they addressed and (2) whether they actually intended to address the issue in a full and meaningful fashion. Hence, their testimony to absolute monotheism, for example, is highly relevant, for they specifically addressed issues regarding theology proper—polytheism, the Trinity, etc. They *intended* to address biblical passages regarding the topic, and they responded to criticisms from other viewpoints.

However, when it comes to the key issues that make up the primary areas of conflict regarding justification by grace through faith alone today, the early fathers show themselves to have embraced viewpoints that were not derived from exegesis of the inspired text but from many and varied other sources. The weight of their testimony, then, must be held against the weight of the consistent witness of Scripture itself, which laid out the doctrine before any of the early fathers put pen to paper. And when we recall that many of those fathers who first created the traditions that so heavily influenced later generations did not even have a complete copy of the New Testament text, we see again the importance of a pan-canonical theology, one based upon the entirety of Scripture. This should also cause us to be tremendously thankful for the work of God in preserving for us the Scriptures to this present day.

CHAPTER 10

Romans 1–3:18: The Foundation—Man in Sin

Before engaging in the exegesis of the text of Romans, it is necessary to offer a defense of the historic Protestant emphasis upon this epistle and its testimony to the nature of justification. It is often said by those who oppose the doctrine of *sola fide* that its supporters make too much of Paul, and especially of Romans, at the expense of the rest of Scripture. The assertion is made that *sola fide* rests upon an unbalanced view of Scripture, one that ignores even the words of the Lord Jesus himself.

Further, it is often noted that Peter warned that the words of Paul are hard to understand, especially regarding salvation itself. Peter wrote ". . . just as also our dear brother Paul wrote to you, according to the wisdom given to him, speaking of these things in all his letters. Some things in these letters are hard to understand" (2 Peter 3:15–16). So why is it that such weight should be placed upon this particular section of sacred Scripture?

First, while Peter did recognize the difficulty accompanying

Paul's writings on the doctrine of salvation, his words in reality communicate just the opposite conclusion to the honest believer who approaches those letters with reverent respect. The whole context of Peter's words bears this out:

> And regard the patience of our Lord as salvation, just as also our dear brother Paul wrote to you, according to the wisdom given to him, speaking of these things in all his letters. Some things in these letters are hard to understand, things the ignorant and unstable twist to their own destruction, as they also do to the rest of the scriptures. Therefore, dear friends, since you have been forewarned, be on your guard that you do not get led astray by the error of these unprincipled men, and fall from your firm grasp on the truth. (2 Peter 3:15–17)

It is not the faithful Christian who is in danger of twisting Paul's words, but the untaught and unstable, who likewise twist *all* ("the rest of") the Scriptures. Not only does Peter recognize Paul's writings as γραφή, Scripture (a most amazing thing to ponder, given that this means Peter clearly recognized that his fellow apostle Paul was being used of God in the same way Isaiah or Jeremiah or even Moses had been, and as *he himself was so being used*), but it is self-evident that he likewise believes Paul's words to be fully understandable to those who are taught and stable. The warning is not that Paul's words, being Scripture, are somehow more difficult than other Scriptures, but that false teachers ("unprincipled men") seek to cause Christians to lose hold of the "firm grasp" they have upon the truth by *twisting* those Scriptures. The fault for the twisting lies in the hearts of the false teachers, not in the text of Paul or any other writer used to give inspired Writ.

The corollary of these words should be fully understood: Scripture is fully capable of equipping the man of God (2 Timothy 3:17) and of giving the Christian a solid hold on truth (2 Peter 3:17). As a result, false teachers seek to twist the Scriptures. This was taking place while the apostles themselves lived and taught and wrote: how much more so after they have passed from the scene (Acts 20:29–30). Scripture forewarns all believers of the constant presence of false teaching and teachers within the context of the church, but it never directs them away from the Scriptures to some other source of sure and certain guidance. The believer who is *taught* and *stable* is promised the capacity to handle the truth. So the idea that we should in some way be suspect of Paul's writings or dismiss them as too difficult finds no basis on Peter's words.

We have already strongly emphasized that any meaningful exegetical approach to Scripture requires us to recognize that some passages of the Word are directly relevant to a particular topic while others are not. The truth that we must interpret passages that merely mention a concept or term in light of others that provide explanations, teaching, and definitions must still be repeated, given the prominence of traditional interpretations and eisegetical errors. A person may well believe one verse to clearly teach a particular viewpoint, but if that interpretation flies directly in the face of the consistent teaching of entire passages of Scripture, extending over many verses or even chapters, obviously such a person must be willing to interpret the single verse in the light of the greater weight and clarity of fuller passages. It is far easier to misinterpret a few words than many. The more context one can provide, the fuller the foundation for interpretation.

This is what makes Romans central to the doctrine of justification in Scripture. Nowhere else, even in Galatians, do we find the same kind of extended, full, purposeful teaching on the subject of how a man is made right before God. It is Paul's intention in the book to provide doctrine, and to do so in the light of possible objections to the Christian truth he is recording.

Every clear and forceful argument involves a solid foundation and a clear direction and order of presentation. Romans is Paul's thought-out, argued, reasoned defense and explanation of the gospel of Jesus Christ. He sends it to the chief city in the empire, knowing that if his mission of reaching the Gentiles is to be fulfilled, Rome is the key. The center of government, commerce, and art, Rome is the hub of the empire, and if the church there can be provided with the firmest foundation in the truth of the gospel, that message will go out to all the known world. (This is why Paul had labored so hard in Ephesus, a chief city of commerce as well, and the result is seen in the founding of churches upriver at Laodicea and Colossae.)

Paul addresses his masterpiece to the church that would give the work the widest possible exposure both by preaching and also copied distribution. Over a century after Paul invested the time to dictate this letter to the Romans (via Tertius, Romans 16:22), Irenaeus likewise spoke of the centrality of the church in Rome as one of the repositories of apostolic tradition, which is, as he defines it, the overriding belief that

> there is one God, Creator of heaven and earth, announced by the law and the prophets; and one Christ, the Son of God. If any one do not agree to these truths, he despises the companions of the Lord; nay more, he despises Christ Himself the Lord; yea, he despises the Father also, and stands self-condemned, resisting and opposing his own salvation, as is the case with all heretics.[1]

This is apostolic tradition in the primitive church, a basic teaching, clearly sub-biblical in the sense of being derived from Scripture and not encompassing anything like an extra-biblical revelation, yet seen as a summary, in almost creedal form, of apostolic teaching. This basic statement is urged by Irenaeus as an argument against the Gnostic heretics who were troubling the Christian church, for they denied this tradition that could be found in every church established by apostles of Christ.

Irenaeus's simple argument is that if those churches that were founded by apostles always believed in one God, Creator of heaven and earth, then it is obvious that the Gnostics, who denied this belief, are not in line with the apostles of Christ and hence have no business calling themselves Christian. The best example Irenaeus can give of how this tradition can be proven to be true is found in the church at Rome. Irenaeus sees Rome as Paul did. Since Christian men from every nation stream in and out of Rome, the beliefs of that church would be pan-catholic, that is,

---

[1]Irenaeus, *Against Heresies*, Book 3, 1:2. See likewise Book 3, 4:2 for a similar rendition of this tradition.

would reflect the beliefs of Christians everywhere. So he writes,

> Since, however, it would be very tedious, in such a volume as this, to reckon up the successions of all the Churches, we do put to confusion all those who, in whatever manner, whether by an evil self-pleasing, by vainglory, or by blindness and perverse opinion, assemble in unauthorized meetings; [we do this, I say,] by indicating that tradition derived from the apostles, of the very great, the very ancient, and universally known Church founded and organized at Rome by the two most glorious apostles, Peter and Paul; as also [by pointing out] the faith preached to men, which comes down to our time by means of the successions of the bishops.[2]

At this point the Latin text is difficult to follow.[3] One translation is as follows:

> For it is a matter of necessity that every Church should agree with this Church, on account of its pre-eminent authority, that is, the faithful everywhere, inasmuch as the apostolical tradition has been preserved continuously by those [faithful men] who exist everywhere.[4]

The contradictory nature of the rendering is obvious: Is it the preeminent authority of the church at Rome itself, or is it that the apostolic tradition has been preserved by "those faithful men who exist everywhere"? Which is why a better rendering, given the context, is:

> For to this Church, on account of more potent principality, it is necessary that every Church (that is, those who are on every side faithful) resort; in which Church ever, by those who are on every side, has been preserved that tradition which is from the apostles.[5]

The point is that the truth has been preserved in Rome

---

[2]Ibid., 3:3:2.

[3]It reads, *Ad hanc enim ecclesiam propter potiorem principalitatem necesse est omnem convenire ecclesiam.*

[4]This is the textual rendition found in *The Ante-Nicene Fathers*, edited by Roberts and Donaldson (I:415). The alternate is found in the editorial footnote on the same page.

[5]Ibid.

because of the many faithful who resort to her from all over the world. She is a mirror of the Christian landscape, and since gnosticism finds no basis in her faith from the beginning (exemplified, as Irenaeus goes on to say, in the letter sent by the church at Rome to the church at Corinth), the Gnostics have no basis to call the apostles their own.

Irenaeus looks back on what Paul foresaw in his own day: the importance of Rome to the evangelistic effort of proclaiming the gospel of grace. As mentioned, this is what prompts Paul's writing of the epistle. It was not that the church was yet suffering from a plague of false teaching, as was the case in the churches in Galatia. Though Paul does warn of false teachers (Romans 16:17–18), it is his intention to provide a positive proclamation of the gospel in his epistle to a church not yet having to deal with the errors that were troubling others.

These considerations explain the format of the letter. This is no hurried note, dashed off to address a question in the local congregation. This is Paul's preaching of the gospel, an ordered, deliberate, logical argument, purposefully written in defense of the gospel of grace. At every turn the apostle shows deep familiarity with the objections his teaching has encountered during the course of his ministry, and he takes pains to provide an apologetic response to his opponents.

Surely we are warranted to believe Paul saw this work as having lasting value for future generations, and hence he wrote with that higher purpose in mind. It is so common for scholars today to reject the idea that the apostles knew they were writing Scripture that it is almost taken as axiomatic that their writings had a very short-range goal. But if one questions that assumed concept and realizes that Paul well knew the church would continue on and would face the very same obstacles and false teachers he himself had faced, the writing of such a work of Scripture, intended to encapsulate and codify the very heart of the gospel message itself, would not only be perfectly reasonable, but utterly necessary.

And so there is every reason to accept this epistle to the faithful at Rome (and through the capital city, to all faithful everywhere) as his *apologia*, the summary statement of the gospel he preached and ultimately died for. As such it could function as nothing less than the foundational source for the doctrine of *sola fide*, as historic Protestant theology has rightly concluded.

There is one further aspect of this apologetic that should be noted. Again, some object to the localization of exegetical studies of any particular doctrine. That is, to focus upon Romans or Galatians is in some fashion to "unfairly skew the data." But such an assumption ignores the nature of inscripturated revelation. Certain biblical passages focus upon certain truths by nature: when Paul writes to the churches in Galatia, the means and method of justification is the key theme of his epistle. Obviously, such a book will carry more data relevant to the topic than will, say, 1 John, with its anti-Docetic emphasis. It is a simple observation that Scripture addresses particular subjects with greater or lesser emphasis in certain places that leads to the proper and right focus upon Romans and Galatians in particular in this study.

ROMANS 1:16–32

SYNOPSIS:

Paul's indictment of the entirety of mankind forms the foundation of the gospel message. There is no good news where the bad news of man's sinful state is not clearly proclaimed *and* perceived. The *results of sin* (the depravity of man) demand a God-centered gospel.

RESOURCES:

C. E. B. Cranfield, *Romans: A Shorter Commentary* (Eerdmans, 1985).

———, "Romans" in *The International Critical Commentary* (T&T Clark, 1980).

James D. G. Dunn, "Romans 1–8" in *The Word Biblical Commentary* (Word, 1988).

Joseph A. Fitzmyer, "Romans" in *The Anchor Bible* (Doubleday, 1992).

Everett F. Harrison, "Romans" in *The Expositor's Bible Commentary* (Zondervan, 1976).

Charles Hodge, *Commentary on the Epistle to the Romans* (Eerdmans, 1983).

Martin Luther, *Commentary on Romans* (Kregel, 1985).

John MacArthur, "Romans 1–8" in *The MacArthur New Testament Commentary* (Moody, 1991).

Douglas Moo, "The Epistle to the Romans," NICNT (Eerdmans, 1996).

Leon Morris, *The Epistle to the Romans* (Eerdmans, 1988).

John Murray, *The Epistle to the Romans* (Eerdmans, 1997).

W. Robertson Nicoll, "Romans" in *The Expositor's Greek Testament* (Eerdmans, 1983).

A. T. Robertson, *Word Pictures in the New Testament*, vol. IV, (Baker, n.d.).

William Sanday and Arthur Headlam, "A Critical and Exegetical Commentary on the Epistle to the Romans" in *The International Critical Commentary* (T&T Clark, 1980).

Thomas R. Schreiner, "Romans" in the *Baker Exegetical Commentary on the New Testament* (Baker, 1998).

Select Bibliography: See Douglas Moo, *The Epistle to the Romans*, xviii–xxv.

MAIN PASSAGE:

1:16 For I am not ashamed of the gospel, for it is God's power for salvation to everyone who believes, to the Jew first and also to the Greek. **1:17** For the righteousness of God is revealed in the gospel from faith to faith, just as it is written, *"the righteous by faith will live."*

1:18 For the wrath of God is revealed from heaven against all ungodliness and unrighteousness of people who suppress the truth by their unrighteousness, **1:19** because what can be known about God is plain to them, because God has made it plain to them. **1:20** For since the creation of the world his invisible attributes—his eternal power and divine nature—have been clearly seen, because they are understood through what has been made. So people are without excuse. **1:21** For although they knew God, they did not glorify him as God or give him thanks, but they became futile in their thoughts and their senseless hearts were darkened. **1:22** Although they claimed to be wise, they became fools **1:23** and exchanged the glory of the immortal God for an image resembling mortal human beings or birds or four-footed animals or reptiles.

1:24 Therefore God gave them over in the desires of their hearts to impurity, to dishonor their bodies among themselves. **1:25** They exchanged the truth of God for a lie and worshiped and served the creation rather than the Creator, who is blessed forever! Amen.

1:26 For this reason God gave them over to dishonorable passions. For their women exchanged the natural sexual relations for unnatural ones, **1:27** and likewise the men also abandoned natural relations with women and were inflamed in their passions for one another. Men committed shameless acts with men and received in themselves the due penalty for their error.

1:28 And just as they did not see fit to acknowledge God, God gave them over to a depraved mind, to do what should not be done. **1:29** They are filled with every kind of unrighteousness, wickedness, covetousness, malice. They are rife with envy, murder, strife, deceit, hostility. They are gossips, **1:30** slanderers, haters of God, insolent, arrogant, boastful, contrivers of all sorts of evil, disobedient to parents, **1:31** senseless, covenant-breakers, heartless, ruthless. **1:32** Although they fully know God's righteous decree that those who practice such things deserve to die, they not only do them but also approve of those who practice them.

1:16

> For I am not ashamed of the gospel, for it is God's power for salvation to everyone who believes, to the Jew first and also to the Greek.

NA[27] Text:

Οὐ γὰρ ἐπαισχύνομαι τὸ εὐαγγέλιον[T], δύναμις γὰρ θεοῦ ἐστιν εἰς σωτηρίαν παντὶ τῷ πιστεύοντι, Ἰουδαίῳ τε πρῶτον καὶ Ἕλληνι.

| [T] του Χριστου D[c] Ψ 𝔐 ¦ 𝔓[26] א A B C D* G 33. 81. 1505. 1506. 1739. 1881. *pc* lat sy co

These words form the initial thesis statement of the epistle. "Gospel" was a term already defined by Paul's day as the message of Jesus Christ (hence the phrase "gospel of Christ" in the majority of manuscripts). The "good news" about Christ is a very specific element in Paul's teaching. This verse indicates that it is something about which some might be tempted to be ashamed, but true believers are not; that it is a divine message, one that embodies God's power; the gospel *saves*; the gospel is directly related to faith; the gospel is for all, Jew and Gentile.

The theme of not being ashamed of the gospel comes from the Lord Jesus and is echoed by Paul. Jesus had solemnly warned His disciples,

> For if anyone is ashamed of me and my words in this adulterous and sinful generation, the Son of Man will also be ashamed of him when he comes in the glory of his Father with the holy angels. (Mark 8:38)

Paul picks up the same term, ἐπαισχύνομαι, that the Lord Jesus used to confess that he is truly a disciple of Christ, for he is not ashamed of the gospel, which would correspond to "my words" in Mark 8:38. The theme of unashamed profession of this gospel is part and parcel of Paul's Christian experience:

> Because of this, in fact, I suffer as I do. But I am not ashamed, because I know the one in whom my faith is set and I am convinced that he is able to protect what has been entrusted to me until that day. (2 Timothy 1:12)

While the world finds the gospel message foolishness (1 Corinthians 1:18), the Christian is not ashamed of the message of the cross. Why? Surely it is to us God's wisdom (1 Corinthians 2:7) or, as Paul puts it here, the very power of God. This is why there can be no shame for the believer who has been transformed by the power of the gospel.

But what does "the power of God" mean? In this context it is God's divine power that accomplishes salvation (εἰς σωτηρίαν, "unto salvation"). Salvation is a divine act: it is something God does, and He does it only through "the gospel." Murray observed,

> The power of God unto salvation of which the gospel is the embodiment is not unconditionally and universally operative unto salvation. It is of this we are advised in the words "to every one that believeth". This informs us that salvation is not accomplished irrespective of faith. Hence the salvation with which Paul is going to deal in this epistle has no reality, validity, or meaning apart from faith. And we are already prepared for the emphasis which is placed upon faith throughout the epistle. The concept of salvation developed in this epistle, therefore, is the *power of God operative unto salvation through faith.* It is this salvation that is proclaimed in the gospel and the gospel as message is the embodiment of this power.[6]

Salvation is accomplished by the gospel, and since salvation is a powerful act, the gospel is described in terms of power.

To everyone who believes is a theme picked up and repeated by Paul over and over and over again, for one of the chief threats he saw to the gospel proclamation and the infant Christian church was a division into Jewish and Gentile churches. This explains his firm denunciation of the hypocrisy of Peter at Antioch recorded in Galatians 2. The weight of the phrase in Paul's writings falls upon the denial of race, class, and gender distinctions. That is, faith is the only means of justification *for anyone,* Jew or Gentile, slave or free, king or servant, male or female. Faith is the lone instrument of justification for all, whoever they are. There must be only one way of justification, one path, one instrument, for if there are multiple ways, there will result multiple churches, multiple congregations. As there is one Christ, one faith, one baptism, and one church, so there is one gospel.

1:17

> For the righteousness of God is revealed in the gospel from faith to faith, just as it is written, "*the righteous by faith will live.*"

---

[6]John Murray, *Romans*, 27–28.

Alternate:

> For in the gospel a righteousness from God is revealed, a righteousness that is by faith from first to last, just as it is written: "The righteous will live by faith."(NIV)

NA[27] Text:

δικαιοσύνη γὰρ θεοῦ ἐν αὐτῷ ἀποκαλύπτεται ἐκ πίστεως εἰς πίστιν, καθὼς γέγραπται, *Ὁ δὲ δίκαιος ἐκ πίστεως ζήσεται.*

Most of the phrases found in verse 17 are repeated in fuller contexts later in Romans (or Galatians). Hence, this initial thesis statement should be viewed in the light of the more complete explanations the apostle provides later in his argument. But a few brief comments are in order.

The fact that the gospel saves Jews and Gentiles alike is the connection to this next verse. For "in it" means "in the gospel." But what is revealed in this gospel? Translations of the phrase δικαιοσύνη θεοῦ *(dikaiosune theou)* differ greatly, as seen above. "The righteousness of God" assumes a particular righteousness, permitting the use of the article when Paul does not include it. "A righteousness from God" comes at the phrase from a different direction, seeing it as something communicated to man with God as its source, its giver. Murray rightly commented:

> So, when the apostle says, "the righteousness of God is revealed", he means that in the gospel the righteousness of God is actively and dynamically brought to bear upon man's sinful condition; it is not merely that it is made known as to its character to human apprehension but that it is manifest in its saving efficacy. This is why the gospel is the power of God unto salvation—the righteousness of God is redemptively active in the sphere of human sin and ruin.[7]

Murray expanded upon the nature of this righteousness:

> Yet it is so intimately related to God that it is a righteousness of divine property and characterized by divine qualities. It is a

[7]Ibid., 29–30.

> "God-righteousness". Because it is such, God is its author; it is a righteousness that must elicit the divine approval; it is a righteousness that meets all the demands of his justice and therefore avails before God. But the particular emphasis rests upon its divine property and is therefore contrasted not only with human unrighteousness but with human righteousness. Man-righteousness, even though perfect and measuring up to all the demands of God's perfection, would never be adequate to the situation created by our sins. This is the glory of the gospel; as it is God's power operative unto salvation so it is God's righteousness supervening upon our sin and ruin. And it is God's power operative unto salvation *because* the righteousness of God is dynamically made manifest unto our justification.[8]

Much likewise has been said concerning the phrase "from faith to faith," or as the NIV renders it (interpretively), "by faith from first to last." One striking understanding of the phrase goes like this:

> It would appear that the clue to the interpretation is provided by Paul himself in a passage that furnishes the closest parallel, namely, 3:22 (cf. Gal. 3:22). There he speaks of "the righteousness of God through faith of Jesus Christ unto all who believe". It might seem that the expression "unto all who believe" is superfluous in this instance because all that it sets forth has been already stated in the expression which immediately precedes, "through faith of Jesus Christ." But the apostle must have some purpose in what seems to us repetition. And the purpose is to accent the fact that not only does the righteousness of God bear savingly upon us *through faith* but also that it bears savingly upon *every one* who believes. It is not superfluous to stress both. For the mere fact that the righteousness of God is through faith does not of itself as a proposition guarantee that faith always carries with it this effect.[9]

In other words, the promise is that faith receives righteousness

---

[8]Ibid., 30.

[9]Ibid., 31–32. There are extensive and useful discussions of the range of meaning that can be attached to δικαιοσύνη in Paul's writings and beyond. Obviously, the key issue is context, and it is an error to attempt to push a *single* definition upon *every* usage. For further useful discussions of the issue, see especially Moo, 79–90, and Schreiner, 58–80.

in every instance. No person who truly believes can fear that his faith will not receive the promise.

1:18

> For the wrath of God is revealed from heaven against all ungodliness and unrighteousness of people who suppress the truth by their unrighteousness.

Alternate:

> The wrath of God is being revealed from heaven against all the godlessness and wickedness of men who suppress the truth by their wickedness. (NIV)

NA[27] Text:
Ἀποκαλύπτεται γὰρ ὀργὴ θεοῦ ἀπ' οὐρανοῦ ἐπὶ πᾶσαν ἀσέβειαν καὶ ἀδικίαν ἀνθρώπων τῶν τὴν ἀλήθειαν ἐν ἀδικίᾳ κατεχόντων.

This passage is connected with the preceding verses through the use of γάρ. Many theories have been proposed as to how this passage relates to the preceding sections, but it seems plain that if one does not automatically exclude the concept of wrath against sin from the gospel, as so many modern interpreters do, the relationship is plain. After introducing the gospel as the power of God, and the centrality of faith to that gospel, Paul begins with an explanation of why the gospel is necessary and why salvation comes by faith. The reason is to be found in the state of man in sin and the wrath of God against that sin.

Ἀποκαλύπτεται is placed in the emphatic position. It is a present tense verb and should be allowed to have its full force in English translation by emphasizing the ongoing action. Simply stating that God's wrath "is revealed" does not provide the full force found in the words of Paul. Wrath against sin is as constant and prevalent as sin itself. Only mercy and grace can withhold the righteous wrath of God against sin and sinners.

ὀργὴ θεοῦ is a rich phrase. Paul speaks of the wrath of God in very similar terms in Romans 2:8, τοῖς δὲ ἐξ ἐριθείας καὶ ἀπειθοῦσι τῇ ἀληθείᾳ πειθομένοις δὲ τῇ ἀδικίᾳ, ὀργὴ καὶ θυμός, "But for those who are factious and do not obey [or, are not obeying] the truth, but obey wickedness, there will be wrath and fury" (RSV). Note the connection of ἀδικίᾳ and ὀργὴ here as well. Ephesians 5:6 and its parallel passage in Colossians 3:6 also speak of the wrath of God coming upon men: διὰ ταῦτα γὰρ ἔρχεται ἡ ὀργὴ τοῦ θεοῦ ἐπὶ τοὺς υἱοὺς τῆς ἀπειθείας, "for because of these things the wrath of God comes upon the sons of disobedience" (NASB). In the same way Paul speaks of the wrath of God coming upon the Jews who are seeking to hinder the preaching of the gospel in 1 Thessalonians 2:16.

ἀπ' οὐρανοῦ: This is divine wrath as it originates "from heaven," i.e., from the abode of God. It comes from a pure and spotless realm into a corrupt and impure one, from the very seat of justice into the presence of the unjust. It is *just* wrath, and no place is given for questioning its presence and its effect. For Paul, it is axiomatic that God *must* judge the world and sin (Romans 3:6).

ἐπὶ πᾶσαν ἀσέβειαν καὶ ἀδικίαν ἀνθρώπων: Paul is unyielding in his teaching. The wrath of God, unlike the irrational rages of the Greek and Roman pantheon, is directed instead toward a well-defined and rational object: *all* the ungodliness and unrighteousness of men. The use of ἐπὶ assures us of this, just as the use of πᾶσαν makes the application universal and unlimited. There is no ungodliness or unrighteousness that is not included in the apostle's words.

ἀσέβειαν speaks to a lifestyle and manner of thought that is marked by impiety. Its meaning is well summarized in Paul's later quotation from the LXX: "There is no fear of God before their eyes" (3:18). It should be noted that this ungodliness speaks of something for which man is culpable. As Paul said in Romans 11:26, "The Deliverer will come from Zion, he will banish ungodliness [ἀσεβείας] from Jacob" (RSV). And most significantly, Paul taught Titus that the grace of God teaches us to renounce all ungodliness and worldly lusts (Titus 2:12: παιδεύουσα ἡμᾶς, ἵνα ἀρνησάμενοι τὴν ἀσέβειαν καὶ τὰς κοσμικὰς ἐπιθυμίας).

ἀδικίαν is even more common in Pauline usage, referring to

unrighteousness, iniquity, and wickedness. It is the true moral opposite of holiness and righteousness. Christians themselves are called to avoid ἀδικίαν, for as Paul says later in Romans 6:13, μηδὲ παριστάνετε τὰ μέλη ὑμῶν ὅπλα ἀδικίας τῇ ἁμαρτίᾳ, "Do not yield your members as instruments of unrighteousness to sin."

ἀνθρώπων: Literally, "of men," though the thought of "human ungodliness and unrighteousness" could be understood. Paul is specific to assert that it is human sin against which the wrath of God is revealed. Men are the image-bearers of God, and men are thus the culpable objects of God's wrath.

τῶν τὴν ἀλήθειαν ἐν ἀδικίᾳ κατεχόντων: This phrase provides a further, and most important, description of the men against whom the wrath of God is directed. Most striking in the apostle's phraseology is the term κατεχόντων. We note the words of Moulton and Milligan: "In enumerating the varied meanings of this interesting verb, it may be well to begin with it as the perfective of ἔχω = 'possess' as in 1 Cor 7[30], 2 Cor 6[10]. . . ."[10] That is, the basic meaning of the term is found in the concept of possession. From this basic meaning (clearly seen in the form of the word itself, i.e., κατά+ἔχω) the semantic range moves to concepts related to "seizing" and from this to the idea of "suppression," its meaning here in Romans 1.[11]

It is important to stress that the men engaging in this activity possess the truth they are actively suppressing. κατεχόντων is a present active participle; τὴν ἀλήθειαν is the object of the action. The men against whom the wrath of God is being expressed are involved in suppressing the truth. Paul will define the content of τὴν ἀλήθειαν in the following verses, and the phrase will be used again in verse 25. The action of suppression does not take place in a vacuum. It is not a morally neutral act. Instead, it takes place in the realm of ἀδικίᾳ, "unrighteousness." The NET speaks of this suppression as being "*by* their unrighteousness," pointing to the

[10]James Hope Moulton and George Milligan, *The Vocabulary of the Greek Testament* (Eerdmans, 1930), 336.

[11]See discussion in Moulton and Milligan, ibid.; in Bauer, Danker, Arndt, and Gingrich, *A Greek-English Lexicon of the New Testament and Other Early Christian Literature*, 3rd ed. (University of Chicago Press, 2000), 532–33, and in *TDNT*, II: 829–30.

means of suppression. But I think the better translation renders it as a locative. The locative phrase indicates the sphere in which the action of the verb takes place, that being the sphere of unrighteousness. This is a wicked suppression, one done with ungodly purpose and intention.

1:19

> . . . because what can be known about God is plain to them; because God has made it plain to them.

Alternate:

> . . . since what may be known about God is plain to them, because God has made it plain to them. (NIV)

NA[27] Text:
διότι τὸ γνωστὸν τοῦ θεοῦ φανερόν ἐστιν ἐν αὐτοῖς· ὁ θεὸς γὰρ αὐτοῖς ἐφανέρωσεν.

τὸ γνωστὸν: This term is normally used simply of an acquaintance, someone who is known. Its most basic meaning is simply "known." Here it means "that which may be known."[12] The term itself does not address whether the fact under discussion is actually known or is only potentially known. Context must define this aspect of the term, and Paul does not leave us wondering.

τοῦ θεοῦ: Paul is not speaking here about anything other than that which may be known "of God." He is addressing the revelation of God and His existence.

φανερόν ἐστιν ἐν αὐτοῖς: That which may be known of God "is manifest," that is, "has been revealed" or "has been made known" or "plain." φανερόν is defined by BDAG as "visible, clear, plainly to be seen, open, plain, evident, known."[13] ἐν αὐτοῖς has been understood as "in them" as well as "among them," that is,

---

[12]BDAG gives as the meaning, "1. *Known* . . . b. of pers.: . . . *acquaintance, friend, intimate*. . . . 2. *Capable of being known, intelligible*." Specifically citing Romans 1:18, we read, "τὸ γνωστὸν τοῦ θεοῦ *what can be known about God*, or *God, to the extent that he can be known*." (BDAG, 204).

[13]Ibid., 1047.

"in their midst." It is not possible to rule out either meaning, though the first understanding could include both a revelation in man's nature itself, as well as that revelation found in creation in general, whereas the second understanding would be limited to the latter aspect. One can find Paul using ἐν αὐτοῖς in both ways. In passages such as Romans 1:24 and 11:17 the meaning "among them" is used. In 2 Corinthians 6:16 and Ephesians 4:18 the meaning "in them" is found. In either case, as the next clause demonstrates, the revelation of τὸ γνωστὸν τοῦ θεοῦ is clear and immediate: those to whom the revelation has been made known.

ὁ θεὸς γὰρ αὐτοῖς ἐφανέρωσεν: Paul here explains how it is that the revelation of God is "clear" and "known." The use of γὰρ closely connects this clause with the preceding one and makes this clause explanatory. God's revelation is clear because God himself has done the revealing. God is the subject of ἐφανέρωσεν; He is the One who does the revealing, and that directly αὐτοῖς, "to them." Pauline usage of ἐφανέρωσεν includes Titus 1:3, ἐφανέρωσεν δὲ καιροῖς ἰδίοις τὸν λόγον αὐτοῦ ἐν κηρύγματι, "At the proper time manifested in his word through preaching"; Colossians 1:26, νῦν δὲ ἐφανερώθη τοῖς ἁγίοις αὐτοῦ, referring to the mystery hidden for ages and generations, "but now made manifest to his saints"; and especially 1 Timothy 3:16, Θεός ἐφανερώθη ἐν σαρκι,[14] "God was manifest in the flesh," where the very Incarnation is described by this term. In none of these cases does ἐφανέρωσεν suggest a mere potentiality, but instead a real and full revelation.

1:20

> For since the creation of the world his invisible attributes—his eternal power and divine nature—have been clearly seen, because they are understood through what has been made. So they are without excuse.

Alternate:

> For from the creation of the world His invisible attributes—His eternal power and divine nature—have been clearly per-

[14]Using the variant reading θεός rather than the textual reading ὅς.

ceived, being understood by means of those things which have been made, with the result that they are without excuse. (Author)

NA[27] Text:

τὰ γὰρ ἀόρατα αὐτοῦ ἀπὸ κτίσεως κόσμου τοῖς ποιήμασιν νοούμενα καθορᾶται, ἥ τε ἀΐδιος αὐτοῦ δύναμις καὶ θειότης, εἰς τὸ εἶναι αὐτοὺς ἀναπολογήτους,

τὰ γὰρ ἀόρατα αὐτοῦ: Again γὰρ signals the connection of this passage with the preceding one. Here Paul expands upon how that which may be known about God has been revealed, explaining the content and extent of τὸ γνωστὸν as well as the means by which this revelation has taken place, that being by τοῖς ποιήμασιν, the things made. He also provides us with the result: no defense, no excuse. "His invisible things" is the literal translation of the phrase. Paul is indicating that these attributes of God are not visible to physical sight, yet their existence is revealed by God to men.

The order of the sentence is probably significant: Paul does not define the "invisible attributes" until after he has asserted that these attributes from the creation of the world by the things made have been clearly perceived and understood. The emphasis falls upon the clarity of the revelation and the fact that this revelation has *always been,* ἀπὸ κτίσεως κόσμου. There has never been a time since creation when His invisible attributes have been "unrevealed."

τοῖς ποιήμασιν νοούμενα καθορᾶται is a difficult phrase. τοῖς ποιήμασιν refers us to the means by which the revelation has taken place, specifically, by creation itself. God has created so that what is created bears testimony to the Creator. But Paul then gives us a description of the clarity of this revelation. νοούμενα is the present passive participial form of νοέω, "perceive, apprehend, understand, gain an insight into."[15] Coupled with καθορᾶται, from καθοράω, "to perceive, notice"[16] it means "is clearly

---

[15]BDAG, 674.
[16]Ibid., 493.

perceived."[17] Again, Paul is referring to the invisible attributes of God, and he asserts plainly that the knowledge of these attributes is not merely potential but actual. That is, by use of the present tense in both the participle and the verb, the use of the indicative mood,[18] and the complementary meanings of the two terms, Paul is asserting that there is an actual reception of the revelation of God's invisible attributes by means of the created things. This is plainly the meaning of the terms, and it is the necessary understanding given that here the apostle is explaining in further detail how it is that he can say that God has "manifested" τὸ γνωστὸν, the things that may be known of God, to men.

ἥ τε ἀΐδιος αὐτοῦ δύναμις καὶ θειότης: With these words Paul more fully explains the extent of what is revealed by the creation—God's eternal power and divine nature—with great clarity. If the question is asked as to what exactly these terms refer to, we might note that Paul provides a self-definition of the terms in the next verse.[19] When he insists that men should have "glorified God and given thanks," he is giving insight, for no matter what else "eternal power" and "divine nature" might entail, they make man responsible for glorifying God as God and giving thanks to Him as Creator. Hence the passage provides a definition that asserts two things: first, the transparency of the revelation; second, the limitation of the revelation.

ἀΐδιος αὐτοῦ δύναμις καὶ θειότης does not exhaust the knowledge of God. That which may be known of God by general revelation is limited by these terms. There is no basis in these words for the "gospel in the stars" type of assertion, where the content of *special revelation* is read into the *general revelation*.

εἰς τὸ εἶναι αὐτοὺς ἀναπολογήτους: The common Pauline structure, εἰς τὸ with the infinitive used to express purpose or

---

[17]Ibid., 674.

[18]I.e., Paul is not presenting a conditional, a subjunctive, or any other kind of doubtful affirmation in the passage.

[19]For the difference between θειότης and θεότης (as used in Colossians 2:9, θεότητος), see Trench's *Synonyms of the New Testament* (Eerdmans, 1983), 7–10. In this instance it is significant to note that Paul does not use the stronger term θεότης, which is reflective of the divine essence (seen fully in Christ), but the more general term, θειότης, which refers to the divine power and majesty. To quote Thayer, "θεότ. *deity* differs from θειότ. *divinity*, as essence differs from quality or attribute" (*The New Thayer's Greek-English Lexicon*, 288).

result, here expressing result. The outcome of the stark *visibility* of the revelation of God to men is that they are ἀναπολογήτους, "without excuse, without defense, without an apologetic" for their rebellion. The Vulgate renders it *inexcusabiles,* "inexcusable."

All pretense has been taken away from man. He cannot plead ignorance, for the revelation (1) has been made to him by God himself (ὁ θεὸς γὰρ αὐτοῖς ἐφανέρωσεν), (2) has been constant and consistent from the beginning of time (ἀπὸ κτίσεως κόσμου), and (3) is currently *being* perceived, and that clearly (νοούμενα καθορᾶται). Indeed, it could be properly understood that it is the intention of the revelation to render man without excuse. This would fit well with the purpose of Paul expressed in his concluding indictment of all of mankind—"for we have already charged that Jews and Greeks alike are all under sin" (Romans 3:9)—and none can make a case *against* their sinfulness in light of the clarity of God's revelation.

1:21

> For although they knew God, they did not glorify him as God or give him thanks, but they became futile in their thoughts and their senseless hearts were darkened.

Alternates:

> . . . for though they knew God, they did not honor him as God or give thanks to him, but they became futile in their thinking, and their senseless minds were darkened. (NRSV)

> For even though they knew God, they did not glorify Him as God, or give thanks to Him as God, but instead they became worthless in their reasonings and their senseless hearts were darkened. (Author)

NA[27] Text:

διότι γνόντες τὸν θεὸν οὐχ ὡς θεὸν ἐδόξασαν ἢ ηὐχαρίστησαν, ἀλλ' ἐματαιώθησαν ἐν τοῖς διαλογισμοῖς αὐτῶν καὶ ἐσκοτίσθη ἡ ἀσύνετος αὐτῶν καρδία.

This is another rich Greek passage that defies simple English phrasing. γνόντες is an aorist active participle syntactically functioning as a circumstantial concessive; that is, the action of the main verb (οὐχ ἐδόξασαν ἢ ηὐχαρίστησαν) is accomplished *in spite of* the action of the participle. τὸν θεὸν is the object of the participle. That which is known to men is God, as Paul has explained in the previous verses. This construction directly asserts the existence of knowledge on the part of those to whom the revelation of God has been made with transparency. The great sinfulness of men in not glorifying God and giving thanks to Him is predicated upon the simple assertion that men knew God but suppressed that knowledge and turned away from it. It is plainly the apostle's teaching that it is a manifest sign of the darkening of the foolish mind of man that he does not glorify God and give thanks, and this view makes sense only in light of the assertion that men knew God and yet struck out on a path of rebellion and rejection.

οὐχ ὡς θεὸν ἐδόξασαν ἢ ηὐχαρίστησαν: Both verbs are functioning together and hence could be rendered, "they did not glorify or give thanks to Him as God." Most translations break the two verbs up because English does not like to use "glorify" without expressing an immediate object. The charge against man, who knows God, is that he does not glorify Him *as God.* There is a kind of glorification of God *as God* that is natural to man as a created being, and it is something against which fallen man fights with all his might. In the same way man is seen to be responsible to give thanks to God as God. Again, it is natural for man to recognize the necessity of thankfulness to God, yet man refuses to give this naturally required thanks. The great sinfulness of this action on man's part is understandable only on the basis of the recognition that men know God exists because God has revealed this truth to them. The depth of the impact of sin is seen as well, for the most natural impulses of the creature man are suppressed in his rebellion against his Maker.

ἀλλ' ἐματαιώθησαν ἐν τοῖς διαλογισμοῖς αὐτῶν: There is a natural reaction to man's rebellion against God and against His revelation. Such heinous sinfulness cannot pass unnoticed. Man's very constitution is impacted by this rejection of God and this refusal to honor and glorify Him. Paul uses the adversative ἀλλ' to introduce what man does *rather than* glorify and give thanks. And while we can see man's actions in the action-noun διαλογισμοῖς, "thoughts" or "reasonings," the verb itself is passive. That is, man's very thoughts and opinions *are rendered* fruitless, vain, and futile. Does Paul have in mind here his later statement, παρέδωκεν αὐτοὺς ὁ θεὸς εἰς ἀδόκιμον νοῦν, "God delivered them over to a reprobate mind" (1:28)? Quite possibly so. In any case, Paul here asserts that the very reasoning powers of man are impacted by this refusal to acknowledge God.

καὶ ἐσκοτίσθη ἡ ἀσύνετος αὐτῶν καρδία: The conjunction of διαλογισμοῖς with καρδία is highly expressive, and for Paul it surely reflects the entirety of the mental aspect of man. The καρδία refers to the very center of man's being, as is seen in Paul's use of the term in Romans 10:8–10, and 1 Corinthians 7:37. Paul uses two terms to describe the impact upon man's mind: ἐματαιώθησαν and ἐσκοτίσθη. Both are most expressive. ἐματαιώθησαν comes from ματαιόω, "render futile/worthless; pass. be given over to worthlessness, think about idle, worthless things, be foolish."[20] The same lexicon translates our passage, "their thoughts became directed to worthless things." The adjectival form is rendered, "idle, empty, fruitless, useless, powerless, lacking truth." ἐσκοτίσθη is the aorist passive of σκοτίζομαι, "become inwardly darkened . . . of the organs of spiritual and moral perception."[21] The picture of the "darkened mind" is quite striking and surely suggests an absence of something that was once there. This portrait is only enhanced by Paul's addition of ἀσύνετος, literally, "without understanding" and therefore, "senseless."[22]

1:22–23

> Although they claimed to be wise, they became fools and exchanged the glory of the immortal God for an image

[20]BDAG, 621.

[21]Ibid., 932.

[22]The use of ἀσύνετος καρδία reminds one of the end product of a life lived outside of the light of God's truth seen in the Lord's own vivid term, σκληροκαρδία, "hardness of heart" (Matthew 19:8; Mark 10:5).

> resembling mortal human beings or birds or four-footed animals or reptiles.

NA[27] Text:
φάσκοντες εἶναι σοφοὶ ἐμωράνθησαν καὶ ἤλλαξαν τὴν δόξαν τοῦ ἀφθάρτου θεοῦ ἐν ὁμοιώματι εἰκόνος φθαρτοῦ ἀνθρώπου καὶ πετεινῶν καὶ τετραπόδων καὶ ἑρπετῶν.

The denial of the truth about God leads man into the ultimate irony: the continued claim to wisdom (one cannot avoid noting the use of σοφοὶ when Paul surely knew many philosophers who posed as lovers of truth) is made while in reality they had become foolish, senseless, lacking the very wisdom they claim to possess.

The ultimate example of foolishness is seen in this passage, where man exchanges[23] the glory of the immortal, incorruptible, imperishable God for mere images of mortal and corruptible men, birds, animals, and reptiles. Here the depravity that results from the suppression of the truth reaches its zenith in open idolatry. Men, knowing they should honor and glorify God, turn that natural desire toward fellow creatures—mere creations. This exchange touches on the very heart of sin: man, the creature, turns away from the Creator and gives what is rightly only to be given to God to what shares the creature's created nature.

Idolatry can be flagrant and open in the sense of the primitive tribal worship of hideous statues, or it can be refined, packaged, and intellectual, as in the modern Western worship of humanistic scholarship or technology. No matter what, any system of thought that does not begin and end with the God who created thought itself is, by definition, idolatrous.

1:24

> Therefore God gave them over in the desires of their hearts to impurity, to dishonor their bodies among themselves.

---

[23]Continue reading for a discussion of the difference between the use of ἤλλαξαν here and μετήλλαξαν in verse 25.

NA*[27] *Text:

Διὸ παρέδωκεν αὐτοὺς ὁ θεὸς ἐν ταῖς ἐπιθυμίαις τῶν καρδιῶν αὐτῶν εἰς ἀκαθαρσίαν τοῦ ἀτιμάζεσθαι τὰ σώματα αὐτῶν ἐν αὐτοῖς.

παρέδωκεν is an action undertaken by God himself. It is no mere coincidence that παραδίδωμι is the same term used of Judas when he "delivered up" the Lord Jesus (Matthew 26:46). God delivers up depraved men ἐν ταῖς ἐπιθυμίαις τῶν καρδιῶν, "in the desires of their hearts," a most frightening statement for any person who has, by the grace of God, been able to see the darkness of their own heart.

The twistedness of sin is seen in that the desires of their hearts result in the dishonoring of their bodies. God, as Creator, designed man to function in a particular fashion. The rebellious creature invests incredible time and energy into finding ways to use his body so as to violate God's law, God's standard. Of course this only results in the damage and despair of the very person engaging in the rebellion, but such is the futility of the depraved mind (1:28).

1:25

> They exchanged the truth of God for a lie and worshiped and served the creation rather than the Creator, who is blessed forever! Amen.

NA*[27] *Text:

οἵτινες μετήλλαξαν τὴν ἀλήθειαν τοῦ θεοῦ ἐν τῷ ψεύδει καὶ ἐσεβάσθησαν καὶ ἐλάτρευσαν τῇ κτίσει παρὰ τὸν κτίσαντα, ὅς ἐστιν εὐλογητὸς εἰς τοὺς αἰῶνας· ἀμήν.

Those who are given over by God to the lusts of their hearts are further described by Scripture as those who μετήλλαξαν τὴν ἀλήθειαν τοῦ θεοῦ ἐν τῷ ψεύδει, those who "exchanged the truth of God for the lie." The term ἤλλαξαν appeared in verse 23 and was translated "exchanged." Yet here it is in the compound form, μετήλλαξαν, the preposition μετά strengthening the concept of exchanging one thing for another.[24] Again the apostle's words are only understandable in light of the acceptance of the fact that men *have* the truth of God but exchange that truth for the lie in unrighteousness. To deny the Creator-creation relationship, which is exactly what Paul presents here, requires that one know what the relationship is before denying it. Therefore, again, the entire passage hangs upon the reality that God *has* revealed himself—not exhaustively, yet with clarity.

As a result of man's unwillingness to retain the truth of God (repeated again in verse 28), he is forced to ascribe worship and reverence to that which by its very nature is worthy of no such thing: the κτίσις. What a horrific picture is here presented: man giving the highest forms of worship and service to the creation. How twisted is the mind that has exchanged the truth of God for the lie.

1:26–27

> For this reason God gave them over to dishonorable passions. For their women exchanged the natural sexual relations for unnatural ones, and likewise the men also abandoned natural relations with women and were inflamed in their passions for one another. Men committed shameless acts with men and received in themselves the due penalty for their error.

It is not necessary to go into quite as much depth with relationship to Paul's catalog of human sins as it is to demonstrate the guilt of man in suppressing the knowledge of God and of twisting the Creator-creation relationship (and hence the exegesis will not be as involved and will not necessitate the Greek text here or in 29–31). Here Paul presents as a clear example of the "twistedness" of the truth-suppressing creature man: the sin of homosexuality. The most natural passion of mankind, the sexual drive, is bent and contorted by the struggle of man in his depravity to "suppress the truth" and "exchange it" for the lie. Knowing that

[24]English does not have a sufficiently wide vocabulary to capture the nuances of many Greek compounds like this. The Vulgate used *mutaverunt* in verse 23 and *commutaverunt* in verse 25.

God has made him in one way, he engages in self-destructive behavior specifically designed to deny the proper function and lifestyle that God has created and decreed. This shows that there is no length to which man will not go to rebel against the *objective fact* of his createdness, including to the point of self-destruction.

1:28

> And just as they did not see fit to acknowledge God, God gave them over to a depraved mind, to do what should not be done.

NA[27] Text:
καὶ καθὼς οὐκ ἐδοκίμασαν τὸν θεὸν ἔχειν ἐν ἐπιγνώσει, παρέδωκεν αὐτοὺς ⸋ὁ θεὸς εἰς ἀδόκιμον νοῦν, ποιεῖν τὰ μὴ καθήκοντα.

|⸋ א* A 0172*

δοκιμάζω, the root of ἐδοκίμασαν, is best translated "did not see fit," with the idea of the NIV being present, "they did not think it worthwhile." ἔχειν has a truly broad semantic range,[25] with BDAG indicating that with the preposition ἐν it means, in this passage, "to acknowledge God." Others suggest "to retain." In either case we have here another description of the same action we have seen before: the suppression of truth, the failure to give glory and thanks, the exchanging of the truth for the lie, etc. Since men did not desire to retain a true knowledge of God, God gave them up to a reprobate mind. It is important to note the order: first is οὐκ ἐδοκίμασαν, "they did not see fit"; then comes παρέδωκεν αὐτοὺς ὁ θεὸς, "God gave them over."[26] We cannot reverse the divine order as revealed in Scripture.

1:29–31

> They are filled with every kind of unrighteousness, wickedness, covetousness, malice. They are rife with envy, murder,

---

[25]See the large number of possibilities in BDAG, 420–22!

[26]One might think the deletion of "God" in א and A is due to the strength of this assertion, but it could also be due to *homoeoteleuton.*

> strife, deceit, hostility. They are gossips, slanderers, haters of God, insolent, arrogant, boastful, contrivers of all sorts of evil, disobedient to parents, senseless, covenant-breakers, heartless, ruthless.

Paul's catalog of the human condition is full, honest, and brutal. Sadly, so many of the listed sins strike modern man as almost trivial: envy, deceit, gossip, boasting, disobedience to parents, being senseless (many *seek* such a state!), covenant-breaking, heartlessness. We note only in passing the use of θεοστυγεῖς, "haters of God," as a tremendously tragic conclusion to a passage that began with διότι τὸ γνωστὸν τοῦ θεοῦ φανερόν ἐστιν ἐν αὐτοῖς, "because that which is known about God is evident within them"(1:19).

1:32

> Although they fully know God's righteous decree that those who practice such things deserve to die, they not only do them but also approve of those who practice them.

NA[27] Text:
οἵτινες τὸ δικαίωμα τοῦ θεοῦ ἐπιγνόντες ὅτι οἱ τὰ τοιαῦτα πράσσοντες ἄξιοι θανάτου εἰσίν, οὐ μόνον αὐτὰ ποιοῦσιν ἀλλὰ καὶ συνευδοκοῦσιν τοῖς πράσσουσιν.

Paul concludes by stating that man is simply mad. Men fully know (ἐπιγνόντες) the result of their actions. They fully know God's decree regarding these things. They fully know that His decree is righteous and just. They fully know that it is proper for God to punish with eternal death those who practice the sins cataloged by Paul in the previous verses. Yet despite this knowledge (another example of the use of the participle as a circumstantial concessive), they not only do these things themselves, but actively engage in encouraging others in the same sinful acts. The process has reached its completion with man, the recipient of the revelation of God's truth, seeking his own destruction in a mindless fit of sinful behavior.

SUMMARY OF EXEGESIS OF ROMANS 1

The preceding investigation has provided us with the following items regarding our subject:

1. That which may be known of God is manifest among men, for God himself has made the revelation (v. 19).
2. This revelation is clear and understood by those to whom it has been made (v. 20).
3. This revelation is limited in scope, revealing God's eternal power and divine nature (v. 20).
4. The result of the clarity of this revelation is that man is held culpable for his rejection of this revelation, that is, he is "without defense" (v. 20).
5. Upon the basis of the aforementioned revelation, Scripture says men know God, but, despite this, they refuse to glorify God or give Him thanks.
6. As a result of man's suppression of this knowledge (vv. 18, 21), man's reasoning is darkened and made futile (v. 21).
7. Men exchange the truth of God, given to them by God himself, for the lie, resulting in idolatry (v. 25).
8. The depth of the depravity of man is compounded by his use of his mental powers to reject God's truth.
9. Man, as a result, twists everything that reminds him of his Creator and the fact of his being a creation. Man is, truly, "totally depraved" in that every aspect of his being is touched by sin.

But Paul is not finished with his proclamation of the bad news. In no way. There is a still more to come, for up to this point the self-righteous Jew could stand next to the apostle and cheer him on. "Indeed, thus live the Gentiles!" the Jew could say. But Paul has another purpose: before he can demonstrate that the means of being made right before God are uniform, that is, that both Jew and Gentile are made right on the same basis, he must, in essence, put both groups into the same boat so that the same means of rescue can be applied.

ROMANS 2

We will not offer a full exegesis of Romans 2 for the simple reason that the main outlines of the chapter are easily discernable, and the one section that calls for a closer examination, 2:11–13, can be properly exegeted without involving in-depth discussion of the surrounding text. However, the context must be established before that passage can be properly addressed.

Paul begins by startling the Jewish reader: "*Therefore* you are without excuse, *whoever you are*, when you judge someone else." Knowing the Jewish attitude, Paul immediately turns to any self-righteous person who fails to see the application of his charge of sinfulness to himself. The Jew may agree with the assertion that God's judgment is "in accordance with truth" against all those who practice the sins cataloged in the first chapter, but he must realize that God's judgment falls upon *all* who break God's law, including the one who thinks that his covenant relationship with God will in some fashion shield him from the same condemnation that comes upon the world.

To fail to acknowledge this truth is to show contempt for God's kindness and patience. God is no friend of hypocrisy, and to extend hearty approval regarding His judgment against such behavior while practicing it yourself results only in the "storing up of wrath" for the coming day of the Lord.

It is upon the mention of the inevitability of the day of judgment that Paul then moves into a discussion of the basis upon which judgment will be rendered. It is vitally important to recognize the context in which we are working. Romans 2:1–3:8 comprises a whole argument meant to convince the Jewish reader that the charge of sinfulness is universal (Romans 3:9) and that the possession of the covenant promises of Israel does not put them in a separate class when it comes to the means of justification.

To make his point Paul will use a number of arguments that draw from common beliefs of the Jews. He begins his apologetic here by establishing the grounds upon which God's justice is to be meted out. This is necessary to establish the universal sinfulness of man *and* the righteousness of God in judging that sin is worthy of death. Missing this simple fact not only cuts the ground out from under the entire argument the apostle presents (making it worthless to his original audience), but it likewise leads to insurmountable exegetical quandaries because it makes Paul self-contradictory, something that should, by definition, cause us to immediately reflect upon the error of such interpretations. Upon what basis will God's righteous judgment be experienced? First and foremost, its universal application has to be established before God's mercy in justification can be understood. So we read,

> **2:6** He will reward each one according to his works: **2:7** eternal life to those who by perseverance in good works seek glory and honor and immortality, **2:8** but wrath and anger to those who live in selfish ambition and do not obey the truth but follow unrighteousness. **2:9** There will be affliction and distress on everyone who does evil, on the Jew first and also the Greek, **2:10** but glory and honor and peace for everyone who does good, for the Jew first and also the Greek.

This is the basic point: judgment is impartial. The Jewish person, who has already been said to be acting in hypocrisy (2:3), is told that only those who "by perseverance in good works seek glory and honor and immortality" will receive eternal life. It is to make a mockery of Paul's entire argument to take such statements out of the context of the demonstration of universal sinfulness and the refutation of the hypocrisy of those who thought their standing or their genetics would gain them eternal life *outside of their true character* and their concern for God's law and create from them an entire methodology of justification. Surely if a person appears before the judgment seat as one who is determined to have sought glory and immortality, that person will receive eternal life, for God's judgments are always just. But if any person appears before Him who has not obeyed the truth but has followed unrighteousness, such a person can only expect wrath and anger, affliction, and distress.

It is Paul's entire thrust, concluded in 3:9, that this is the end of all flesh, "for all have sinned and fall short of the glory of God" whether Jew or Gentile (3:23). Therefore, he asserts, affliction and distress will come upon everyone, whether Jew or Gentile. God's judgment is impartial and just. This is step 1 in coming to the final conclusion: All have sinned; hence, all are in need of a means of justification based on God's grace, not on our merit.

> **2:11** For there is no partiality with God. **2:12** For all who have sinned apart from the law will also perish apart from the law, and all who have sinned under the law will be judged by the law. **2:13** For it is not the ones who hear the law who are righteous before God, but those who do the law will be declared righteous.

NA[27] Text (verse 13):
οὐ γὰρ οἱ ἀκροαταὶ νόμου δίκαιοι παρὰ τῷ θεῷ, ἀλλ' οἱ ποιηταὶ νόμου δικαιωθήσονται.

Sin brings judgment whether one is apart from the law (i.e., a Gentile to whom the law was not given in the same manner it was given to the Jew) or "under the law." Verse 13 is an expansion of the thought in 12b: those who have sinned under the law will be judged by means of that law. This seems too obvious for statement, but it was not. Many Jews saw the law not as a guide for righteous living but as a mark of covenant blessings taken so for granted that the moral demands were no longer relevant, or at least they believed they would not be applied with the stricture expected of non-Jews.

That these are the self-righteous Jews Paul has in mind is clear from 2:17–24. So if one has just announced to such a self-righteous Jew that God's judgment will fall with equal severity upon the Jew who sins under the law, what further explanation and expansion could be offered to cut off any of the objections that might be raised? This is the essence of verse 13.

The connection to the preceding thought of verse 12 is established by γὰρ, "for." Why will judgment come upon even the Jew who sins under the law? Because of a basic principle of justice. Being a "hearer of law" (οἱ ἀκροαταὶ νόμου) will not justify. There is a contrast here between the hearer of law and the doer of law. The first would refer to the Jews who hear the law as part of the regular services of worship in the synagogue. As such they were privileged indeed to hear the law read each Sabbath day.

But to hear without doing is futile. Paul points to the same inherent contradiction that James attacks when he speaks of being a *doer* of the word rather than a mere *hearer* (James 1:22), using the very same term for "hearers." Both recognize the natural inconsistency of hearing God's law and yet not obeying it and thereby doing what it commands. Possession of the law without obedience is worthless. Hearing without obeying cannot bring justification, no matter how strongly the Jew might believe his covenant status in some way made him right with God. The Jew knows the truth of the statement that it is the doer of the law who receives justification from God.

There is no reason at all, given the context, for any confusion to exist regarding verse 13b, as if Paul is here setting up the idea that law-keeping is the means of justification. Nor is there any reason to think Paul is introducing a hypothetical. He is simply stating a truism, a basic, obvious fact that flows from the contrast between hearing and doing. The context precludes anything more than the recognition that doing is demanded by the law, not mere hearing. Paul will, of course, clearly address the issue of the means of justification once he has established the universal need thereof: at this point he is stripping away every excuse and objection he has encountered during the course of his own ministry. John Murray wrote regarding this passage,

> The apostle is undoubtedly guarding against that perversion so characteristic of the Jew that the possession of God's special revelation and of the corresponding privileges would afford immunity from the rigour of the judgment applied to others not thus favoured. He speaks of "the *hearers* of the law" because it was by hearing the Scriptures read that the mass of the people of Israel became acquainted with them and in that sense could be said to *have* the law. . . .
>
> It is quite unnecessary to find in this verse any doctrine of justification by works in conflict with the teaching of this epistle in later chapters. Whether any will be actually justified by works either in this life or at the final judgment is beside the

apostle's interest and design at this juncture. The burden of this verse is that not the hearers or mere possessors of the law will be justified before God but that in terms of the law the criterion is *doing*, not hearing. The apostle's appeal to this principle serves that purpose truly and effectively, and there is no need to import questions that are not relevant to the universe of discourse.[27]

And Douglas Moo likewise observed,

Paul explains why even those who possess the law will nevertheless be condemned when they sin. It is because the law can justify only when it is obeyed; reading it, hearing it taught and preached, studying it—none of these, nor all of them together, can justify. . . . God's abhorrence of any hearing of the law without doing it is a very customary teaching. . . . Whereas the principle in these examples has a hortatory purpose—to encourage obedience to the law or to the Word of God—Paul uses the principle to remind Jews of the standard of God's judgment. Only those who are "*doers* of the law" will be declared right in the judgment.

The question arises here again: Who are those whom Paul views as vindicated in the judgment by their doing of the law? . . . We think it more likely that Paul is here simply setting forth the standard by which God's justifying verdict will be rendered. This verse confirms and explains the reason for the Jews' condemnation in 12b; and this suggests that its purpose is not to show how people can be justified but to set forth the standard that must be met if a person is to be justified.

As he does throughout this chapter, Paul presses typical Jewish teaching into the service of his "preparation for the gospel." Jews believed that "doing" the law, or perhaps the intent to do the law, would lead, for the Jew already in covenant relationship with God, to final salvation. Paul affirms the principle that doing the law can lead to salvation; but he denies (1) that anyone can so "do" the law; and (2) that Jews can depend on their covenant relationship to shield them from the consequences of this failure.[28]

---

[27]Murray, *Romans*, 71.
[28]Moo, *Romans*, 147–48.

The self-righteous Jew who is here reminded that the mere possession of law does not make one right with the Lawgiver has this truth brought home to him with striking clarity in the following verses:

> **2:17** But if you call yourself a Jew and rely on the law and boast of your relationship to God **2:18** and know his will and approve the superior things because you receive instruction from the law, **2:19** and if you are convinced that you yourself are a guide to the blind, a light to those who are in darkness, **2:20** an educator of the senseless, a teacher of little children, because you have in the law the essential features of knowledge and of the truth—**2:21** therefore you who teach someone else, do you not teach yourself? You who preach against stealing, do you steal? **2:22** You who say not to commit adultery, do you commit adultery? You who abhor idols, do you rob temples? **2:23** You who boast in the law dishonor God by transgressing the law! **2:24** For just as it is written, "*the name of God is being blasphemed among the Gentiles because of you.*"

To hear the law and not do the law results in the name of God being blasphemed, so unnatural and self-contradictory is such a situation. This is the essence of Paul's attack in this passage: to demonstrate that the Jew who would excuse himself from the universal sinfulness of man outlined in the first chapter is, in fact, just as guilty as the Gentile who makes no claim to a covenant relationship with God. Truly the truth of man's state is simple: All, Jew and Gentile, have sinned and have fallen short of the glory of God.

PAUL'S SUMMARY ARGUMENT: ROMANS 3:9–18

Paul continues closing every avenue of excuse for his brethren according to the flesh, the Jews. He insists that "true Judaism" is not a matter of externals but of the internal operation of the Spirit of God in the circumcision of the heart itself (2:29). This is followed with a discussion of the advantages the Jews had in having been entrusted with the "oracles of God" and how their unbelief has not nullified the faithfulness of God (a topic he will return to in the early verses of Romans 9). When Paul's imaginary objector reappears in 3:5, Paul's response shows the fundamental necessity of justice in the world, for he retorts, "For otherwise how could God judge the world?" That God *will* and *must* judge is a given in the biblical worldview.

Finally, having addressed the key objections to man's sinfulness, Paul launches his final assault by stringing together a lengthy catena of passages of the testimony of Scripture itself to the sinfulness of man. He puts all of humanity under judgment so that the means of redemption, the message of faith, can be preached to every individual *on the same grounds.* Without this initial establishment of the bad news, the presentation of justification by faith that follows would make no sense at all.

> **3:9** What then? Are we better off? Certainly not, for we have already charged that Jews and Greeks alike are all under sin,
> **3:10** just as it is written:
> "*There is no one righteous, not even one,*
> **3:11** *there is no one who understands,*
> *there is no one who seeks God.*
> **3:12** *All have turned away,*
> *they have together become worthless;*
> *there is no one who shows kindness, not even one.*"
> **3:13** "*Their throats are open graves,*
> *they deceive with their tongues,*
> *the poison of asps is under their lips.*"
> **3:14** "*Their mouths are full of cursing and bitterness.*"
> **3:15** "*Their feet are swift to shed blood,*
> **3:16** *ruin and misery are in their paths,*
> **3:17** *and the way of peace they have not known.*"
> **3:18** "*There is no fear of God before their eyes.*"

It would be a major error to miss the apostle's context and seek refuge in doing what Paul is clearly *not* doing. His point is to be derived from the entirety of the testimony to sin, not from a close examination of each passage. Some have missed Paul's point by attempting to dissect each quotation, isolate the context from which it was taken, and in essence limit the accusation of sin inherent in the passages. But surely this is not Paul's intention. Instead, we are given his own interpretation right at the start in the words "for we have already charged that Jews and Greeks alike are all under sin, just as it is written. . . ." We will see in verse 19 that Paul is using an argument from the greater to the lesser: these verses are applicable directly to the Jews because they come from the Scriptures entrusted to them, and if this is true of God's people, who have a clear revelation of God's will in His law, how much more the Gentiles?

The weight of the combination of these passages is almost overwhelming. The terms used are extensive and unyielding. First is the denial of the existence of a righteous man, drawing from (and paraphrasing slightly) Psalm 14:1–3. In the context in which he places it, Paul is saying *every* Jew and Gentile has fallen short of righteousness and understanding. There is no righteous man, "not even one." Obviously Paul here refers to the absolute standard of judgment, the charge of sin, and not the moral righteousness of a Job or a Zechariah.

The next two phrases support this conclusion, as we are told there is "no understanding one" (οὐκ ἔστιν ὁ συνίων) and no "God-seeker" (οὐκ ἔστιν ὁ ἐκζητῶν τὸν θεόν), again drawn from Psalm 14. While συνίημι is used in the LXX to render Hebrew verbs of prosperity and success, here Paul interprets it to refer to the understanding that leads to life and righteousness. The assertion that there is no "God-seeker," or "there is no one who seeks after God," fulfills the idea of lacking understanding or wisdom. One cannot help but think of the depraved mind of Romans 1:28. The very phrase is filled with despair: *all* of those made in the image of God lack understanding; all those created by God do not seek Him (rather, as Paul has already explained, they suppress the knowledge they have of Him).

But one might well ask why Paul begins his concluding argument with such words. For indeed, if there is none who has understanding, none who seeks after God, then there can only be one basis upon which salvation can be based: the mercy and grace of God. All will be dependent upon God's grace; none will be able to stand above the others. It is central to the demonstration of the universal sinfulness of man and the absolute necessity of grace for the true *sinfulness of sin* to be announced.

The catena continues with highly descriptive phrases, focusing upon the twistedness and depravity of man. The passage reaches a crescendo in the recognition of the violence of man. Ruin and misery accompany man, and the path of peace man does not know. Surely there is a progression here: if man does not seek after God, he will end up seeking after his own desires and lusts, resulting in murder, misery, and havoc.

The final charge laid at the feet of mankind is "there is no fear of God before their eyes." Pots in rebellion against their Potter; creatures in insurrection against their Creator. This is the state of man.

The establishment of the *need* of fallen man now complete, Paul can now turn to the gracious provision in Christ Jesus.

CHAPTER 11

Romans 3:19–31: The Gospel Stated

SYNOPSIS:

Romans 3:19–31 comprises the initial proclamation of the gospel of God's grace. It follows the demonstration of man's deadness in sin and his inability to obtain righteousness in and of himself. The focus is upon the means of justification, the nature of God's act of justifying the sinner, and the basis upon which God can declare a sinner righteous, that being the atoning work of Christ on the cross.

RESOURCES, BACKGROUND ISSUES, AND BIBLIOGRAPHY:

See listing in chapter 10, pages 143–144.

MAIN PASSAGE:

3:19 Now we know that whatever the law says, it says to those who are under the law, so that every mouth may be silenced and the whole world may be held accountable to God. **3:20** For *no one* *is declared righteous before him* by the works of the law, for through the law comes the knowledge of sin.

3:21 But now apart from the law the righteousness of God (which is attested by the law and the prophets) has been disclosed—**3:22** namely, the righteousness of God through the faithfulness of Jesus Christ for all who believe. For there is no distinction, **3:23** for all have sinned and fall short of the glory of God. **3:24** But they are justified freely by his grace through the redemption that is in Christ Jesus. **3:25** God publicly displayed him as a satisfaction for sin by his blood through faith. This was to demonstrate his righteousness, because God in his forbearance had passed over the sins previously committed. **3:26** This was also to demonstrate his righteousness in the present time, so that he would be just and the justifier of the one who lives because of Jesus' faithfulness.

3:27 Where, then, is boasting? It is excluded! By what principle? Of works? No, but by the principle of faith! **3:28** For we consider that a person is declared righteous by faith apart from the works of the law. **3:29** Or is God the God of the Jews only? Is he not the God of the Gentiles too? Yes, of the Gentiles too! **3:30** Since God is one, he will justify the circumcised by faith and the uncircumcised through faith. **3:31** Do we nullify the law through faith? Absolutely not! Instead we uphold the law.

3:19

> Now we know that whatever the law says, it says to those who are under the law, so that every mouth may be silenced and the whole world may be held accountable to God.

NA[27] Text:
οἴδαμεν δὲ ὅτι ὅσα ὁ νόμος λέγει τοῖς ἐν τῷ νόμῳ λαλεῖ, ἵνα πᾶν στόμα φραγῇ καὶ ὑπόδικος γένηται πᾶς ὁ κόσμος τῷ θεῷ·

"We know" indicates that Paul is referring to a given, something that is not controversial. The passages he has just cited are all from the Hebrew Scriptures, those which were entrusted to the Jews (3:2). What "the law" says, it says to those who are "in the law" (literally), which would seemingly limit the preceding section to the Jews. But this is contrary to Paul's own stated purpose (3:9). Instead, as mentioned, it seems Paul is using an argument from the greater to the lesser in this verse. If the Scriptures condemn the Jews in these words, how much more those who do not have the Scriptures? Hence, "so that every mouth may be silenced" could be paraphrased "So if the Jews are thus condemned, so all the world likewise is liable to judgment."

πᾶν στόμα (*pan stoma*, "every mouth") is the parallel to 3:9's "Jew and Gentile." Every mouth is to be shut, that is, all excuse-making is ended. The whole world is rendered accountable (ὑπόδικος) before God. Douglas Moo put it this way:

> The terminology of this clause reflects the imagery of the courtroom. "Shutting the mouth" connotes the situation of the defendant who has no more to say in response to the charges brought against him or her. The Greek word translated "accountable" occurs nowhere else in the Scriptures, but is used in extra-biblical Greek to mean "answerable to" or "liable to prosecution," "accountable." Paul pictures God both as the one offended and as the judge who weighs the evidence and pronounces the verdict. The image, then, is of all humanity standing before God, accountable to him for willful and inexcusable violations of his will, awaiting the sentence of condemnation that their actions deserve.[1]

The silence of the sinner is a vital part of what we might call the preparatory work of the proclamation of man's culpability and depravity. *It is only in the silence of agreement with God's just sentence on sin and sinners that the gospel message can be heard.* The position this conclusion holds as the transition into the proclamation of the gospel of grace shows how vital it is to understand the necessity of the rejection of all forms of self-righteousness.

3:20

> For *no one is declared righteous before him* by the works of the law, for through the law comes the knowledge of sin.

---

[1]Moo, *Romans*, 205.

NA*[27] *Text:
διότι ἐξ ἔργων νόμου οὐ δικαιωθήσεται πᾶσα σὰρξ ἐνώπιον αὐτοῦ, διὰ νόμου ἐπίγνωσις ἁμαρτίας.

Romans 3:20 is a vital transitional verse that, almost in passing, provides an inspired explanation of the role of law and the nature of "works of law" in Paul's thinking. Despite a tremendous amount of very imaginative speculation on the part of some in modern scholarship, the intention of the apostle is quite clear. Only by seeking some "new" understanding can his point be missed. The passage provides a vital framework in which the rest of this passage must be seen.

One could summarize the entire section by stating "The function of the law has never been to justify, but to reveal sin. Therefore, law-keeping will never justify anyone." The function of the law is taken as a given: to give true knowledge (ἐπίγνωσις) of sin.

> "Knowledge of sin," on the other hand, does not simply mean that the law defines sin; rather, what is meant is that the law gives to people an understanding of "sin" (singular) as a power that holds everyone in bondage and brings guilt and condemnation. The law presents people with the demand of God. In our constant failure to attain the goal of that demand, we recognize ourselves to be sinners and justly condemned for our failures.[2]

Because this is the role of law, it is in fact a perversion of law to attempt to make it function in a way God never intended. God did not intend to make men right with himself by law, and thus no flesh (a truly universal phrase) will ever be justified *in His sight* (a key phrase) by law, for this would violate God's purpose.

Verse 20 continues the thought of 19, providing the explanation as to why the law closes every mouth and shuts off every excuse on the part of sinful man. The law brings the knowledge of sin. Those who have only the law, and not faith in the one who justifies the ungodly, can only receive one thing from law: condemnation. The function of the law in bringing all the world into

---

[2]Ibid., 210.

a state of accountability before God is not some mistake—it was God's purpose from the start.

The phrase "by the works of the law" (ἐξ ἔργων νόμου) has been the subject of much discussion. (An extended examination of this phrase as it relates to the most popular means of denying *sola fide* is included later.) The prevalence of the phrase in Paul's specifically soteriological teaching shows that it was a general term he used in his teaching and preaching ministry with great regularity. But one thing to be noted is that while it appears here with "of law" (νόμου), it appears often without the modifier without any indication that the meaning is substantially different. That is, when one realizes that "law" for Paul is something that is good (Romans 7:12, 16; 1 Timothy 1:8) and holy and just, something that is established when we understand its true purpose and function (Romans 3:31), we will see that works of law are any and all works that are done in accordance with God's moral prescriptions.

There can be no higher law by which to do "higher works of law" that could possibly justify us. This being the case, whether Paul says "by works *of law*" or simply "by works," in either case he is referring to works done in accordance with a standard with an eye to receiving something from God (see especially Romans 4:4–8). Douglas Moo bears this out:

> "Works of the law," then, as most interpreters have recognized, refers simply to "things that are done in obedience to the law." Paul uses the phrase "works of the law" instead of the simple "works" because he is particularly concerned in this context to deny to Jews an escape from the general sentence pronounced in v. 19. But, since "works of the law" are simply what we might call "good works" defined in Jewish terms, the principle enunciated here has universal application; nothing a person does, whatever the object of obedience or the motivation of that obedience, can bring him or her into favor with God. It is just at this point that the significance of the meaning we have given "works of the law" emerges so clearly. Any restricted definition of "works of the law" *can* have the effect of opening the door to the possibility of justification

> by works—"good" deeds that are done in the right spirit, with God's enabling grace, or something of the sort. This, we are convinced, would be to misunderstand Paul at a vital point.[3]

"By works of law" (ἐξ ἔργων νόμου), then, refers to actions done in obedience to the law of God. The person pursuing works of law is described by Paul in his letter to the Galatians (5:4) as οἵτινες ἐν νόμῳ δικαιοῦσθε, those who are "seeking to be justified by law." The idea of seeking justification or righteousness by means of human activities in accordance with a rule of living also appears later in Paul's letter to the Romans when he says,

> **9:30** What shall we say then?—that the Gentiles who did not pursue righteousness obtained it, that is, a righteousness that is by faith, **9:31** but Israel even though pursuing a law of righteousness did not attain it. **9:32** Why not? Because they pursued it not by faith but (as if it were possible) by works. . . . **10:3** For ignoring the righteousness that comes from God, and seeking instead to establish their own righteousness, they did not submit to God's righteousness. **10:4** For Christ is the end of the law, with the result that there is righteousness for everyone who believes.

Note that Israel "pursued" righteousness, seeking to gain something by "a law of righteousness" and "as if it were . . . by works." They were "seeking . . . to establish their own righteousness" by their activities, their works. But, as in the rest of his theology, Paul contrasts the activities of the Israelites in seeking and doing with the only way of justification God has provided: faith, belief. The pursuit of righteousness by work is specifically said to be impossible: Only by faith is the goal of a right standing with God obtained.

Yet lengthy passages such as this demonstrate the consistency in seeing each reference to "by works," "by works of law," etc. as referring to any and all attempts to engage in righteous activities that result in a change in one's standing with God. Such meritorious works are contrasted with the only true way of justification: faith. Murray's *Romans* puts it this way:

[3]Ibid., 209.

> Justification is through the redemption that is in Christ Jesus; it is not through any price of ours; it is the costly price that Christ paid in order that free grace might flow unto the justification of the ungodly.[4]

We should also see the connection between "will be justified" (NASB) here and Romans 2:13, which we noted previously. When the two passages are placed together it is clear that the apostle never intended to teach that those who "do the law" will hear the sentence of "just" on the basis of their so doing. Instead, Paul says that "no one" (literally "no flesh," πᾶσα σὰρξ) will be justified by the law, for that is not the function of the law in God's economy. "No flesh" probably refers to Jew and Gentile—a fully universalistic reference that denies the possibility of *anyone* gaining righteousness by any means outside of the single way of faith in Christ.

One phrase sometimes lost in the reading that has great importance is "before Him" or "in His sight" (ἐνώπιον αὐτοῦ). This places the action of justification firmly before the throne of God, not in the realm of human affairs or activities. To be justified before men is something obviously very different than to be justified before God. One might think of it as "justified in the divine realm over against the merely human." This is important in considering James 2:14–26 as well as when we think of how it is a Christian lives out a godly life.

EXCURSUS ON "WORKS OF LAW"

It is often said that justification by faith is in error because it misunderstands Paul's use of the phrase "works of law." The general idea is that Paul is speaking solely of works of Jewish law and that the spectrum of the law under consideration is primarily that element of the law fulfilled in Christ, the ceremonial law. Many aberrant groups that cling to the Bible as a religious authority (but also overthrow its ultimate authority through the addition of

[4]Murray, *Romans*, 115.

other authorities in the form of men, groups, traditions, or other Scriptures) will promote a works-salvation system by dismissing the Pauline teachings either as too difficult to understand or, more often, by assuring their followers that Paul was only saying we no longer have to observe Jewish ceremonies. The argument can become quite involved and polished.

Jonathan Edwards, one of the greatest theological minds of the modern era, addressed the common objection that the "works of law" noted by Paul are merely those works of the ceremonial Jewish law, and that therefore we have warrant for binding works of some *other* kind of law upon men in the matter of justification. His insights are well worth a close examination:

> But that the apostle does not mean only works of the ceremonial law, when he excludes works of the law in justification, but also the moral law, and all works of obedience, virtue, and righteousness whatsoever, may appear by the following things:
>
> 1. The apostle does not only say that we are not justified by the works of the law, but that we are not justified by works, using a general term. . . . From all these there is no reason in the world to understand the apostle to mean anything other than works in general as correlates of a reward, or good works, or works of virtue and righteousness.
>
>   When the apostle says we are not justified or saved by works, without any such term annexed as "the law," or any other addition to limit the expression, what warrant does anyone have to confine it to works of a particular law or institution, excluding others?[5]

Edwards then in the second place quite rightly observes that when Paul speaks of the transgression of men in Romans 3, he speaks of transgressions of the *moral* law, not the *ceremonial.* Then, given the conclusion in 3:19–20, where the *moral* law has brought all under sin, obviously, it is then impossible to avoid seeing that the statement "Therefore, by the deeds of the law shall no flesh be justified in His sight" (3:20 KJV) *must* include the moral law at the very least, and that it *exemplifies* the moral law in reality. And

[5]Jonathan Edwards, *Justification by Faith Alone* (Soli Deo Gloria, 2000), 38–39.

so he concludes, "And therefore our breaches of the moral law argue simply that we cannot be justified by the law that we have broken."[6]

His third argument is likewise compelling: In the preceding sections of Romans "the law" was the moral law, as in Romans 2:12, where it is obviously not the ceremonial law that is in view. But he is not finished:

> 4. It is evident that when the apostle says we cannot be justified by the works of the law he means the moral as well as the ceremonial law, by his giving this reason for it, that "by the law is the knowledge of sin" (Romans 3:20). . . . It is a miserable shift, and a violent force put upon the words, to say that the meaning is that by the law of circumcision comes the knowledge of sin, because circumcision, signifying the taking away of sin, puts men in mind of sin.
> 5. It is evident that the apostle does not mean only the ceremonial law, because he gives this reason why we have righteousness and a title to the privilege of God's children: not by the law, but by faith, in that "the law worketh wrath." . . . Now the way in which the law works wrath, by the apostle's own account in the reason he himself annexes, is by forbidding sin and aggravating the guilt of the transgression.
> 6. It is evident that, when the apostle says we are not justified by the works of the law, he excludes all our own virtue, goodness, or excellence. This is evident by the reason he gives: that boasting might be excluded (Romans 3:26–28). . . . If we are not justified by works of the ceremonial law, how does that exclude boasting, as long as we are justified by our own excellence, or virtue and goodness of our own, or works of righteousness which we have done?
> 7. The next reason given by the apostle why we can be justified only by faith, and not by the works of the law, comes in Galatians 3. When he says that "they that are under the law are under the curse," he makes it evident that he does not mean only the ceremonial law.[7]

---

[6]Ibid., 40.
[7]Ibid., 41–46.

Each of these considerations would be enough, but taken as a whole they make the case quite clear. There is no basis whatsoever in the text or argument of Paul for the artificial limitation of "works of law" to a narrow subset that can somehow be eclipsed or, worse, replaced by some new set of laws or duties. In fact, there is a subtle though pervasive antinomianism involved in the argument that attempts to get around Paul's contrast between meritorious law-keeping and the abandonment of self-righteousness that is true, saving faith. That is, one must in some way denigrate the law of God to say it has now been eclipsed by some "higher" law that in some way better reveals God's moral will for man.

Surely this was not Paul's view. Instead, he well knew the supremacy of the law in that department, but he also knew the law was not given to justify; rather, it was to give us knowledge of sin, to lead us to Christ, that we might be justified, not by observing its precepts, but by faith in the One who fulfilled the law in our place (Galatians 3:25).

3:21

> But now apart from the law the righteousness of God (which is attested by the law and the prophets) has been disclosed—

NA*[27] *Text:
Νυνὶ δὲ χωρὶς νόμου δικαιοσύνη θεοῦ πεφανέρωται μαρτυρουμένη ὑπὸ τοῦ νόμου καὶ τῶν προφητῶν. . . .

Having used the law to bring all to a point of accountability and guilt, and having insisted that the law cannot justify but only convict, the apostle separates the discussion from the law by starting verse 21, "But now apart from the law . . ." The action of the main verb, "has been disclosed" or "manifested," is accomplished "without law" (χωρὶς νόμου), apart from the function of the law. The "righteousness of God" is revealed apart from law. Certainly, then, Paul does not speak of the general revelation that God, in himself, is righteous, for the law's equity and holiness does witness this very thing. Instead, this is a righteousness defined in the next verse as that which is "through faith" in Jesus Christ.

Many have been the suggestions as to exactly what this phrase means. Some have suggested it is a righteousness *from* God (which is true, as far as it goes). Others have said it is a righteousness that God approves (over against a works-oriented one that He would not), and again, this is true, to an extent. Others have suggested a righteousness that "works" in accomplishing salvation, and that is true as well. But none of these can, in and of itself, capture the fullness of the phrase. Murray explains,

> Yet it is so intimately related to God that it is a righteousness of divine property and characterized by divine qualities. It is a "God-righteousness". Because it is such, God is its author; it is a righteousness that must elicit the divine approval; it is a righteousness that meets all the demands of his justice and therefore avails before God. But the particular emphasis rests upon its divine property and is therefore contrasted not only with human unrighteousness but with human righteousness. Man righteousness, even though perfect and measuring up to all the demands of God's perfection, would never be adequate to the situation created by our sins. This is the glory of the gospel; as it is God's power operative unto salvation so is it God's righteousness supervening upon our sin and ruin. And it is God's power operative unto salvation *because* the righteousness of God is dynamically made manifest unto our justification. Nothing serves to point up the effectiveness, completeness, and irrevocableness of the justification which it is the apostle's purpose to establish and vindicate than this datum set forth at the outset—the righteousness which is unto justification is one characterized by the perfection belonging to all that God is and does. It is a "God-righteousness".[8]

More information will be given about the exact nature of this "God-righteousness" in the following passages. For now, it is important to know that for Paul, this is a righteousness apart from law that is witnessed *by* the law and the prophets! But here Paul speaks of "law and prophets" in the standard formula for the Scriptures, the Old Testament. The apostle affirms the

[8]Murray, *Romans*, 30–31.

consistency of his message with the inspired Scriptures of the church. There is no room at all in the apostolic preaching for any denigration of the utter authority *and integrity* of the Old Testament *as a body of divine revelation.* Paul had no concept of the Old Testament as a collection of human writings that had undergone extensive revision and editing so as to no longer present any coherent, consistent truth. Instead, he insists that the righteousness of God he proclaims is fully in harmony with the ancient Scriptures of the Jewish people.

3:22

> . . . namely, the righteousness of God through the faithfulness of Jesus Christ for all who believe. For there is no distinction . . .

Alternate:

> . . . even the righteousness of God through faith in Jesus Christ for all those who believe; for there is no distinction. (NASB)

NA[27] Text:
. . . δικαιοσύνη δὲ θεοῦ διὰ πίστεως Ἰησοῦ Χριστοῦ εἰς πάντας τοὺς πιστεύοντας. οὐ γάρ ἐστιν διαστολή . . .

Verse 22 begins with a restatement of the righteousness Paul is presenting (the NET giving the appositive translation, "namely"). But immediately the issue of how to translate the phrase "through faith in Jesus Christ" (διὰ πίστεως Ἰησοῦ Χριστοῦ) arises. The NET consistently takes the genitive as a subjective, "the faithfulness of Jesus Christ," while most translations follow the objective, "faith of [in] Jesus Christ." Daniel Wallace summarizes the evidence and admits that "while the issue is not to be solved via grammar" he does feel "on balance grammatical considerations seem to be in favor of the subjective gen[itive] view."[9] But most feel the contextual argument overrides the grammatical one. As Fitzmyer's *Romans* states:

> The sense of the gen. is disputed. Some commentators would understand it as subjective. . . . Such interpreters appeal to 3:3 ("the faith of God"), 4:12, 16 ("the faith of Abraham"), where there is mention of the faith *of* an individual, not faith *in* an individual.
>
> While this interpretation might seem plausible, it runs counter to the main thrust of Paul's theology. Consequently, many commentators continue to understand the gen. as objective, "through faith in Jesus Christ," as in 3:26; Gal 2:16, 20; 3:22; Phil 3:9; cf. Eph 3:12. . . . Indeed, as Dunn rightly notes (*Romans,* 166), Paul does not draw attention to Christ's faithfulness elsewhere in the extended exposition of Romans, even where it would have been highly appropriate, especially in chap. 4, where Abraham's *pistis* is the model for the believer. Paul is not thinking of Christ's fidelity to the Father; nor does he propose it as a pattern for Christian conduct. Rather, Christ himself is the concrete manifestation of God's uprightness, and human beings appropriate to themselves the effects of that manifested uprightness through faith in him.[10]

Likewise Douglas Moo notes the arguments in favor of the subjective genitive but concludes,

> Despite these arguments, the traditional interpretation of the phrase is preferable. The linguistic argument in favor of the alternative rendering is by no means compelling. In addition, contextual considerations favor the objective genitive in Rom.

---

[9]Daniel Wallace, *Greek Grammar Beyond the Basics* (Zondervan, 1996), 116. Wallace gives as a summary of the modern support for the subjective viewpoint as follows: R. N. Longenecker, *Paul, Apostle of Liberty* (New York: Harper & Row, 1964), 149–52; G. Howard, "The 'Faith of Christ,' " *ExpTim* 85 (1974) 212–15; S. K. Williams, "The 'Righteousness of God' in Romans," *JBL* 99 (1980), 272–78; idem, "Again *Pistis Christou,*" CBQ 49 (1987), 431–47; R. B. Hays, *The Faith of Jesus Christ: An Investigation of the Narrative Substructure of Galatians 3:1–4:11* (SBLDS 56; Chico: Scholars, 1983); M. D. Hooker, "Πίστις Χριστοῦ," NTS 35 (1989), 321–42; R. B. Hays, "ΠΙΣΤΙΣ and Pauline Christology: What Is at Stake?" *SBL 1991 Seminar Papers,* 714–29; B. W. Longenecker, "Defining the Faithful Character of the Covenant Community: Galatians 2.15–21 and Beyond," preliminary draft of a paper presented in Durham, England, 1995.

[10]Fitzmyer, *Romans,* 345.

> 3:22. While the Greek word *pistis* can mean "faithfulness" (see 3:3), and Paul can trace our justification to the obedience of Christ (5:19), little in this section of Romans would lead us to expect a mention of Christ's "active obedience" as basic to our justification. Moreover, *pistis* in Paul almost always means "faith"; very strong contextual features must be present if any other meaning is to be adopted. But these are absent in 3:22. If, on the other hand, *pistis* is translated "faith," it is necessary to introduce some very dubious theology in order to speak meaningfully about "the faith exercised by Jesus Christ." Finally, and most damaging to the hypothesis in either form, is the consistent use of *pistis* throughout 3:21–4:25 to designate the faith exercised by people in God, or Christ, as the sole means of justification. Only very strong reasons would justify giving to *pistis* any other meaning in this, the theological summary on which the rest of the section depends.[11]

So taking the translation of the NASB as normative,[12] we here have an affirmation that the righteousness found in the gospel is the God-righteousness that comes by means of faith in Jesus Christ to every believer, Jew or Gentile. It is faith that is the sole avenue through which this righteousness comes and that for all people. There is not one righteousness for the Jew, derived from law, and another for the Gentile, derived from faith. And that one righteousness of God can only be obtained in one way by all men, Jew or Gentile—by faith.

A testimony to the deity of Christ is found in the use of the term "faith" here in Romans 3:22. When Paul speaks of saving faith in Romans 4:5, the object is "the God who justifies," and in context this would be the Father. Yet here we have saving faith expressed with the object being Jesus Christ.[13] Surely such faith could not be placed in a mere creature.

---

[11]Moo, *Romans*, 225.

[12]We have done this throughout the work, noting the objective translation whenever the NET gives the subjective.

[13]Assuming the objective genitive. No such testimony is to be derived from the subjective, though the fact that Christ's faithfulness is never failing would be a testimony to His divine nature.

3:23

. . . for all have sinned and fall short of the glory of God.

NA*[27] *Text:
πάντες γὰρ ἥμαρτον καὶ ὑστεροῦνται τῆς δόξης τοῦ θεοῦ

This passage, so often cited without its surrounding context, fills out the meaning of "there is no distinction" from 3:22. There is no distinction in the matter of receiving the righteousness of God by faith, whether Jew or Gentile, for all men have sinned and fallen short of the glory of God. All, then, are placed in the exact same position and must have the exact same remedy for their fall: the righteousness of God that comes by faith in Christ Jesus. It is surely true that all have sinned, but that argument was presented and concluded in 3:9–20. This passage is actually drawing on that already established fact of man's sinfulness to emphasize that there cannot be more than one way of justification. Jew and Gentile must stand shoulder to shoulder in this matter. There is only one way of salvation.

3:24

But they are justified freely by his grace through the redemption that is in Christ Jesus.

NA*[27] *Text:
δικαιούμενοι δωρεὰν τῇ αὐτοῦ χάριτι διὰ τῆς ἀπολυτρώσεως τῆς ἐν Χριστῷ Ἰησοῦ·

Matthew recorded the crucifixion of the Lord Jesus Christ almost in passing, using a participial phrase to note the greatest event in human history (Matthew 27:35). Participial phrases often carry tremendous theological weight, and Romans 3:24 ranks with Matthew's words at the top of the list of the most important. This passage embodies a summary of the gospel as full as any other single passage in all the inspired Word.

The thrust of the phrase is clear and unambiguous. All who

are justified experience this work of God (1) freely, (2) by His grace, and (3) through the redemption that is in Christ Jesus. Each phrase encapsulates an entire spectrum of Christian truth regarding the gospel.

But before those issues can be explored, a question exists as to how to relate the present participle "being justified" (δικαιούμενοι) to what has come before. One way of doing this is to subordinate the verbs of the previous verse to it: "since all have sinned and fall short of the glory of God; they are now justified by his grace as a gift," as in the NRSV. We would be quick to agree with Moo, however, in pointing out that "all" in this connection "indicates not universality ('everybody') but lack of particularity ('anybody')."[14] Anyone who is justified experiences this in only one way: the freedom of grace.

This observation of the intention of Paul also explains the present tense of the participle. Obviously, the apostle is not here describing a process of justification over time in the life of an individual.[15] The participle is describing the act of justification on the part of God regarding sinners as a whole. No other tense would properly address the statement that is being made. The time frame of justification with relationship to the individual believer is laid out with more than sufficient clarity in Romans 4–5 to avoid any confusion in this verse.

Next, the meaning of "to justify" comes through clearly in these words as well. Surely no idea of subjective change or provisional status with God can fit with the freedom of grace in Christ that is asserted to be the very means by which this action takes place. It is a tremendous stretch to read the text "Being subjectively made pleasing to God as a gift by His grace." Instead, the focus is solely upon God. Justification is His gracious and free declaration, and it is made possible solely because of the redemptive work of Christ. As stated in Moo's *Romans*,

> As Paul uses it in these contexts, the verb "justify" means not "to make righteous" (in an ethical sense) nor simply "to treat

[14]Moo, *Romans*, 227.

[15]Some have actually missed Paul's point and based a dogmatic assertion regarding justification as an ongoing process on passages such as this.

> as righteous" (though one is really not righteous), but "to declare righteous." No "legal fiction," but a legal reality of the utmost significance, "to be justified" means to be acquitted by God from all "charges" that could be brought against a person because of his or her sins. This judicial verdict, for which one had to wait until the last judgment according to Jewish theology, is according to Paul rendered the moment a person believes. The act of justification is therefore properly "eschatological," as the ultimate verdict regarding a person's standing with God is brought back into our present reality.[16]

Paul finds another way to express "without works" by attaching "freely" or "as a gift" (δωρεὰν) to God's action of justification. Given that "by His grace" carries within itself the same idea of "free" and "gift," Paul is piling on the adjectives so as to safeguard the very heart of his message of grace. The action of God in declaring the believer justified is done freely in the nature of a gift.

Gifts are given without cost or price. The person who receives this kind of gift is not expecting it, nor does he put himself in a position of making it more likely that such a gift will be given. The freedom of the gift is intimately connected with the freedom of the giver. A person who gives a gift is free in choosing *to whom* it is given, and surely it is no longer a gift if, in fact, there are conditions attached to the receipt of it. If there is anything *in the person* that merits or attracts this gift, it is no longer free, nor is it a gift.

> God's justifying verdict is totally unmerited. People have done, and can do, nothing to earn it. This belief is a "theological axiom" for Paul and is the basis for his conviction that justification can never be attained through works, or the law (cf. Rom. 4:3–5, 13–16; 11:6), but only through faith. Once this is recognized, the connection between v. 22a and v. 24 is clarified; that justification is a matter of grace on God's side means that it must be a matter of faith on the human side. But the gracious nature of justification also answers to the dilemma of people who are under the power of sin (v. 23).[17]

---

[16]Moo, *Romans*, 227–28.
[17]Ibid., 228.

At this point Moo quotes Blaise Pascal, who with insight characteristic of the Jansenist movement that impacted him so much, wrote in his wonderful *Pensees,* "Grace is indeed needed to turn a man into a saint; and he who doubts it does not know what a saint or a man is" (#508).

All of salvation flows from the grace of God, but it is a great mistake to think that this simply means grace gives rise to a general "salvific intent." Paul says that the actual justification of the believer is an action of that grace, not merely a hoped-for result of that grace. God justified "by grace." Grace is not only the unmerited favor of God (Paul's use excluding all concepts of merit or work, Romans 11:6), but in this case it is the *de*merited favor of God, for it is extended to those who are, as we have seen, enemies of God. These are not merely at a moral neutral point who are given something they did not deserve. These are convicted criminals, justly condemned, who find in the grace and mercy of the very one they sinned against the key to their pardon and freedom freely offered.

> The free and sovereign graciousness of the act is the positive complement to that which had been asserted in verse 20 that "from the works of the law no flesh will be justified" in God's sight. No element in Paul's doctrine of justification is more central than this—God's justifying act is not constrained to any extent or degree by anything that we are or do which could be esteemed as predisposing God to this act. And not only is it the case that nothing in us or done by us constrains to this act but all that is ours compels the opposite judgment—the whole world is brought in guilty before God *(cf.* vss. 9, 19). This action on God's part derives its whole motivation, explanation, and determination from what God himself is and does in the exercise of free and sovereign grace. Merit of any kind on the part of man, when brought into relation to justification, contradicts the first article of the Pauline doctrine and therefore of his gospel. It is the glory of the gospel of Christ that it is one of free grace.[18]

[18]Murray, *Romans,* 115.

Hence, the propriety of describing grace as *de*merited favor, that favor given to the one who is more than merely undeserving.

But how can even the power of grace pardon and justify and yet God remain holy? Paul teaches that justification takes place "through the redemption which is in Christ Jesus." Grace does not simply wish the sin problem away. It does not make a mockery of God's holiness and the demands His law makes against the rebel sinner. No, grace can save only *through* the redemptive work grace itself provides in Jesus Christ. As Murray stated,

> Redemption has not only been wrought by Christ but in the Redeemer this redemption resides in its unabbreviated virtue and efficacy. And it is redemption thus conceived that provides the mediacy through which justification by God's free grace is applied.[19]

Redemption is located in Christ Jesus. We rarely think of it in these terms, but it is an accurate idea. The concept of redemption existing outside of Christ is foreign to Christianity. There is no room for the idea of pluralism, "many roads to heaven," for those who flee to Christ for redemption. The very idea of another place of redemption makes no sense whatsoever. Redemption is either in Him or it is not—it cannot be there *and* somewhere else. As Paul would say elsewhere, if righteousness can come through another avenue (the law), then Christ died needlessly (Galatians 2:21).

But if this is the case, then it must follow that the redemption that is in Christ is *sufficient for the work of grace in the salvation of God's people.* There is nothing lacking in the work of Christ. Grace is able to bring about the justification (and hence, in light of Romans 8:30, the glorification) of all God's people because it has a perfect redemption to apply. Indeed, if grace were to fail to save, it would point to an insufficiency in the grounds of its work. But such is impossible, since the work that allows God to graciously justify sinners is the perfect work of Christ on the cross (Hebrews 10:10–14).

---

[19]Ibid., 116.

3:25–26

> God publicly displayed him as a satisfaction for sin by his blood through faith. This was to demonstrate his righteousness, because God in his forbearance had passed over the sins previously committed. This was also to demonstrate his righteousness in the present time, so that he would be just and the justifier of the one who lives because of Jesus' faithfulness.

NA[27] Text:
ὃν προέθετο ὁ θεὸς ἱλαστήριον διὰ τῆς πίστεως ἐν τῷ αὐτοῦ αἵματι εἰς ἔνδειξιν τῆς δικαιοσύνης αὐτοῦ διὰ τὴν πάρεσιν τῶν προγεγονότων ἁμαρτημάτων ἐν τῇ ἀνοχῇ τοῦ θεοῦ, πρὸς τὴν ἔνδειξιν τῆς δικαιοσύνης αὐτοῦ ἐν τῷ νῦν καιρῷ, εἰς τὸ εἶναι αὐτὸν δίκαιον καὶ δικαιοῦντα τὸν ἐκ πίστεως Ἰησοῦ.

Upon making reference to the redeeming work of Christ, Paul then explains the nature of that redeeming work. He says Christ was displayed by God (the Father) as a "satisfaction for sin" or more commonly, "a propitiation in His blood" (NASB). Some object to the translation "propitiation" because this word refers to a sacrifice that both takes away the guilt of sin and that assuages wrath.[20] Contemporary liberal theology has no place for wrath, only love. A God of wrath does not fit into liberalism, for the God of liberalism, seemingly, can look upon sin and evil with a wide, loving smile. Sadly, many evangelicals are likewise very uncomfortable with the wrath of God, preferring to keep it in the shadows, leaving it only for those who want to go deep into theology. For these, the worry is offending the sensibilities of modern men. Yet the wrath of God is just as real as the love of God, and only a desire for God to be less personal than His creatures can justify the denial of the clear biblical witness to the wrath of God against sin.[21]

The Old Testament (Septuagint) background of the term translated "propitiation" (ἱλαστήριον) is most enlightening:

---

[20]See the extensive discussion in Morris, *The Apostolic Preaching of the Cross*, 144–213.
[21]See the previous discussion on this issue in chapter 6.

In the OT and Jewish tradition, this "mercy seat" came to be applied generally to the place of atonement. By referring to Christ as this "mercy seat," then, Paul would be inviting us to view Christ as the New Covenant equivalent, or antitype, to this Old Covenant "place of atonement," and, derivatively, to the ritual of atonement itself. What in the OT was hidden from public view behind the veil has now been "publicly displayed" as the OT ritual is fulfilled and brought to an end in Christ's "once-for-all" sacrifice. This interpretation, which has an ancient and respectable heritage, has been gaining strength in recent years. It is attractive because it gives to *hilastarion* a meaning that is derived from its "customary" biblical usage, and creates an analogy between a central OT ritual and Christ's death that is both theologically sound and hermeneutically striking.[22]

Murray touches upon this issue as well:

Redemption contemplates our bondage and is the provision of grace to release us from that bondage. Propitiation contemplates our liability to the wrath of God and is the provision of grace whereby we may be freed from that wrath. It is wholly consonant with Paul's teaching in this epistle that he should enunciate the provision of God's grace unto our justification in this way. For he had begun his demonstration that the whole human race is under sin with the affirmation that "the wrath of God is revealed from heaven upon all ungodliness and unrighteousness of men" (1:18).[23]

Today's man often mocks the concept of atonement. Robert Funk, the founder and primary mover of "The Jesus Seminar," has written,

The doctrine of the atonement—the claim that God killed his own son in order to satisfy his thirst for satisfaction—is subrational and subethical. This monstrous doctrine is the stepchild of a primitive sacrificial system in which the gods had to be

[22]Moo, *Romans*, 232–33. See his footnote 68 on page 233 for responses to those who object to the identification of ἱλαστήριον as "mercy seat."

[23]Murray, *Romans*, 116.

appeased by offering them some special gift, such as a child or an animal.[24]

Writers opposed to the Christian faith often allege that the ideas of wrath, propitiation, and sacrifice are no longer relevant (as if culture functions as the standard of truth to which God must conform). Enemies of the faith often point to the alleged parallel between the biblical doctrine of atonement and the ancient pagan religions that required sacrifice, whether animal or human. But it has been rightly pointed out that the Christian doctrine of atonement is significantly different than that of the religions of men. While in paganism sacrifices make it possible for the deity to be forgiving, in Christianity God himself provides the propitiation because of His grace and mercy. Combine this truth with radical monotheism, and the oft-alleged "pagan connection" is seen to be a mere shadow without substance.

The blood of Christ brings forgiveness of sins. Hodge's *Commentary on Romans* states,

> *The blood* of Christ is an expression used in obvious reference to the sacrificial character of his death. It was not his death as a witness or as an example, but as a sacrifice, that expiates sin. And by *his blood*, is not to be understood simply his death, but his whole work for our redemption, especially all his expiatory sufferings from the beginning to the end of his life. . . . It is evident from this statement, that Paul intended to exclude from all participation in the meritorious ground of our acceptance with God, not only those works performed in obedience to the law, and with a legal spirit, but those which flow from faith and a renewed heart.[25]

The apostle goes on to assert the righteousness of God in having entered into relationship with men (such as Abraham) who had faith in Him even before the sacrifice of Christ. God "passed over" the sins "previously committed," not by simply dismissing them, but by exercising forbearance in light of the certainty of the

[24]"The Coming Radical Reformation: Twenty-one Theses" by Robert Funk, *www.westarinstitute.org/Periodicals/4R_Articles/Funk.theses/funk_theses.html*

[25]Hodge, *Commentary on Romans*, 94.

sacrifice of Christ.[26] The public display of the propitiatory death of Christ, then, becomes a "demonstration" that God has been righteous to "forbear" His punishment of the sins of those who lived before Christ and had faith in the promises of God.

Clearly the concern of the apostle is to express forcefully the essential justness of God in His dealings with the sin of His people. This is seen in the "so that he" (εἰς τὸ εἶναι αὐτὸν) phrase that introduces the purpose of the demonstration of the sacrifice of Christ. Paul says that God is just. In his mind, such is foundational to the very functioning of the universe (Romans 3:6; Psalm 94:1–4; 97:2). The death of Christ proves God's justice, and it also allows him to be the Justifier of the one who believes in Jesus.[27]

> It is likely that "the justifier" is not coordinate with "just"—"just and justifying," nor instrumental to it—"just by means of justifying," but concessive—"just even in justifying." Paul's point is that God can maintain his righteous character ("his righteousness" in vv. 25 and 26) even while he acts to justify sinful people ("God's righteousness" in vv. 21 and 22) because Christ, in his propitiatory sacrifice, provides full satisfaction of the demands of God's impartial, invariable justice. To be sure, this way of viewing the atonement is out of fashion these days, frequently being dismissed as involving ideas completely foreign to the biblical teaching about God's sovereignty and love.[28]

The term "the Justifier" is repeated in Romans 4:5, where the justified are the ungodly, showing that "the one who believes in Jesus" and "the ungodly" are the same group. To call God the Father "the Justifier" is similar to calling the Son "the Savior" and the Spirit "the Sanctifier." Each is a divine work. God the Father is the Justifier of the one who has faith in Jesus *and no one else.* It is this divine freedom that leads Paul directly into the next point.

---

[26]Those who deny to God perfect and complete knowledge of future events would not be able to make such a statement.

[27]The NET's consistent translation of the genitive as a subjective is particularly poor here, for surely it is not the faithfulness of Christ that is in view here, but the identification of the one who has faith in Christ.

[28]Moo, *Romans*, 242.

3:27

Where, then, is boasting? It is excluded! By what principle? Of works? No, but by the principle of faith!

NA[27] Text:
Ποῦ οὖν ἡ καύχησις; ἐξεκλείσθη. διὰ ποίου νόμου; τῶν ἔργων; οὐχί, ἀλλὰ διὰ νόμου πίστεως.

If God is the Justifier not of the one who works, obtains, or by some other means merits anything from God, but instead of the one who *believes*, how can there be any reason for boasting (καύχησις)? Boasting is excluded, shut out (ἐξεκλείσθη).

> Paul's point is that the narrow focus of most of his fellow Jews on the Mosaic law as the system within which their relationship to God was established gives rise to an implicit "boast" in human achievement; what a person does in obedience to the law becomes, in some sense and to varying degrees, critical to one's "righteousness." Once it is seen, however, that God's righteousness comes to people "apart from the law," there can be no more cause for any pride in human achievement.[29]

Boasting is excluded by a law of faith that is directly contrasted with a law of works. The faith-works contrast will only grow stronger in the following verses (and come to its strongest expression in 4:4–5). Man has no basis for boasting, for there is nothing in the nature of faith that can possibly provide a ground for pride:

> This result obviously could not follow from any plan of justification that placed the ground of the sinner's acceptance in himself, or his peculiar advantages of birth or ecclesiastical connection; but it is effectually secured by that plan of justification which not only places the ground of his acceptance entirely out of himself, but which also requires, as the very condition of that acceptance, an act involving a penitent acknowledgment of personal ill-desert, and exclusive dependence on the merit of another.[30]

---

[29]Ibid., 249.
[30]Hodge, *Commentary on Romans*, 100.

One may truly ask how Paul could express himself with any further clarity on the *freedom* and *graciousness* of the divine act of justification than he has in Romans 3:20–27. And so it is fitting that at this point a conclusion is presented that he then proves by the extended scriptural argument today identified as Romans 4.

3:28

For we consider that a person is declared righteous by faith apart from the works of the law.

Alternate:

For we maintain that a man is justified by faith apart from works of the Law. (NASB)

NA[27] Text:
λογιζόμεθα γὰρ δικαιοῦσθαι πίστει ἄνθρωπον χωρὶς ἔργων νόμου.

This passage, the charter of *sola fide,* is so only as it functions as the summary and conclusion of the preceding arguments. When one considers what has been said before, it is clear that this passage does indeed teach faith alone. The long list of phrases Paul has brought into play already defines what he means by "justified by faith apart from works of law."

We have already seen works of law denied a place in justification in 3:20. God's righteousness was said to be manifested apart from the law in 3:21. He has said that justification is a free act, a gracious act, one that flows from the redemptive work of Christ, in 3:24. He has described God as the Justifier of the one who has faith in Jesus, based upon the propitiation in Christ's blood (3:25–26).

So when Paul excludes all boasting in 3:27, and then concludes that we are "justified by faith apart from works of law," it is surely understandable why many, as we will see, have understood Paul to be saying that the *only* way of justification is by faith, for that is surely Paul's entire point! And that is what *sola fide* means: faith alone, faith as the *only* means of justification, without mixture, without merit, without price. So clear is this assertion that many in church history have drawn it out:

> As in 3:20, what is meant is not certain kinds of works, or works viewed in a certain light, but anything a person does in obedience to the law and, by extrapolation, anything a person does. This being the case, Luther's famous addition of *sola* ("alone") to *fide* ("faith")—in which he was preceded by others, including Thomas Aquinas—brings out the true sense intended by Paul. A serious erosion of the full significance of Paul's gospel occurs if we soften this antithesis; no works, whatever their nature or their motivation, can play any part in making a sinner right with God.[31]

Fitzmyer[32] quotes Bellarmine, who lists eight patristic uses of "faith alone," including Origen, Hilary, Basil,[33] Ambrosiaster, John Chrysostom, Cyril of Alexandria, Bernard, and Theophylact. He also notes that Lyonnet added two others, Theodoret and Thomas Aquinas. Charles Hodge provides Protestant affirmation of this information:

> From the nature of the case, if justification is by faith, it must be by faith alone. Luther's version, therefore, *allein durch den glauben*, is fully justified by the context. The Romanists, indeed, made a great outcry against that version as a gross perversion of the Scriptures, although Catholic translators before the time of Luther had given the same translation. So in the Nuremberg Bible, 1483, "Nur durch den glauben." And the Italian Bibles of Geneva, 1476, and of Venice, 1538, *per sola fide.*[34]

---

[31]Moo, *Romans*, 249–50.

[32]Fitzmyer, *Romans*, 360–61.

[33]Given the frequency of the charge against Luther, it is enlightening to note the actual words of Basil in this regard: Αὔ γὰρ δὴ ἡ τελεία καὶ ὁλόκληρος καύχησις ἐν Θεῷ, ὅτε μήτε ἐπὶ δικαιοσύνῃ τις ἐπαίρεται τῇ ἑαυτοῦ, ἀλλ' ἔγνω μὲν ἐνδεῆ ὄντα ἑαυτὸν δικαιοσύνης ἀληθοῦς, πίστει δὲ μόνῃ τῇ εἰς Χριστὸν δεδικαιωμένον (Basil of Caesarea, *Homilia XX, Homilia de Humilitate*, §3, PG 31:529). The words "πίστει δὲ μόνῃ . . . δεδικαιωμένον" were penned more than a thousand years before Luther translated Romans 3.28.

[34]Hodge, *Commentary on Romans*, 100.

So we are perfectly warranted to read Paul's words as "faith alone," *for how else could it possibly be understood?* Can we seriously look at this passage in its context and say Paul means that we are justified by faith along with something else? Surely not! Justification is by faith. There is no other doctrine in Paul; hence, to say "alone" is simply to say "There is no other means."

Paul does not say that "I, Paul, maintain," but "we maintain," speaking either for the apostles as a whole or, in a broader sense, for all Christians. This conclusion is for all Christians, at all times, and since it defines for Paul a vital element of the very gospel itself, its importance should not be overlooked. Justification by faith is here stated, as one has pointed out:

> Justification by works always finds its ground in that which the person is and does; it is always oriented to that consideration of virtue attaching to the person justified. The specific quality of faith is trust and commitment to another; it is essentially extraspective and in that respect is the diametric opposite of works. Faith is self-renouncing; works are self-congratulatory. Faith looks to what God does; works have respect to what we are. It is this antithesis of principle that enables the apostle to base the complete exclusion of works upon the principle of faith. Only faith has relevance within that gospel delineated in verses 21–26. And, if faith, then it is "without works of law". It follows therefore that "by faith alone" is implicit in the apostle's argument. Luther added nothing to the sense of the passage when he said "by faith alone".[35]

3:29–30

> Or is God the God of the Jews only? Is he not the God of the Gentiles too? Yes, of the Gentiles too! Since God is one, he will justify the circumcised by faith and the uncircumcised through faith.

---

[35]Murray, *Romans*, 123.

NA*[27] *Text:
ἢ Ἰουδαίων ὁ θεὸς μόνον; οὐχὶ καὶ ἐθνῶν; ναὶ καὶ ἐθνῶν, εἴπερ εἷς ὁ θεὸς ὃς δικαιώσει περιτομὴν ἐκ πίστεως καὶ ἀκροβυστίαν διὰ τῆς πίστεως.

The emphasis upon the lack of works of obedience to law in verse 28 would immediately raise objections from the Judaizers, so Paul is ready with a quick answer. Since the Jews would confess Yahweh to be God of *all* creation, and hence all men, it would follow that that one God would justify all men in the same fashion, on the same basis, and that basis is plainly stated to be *faith* for Jew or Gentile.[36]

3:31

> Do we then nullify the law through faith? Absolutely not! Instead we uphold the law.

NA*[27] *Text:
νόμον οὖν καταργοῦμεν διὰ τῆς πίστεως; μὴ γένοιτο· ἀλλὰ νόμον ἱστάνομεν.

But if it is true that justification is by faith without works of law, does this not render the law useless and void? Not at all. The answer to the objection is found in the *nature* of the law and the *purpose* for which it was given. Paul began this section by stating that the law gives us knowledge of sin (Romans 3:20). That is its purpose. So when we say that a man is justified by faith alone, we are in fact establishing (ἱστάνομεν) the function of the law, for it reveals that all are sinners, all are condemned, all are helpless, and there is no way of salvation in self-righteousness. Murray was exactly right when he wrote,

> In the sustained argument of the preceding verses the negation of works of law as having any instrumentality or efficiency

---

[36]As to why Paul uses two different prepositions, ἐκ for the circumcised and διὰ for the uncircumcized, many, many suggestions have been offered, but it is probably best to simply view it as a stylistic variation, little more.

> in justification has in view works performed in obedience to divine commandment and therefore the law contemplated is the law of commandment from whatever aspect it may be regarded. What is in view is law as commanding to compliance and performance. And the insistence of the apostle is that *any* works in performance of *any* such commandment are of no avail in justification. The question is then: does this abrogate the law of commandment and make it irrelevant and inoperative in every respect? Paul's answer is in terms of his most emphatic formula of denial. He recoils with abhorrence from the suggestion and says: "God forbid". Having thus rejected the supposition he says apodictically the affirmative opposite: "Yea, we establish the law".[37]

This is likewise vital to maintaining the proper balance in the Christian life regarding the law as well. Paul is no antinomian: the law is just and holy and good, but one must understand its purpose and reason. The Christian can look to the law as a guide in knowing what is pleasing to God. We have clear instruction regarding how we are to think of God, how we are to think of our neighbor, and how we are to behave.

Romans 3:20–31 provides the heart of Paul's teaching on the subject of justification. Romans 4:1–5:10 then provides an extended biblical defense, an apologetic, for the heart of the doctrine expressed in 3:20–31. Often an apologetic defense will clarify key issues in the light of objections and attacks. And this is exactly what takes place in the fourth chapter of Romans.

[37]Murray, *Romans*, 126.

CHAPTER 12

Romans 4:1–12: The God Who Justifies

SYNOPSIS:

Romans 4:1–12 contains Paul's biblical defense of the gospel of grace he has proclaimed in 3:19–31. It presents his key proof text, Genesis 15:6, and provides his own inspired interpretation and commentary. Elemental issues regarding the nature of justification, saving faith, and forgiveness of sins are addressed with a force commensurate with the apologetic nature of the passage.

RESOURCES, BACKGROUND ISSUES, AND BIBLIOGRAPHY:

See listing in chapter 10, pages 143–144.

MAIN PASSAGE:

4:1 What then shall we say that Abraham, our ancestor according to the flesh, has discovered regarding this matter? **4:2** For if Abraham was declared righteous by the works of the law, he has something to boast about (but not before God). **4:3** For what does

the scripture say? "*Abraham believed God, and it was credited to him*
as righteousness." **4:4** Now to the one who works, his pay is not
credited due to grace but due to obligation. **4:5** But to the one
who does not work, but believes in the one who declares the ungodly righteous, his faith is credited as righteousness. **4:6** So even
David himself speaks regarding the blessedness of the man to
whom God credits righteousness apart from works:
4:7 *"Blessed are those whose lawless deeds are forgiven, and whose sins*
are covered;
4:8 *blessed is the one against whom the Lord does not count sin."*

4:9 Is this blessedness then for the circumcision or also for the
uncircumcision? For we say, "*faith was credited to Abraham as righ-*
teousness." **4:10** How then was it credited to him? Was he circumcised at the time, or not? No, he was not circumcised but uncircumcised! **4:11** And he received the sign of circumcision as a seal
of the righteousness that he had by faith while he was still uncircumcised, so that he would become the father of all those who
believe but have never been circumcised, that they too could have
righteousness credited to them. **4:12** And he is also the father of
the circumcised, who are not only circumcised, but who also walk
in the footsteps of the faith that our father Abraham possessed
when he was still uncircumcised.

4:1–3

NA*[27] *Text:
Τί οὖν ἐροῦμεν εὑρηκέναι Ἀβραὰμ τὸν προπάτορα ἡμῶν κατὰ σάρκα; εἰ γὰρ Ἀβραὰμ ἐξ ἔργων ἐδικαιώθη, ἔχει καύχημα, ἀλλ᾽ οὐ πρὸς θεόν. τί γὰρ ἡ γραφὴ λέγει; *ἐπίστευσεν δὲ Ἀβραὰμ τῷ θεῷ καὶ ἐλογίσθη αὐτῷ εἰς δικαιοσύνην.*

Paul introduces his biblical defense of justification by grace through faith without works by asking "What then shall we say?" He invites his opponents to reason with him on the basis of the inspired text. He goes immediately to the greatest figure in the history of Israel outside of Moses, the great patriarch Abraham.

For if Abraham was declared righteous by . . . works: Paul presents a hypothetical situation. If it were possible for Abraham to be justified *by works* (ἐξ ἔργων), then he would have grounds for boasting, the very thing Paul has insisted in 3:27 is shut out, utterly excluded from the Christian gospel (1 Corinthians 1:30–31). And since the context of Abraham excludes works of the Mosaic law (coming long before the giving of that law), we can see that it is an error to artificially limit the scope of "works" to "works done in obedience to Mosaic law."

but not before God: even the hypothetical idea of boasting before God is too much for the apostle. There can be no boasting before God in any situation, and especially that of Abraham, for the Word tells us exactly how it was that he was justified. But note again this use of "before God" (πρὸς θεόν), for we have already seen that this is the realm in which justification relating to salvation takes place.

Paul then turns to the Scriptures (ἡ γραφὴ). That this is such a common action of the apostles should not result in our missing the weight of these words. The apostles find in the Scriptures (which for them would be the twenty-two books of the Hebrew Scriptures,[1] corresponding to the thirty-nine books of the Protestant canon) ultimate and final religious authority. Their appeal to the Bible is a testimony to the fact that they and their opponents, the Judaizers, both accepted the reality of a divine revelation from God. Scriptural citations were considered to be fully authoritative and without appeal.

The citation is from the Septuagint translation of Genesis 15:6, the version that his readers would know and use.

4:4–5

> Now to the one who works, his pay is not credited due to grace but due to obligation. But to the one who does not work, but believes in the one who declares the ungodly righteous, his faith is credited as righteousness.

---

[1]See the discussion of the issue of the Old Testament canon in Roger Beckwith, *The Old Testament Canon of the New Testament Church* (Eerdmans, 1985).

NA[27] Text:

τῷ δὲ ἐργαζομένῳ ὁ μισθὸς οὐ λογίζεται κατὰ χάριν ἀλλὰ κατὰ ὀφείλημα, τῷ δὲ μὴ ἐργαζομένῳ πιστεύοντι δὲ ἐπὶ τὸν δικαιοῦντα τὸν ἀσεβῆ λογίζεται ἡ πίστις αὐτοῦ εἰς δικαιοσύνην·

Immediately upon the heels of the citation of the passage we are provided what can only be called an inspired interpretation of Genesis 15:6. Interestingly, Paul will not return to the specific context of Genesis until verse 9, but each verse between 3 and 9 is directly related to Paul's understanding of what Genesis 15:6 is saying. Before getting into the fine points of this vital passage, we should see what the original readers of the letter would have seen. That is, there is a complete 180° contrast between the person being described in verse 4 and the one in verse 5. This can be seen by placing the first few words of each verse in direct contrast to the other:

Verse	Greek Text	English Text
Verse 4	τῷ δὲ ἐργαζομένῳ	But to the working one
Verse 5	τῷ δὲ μὴ ἐργαζομένῳ	But to the not working one

What is not always clear to the reader is that Paul purposefully uses the exact same participial phrase in the two verses, only in verse 5 he uses the direct *negation* thereof. So it is plainly his intent to provide a black and white contrast between the two individuals presented in each verse. And why is this important? Because we find in these verses the clearest explication in all of Paul's writings of what it means to *work* and, in contrast to that, *to believe.* The effort he puts into making that contrast as strong as possible answers many of the attempts by modern men to insert *some* kind of meritorious works into the doctrine of justification.

Now to the one who works: Paul uses a participle to describe the "working one." The illustration is drawn from the normal life of those who would be reading his letter. A person who works is an employee, maybe in those days an artisan, merchant, teacher. The picture is of a person who engages in regular human activity so as to receive a reward—pay. Paul uses the normal Koine term for wage, *misthos* (μισθὸς), when he says the "pay" is not "credited due to grace." He is speaking of the legal, necessary giving of pay to the employee who has worked for it. When a person engages in this kind of work, the pay is not credited due to grace, i.e., as a gift (Paul uses his normal word for "grace" here, χάριν).

No employer walks up to an employee, pays him what is due, and says "Here is a gift." *It was earned.* And that is exactly what Paul says when he says it is credited "due to obligation." Literally it is "according to what is owed" (κατὰ ὀφείλημα), a term often used to refer to that which is given in payment of a debt. The pay is not "reckoned" or "imputed" according to grace but according to debt—this is the literal idea. Part of the meaning of "working" is that it results in a debt being incurred. This will become very important.

It should also be noted that just as Paul uses the theologically rich term "grace" in this rather mundane, daily example of working and receiving pay, he also uses another of his favorite terms, "reckon" or "impute" (λογίζεται). The reason for this usage is close at hand: he intends to contrast this kind of working-for-reward with the means of justification in verse 5.

We noted in 4:2 that Paul uses "of works." We now see the definition of the works, even "works of law," to which he refers. The key element of "working" is not the standard by which one labors (i.e., Mosaic law, or some other law). As we have asserted, there is no higher standard than God's law to which Paul could possibly refer us as to moral behavior. The law is just and holy and good, and it shows us our sin. The primary element of "working," then, is the attitude and goal of the one doing the work. The "working one" in 4:5 is seeking to gain something by the work that is done. This becomes the contrast with verse 5.

But to the one who does not work: The phrase is defined in its own context. There is no reason to be confused between this verse and such passages as Ephesians 2:10, for both are easily understood in their native contexts. This phrase is the contrast to verse 4: whatever is inherent in the idea of "working" so that the result is *debt* (ὀφείλημα) is completely negated in verse 5. And why *must* this be understood? Because Paul is defining what it means to have saving faith. Upon giving the negative, "does not work," he then gives the positive, "but believes." *The polar opposite of working so as to create a situation of debt is believing.* There are few more important truths than this, for the vast majority of confusion and false teaching on the subject of justification misses this very point!

The believing of which Paul speaks is, by the contrast he draws here, a belief that creates no debt, that brings no plea, that makes no offer or bargain. It is the empty hand of faith. It hides no bribe, makes no effort at earning or coercing anything from God. It knows its bankruptcy and does not conceal it. All acts of obedience to a law performed so as to gain a right standing with God in any way, shape, or form *violate the definition of the faith that brings justification presented here.* This passage slams the door on any and all works-salvation schemes that attempt to pay lip service to grace by saying it is necessary but insufficient outside of the addition of *some* level of human works.

> That God acts toward his creatures graciously—without compulsion or necessity—is one of Paul's nonnegotiable theological axioms. He uses it here to show that the faith that gained righteousness for Abraham was a faith that excluded works. For many of us, accustomed by four centuries of Protestant theology to the Pauline "faith vs. works" contrast, this point might appear mundane. But it flew in the face of the dominant Jewish theology of the day, which joined faith and works closely together, resulting in a kind of synergism with respect to salvation.[2]

The faith that saves is a faith that clings in helpless dependence upon another: the God who justifies.

Exegetical commentaries agree on the intention of the apostle here. Charles Hodge said,

> *But to him that worketh not,* τῷ δὲ μὴ ἐργαζομένῳ. That is, to him who has no works to plead as the ground of reward; πιστεύοντι δὲ ἐπὶ κ.τ.λ., *but believeth upon, i.e.* putting his trust upon. The faith which justifies is not mere assent, it is an act

[2]Moo, *Romans*, 263.

> of trust. The believer confides upon God for justification. He believes that God will justify him, although ungodly; for the object of the faith or confidence here expressed is ὁ δικαιῶν τὸν ἀσεβῆ, he who justifies the ungodly. Faith therefore is appropriating; it is an act of confidence in reference to our own acceptance with God.[3]

Likewise, John Murray focused upon the clear contrast and asserted,

> The antithesis is therefore between the idea of compensation and that of grace—the worker has compensation in view, he who does not work must have regard to grace. . . . The description given in verse 5, "him who justifies the ungodly" is intended to set off the munificence of the gospel of grace. The word "ungodly" is a strong one and shows the magnitude and extent of God's grace; his justifying judgment is exercised not simply upon the unrighteous but upon the ungodly.[4]

And C. E. B. Cranfield added,

> The sense intended by τῷ . . . μὴ ἐργαζομένῳ here would seem to be "to him who does no works which establish a claim on God" or "to him who has no claim on God on the ground of works," and, by contrast, τῷ . . . ἐργαζομένῳ in the previous verse would seem to mean "to him who does works which establish a claim on God" (there being no such man, according to Paul, Jesus Christ alone excepted). . . . Calvin was of course right to observe that Paul has no intention of discouraging the doing of good works (p. 84). τῷ . . . μὴ ἐργαζομένῳ does not imply that Abraham did no good works, but only that he did none which constituted a claim on God.[5]

The saving faith that is contrasted with works always has the same object: *but believes in the one who declares the ungodly righteous.* God, the Justifier of the ungodly, is the object of saving faith. Just as Abraham believed Yahweh, so every person who will hear God's

[3]Hodge, *Commentary on Romans,* 113.
[4]Murray, *Romans,* 132–33.
[5]Cranfield, *Romans,* 1:232.

declaration of right standing with Him will do so only upon belief in Him and His promises.

But it is right here that many stumble, for the ones who are declared righteous are the *ungodly.* The person whose mouth has yet to be closed, who has not yet come to fully understand his sin and its guilt, may not understand just how precious it is that Paul inserted those two words, "the ungodly," at this point. It is not the godly, the righteous, who need to hear about the God who justifies (as if such even exist outside of their own self-deception). God justifies the ungodly. Such an assertion runs directly counter to everything man's religions teach. Men believe themselves capable of cleaning themselves up, of doing good works so as to receive from God the sentence of justification. One cannot help but think of these words from Roman Catholic writer Ludwig Ott:

> The reason for the uncertainty of the state of grace lies in this: that without a special revelation nobody can with certainty of faith know whether or not he has fulfilled all the conditions which are necessary for achieving justification.[6]

Paul's response to such an assertion would be twofold. First, the conditions necessary for achieving justification were accomplished in our place by Jesus Christ, who alone fulfilled the law perfectly. Second, no person can fulfill conditions to "achieve" justification in the sense Ott is presenting it here. The sole condition for the sinner to receive justification from God is a faith that is here contrasted in the strongest terms with any idea of merit or work. And the only one who needs to look for this kind of justification is the one who knows himself to be ungodly, incapable of good in the sight of God. Jonathan Edwards commented,

> It is as much as if the apostle had said, "As for him who works, there is no need of any gracious reckoning or counting it for righteousness, and causing the reward to follow as if it were a righteousness; for if he has works, he has that which is a righteousness in itself, to which the reward properly belongs."[7]

---

[6]Ludwig Ott, *Fundamentals of Catholic Dogma* (TAN, 1974), 262. This may explain why Catholic commentator Fitzmyer passes over verse 4 with barely three sentences, missing the vital importance of the contrast of verses 4 and 5 (*Romans,* 374).

[7]Jonathan Edwards, *Justification by Faith Alone* (Soli Deo Gloria, 2000), 3.

Modern religious movements have likewise faltered at this point. Joseph Smith, the founder of Mormonism, was so scandalized by the idea of God justifying the ungodly that in his *Inspired Translation* he completely rewrote the verse and inserted a negation so that for his followers the object of faith is the God who does *not* justify the ungodly![8]

4:6

> So even David himself speaks regarding the blessedness of the man to whom God credits righteousness apart from works.

NA[27] Text:
καθάπερ καὶ Δαυὶδ λέγει τὸν μακαρισμὸν τοῦ ἀνθρώπου ᾧ ὁ θεὸς λογίζεται δικαιοσύνην χωρὶς ἔργων.

Paul is not leaving Genesis 15:6 and Abraham. He is simply bringing in further confirmation from a statement of David. He is not shifting the focus to David, to David's life, or anything of the kind.

> The appeal to David and to the psalm which is here attributed to him is not, however, independent of that demonstration drawn from the case of Abraham. It is confirmatory or, to use Meyer's expression, "accessory".[9]

Paul is very specific in his understanding of the quotation he provides from Psalm 32 (Psalm 31 in the Septuagint). He says David spoke of a particular kind of blessing (μακαρισμὸν) upon a certain "man" (ἀνθρώπου). He does not say this blessing was limited to, or even focused upon, David. The use of "man" indicates a wider context than David, or even Abraham. Rather, this is a blessing that belongs to all men and women to whom righteousness is imputed apart from, separate from, works.

This gives us yet another "inspired interpretation" of an Old

---

[8]This is consistent with his own writings. For example, Moroni 10:32 in the *Book of Mormon* contains these words: "And if ye shall deny yourselves of all ungodliness, and love God with all your might, mind and strength, then is his grace sufficient for you. . . ."

[9]Murray, *Romans*, 133.

Testament passage. Paul gives us the proper understanding up front, so to speak: he quotes Psalm 32 solely to illustrate the imputation of righteousness "apart from works" (χωρὶς ἔργων), for this is supportive of the thesis he continues to demonstrate regarding the means by which Abraham himself was justified. To attempt to go back into the life of David and undercut the apostle's own interpretation of these words by pointing to some actions David engaged in is to question Paul's own understanding of the texts and his own authority as an apostle in this passage.

Surely this section supports the previously demonstrated teaching that imputation does not subjectively change people but instead treats them as if they are in possession of what is imputed to them. Hodge commented,

> The words are λέγει τὸν μακαρισμὸν, *utters the declaration of blessedness* concerning the man, [etc.] *whom God imputeth righteousness without works,* that is, whom God regards and treats as righteous, although he is not in himself righteous. The meaning of this clause cannot be mistaken. "To impute sin," is to lay sin to the charge of any one, and to treat him accordingly, as is universally admitted; so "to impute righteousness," is to set righteousness to one's account, and to treat him accordingly. This righteousness does not, of course, belong antecedently to those to whom it is imputed, for they are ungodly, and destitute of works. Here then is an imputation to men of what does not belong to them, and to which they have in themselves no claim. To impute righteousness is the apostle's definition of the term to *justify.* It is not making men inherently righteous, or morally pure, but it is regarding and treating them as just. This is done, not on the ground of personal character or works, but on the ground of the righteousness of Christ.[10]

4:7–8

> *"Blessed are those whose lawless deeds are forgiven, and whose sins are covered; blessed is the one against whom the Lord does not count sin."*

---

[10]Hodge, *Commentary on Romans,* 115.

NA*[27] *Text:

μακάριοι ὧν ἀφέθησαν αἱ ἀνομίαι καὶ ὧν ἐπεκαλύφθησαν αἱ ἁμαρτίαι· μακάριος ἀνὴρ ⸀οὗ οὐ μὴ λογίσηται κύριος ἁμαρτίαν.

| ⸀ ᾧ ℵ² A C D² F Ψ 33. 1881 𝔐 ¦ *txt* ℵ* B D* G 1506. 1739 *pc*

The quotation provided by Paul is directly from the Septuagint, word for word. The triad of blessings is not upon three different men but upon the same man to whom Paul refers. Therefore, the three descriptions are to be taken together: the forgiveness of the lawless deeds is equivalent to the covering of sins. And if this is the case, then both of these are equivalent to the non-imputation of sins in verse 8.

John Murray, combining depth of scholarship with the passion of the believing theologian, saw the centrality of this section of Scripture to the definition of justification by faith. His comments[11] are not only worthy of citation, but of close examination:

> What David spoke of in terms of the non-imputation and forgiveness of sin Paul interprets more positively as the imputation of righteousness.

This is a vitally important observation: Paul defines the words of David as referring to the blessedness of the imputation of righteousness apart from works, but the only imputation spoken of in the citation from Psalm 32 is that of the *non-imputation* of sin (4:8). Protestant exegetes have often pointed to the reality of "double imputation," that is, of the imputation of the righteousness of Christ to the believer *and* the imputation of our sins to Christ, the necessary corollary to the *non-imputation* of sins to those who have faith in Jesus.

> And the blessed man is not the man who has good works laid to his account but whose *sins* are *not* laid to his account. David's religion, therefore, was not one determined by the concept of good works but by that of the gracious remission of sin, and the blessedness, regarded as the epitome of divine favour, had no affinity with that secured by works of merit.

[11]The following citations are from Murray, *Romans*, 133–35.

Murray is again referring to the Roman Catholic concept of doing good works in a state of grace with the result that these good works are meritorious in God's sight. He rightly denies this is Paul's view, for the biblical view is wholly based upon the gracious remission of sins and the perfection of *imputed* righteousness, not inherent or "state of grace" righteousness.

> When Paul speaks of God as "imputing righteousness" (vs. 6), he must be using this expression as synonymous with justification. Otherwise his argument would be invalid. For his thesis is justification by faith without works. Hence to "impute righteousness without works" is equivalent to justification without works. . . . When Paul derives his positive doctrine of justification, in terms of the imputation of righteousness (vs. 6), from a declaration of David that is in terms of the remission and non-imputation of sin (vss. 6, 7) and therefore formally negative, he must have regarded justification as correlative with, if not as defined in terms of, remission of sin. This inference is conclusive against the Romish view that justification consists in the infusion of grace. Justification must be forensic, as remission itself is.

The last line in the above citation should be repeated. If Murray is rightly following the argument of the apostle, as he most assuredly is, the argument is indeed conclusive. Paul has not moved to some other issue than justification by citing David's words. He is still speaking of justification, the imputation of righteousness apart from meritorious works. Paul, then, is saying that the remission of sin and the non-imputation of sin of 4:5–8 is correlative with the doctrine of justification he is defending.

Therefore, since remission of sin is, beyond all dispute and question, a forensic declaration, so too must justification be a forensic declaration on the part of God. No one can possibly deny that to remit sin is to speak of an action that requires a judge with the authority to pronounce sentence and then to remit sentence. So if remission of sin is being seen by the apostle as correlative with justification, it follows that justification is, as we have already proven but now confirm beyond dispute, a forensic, legal declaration on the part of God the Father regarding the believer, based upon the work of another, the Lord Jesus Christ.

> The appeal to David and to Psalm 32:1, 2, in addition to that said of Abraham, is for the purpose of demonstrating that what the Scripture conceives of as the epitome of blessing and felicity is not the reward of works but the bestowment of grace through faith. Blessedness consists in that which is illustrated by the remission of sins and not by that which falls into the category of reward according to merit.

Murray has touched upon the key difference between those who come to these passages with their traditions and systems of authority and those who come with a commitment to *sola scriptura* and a desire to hear *only* what is spoken by the Holy Spirit in the Scriptures. Man's religions focus upon man—man's works, man's merits—and limit God to the gracious "way-maker," who works out a plan but then leaves it to the creature to succeed or fail, as the case may be. Yet the apostle saw that such systems miss the heart and soul of what God has done in Christ. The greatest blessing is not receiving sufficient grace so as to be able to do good works in a state of grace so as to receive, at least in part, a reward of eternal life. The greatest blessing is to be forgiven of sin.

WHO IS THE BLESSED MAN?

This brings us to a question that must be answered by every person who believes the Bible to be God's Word: Who is the blessed man of Romans 4:8? The apostle tells us the blessed man in 4:6 is the one to whom God imputes righteousness apart from works. But verse 8, as we have seen, defines this in terms of non-imputation of sin. So who is this man?

The religions of man cannot answer this question. Man's religions, centered as they are upon man's works and merits and will, must, as a result, lack a perfect Savior who can save in and of himself, without the aid of the creature. Their systems, drawing from the nearly universal synergism of human religiosity, always make room for man's success or failure in "doing things"—

whether they be called sacraments, rituals, works, or good deeds—so that the final outcome of salvation is always in doubt. And if these systems contain any kind of belief in a punishment after life, there must be some means of holding man accountable for the sins committed during life. Without a perfect sin-bearer, the issue of unforgiven sin, rightly imputed to the one who committed it, must have resolution.

But it is just here that the question we are asking comes into full play. Who is the blessed man to whom the Lord will not impute sin? If a religion claims to follow the Bible and yet has no meaningful answer to this question, its error is immediately manifest. But before we press the question home, there are two issues about the passage itself that must be addressed.

First, as was noted above, there is a textual variant in the underlying Greek text. The *Majority Text* (and hence the KJV and NKJV) reads, "*to whom* the Lord shall not impute sin," following the reading of ᾧ, *to whom.* The *Nestle-Aland* text, and thus modern translations such as the NASB and NIV, reads "*whose sin* the Lord will not take into account." The NET, while following the *Nestle-Aland* text, in essence takes a middle road, interpreting the phrase in such a way as to render the variant meaningless, and truly, there is no real difference in the two readings as far as the actual thrust of the passage goes.[12]

The second issue is how we should understand the phrase οὐ μὴ λογίσηται κύριος ἁμαρτίαν, "the Lord will not impute sin." Commentaries, even the best, are almost silent in discussing this issue. Often Old Testament citations are passed over unless there is a reason to go into some discussion of their text. It is taken almost as a given that the writer uses the form of the Septuagint as a default text, and only if there is an alteration is much attention devoted to the grammar and syntax of the citation. But at this point we wish to suggest that something important must be noted in the syntax of the passage.

οὐ μὴ λογίσηται is an aorist subjunctive, sometimes called the

---

[12]The LXX reads as the *NA*[27] with οὗ. Some argue that the later manuscripts were attracted to the use of ᾧ because it appears in verse 6, "*to whom* God credits righteousness apart from works." In either case, the meaning is clear.

emphatic negation subjunctive,[13] the strongest form of denial. Given the base meaning of the subjunctive, the aorist subjunctive *denies the possibility of a future event.* That is, it denies potentiality, saying something simply cannot and will not be. The aorist subjunctive is used primarily in the sayings of Jesus (John 6:37; 10:28; 11:26) and in quotations from the Septuagint, such as here. It is often soteriologically significant; that is, Jesus twice denies He will ever fail in His work of salvation by using the aorist subjunctive (John 6:37; 10:28), and other passages such as Hebrews 13:5 fall into the same category.

Now, if we take the classic meaning of the aorist subjunctive in this passage, we have the nature of the blessing being defined as the denial of the possibility of the imputation of sin to the believer. The immediate question that arises is, Does this refer solely to past sins, so that what is being said is that God will not impute past sins to one who has been forgiven? Or is there something more here? Is the aorist subjunctive saying this blessedness is found in the non-imputation of sin *ever*? That is, do we have warrant, in the grammar or in the context, to say that the aorist subjunctive is here referring to the denial of the possibility of there *ever* being imputation of sin?

On the basis of the strict grammar itself, the issue could not be decided, for the question is not about what the aorist subjunctive indicates, but it is about the meaning of the word "sin" and whether that is referring to past sin only or all of a person's sin. In either case, that sin cannot, in any fashion, be imputed to the believer.

But there is indication in the passage that Paul has chosen this text from Psalm 32 specifically to make the very point that the believer's sin *en toto* will never be imputed to him. The signs that point to this conclusion are two.

First, Paul ends his quotation in the middle of a verse in Psalm 32. He chose what he cited for a reason, and surely he knew what the aorist subjunctive indicated. Second, join this with the fact that we already know Paul is interpreting the non-imputation of sin in 4:8 as the direct equivalent of the *imputation of righteousness*

[13]See the discussion in Wallace, *Greek Grammar Beyond the Basics,* 468–69.

apart from works from 4:6, and the key fact is then brought into play. Is the righteousness that is imputed to the believer one that is merely a "now" righteousness that can be undone by a single act of disobedience, or is it a perfect righteousness, the righteousness of Christ, that cannot be added to or diminished? We have already seen that it is the righteousness of God, so it would follow that if the imputation of this righteousness results in the perfect salvation of all those who receive it, then the corresponding non-imputation of sin would have to refer to *all* the sin of the individual, not just sins up to a certain point.

This becomes very clear in light of Paul's stated belief that the Father made the sinless Son "sin on our behalf," with the express purpose being that we would, as a result, be made "the righteousness of God in Him" (2 Corinthians 5:21 NASB). If Christ is made sin, the question is, What sin? The only answer is, The sin that is never imputed to the blessed man!

And so with these issues addressed, we ask the question again: Who is the blessed man? The blessed man in Paul's context is the believer, the one who, having given up all hope of personal righteousness, has put his or her faith and trust in the God who justifies the ungodly. This one is imputed a perfect righteousness, his or her sins having been borne substitutionarily by Christ on the cross. This is the blessed man.

4:9–10

> Is this blessedness then for the circumcision or also for the uncircumcision? For we say, "*faith was credited to Abraham as righteousness.*" How then was it credited to him? Was he circumcised at the time, or not? No, he was not circumcised but uncircumcised!

NA[27] Text:

Ὁ μακαρισμὸς οὖν οὗτος ἐπὶ τὴν περιτομὴν ἢ καὶ ἐπὶ τὴν ἀκροβυστίαν; λέγομεν γάρ, ἐλογίσθη τῷ Ἀβραὰμ ἡ πίστις εἰς δικαιοσύνην. πῶς οὖν ἐλογίσθη; ἐν περιτομῇ ὄντι ἢ ἐν ἀκροβυστίᾳ; οὐκ ἐν περιτομῇ ἀλλ' ἐν ἀκροβυστίᾳ·

This section sets up the next of Paul's main points regarding

Genesis 15:6 and the justification of Abraham. He well knew the kind of response he had gotten, probably in the public disputations he had undertaken against the Jews, when he presented his proof regarding Abraham's justification. "But Abraham was before the law, so it is not fair to use him as an example. Besides, Abraham did receive circumcision, which shows he didn't simply believe." Paul's rebuttal of this, and any other system that attempts to place Abraham's justification at differing times in his life, falls under the simple consideration he introduces in these verses.

The "blessedness" to which verse 9 refers goes back to the imputation of righteousness apart from works. When did Abraham receive this imputed righteousness? Was it before he was circumcised or after? The answer is obvious: the scriptural narrative tells us the specific event of Genesis 15:6 took place before Abraham received circumcision. The imputation of righteousness, then, *preceded* the giving of the sign of the covenant. Abraham was justified by faith before he became circumcised.

> Hence in the matter of justification and of the faith that was unto justification circumcision was no factor at all, not even in the sense of a conditioning circumstance. This is the force of the lesson which is derived from the sequence in the history of Abraham. It is more than the question of temporal sequence; it is that circumcision had nothing whatsoever to do with Abraham's faith or justification.[14]

While this may seem a small point to many, it is an important observation in light of the ingenuity of man who is constantly attempting to find a way around God's way of justification. One particularly appealing argument goes like this: Abraham was indeed justified in Genesis 15:6, but he had been justified back in Genesis 12 (in light of Hebrews 11:8) when he responded in faith to God's command to leave Ur, and he was justified again in Genesis 22 (drawing from James 2:21) when he offered Isaac upon the altar. So does it not follow that justification is not a once-for-all thing,

---

[14]Murray, *Romans,* 137.

but is iterative in the sense that it happened in Abraham's life at least three times (and probably more that are not recorded)? This view would seem to indicate that Abraham fell away and lost his justification between each incident, though that is not often made a part of the argument.

So what can be said in response? The writer to the Hebrews says that Abraham acted in faith in responding to God's call to leave Ur of the Chaldees. However, saving faith always has an object, and the object of saving faith in Abraham's life was the promise given him in Genesis 15, not Genesis 12. And as we will show in our exegesis of James 2, the justification spoken of there is in a completely different context than that of Romans and Galatians. Still, however, the argument carries weight for many who are seeking a way out of the biblical teaching on the subject.

The fundamental error of the argument thus presented is really quite simple: it is not an argument *from* Scripture; it is an argument *against* Scripture. That is, the person presenting this argument has a problem with Paul's interpretation of Genesis 15:6 and is, in fact, arguing just as Paul's opponents would have in the same position. To argue against an apostle of the Lord Jesus Christ only shows that one's theology is in error from its very inception.

But beyond the observation that this is an argument against Paul (and hence against Protestant theology, which follows his teaching), it is also a flawed argument. Paul's entire point is based upon justification being a forensic declaration that takes place one time in the believer's life. If, in fact, justification is ongoing, or repetitive, or iterative, then Paul's entire point collapses, and one can almost hear the laughter of his Jewish opponents.

Yet this is not an option for the consistent interpreter of the Bible. If Romans is Scripture, then it follows that justification in Abraham's life took place at a point in time prior to circumcision, not afterward. Since Abraham received that sign in Genesis 17, when Ishmael was thirteen years of age, Paul *cannot* be saying that Abraham was again justified in Genesis 22. And the justification that was his in Genesis 15:6 cannot be a "re-justification" after having been initially justified in Genesis 12, since this, too, would undercut Paul's entire position with his opponents. They could then point to Abraham's act of obedience in leaving Ur as evidence *against* Paul's stated thesis: Justification is by grace through faith without works. Justification, then, *must* be a point-in-time declaration, not a process that is repeated, or else Romans 4:1–8 is not inspired Scripture. To say otherwise is to make a complete mockery of the entirety of Romans 4.

4:11–12

> And he received the sign of circumcision as a seal of the righteousness that he had by faith while he was still uncircumcised, so that he would become the father of all those who believe but have never been circumcised, that they too could have righteousness credited to them. And he is also the father of the circumcised, who are not only circumcised, but who also walk in the footsteps of the faith that our father Abraham possessed when he was still uncircumcised.

NA*[27] *Text:
καὶ σημεῖον ἔλαβεν περιτομῆς σφραγῖδα τῆς δικαιοσύνης τῆς πίστεως τῆς ἐν τῇ ἀκροβυστίᾳ, εἰς τὸ εἶναι αὐτὸν πατέρα πάντων τῶν πιστευόντων δι᾽ ἀκροβυστίας, εἰς τὸ λογισθῆναι καὶ αὐτοῖς τὴν δικαιοσύνην, καὶ πατέρα περιτομῆς τοῖς οὐκ ἐκ περιτομῆς μόνον ἀλλὰ καὶ τοῖς στοιχοῦσιν τοῖς ἴχνεσιν τῆς ἐν ἀκροβυστίᾳ πίστεως τοῦ πατρὸς ἡμῶν Ἀβραάμ.

These concluding verses explain how Abraham, by that one act of faith, has become a father to many nations in fulfillment, obviously, of the promise to which he responded in faith, found in Genesis 15:5:

> And He took him outside and said, "Now look toward the heavens, and count the stars, if you are able to count them." And He said to him, "So shall your descendants be." (NASB)

But Abraham becomes the father of *all* who believe, Jew or Gentile, for both stand before God justified in the exact same way: by faith. Abraham was righteous, by faith, *before* he received circumcision. That work added nothing to his imputed righteousness. God arranged it this way specifically so that he could be seen as a father to all who, like him, believe without being circumcised, so that they could see that they could have righteousness imputed to them, just as he did. But likewise, he is a father to the Jew who follows him in the matter of having faith in the living God. Obviously, Paul believed one could receive the sign of circumcision and not have personal faith, as his main opponents had the sign but not the faith. Such would be inconsistent, to be sure, as Murray points out:

> For if circumcision signified faith, the faith must be conceived of as existing prior to the signification given and, in a way still more apparent, a seal or authentication presupposes the existence of the thing sealed and the seal does not add to the content of the thing sealed.[15]

Obviously not all who were circumcised were of faith. But those who *did* believe received justification on the exact same basis as the Gentiles. No difference could possibly exist.

THE CASE OF PHINEHAS

Is it not the case, though, that Paul is here engaging in unfair use of the Old Testament text? Some seem to suggest so in light of Psalm 106. Here we read in verses 30–31:

> Then Phinehas stood up and interposed,
> And so the plague was stayed.
> And it was reckoned to him for righteousness,
> To all generations forever. (NASB)

This psalm is referring to the incident recorded in Numbers 25:6–13:

> **6** Then behold, one of the sons of Israel came and brought to

---

[15]Ibid.

> his relatives a Midianite woman, in the sight of Moses and in the sight of all the congregation of the sons of Israel, while they were weeping at the doorway of the tent of meeting. **7** When Phinehas the son of Eleazar, the son of Aaron the priest, saw it, he arose from the midst of the congregation and took a spear in his hand, **8** and he went after the man of Israel into the tent and pierced both of them through, the man of Israel and the woman, through the body. So the plague on the sons of Israel was checked. **9** Those who died by the plague were 24,000. **10** Then the Lord spoke to Moses, saying, **11** "Phinehas the son of Eleazar, the son of Aaron the priest, has turned away My wrath from the sons of Israel in that he was jealous with My jealousy among them, so that I did not destroy the sons of Israel in My jealousy. **12** Therefore say, 'Behold, I give him My covenant of peace; **13** and it shall be for him and his descendants after him, a covenant of a perpetual priesthood, because he was jealous for his God and made atonement for the sons of Israel' " (NASB).

Surely the parallels are quite clear, especially when one considers that the Hebrew text of Psalm 106:31 is almost identical to that of Genesis 15:6, and the Septuagint rendering of the two passages is identical (καὶ ἐλογίσθη αὐτῷ εἰς δικαιοσύνην). If Phinehas was justified on the basis of what he did (an action), then clearly Paul is mistaken. Is this the case? Murray answers in the negative and argues as follows,

> We must, however, recognize the difference between the two cases (Gen. 15:6 and Psalm 106:31). In the case of Phinehas it is an act of righteous zeal on his part; it is a deed. He was credited with the devotion which his faith in God produced—righteousness in the ethical and religious sense. But that which was reckoned to Abraham is of a very different sort. It is in Paul's interpretation and application of Genesis 15:6 this becomes quite patent. Paul could not have appealed to Psalm 106:31 in this connection without violating his whole argument. For if he had appealed to Psalm 106:31 in the matter of *justification*, the justification of the ungodly (*cf.* vs. 5), then the case of Phinehas would have provided an inherent contradiction and would have demonstrated *justification* by a

> righteous and zealous act. Though then the formula in Genesis 15:6 is similar to that of Psalm 106:31, the subjects with which they deal are diverse. Genesis 15:6 is dealing with *justification*, as Paul shows; Psalm 106:31 is dealing with the good works which were the fruit of faith. This distinction must be kept in view in the interpretation of Genesis 15:6, particularly as applied by Paul in this chapter.[16]

Murray's interpretation takes something for granted that is no longer foundational in many circles: the accuracy, consistency, and inspiration of Paul as an apostle of Jesus Christ and as an instrument in the writing of Scripture. *If* Paul is an apostle, and *if* Romans is subject to the same divine and miraculous superintendence that Peter describes as "men carried along by the Holy Spirit spoke from God," then it follows inexorably that to confuse the meaning and context of Abraham's faith in the promise of God in Genesis 15:6 with the zeal of Phinehas and his reward is to make Scripture contradict Scripture.

Those who would point to this passage as subversive of *sola fide* likewise ignore a few other issues. The context of Genesis 15:6 is clearly that of God giving the promise to Abraham so that his faith is in that promise, a point Paul will stress in the rest of the chapter. There is no promise in Numbers 25 or Psalm 106. Abraham places faith in God as one capable of keeping His promises. Phinehas acts upon God's law and brings punishment upon evildoers, and as a result is rewarded. The righteousness he receives is, however, defined in the context quite differently than what we have in Genesis 15:6. Phinehas was already a man of faith, and his jealousy for the glory of God resulted in his receipt of a "covenant of peace" and a "covenant of a perpetual priesthood."

This was not Phinehas's initial encounter with God or with faith in Him. As a zealous, obedient, believing priest, Phinehas's action was not spurred on by a promise from God, but from zeal to punish sin in the congregation. The *zedekah* he receives in

---

[16]Ibid., 131.

response is defined in context as reward for his jealousy for God, not as a right standing before God, something he would have to have already had by definition to stand before the Lord as a priest.

CHAPTER 13

Romans 4:13–5:1: Justification Applied

SYNOPSIS:

Romans 4:13–5:1 provides the application of the theology of Romans 3:20–31 and the apologetic defense of that theology in 4:1–12. This is an extended discussion of the supremacy of the *promise* to the law and how if one makes observance of the law the means of securing righteousness, then the promise is void, grace is undone, and the gospel loses its power.

Due to the length of the section not all verses will be exegeted closely, and the Greek text will be provided only for those passages that warrant it.

RESOURCES, BACKGROUND ISSUES, AND BIBLIOGRAPHY

See listing in chapter 10, pages 143–144.

MAIN PASSAGE:

4:13 For the promise to Abraham or to his descendants that he would inherit the world was not fulfilled through the law, but through the righteousness that comes by faith. **4:14** For if they become heirs by the law, faith is empty and the promise is nullified. **4:15** For the law brings wrath, because where there is no law there is no transgression either.

4:16 For this reason it is by faith that it may be by grace, with the result that the promise may be certain to all the descendants—not only to those who are under the law, but also to those who have the faith of Abraham, who is the father of us all **4:17** (as it is written, "*I have made you the father of many nations*"). He is our father in the presence of God whom he believed—the God who makes the dead alive and summons the things that do not yet exist as though they already do. **4:18** Against hope Abraham believed in hope with the result that he became *the father of many nations* according to the pronouncement, "*so will your descendants be.*" **4:19** Without being weak in faith, he considered his own body as dead (because he was about one hundred years old) and the deadness of Sarah's womb. **4:20** He did not waver in unbelief about the promise of God but was strengthened in faith, giving glory to God. **4:21** He was fully convinced that what God promised he was also able to do. **4:22** So indeed it was credited to Abraham as righteousness. **4:23** But it is not written that *it was credited to him* only for Abraham's sake, **4:24** but also for our sake, to whom it will be credited, those who believe in the one who raised Jesus our Lord from the dead. **4:25** He was given over because of our transgressions and was raised for the sake of our justification.

5:1 Therefore, since we have been declared righteous by faith, we have peace with God through our Lord Jesus Christ.

4:13–15

Having presented Abraham as the model of faith for Jew and Gentile alike, Paul now presses his point home by demonstrating the superiority of "promise" (ἐπαγγελία), as found in Genesis 15:5, to "law," which came after the promise. The fact that the promise *precedes* the law is important in Paul's thinking. Fitzmyer rightly recognizes this:

Abraham's status of justification before God not only did not depend on his adoption of circumcision, but did not depend even on his observance of the law. Indeed, God's promise to Abraham came independently of the law. Thus Paul draws a third argument from the story in Genesis. He now exploits another element of the Genesis story, the promise made to Abraham for the future that he would have a numberless progeny, a progeny not limited to those who would be descended from him physically, but a progeny of believers drawn from all of the nations. The passing on of this benefit of God's promise to Abraham's offspring could not depend on the law. Paul realizes that the law could not be the norm of justification, for it would undo the role of faith.[1]

In verse 13 Paul insists that the promise to Abraham did not come through law but through the righteousness "that comes by faith." He continues the strong contrast between works/law and grace/faith that runs through the entire passage. If it is otherwise, he argues in verse 14, and being an heir with Abraham of the promise comes from law, the only possible conclusion to be drawn is that the faith Abraham showed in the promise *before* the law is "emptied" or "made void," an obvious impossibility in light of Genesis 15:6. This assertion likewise proves that one cannot mix faith and acts of obedience as the grounds of righteousness, for this would involve the emptying of faith.

The antithesis between saving faith and works of any kind, already established, is now illustrated in a variety of ways. Indeed, the apostle says that if those who are "of law" are heirs, the promise is nullified, destroyed, rendered useless. There is no middle ground, no neutrality, in Paul's thinking. It is either faith *alone*, or it is nothing.

The reason law cannot be an avenue by which the promise comes to the heirs is obvious: it was never intended to function in that way. The law brings wrath, not promise, not justification. But what does it mean to say that "for the law brings wrath, because where there is no law there is no transgression either"? Murray comments,

---

[1]Fitzmyer, *Romans*, 383.

Without law there would be no sin, for sin consists in the transgression of the law. In our sinful situation, therefore, there is always transgression of the law and it is this transgression that evokes the wrath of God. The sequence of the thought is: law existing, sinful men transgressing law, the wrath of God provoked to exercise by transgression. Paul's enunciation of this is condensed; that is why he says "the law works wrath"; it works wrath only, however, because of the transgression.

This consideration that the law works wrath is pertinent to the hypothesis which Paul had stated in the preceding verse. For if it is the *wrath* of God that the law works, then there cannot be *by law* the favour which faith and the promise presuppose; by law the context of faith and promise is eliminated, the opposite comes into operation, and faith and promise are thus made void.[2]

4:16–17a

For this reason it is by faith that it may be by grace, with the result that the promise may be certain to all the descendants—not only to those who are under the law, but also to those who have the faith of Abraham, who is the father of us all (as it is written, "*I have made you the father of many nations*").

NA*[27] *Text:

Διὰ τοῦτο ἐκ πίστεως, ἵνα κατὰ χάριν, εἰς τὸ εἶναι βεβαίαν τὴν ἐπαγγελίαν παντὶ τῷ σπέρματι, οὐ τῷ ἐκ τοῦ νόμου μόνον ἀλλὰ καὶ τῷ ἐκ πίστεως Ἀβραάμ, ὅς ἐστιν πατὴρ πάντων ἡμῶν, καθὼς γέγραπται ὅτι *πατέρα πολλῶν ἐθνῶν τέθεικά σε* . . .

Since the law works wrath, it must be that justification is "from faith" (ἐκ πίστεως, in contrast with ἐκ νόμου, "from law" in verse 14). But then we have the additional integral phrase "that it may be by grace" (ἵνα κατὰ χάριν). It is important to plot the flow of thought: Because law works wrath, justification is by faith. It is by faith so that it may be by, or in accordance with, grace. Since it is by grace, the promise will be certain or guaranteed to all the

[2]Murray, *Romans*, 144.

descendants, to both Jew and Gentile. Or in simpler form, it is by faith so that it can be by God's grace so that the promise will be guaranteed to every believer, Jew or Gentile. To break the chain at any point leads to only one result: the promise is no longer certain to anyone. And this is exactly what we see in the religions of men: the uncertainty of their relationship with God is due to the fact that they insert man's actions, merits, and decisions into the mix, resulting in a synergistic soteriology.

Justification by faith is commensurate with grace, and only with grace. There is a fundamental contradiction between faith and works, and between grace and law. Only the empty hand of faith fits in God's powerful hand of grace. Like a key that only fits in a particular lock, so faith is the sole key that matches the lock of grace. One can attempt to get the key of works and law into the lock of grace all day long, but it will never work. Works and law are not "in accordance with" grace. Only faith is.

> Since law works wrath in view of transgression, law knows no grace. Therefore the inheritance cannot be of law and those who are of law cannot be the heirs. The only alternative is the principle of faith and so the inheritance is of faith in order that it might be by grace. Faith and grace cohere; law and the promised inheritance are contradictory.[3]

The perfect correlation of faith and grace results in the establishment, certitude, and guarantee of the promise to all the descendants. Why? A promise based upon accomplishment in light of a legal standard cannot be guaranteed! The law places the burden upon the one who is *working*, while grace places the burden upon *the One who graciously justifies!* One leads to a man-centered religion, the other to a God-centered one. One leads to a "do this, do this, and hope you make it" plan of salvation, the other to a "God has done this, the promise is sure" gospel. The promise is true for Jew[4] or Gentile, for all who by grace through faith trust in the promise of God in Jesus Christ.

---

[3]Ibid.

[4]The phrase "who are of the law" in this verse must refer not to those who seek justification by law, as it has meant in other passages, but to Jews in general, since the other group mentioned is placed along with those who are of the faith of Abraham. See Murray, *Romans*, 144–45, and Moo, *Romans*, 278–79.

4:17b–20

The next four verses focus upon the experience of faith in Abraham's life at the time of the giving of the promise, especially that the faith he exercised was one that was contradictory to the situation that appeared before his eyes. God's promise did not seem to have any high probability of taking place as Abraham saw the situation, yet he "grew strong in faith" and by so doing gave glory to God by believing what He said.

4:21–22

> He was fully convinced that what God promised he was also able to do. So indeed it was credited to Abraham as righteousness.

The object of Abraham's saving faith was the God who is able to fulfill the promises He has made. Paul has said that Abraham believed in the God who justifies the ungodly, and here we have the connection between the promise of God and the act of justification itself. It was this kind of radical faith, based upon the character of God as the one saving and not upon the facts as he saw them (his age, the age of Sarah, etc.), that is imputed to Abraham as righteousness (verse 22, quoting again Genesis 15:6).

4:23–24

> But it is not written that *it was credited to him* only for Abraham's sake, but also for our sake, to whom it will be credited, those who believe in the one who raised Jesus our Lord from the dead.

NA[27] Text:
Οὐκ ἐγράφη δὲ δι᾽ αὐτὸν μόνον ὅτι *ἐλογίσθη αὐτῷ* ἀλλὰ καὶ δι᾽ ἡμᾶς, οἷς μέλλει λογίζεσθαι, τοῖς πιστεύουσιν ἐπὶ τὸν ἐγείραντα Ἰησοῦν τὸν κύριον ἡμῶν ἐκ νεκρῶν.

Paul says that the recording of these words regarding the imputation of righteousness on the exercise of faith was not simply for the sake of Abraham and his relationship to God, but that it was the Spirit's intention that we, who long after Abraham's day believe in God as he did, should be benefited by these words. Abraham's faith in God, who brought life out of Abraham's dead body, is likened to our faith in Him who raised Jesus our Lord from the dead. *Never* is saving faith focused upon man or what man does, but always upon the all-powerful God who accomplishes His will in all things.

> This is to say that not only was Abraham justified by faith but all who believe after the pattern of Abraham will also be justified by faith. . . . Our faith likewise is focused upon God in the character that is exemplified by the miracle of the resurrection of Jesus from the dead.[5]

But someone may ask why it is that it seems Paul refers to a *future* imputation (i.e., "to whom it will be credited") when he uses a present tense term to describe the believers ("those who believe"). The answer is easily seen when one considers the shift in time frame. The "to whom it will be credited" is still in Abraham's time frame, yet this transitions in the description of those who believe, for the object of faith is now "fuller" than it was for Abraham, as we believe in the One who raised Jesus our Lord from the dead. Moo comments, "Paul looks at our justification from the standpoint of the promise to Abraham: Christians are those who eventually experienced the justification promised to him."[6]

4:25

> He was given over because of our transgressions and was raised for the sake of our justification.

NA[27] Text:

ὃς παρεδόθη διὰ τὰ παραπτώματα ἡμῶν καὶ ἠγέρθη διὰ τὴν δικαίωσιν ἡμῶν.

---

[5]Murray, *Romans*, 153.
[6]Moo, *Romans*, 287.

When the apostle makes reference to Christ, he then describes the Savior's role in our salvation. He connects the "giving over" or deliverance of Christ in relation to our transgressions, focusing upon the sacrifice that takes away sin. But then he says Christ was raised for our justification. Without a living Savior as final and full proof of the faithfulness of God to His promises, faith would not have a proper object. Hodge has put it this way,

> With a dead Saviour, a Saviour over whom death had triumphed and held captive, our justification had been for ever impossible. As it was necessary that the high priest, under the old economy, should not only slay the victim at the altar, but carry the blood into the most holy place, and sprinkle it upon the mercy-seat; so it was necessary not only that our great High Priest should suffer in the outer court, but that he should pass into heaven, to present his righteousness before God for our justification. Both, therefore, as the evidence of the acceptance of his satisfaction on our behalf, and as a necessary step to secure the application of the merits of his sacrifice, the resurrection of Christ was absolutely essential, even for our justification.[7]

5:1

> Therefore, since we have been declared righteous by faith, we have peace with God through our Lord Jesus Christ.

Alternates:

> Therefore, since we have been justified through faith, we have peace with God through our Lord Jesus Christ. (NIV)

> Therefore, having been justified by faith, we have peace with God through our Lord Jesus Christ. (NASB)

NA[27] Text:

Δικαιωθέντες οὖν ἐκ πίστεως εἰρήνην ⸀ἔχομεν πρὸς τὸν θεὸν διὰ τοῦ κυρίου ἡμῶν Ἰησοῦ Χριστοῦ

[7]Hodge, *Commentary on Romans,* 129.

| ⸀ -χωμεν ℵ* B C D K L 33. 81. 630. 1175. 1739* *pm* lat bo; Mcion^{T} ¦ *txt* ℵ^{1} B^{2} F G P Ψ 0220^{vid}. 104. 365. 1241. 1505. 1506. 1739^{c}. 1881. 2464. *l* 846 *pm* vg^{mss}

Romans 5:1 marks the transition from the demonstration of the *doctrine* of justification to the *application* of justification. But it is not a sudden shift, and we can gain much theological insight from the passage. In fact, the very form of the transition ("Therefore, having been justified . . .") is rich in wisdom regarding the topic before us.

The NET and NIV both render the aorist participle *dikaiothentes* (δικαιωθέντες) as "since we have," with the NIV choosing "been justified through faith" and the NET going with "been declared righteous by faith." The NASB's "having been justified by faith" is only slightly more literal. In each of these translations, we see one of the key elements of the passage: *the declaration of justification is in the past.* That is, the aorist participle, syntactically speaking, refers to an action that is *antecedent to* the action of the main verb, here *echomen* (ἔχομεν).[8] As Fitzmyer observed,

> *now that we are justified through faith.* Lit., "justified from faith," expressed by the aor. pass. ptc., which connotes the once-for-all action of Christ Jesus on behalf of humanity. What is stated at the beginning of this verse is a summation of the latter section of part A, especially 3:22–26.[9]

The relationship between justification and having peace is clear: *because* we have been justified through faith as an action in the past, we now have, as a present possession, peace (εἰρήνην) with God.

There can be no doubt what lies behind Paul's use of the term "peace" in this passage. The Jew steeped in Scripture knew full well the meaning of *shalom* (שָׁלוֹם). It does not refer merely to a cessation of hostilities (though surely it means this as well, and

---

[8]Some aorist participles can express a simultaneous action, but in this case the aorist participle with the present tense verb clearly refers to an antecedent action, as all meaningful translations recognize. Aorist participles are routinely and regularly antecedent in their time to the main verb of the sentence. They can be contemporaneous in action, but they are so with (1) other aorists and (2) what is called a "historical present." Romans 5:1 fits in neither category, hence, the translation.

[9]Fitzmyer, *Romans*, 395.

such is true of justification, for the *reason* for hostility is removed in the work of Christ). It is not a temporary cease-fire. *Shalom* would not refer to a situation where two armed forces face each other across a border, ready for conflict, but not yet at war. *Shalom* refers to a fullness of peace, a wellness of relationship. It has a strong positive element. Those systems that proclaim a man-centered scheme of justification cannot explain the richness of this word. They cannot provide *peace* because a relationship that finds its source and origin in the actions of imperfect sinners will always be imperfect itself. Only the gospel of Christ, which says that Christ is our all-in-all, that Christ is the powerful Savior, that Christ is able to save completely (Hebrews 7:25), can provide for true peace. This theme was prevalent in the older, theologically oriented commentaries:

> The phrase εἰρήνην ἔχομεν πρὸς τὸν θεὸν, *we have peace in regard to God*, properly means, God is at peace with us, his ὀργή (wrath) towards us is removed. It expresses, as Philippi says, "not a state of mind, but a relation to God." It is that relation which arises from the expiation of sin, and consequently justification. We are no longer his enemies, in the objective sense of the term . . . but are the objects of his favour.[10]

Justified by faith as a past action, resulting, infallibly, invariably, in peace with God: Paul will repeat this theme in Romans 8:30, where he will say that those who are justified by God will, without fail, be glorified by Him as well. The Christian can speak as the apostle Paul, "I *have been* justified by faith. I have peace with God through my Lord and Savior, Jesus Christ."

THE TEXT OF ROMANS 5:1: INDICATIVE OR SUBJUNCTIVE?

The New Testament is the most accurate ancient text known to man. Modern scholars have an embarrassing amount of textual

---

[10]Hodge, *Epistle to the Romans*, 132.

data in the manuscript tradition with which to work. The overall textual purity and certainty of the original readings far surpass any other document of antiquity.

However, there are a relatively small number of textual variants in the manuscript tradition of the New Testament that call for close study. Romans 5:1 is one of these. Not only does it present a theologically relevant issue, but it likewise presents a variant that pits the external documentation against the internal considerations. Despite the issues involved, a wide and bipartisan group of scholars all agree: the actual reading is not difficult to discern.

The variant reading information is provided with the *NA*[27] text above. The difference amounts to all of one letter, but that one letter determines if the reading contains an indicative verb or a subjunctive verb. The subjunctive form of the verb is ἔχωμεν, and the indicative is ἔχομεν. The difference is basic: the subjunctive has the ω (the Greek letter omega), while the indicative has ο (the Greek letter omicron). In a very general sense, the subjunctive would be translated "Let us have peace with God," while the indicative is translated "We have peace with God."

Unfortunately, 𝔓[46], one of the most important witnesses to the text of the Pauline letters, begins at Romans 5:17 and therefore cannot help us with this variant. The great uncials, ℵ, A, and B, each give the subjunctive reading. However, both ℵ and B have the subjunctive in the original hand, with an immediate correction by the first corrector. The problem is, we cannot know with certainty the amount of time that passed between the original writing and the first correction: sometimes the first corrector represents an almost immediate correction, sometimes decades have passed since the original writing.

This is significant in this variant, since the difference between the two words can be understood simply as an error of hearing. That is, if the scribe was copying as the text was being read to him, the difference in pronunciation between the two forms would have been quite minimal. But even if these manuscripts were written by someone who was copying directly from an exemplar (an original document before them), the difference in the two forms could be easily explained as an error of sight.

Interestingly enough, the *Majority Text* is split on this variant. The *Majority Text*, edited by Hodges and Farstad, gives the indicative form as its reading, but notes that there is a split in the manuscript tradition upon which they lean.

Some writers, for primarily theological reasons, focus upon the variant in an attempt to remove Romans 5:1 from the field of battle, so to speak. But as mentioned, there is a truly bipartisan agreement on how the variant should be read. The following sources span a wide variety of theological beliefs, but all come to the same conclusion:

> The better Greek MSS (ℵ*, A, B*, C, D, K, L, 33, 81, 1175) read *echōmen* the pres. subjunct., "let us have peace with God," as Kuss, Lagrange, and Sanday and Headlam prefer to read the text. That would introduce a paraenetic nuance, and it has been so understood by patristic writers and others, making it the equivalent of *phylassien eirēnēn,* "keep peace" (with God), i.e., "let us now give evidence of this justification by a life of peace with God." But N-A[26] and most modern commentators prefer the reading *echomen,* the pres. indic., "we have peace" (as in MSS ℵ[1], B2, F, G, P, Ψ, 0220), regarding the confusion of *o* with *ō* as auditory on the part of the copyist. Thus Paul's utterance is a statement of fact expressing an effect of justification, which suits the context better than the hortatory subjunctive. Here Paul is not exhorting human beings to manifest toward God a peaceful attitude, but is instead stating the de facto situation in which they find themselves, one of peace and reconciliation issuing from his grace and mercy and guaranteeing the hope of salvation, for they are no longer under wrath.[11]

> Though the indicative ἔχομεν is a good deal less strongly attested than the subjunctive ἔχωμεν, it is almost certainly to be preferred on the ground of intrinsic probability. It is clear from v. 10f that Paul regards the believer's peace with God as a fact. It would therefore be inconsistent for him to say here

[11]Fitzmyer, *Romans,* 395. Likewise, the Roman Catholic *Jerome Biblical Commentary* (Prentice-Hall, 1968), II:305, says of this same variant, "The pres. indic. *echomen* ('we have' [peace]) is preferred by modern commentators to the pres. subj. *echōmen* ('let us have'), which, though better attested, is an obvious scribal correction."

"let us obtain peace" (Paul would anyway hardly think of peace with God as something to be obtained by human endeavour). If the subjunctive is read, we must understand it in some sense as "let us enjoy the peace we have" or "let us guard the peace we have" (cf., e.g., Origen, Chrysostom). But this is not free from objection; for it would surely be strange for Paul, in such a carefully argued writing as this, to exhort his readers to enjoy or to guard a peace he has not yet explicitly shown to be possessed by them. While it is of course true that considerations such as have just been mentioned could easily have led to the substitution of the indicative for the subjunctive, a deliberate alteration in the opposite direction would also be understandable, since a copyist might well have felt that, after so much doctrinal statement, an element of exhortation was called for. But, since the difference in pronunciation between *ο* and *ω* was slight, a change in either direction could easily occur, whenever in the transmission of the text dictation was employed (cf. the textual variations in, e.g., 6.2; 14.19; I Cor 15.49).[12]

The context of vv. 1–11 suggests ἔχομεν. The better attestation of ἔχωμεν is offset by the fact that in R. 14:19 there is better attestation of the impossible indic[ative] διώκομεν instead of the conj., which alone is possible. In manuscript tradition there is an uncontrollable vacillation between the indic. and conj. of the 1st pers. plur.[13]

Although the subjunctive *ἔχωμεν* . . . has far better external support than the indicative *ἔχομεν*. . . , a majority of the Committee judged that internal evidence must here take precedence. Since in this passage it appears that Paul is not exhorting but stating facts ("peace" is the possession of those who have been justified), only the indicative is consonant with the apostle's argument.[14]

The general agreement of scholars from all viewpoints and backgrounds is a strong testimony to the indicative reading that is found in the vast majority of modern commentators.

---

[12]C. E. B. Cranfield, *Commentary on Romans* (T&T Clark, 1975), 257.
[13]Werner Foerster in *TDNT* (Eerdmans, 1964), II:416.
[14]Bruce Metzger, *A Textual Commentary on the Greek New Testament* (UBS, 1975), 511.

CHAPTER 14

Romans 8:28–34: Justification in the Golden Chain of Redemption

SYNOPSIS:

Romans 8:28–34 comprises what is called the Golden Chain of Redemption. Its relevance to the doctrine of justification is obvious, as here the doctrine is placed directly in connection with other great themes in the gospel: predestination, calling, glorification. Then, the verb "to justify" appears in the context of the courtroom, clearly establishing the forensic/legal nature of the term in Paul's usage.

RESOURCES, BACKGROUND ISSUES, AND BIBLIOGRAPHY:

See listing in chapter 10, pages 143–144.

MAIN PASSAGE:

8:28 And we know that all things work together for good for
those who love God, who are called according to his purpose, **8:29**
because those whom God foreknew he also predestined to be

conformed to the image of his Son, that his Son would be the firstborn among many brothers and sisters. **8:30** And those God predestined, he also called; and those he called, he also justified; and those he justified, he also glorified.

8:31 What then shall we say about these things? If God is for us, who can be against us? **8:32** Indeed, he who did not spare his own Son, but gave him up for us all—how will he not also, along with him, freely give us all things? **8:33** Who will bring any charge against God's elect? It is God who justifies. **8:34** Who is the one who will condemn? Christ is the one who died (and more than that he was raised), who is at the right hand of God, and who also is interceding for us.

8:28–30

NA*[27] *Text:

Οἴδαμεν δὲ ὅτι τοῖς ἀγαπῶσιν τὸν θεὸν πάντα συνεργεῖ εἰς ἀγαθόν, τοῖς κατὰ πρόθεσιν κλητοῖς οὖσιν. ὅτι οὓς προέγνω, καὶ προώρισεν συμμόρφους τῆς εἰκόνος τοῦ υἱοῦ αὐτοῦ, εἰς τὸ εἶναι αὐτὸν πρωτότοκον ἐν πολλοῖς ἀδελφοῖς· οὓς δὲ προώρισεν, τούτους καὶ ἐκάλεσεν· καὶ οὓς ἐκάλεσεν, τούτους καὶ ἐδικαίωσεν· οὓς δὲ ἐδικαίωσεν, τούτους καὶ ἐδόξασεν.

This passage is so tremendously rich in theological meaning and insight that a full exegesis, including examination of such words as "foreknown" and "predestined" and "called," could easily extend to the size of a full book in and of itself. Our purposes, however, can be fulfilled by noting these issues only as they relate to the doctrine of justification.

Romans 8:28 cannot be understood outside of a view of God that accepts His utter sovereignty over all that He has made (Ephesians 1:11). The promise of all things "working together for good" for God-lovers requires a God who is not merely the Great Observer in the Sky, but a Sovereign King whose decree forms the very fabric of time. Those who love God are defined in the next phrase as those who are the "called" (κλητοῖς). This term will come up in verse 30 when Paul will say that all those God predestines he calls. Those who are called are called not for anything in them, but solely on the basis of God's purpose (κατὰ πρόθεσιν).

Upon making reference to those He himself had called, who are as a result God-lovers, Paul speaks of God *foreknowing* (προέγνω) them and then predestining them to conformance to the image of His Son. English speakers tend to read into such terms as "foreknown" the *transparent* meaning of the English word. But foreknowing is an *action* on God's part—something God *does*. It is not a passive element, where God is simply sitting back and receiving knowledge of future events. And each time the term is used in the New Testament with God as the one doing it, it has, invariably, *persons* as the direct object of the verb.[1] God foreknows people, not events.

So what does "foreknow" mean?[2] In light of the meaning of "to know" in the Old Testament (which often carries the meaning of "have a relationship with" and then "to choose") and also how it is used here, it refers to God's choosing to enter into loving relationship with the elect prior to their even coming into existence, that is, from eternity past. The key affirmation made here is that it is God's purpose that determines who is called (8:28), and it is God's action of actively foreknowing that leads to His actively predestining to salvation, including being conformed to the image of Christ.

The "golden chain" then begins in verse 29 with the divine actions of foreknowing and predestining, and it continues in verse 30 with the next three links—calling, justification, and glorification. Again these are all verbs that are (1) past tense (presenting the certainty of these events from the divine perspective) and (2) active in voice (these are things God does). The repetitive use of "those" or "those whom" (οὓς . . . τούτους) indicates that Paul has the same group in mind throughout: the elect. Those who receive the divine action of foreknowing in verse 29 likewise receive the divine action of glorification in verse 30.

---

[1]In Romans 8:29 the direct object is the elect (a personal direct object). In Romans 11:2 it is His people "whom He foreknew." And in 1 Peter 1:20 the one who was "foreknown" is Christ himself.

[2]This issue is discussed more fully in my *The Potter's Freedom* (Calvary Press, 2000), 195–200.

Two important truths regarding justification flow from considering this passage of sacred Scripture. First, *justification always and in every instance leads to glorification. All* those who are justified (divine action, God is the subject, man the object) are also glorified (divine action, God is the subject, man the object). Most religious systems that claim the Bible as an authority and yet violate its teachings hold that you can be justified and yet lost unless you do certain things to maintain your justification. Scripture knows nothing of such a scheme. God justifies, God glorifies, and those to whom He does the first He does the second.

Second, *God justifies only those He calls.* This is looking the other direction from the preceding fact. That is, just as justification infallibly leads to glorification (and only those who are justified can possibly be glorified), so too *only* those who are called are justified. What is the significance of this? If justification is something that God does unfailingly to all those He foreknows, predestines, and calls, then it is obviously not something dependent upon a synergistic scheme for accomplishment. This also touches upon the nature of faith as a gift: if saving faith were not a gift, but were a general capacity, the specificity of justification seen in this passage would not be possible. The truth of the divine prerogative in salvation runs both directions in the golden chain of redemption.

8:31–32

> What then shall we say about these things? If God is for us, who can be against us? Indeed, he who did not spare his own Son, but gave him up for us all—how will he not also, along with him, freely give us all things?

NA[27] Text:
Τί οὖν ἐροῦμεν πρὸς ταῦτα; εἰ ὁ θεὸς ὑπὲρ ἡμῶν, τίς καθ' ἡμῶν; ὅς γε τοῦ ἰδίου υἱοῦ οὐκ ἐφείσατο ἀλλὰ ὑπὲρ ἡμῶν πάντων παρέδωκεν αὐτόν, πῶς οὐχὶ καὶ σὺν αὐτῷ τὰ πάντα ἡμῖν χαρίσεται;

The proclamation of the work of God in salvation prompts Paul to ask what could possibly be said in response to these things.

God's work is sure, and all the glory goes to Him. No one will thwart Him. "If God is for us, who can be against us?" is a question that has no meaningful answer, for while the entirety of the world may ally itself against God's people, that is nothing compared to the Almighty being on our side. But Paul uses the first person plural, "us." Who is the "us"? The context will answer this question shortly.

How has God shown himself to be "for us"? Verse 32 answers this with some of the greatest truths of the gospel. The Father did not spare His own Son! He "delivered Him over for us all." Interestingly the phrase "in our behalf" (ὑπὲρ ἡμῶν) is placed first, putting some kind of emphasis upon the *substitutionary* element of the atonement of Christ in behalf of "us." As Murray put it,

> The Father contemplated all on behalf of whom he delivered up the Son in the distinctiveness of the sin, misery, liability, and need of each. If we had been submerged in the mass, if we had not been contemplated in the particularity that belongs to each of us, there would be no salvation. The Father had respect to all of us when he delivered up the Son.[3]

The giving of the Son on behalf of God's people is the fullest, most inarguable demonstration of His being *for us* that could possibly be given. And in light of the giving of His Son in our place, does it not follow that He will not *along with Him* freely give us all things? His point is obvious: God is *for* us and will not withhold from us anything necessary to life and godliness. He has given us Christ, in whom are hidden all the treasures of wisdom and knowledge, who has become to us our all-in-all. Murray commented,

> If the Father did not spare his own Son but delivered him up to the agony and shame of Calvary, how could he possibly fail to bring to fruition the end contemplated in such sacrifice. The greatest gift of the Father, the most precious donation given to us, was not things. It was not calling, nor justification, nor even glorification. It is not even the security with which the apostle concludes his peroration (vs. 39). These are

[3]Murray, *Romans*, 325.

> favours dispensed in the fulfillment of God's gracious design. But the unspeakable and incomparable gift is the giving up of his own Son. So great is that gift, so marvellous are its implications, so far-reaching its consequences that all graces of lesser proportion are certain of free bestowment. . . . Since he is the supreme expression and embodiment of free gift and since his being given over by the Father is the supreme demonstration of the Father's love, every other grace must follow upon and with the possession of Christ.[4]

8:33

> Who will bring any charge against God's elect? It is God who justifies.

NA[27] Text:

τίς ἐγκαλέσει κατὰ ἐκλεκτῶν θεοῦ; θεὸς ὁ δικαιῶν·

God has given the Son in the place of His people. Who, then, can bring a charge against God's elect? The phrase "elect of God" defines the "us" that has been seen throughout the preceding verses:

> The extent of "us all" is defined by the context. The denotation is the same as that of verse 31 and "us all" of verse 32 cannot be more inclusive than the "us" of verse 31. The "us" of verse 31 are those spoken of in the preceding verses, expressly identified as the foreknown, predestinated, called, justified, glorified. And, furthermore, the succeeding context specifies just as distinctly those of whom the apostle is speaking—they are God's elect (vs. 33), those on behalf of whom Christ makes intercession (vs. 34), those who can never be separated from the love of Christ (vss. 35, 39). The sustained identification of the persons in these terms shows that this passage offers no support to the notion of universal atonement. It is "for all of us" who belong to the category defined in the context that Christ was delivered up.[5]

---

[4]Ibid., 326.
[5]Ibid., 325.

The phrase "bring a charge" (ἐγκαλέσει) is a legal term. It is used in numerous ancient texts in this very context.[6] At this point Paul puts the conversation squarely in the court of law. To bring a charge against God's elect is to engage in formal legal proceedings. Paul's question is rhetorical, meant to indicate the impossibility of the proposed action. There is no answer to the question "Who?" for none are able to come forth with any hope of success. The reason is obvious. The Greek reads, ". . . elect of God? God the justifier," with the two forms of "God" appearing in direct contact with each other (θεοῦ; θεὸς). Who can find success in bringing a charge against God's elect people when God himself has pronounced them righteous? God is the Justifier, and He is also the judge before whom the charge must be heard!

> Many accusers are envisaged, but their accusations are of no account since God has pronounced his justifying sentence. There is no appeal from his tribunal. The charges of all others are worthy only of contempt.[7]

It is common to see as the background of Paul's words the Old Testament prophecy of Isaiah. In Isaiah 54:17 we read,

> "No weapon that is formed against you will prosper;
> And every tongue that accuses you in judgment you will condemn.
> This is the heritage of the servants of the Lord,
> And their vindication is from Me," declares the Lord. (NASB)

Not only does the passage speak of accusations against the servants of the Lord, but Yahweh says that their vindication is from Him. The Hebrew uses *zedekah*, and the Septuagint has δίκαιοι. The parallel is even stronger with these words from Isaiah 50:8–9:

> He who vindicates Me is near;
> Who will contend with Me?
> Let us stand up to each other;
> Who has a case against Me?

---

[6]Moulton and Milligan, *The Vocabulary of the Greek Testament,* 179.
[7]Murray, *Romans,* 327.

Let him draw near to Me.
Behold, the Lord GOD helps Me;
Who is he who condemns Me?
Behold, they will all wear out like a garment;
The moth will eat them. (NASB)

Again the same complex of terms appears in the Hebrew and Septuagint. Likewise, when we move to the context of 8:34, where the one who condemns is introduced, similar terminology appears in the Septuagint of Isaiah 50:9. The servant of God can speak of God's help, so that he can ask "Who is he who condemns me?"

But we cannot overemphasize that the meaning of "justifies" in Romans 8:33 simply cannot be anything other than forensic in nature. The conjunction of "charge" and "justify" (ἐγκαλέσει / δικαιῶν) renders incomprehensible any idea of justify as an "infusion of grace" or a subjective, inward change, such as sanctification. How would it be impossible to bring a charge against God's elect (the point of the verse) if "justifying" is not a legal declaration? But this is not all: the context gives more compelling evidence that this is the case.

8:34

Who is the one who will condemn? Christ is the one who died (and more than that he was raised), who is at the right hand of God, and who also is interceding for us.

NA[27] Text:
τίς ὁ κατακρινῶν; Χριστὸς Ἰησοῦς ὁ ἀποθανών, μᾶλλον δὲ ἐγερθείς, ὃς καί ἐστιν ἐν δεξιᾷ τοῦ θεοῦ, ὃς καὶ ἐντυγχάνει ὑπὲρ ἡμῶν.

The rhetorical question moves forward: "Who is the one who will condemn?" "Condemn" (κατακρινῶν) is again unquestionably legal in its use, both in this context and in extra-biblical writings.[8] But it moves beyond the initial bringing of a charge to the

[8]Moulton and Milligan, 328.

actual sentence of condemnation. There is a parallel between the "one who will condemn" and the "one who died" (ὁ κατακρινῶν / ὁ ἀποθανών). Who is the condemning one, when Christ is the one who died and rose again? Who can speak a word of condemnation (cf. Romans 8:1) against the elect of God when Christ has died in their place? And even more than this, after He has been raised from the dead and has entered into the very presence of the Father, who is there to intercede for them?

> The apostle's appeal to the exalted glory, authority, and dominion is related directly to the assurance of the security belonging to the elect of God. Since he has all authority in heaven and in earth, no adverse circumstance or hostile power can wrench his people from his hand or separate them from his love. . . . Only here and in Hebrews 7:25 is the heavenly intercession of Christ expressly mentioned. But it is implied in other passages (cf. John 14:16; I John 2:1; possibly Isa. 53:12).[9]

But notice that the apostle returns to the personal "us," having identified the "us" as the elect of God in verse 33. This adds a tremendously intimate aspect to the assertion that Christ's love and concern for His people is ongoing.

> And the evidence will demonstrate that every need of the believer and every grace requisite to consummate his redemption are brought within the scope of Christ's intercession (*cf.* Heb. 7:24, 25). We may not regard this as mythical any more than may we regard as mythical the resurrection and exalted glory of our Redeemer. . . . For nothing serves to verify the intimacy and constancy of the Redeemer's preoccupation with the security of his people, nothing assures us of his unchanging love more than the tenderness which his heavenly priesthood bespeaks and particularly as it comes to expression in intercession for us.[10]

However, the glory of the doctrine should not keep us from noting that *the forensic context is ongoing*. The term Paul uses to

[9]Murray, *Romans,* 329.
[10]Ibid., 329–30.

express Christ's intercession for us (ἐντυγχάνει) is, not at all surprisingly by now, used in secular writings in legal documents and proceedings.[11] This again establishes the legal nature of justification, and it surely exposes the error of those who insist that the court of law is an inappropriate context for the expression of the work of God in Christ. Some maintain that the only context in which we should speak of God's loving work of redemption in Christ is that of the family, hence, to speak of adoption, sonship, forgiveness, the Fatherhood of God, etc. But the Spirit of God inspired the apostle Paul to safeguard the truths of the gospel of Jesus Christ by placing them in contexts that would preclude the inclusion of man's concepts of merit and works while clearly explaining the truth of justification.

There is nothing contradictory between confessing that justification is a forensic, legal action on the part of God the Father, based on the work of Christ the Son, and recognizing the love of God that is shed abroad in our hearts, the intimacy of adoption, the deeply personal nature of what it means to call God "Father." The Spirit placed *both* contexts in Scripture, and we are the ones who are harmed when we choose to embrace one to the exclusion of the other.

---

[11] Moulton and Milligan, 219.

CHAPTER 15

Accursed of God: The Gospel Brings Judgment

SYNOPSIS:

The prolegomena of Galatians may not provide the depth of information found in Romans, but without a doubt it provides the strongest case for the centrality of the gospel to the Christian faith of any biblical passage. Its presence in the canon of Scripture precludes any possibility of any kind of pluralistic "gospel" claiming fidelity to the Bible. It is clear and unambiguous. A false gospel does not save, and the truth of the gospel is precious in God's sight (and therefore in the sight of any person who loves God). God's curse falls upon the person who seeks to pervert the gospel and preach a counterfeit message in its place. Given that Paul then goes on to focus upon the very same issues in Galatians that gave rise to the primary passages already examined in Romans, the importance of these considerations is clear.

RESOURCES:

James Montgomery Boice, "Galatians" in *The Expositor's Bible Commentary* (Zondervan, 1976).

F. F. Bruce, "Commentary on Galatians" in *The New International Greek Testament Commentary* (Eerdmans, 1982).

Ernest D. Burton, "A Critical and Exegetical Commentary on the Epistle to the Galatians" in *The International Critical Commentary* (T&T Clark, 1988).

Ronald Y. K. Fung, "The Epistle to the Galatians" in *The New International Commentary on the New Testament* (Eerdmans, 1988).

William Hendriksen, "Exposition of Galatians" (Baker, 1968).

J. B. Lightfoot, *The Epistle of St. Paul to the Galatians* (Hendrickson, 1981).

Richard N. Longenecker, "Galatians" in *The Word Biblical Commentary* (Word, 1990).

Martin Luther, *Commentary on Galatians* (Kregel, 1979).

John MacArthur, "Galatians" in *The MacArthur New Testament Commentary* (Moody Press, 1987).

J. Louis Martyn, "Galatians: A New Translation with Introduction and Commentary" in *The Anchor Bible* (Doubleday, 1997).

Leon Morris, *Galatians: Paul's Charter of Christian Freedom* (InterVarsity, 1996).

MAIN PASSAGE:

1:6 I am astonished that you are so quickly deserting the one who called you by the grace of Christ and following a different gospel—**1:7** not that there is another gospel, but there are some who are disturbing you and wanting to distort the gospel of Christ. **1:8** But even if we or an angel from heaven should preach a gospel contrary to the one we preached to you, let him be condemned to hell! **1:9** As we have said before, and now I say again, if any one is preaching to you a gospel contrary to what you received, let him be condemned to hell!

1:10 Am I now trying to gain the approval of people or of God? Or am I trying to please people? If I were still trying to please people, I would not be a slave of Christ!

1:11 Now I want you to know, brothers and sisters, that the gospel I preached is not of human origin. **1:12** For I did not receive it or learn it from any human source; instead I received it by a revelation of Jesus Christ.

If Romans gives us the height of Paul's theological reflection, then Galatians reveals his passion for the gospel as none other. Gone is the neat orderliness of Romans. In its place is the rushed emotion of one who sees his audience in great danger of spiritual catastrophe. Words pour quickly from his pen; transitions are brief, hurried, sometimes forgotten. Verbs are neglected as the author rushes to warn his readers of their jeopardy. And when Paul speaks of those who are perverting the gospel of grace, some of the harshest words in the entirety of Scripture are placed before us.

The presence of the phrase ἡ ἀλήθεια τοῦ εὐαγγελίου ("the truth of the gospel") and the calling down of the very ἀνάθεμα *(anathema)* of God upon those who would preach a different gospel and pervert the gospel of Christ show, beyond doubt, that Paul is deadly serious in his teaching and concern. These elements make Galatians most out of step with modern culture, for not only does Paul believe there is one true gospel (over against the contemporary denial of objective truth about *anything* and *especially* about religious matters), but he makes it a matter of *morals* and *salvation* what one does with that gospel! As such, Galatians cuts deeply across the modernistic attempt to make room for many gospels.

1:6–7a

> I am astonished that you are so quickly deserting the one who called you by the grace of Christ and following a different gospel—

Alternate:

> I am amazed that you are so quickly being moved from the One who called you by the grace of Christ unto another gospel. (Author)

NA*[27] *Text:
Θαυμάζω ὅτι οὕτως ταχέως μετατίθεσθε ἀπὸ τοῦ καλέσαντος ὑμᾶς ἐν χάριτι Χριστοῦ εἰς ἕτερον εὐαγγέλιον, ὃ οὐκ ἔστιν ἄλλο, . . .

Galatians has one of the shortest salutations of all of Paul's letters. The brevity of the introduction is certainly in character for the rest of the letter. The book carries a great deal of energy in its words. The author was obviously agitated—angry—emotionally upset—when he wrote it. The short, choppy sentences move at breakneck speed. Some of Paul's normal style is missing (compare, for example, the far more "dignified" presentations of some of the same concepts in Romans and Ephesians). He has something he needs to say, and he is going to say it. Some of the bluntest language in all the New Testament is found in Galatians (see, for example, 1:6–9; 3:1; 5:12); indeed, some blush at the force with which Paul expresses himself. What caused the apostle to the Gentiles to act the way he did?

The text leads us to believe that it was the incredible importance of the purity of the gospel that drove Paul to write Galatians. The very salvation of those people with whom he had labored (4:19) was at stake. The language he uses, the style that is his, shows clearly that nothing was of a higher priority to him than the true nature of the gospel itself. In all of Paul's other epistles, he follows his salutation with words of commendation and assurances of his continuing prayer for the Christians in the church in that city or in those cities to which the letter is addressed. Even when writing to Corinth, in the midst of great difficulties and immorality in the church, he does this. Only in Galatians is there no positive word, no commendation. The issue is too important for anything to get in the way of immediate correction, immediate warning.

He begins by saying that he is *amazed* at the Galatians. The term speaks of absolute wonderment and shock. He is dumbfounded by their actions. What causes this? "You are so quickly deserting the one who called you." The term translated "quickly" can either refer to quickness in the sense of a short period of time (which would have bearing upon just when the epistle was written, for this would seemingly indicate a short period of time between the initial evangelization of these churches and their subsequent moving away from the truth of the gospel), or it can refer instead to the ease with which they were being convinced of another teaching. In either case, Paul is astounded at their instability, their fickleness.

The Galatian believers, in their acceptance of this "other gospel," are, in the alternate translation, "being moved from the One who called them." The term is often translated as a middle reflexive, which would yield the translation, "you are moving yourselves." However, despite the good evidence for this among scholars, others point out that the blame for this defection is primarily placed by Paul upon the false teachers, for it is they who are actively *troubling* the Christians in Galatia. Hence, a more consistent rendering would be to take the verb as a passive, as in the alternate translation.

Any movement away from the true gospel, according to Paul, is a movement away from God himself, who called each believer by the grace of Christ. Here is defection of the gravest sort, resulting in terrible guilt both for those who would encourage such treason as well as for those who would abandon their faith. Paul does not indicate that these Galatians have gone to a point of no return, and if they heeded the warnings of this letter they certainly could have turned back from their course of destruction. However, the truth remains that one cannot substitute *another gospel* and claim to be moving closer to God. God's truth and the gospel cannot be separated from each other.

The concept of God being the Sovereign of the entire universe that underlies Paul's thinking here is sadly foreign to postmodern man. God is true. Since the eternal, personal God of the Bible exists, then truth exists as well. Truth is absolute—it is defined by God's being. Man is not the measure of truth. If God reveals something to be true, then it is true, irrespective of whether man accepts it as true or not.

Here, the *gospel* of God is true. If a man does not accept this gospel, or opts for "another gospel," then he is, by so doing, moving *away from* (ἀπὸ) God. His beliefs are false. The fact that so many who today claim to be Christian and yet deny that the gospel can be defined with sufficient clarity to allow one to say "this is true teaching and this is false teaching" shows how deeply the humanistic/naturalistic worldview has invaded the church.

Foundational to the gospel of God is the description of God as τοῦ καλέσαντος, "the One who calls." God is presented as sovereign in salvation, as the One who initiates the entire process that the Galatians are now trying to short-circuit. And how did God call them? "By the grace of Christ" is Paul's answer. The grace of God is, in Paul's vocabulary, used interchangeably with the grace of Christ, since in his mind there is no difference between the two (just as he uses "the Spirit of Christ" and the "Spirit of God" interchangeably, e.g., Romans 8:9). The very calling of God is described as an action of grace and mercy. God is under no obligation to call anyone outside of His grace. That Paul can, without elaboration, mention this suggests that it was something he expected to be understood by his readers.

"Unto another gospel, which is not another" (εἰς ἕτερον εὐαγγέλιον, ὃ οὐκ ἔστιν ἄλλο) brings us to a discussion of just what Paul means by "another gospel" followed immediately by the negation of the possibility of there actually being another gospel. Paul uses two different words in the Greek text, both of which are translated "another." The first, *heteros*, normally refers to another of *a different kind.* The second, *allos*, normally refers to another *of the same kind.* Many commentators point out these differing meanings, drawing the conclusion that Paul is basically saying that this other gospel is not a gospel *of the same kind* as the true, biblical gospel of Christ, and this may well be true.

Other interpreters, however, note that this differentiation between *heteros* and *allos* is not ironclad, and they point specifically to 2 Corinthians 11:4, where Paul writes, "For if one comes proclaiming another [*allos*] Jesus whom we have not proclaimed, or another [*heteros*] spirit which you have not received, or another [*heteros*] gospel which you have not received, you might well put up with them." Further examination of the usage of the terms, as J. B. Lightfoot wrote, reveals that "while *allos* is generally confined to a negation of identity, *heteros* sometimes implies the negation of resemblance."[1] So in 2 Corinthians 11:4 this would indicate a different identity of this "other Jesus," while the other spirit and the other gospel are of a different kind, lacking a true resemblance to the real thing.

John also uses *allos* in an important way. In John 14:16 Jesus said, "And I will ask the Father, and He will give you another [*allos*] Helper, that He may be with you forever" (NASB). The usage of *allos* in 2 Corinthians 11:4 would fit well here: the Spirit is another from Jesus as far as identity is concerned, yet He is the same kind of Comforter as Jesus is. Therefore, as used here in Galatians 1:6–7, it would seem that the differentiation between *allos* and *heteros* is purposeful and would, given what follows, indicate that this "other gospel" is not another of the same kind or identity, but is another of a different kind, a *non-gospel.*

Clearly for Paul there cannot be more than one εὐαγγέλιον (*euaggelion,* "gospel"). Either one has the *gospel of Christ* or one does not have any gospel at all. Therefore, the gospel itself must be definable so that the false pretenders can be identified. This seems rather obvious: if one cannot say "This is the gospel, and that is not," then Paul's assertions throughout this epistle are senseless. Yet it is just this ability to define the gospel that seems to have been lost in our modern situation. There are *so many* false concepts of the gospel that confusion reigns supreme, and anyone who claims to be able to make heads or tails of the situation is immediately looked at with suspicion. Beyond this, many cultic groups claim that all presentations of the "gospel" other than their own are perversions and are false. One does not want to be in the same company as the false teachers.

So it has become fashionable to allow for wide divergence concerning the nature of the gospel. Often this willingness to compromise is cloaked under the banner of false humility. "Well, there are many good men who disagree about the nature of the gospel, and I certainly recognize my own limitations and know how I could quite possibly be wrong, so it would be wrong of me

---

[1]J. B. Lightfoot, *Galatians,* 76.

to be so dogmatic as to charge others with false teaching." This disease is, quite clearly, epidemic.

Yet, someone might say, is it not true that we are prone to make mistakes? Are we not liable to be influenced deeply by our own traditions, our own backgrounds? In light of this, and given that, unlike Paul, we have not received a direct revelation of the gospel from Jesus Christ but are dependent upon a written record, would it not be wise to be a bit more generous toward others when it comes to differences about the gospel? As the argument goes, we have less assurance of the truth than Paul did.

There is a subtle yet fatal flaw in this reasoning. It is an error that is so basic to understanding the sickness of the modern professing church that we must take the time to point it out. If what was said above is true, then what logically follows is that we are in a position where we cannot be certain about the gospel message. But is this not the same as saying that the means by which *we* know the gospel, that is, by the Scriptures, is somehow insufficient to give us the same confidence and surety? Are we not in actuality saying that the Bible is flawed, incapable of truly defining the gospel so as to allow us to resist false perversions thereof? Most assuredly! This most often comes under the guise of teaching that points out the "difficult passages" and, on the basis of these, asserts that for *anyone* to claim to know the message of the Bible, outside of some very nebulous concepts, is to claim to know the unknowable.

Since the Bible has been so savagely attacked both from without the church (under the banner of science, philosophy, or humanism) and from within the professing church (under the guise of liberalism), much of its authority has vanished from many Protestant denominations. Therefore, the strong denunciation of false gospels is lacking in modern preaching. This has opened the door wide for all kinds of false teaching to flood the churches, washing away the bold, powerful proclamation that marks a church that is committed to the authority of the Word of God, the Bible.

The loss of trust and confidence in the Bible as the Word of God is directly related to the unpopularity of preaching against false doctrine or teaching. If one does not believe that there is an authoritative source of God's truth that is sufficiently clear and understandable to communicate that truth, one will hardly have any basis upon which to identify false teaching.

The fact that Paul had no problem in calling the teaching of the Galatian leaders a "non-gospel" should tell us that he was not laboring under the impression that the gospel was unclear or unknowable. If we follow his lead as it is presented to us in his letter to the Galatian churches, we too shall be able to warn others against those teachings that could, quite clearly, bring them into eternal damnation.

1:7b

> . . . but there are some who are disturbing you and wanting to distort the gospel of Christ.

Alternate:

> . . . except there are those who are troubling you and are wishing to change the gospel of Christ. (Author)

NA[27] Text:

. . . εἰ μή τινές εἰσιν οἱ ταράσσοντες ὑμᾶς καὶ θέλοντες μεταστρέψαι τὸ εὐαγγέλιον τοῦ Χριστοῦ.

but there are some who are disturbing you: Nowhere will Paul directly address the false teachers who are troubling the Galatians. He addresses only the believers, and he refers to these others in the third person. In fact, it seems clear that Paul desired no friendly contact or ecumenical discussions with the teachers in Galatia. He was not going to go over and have a little chat about the issues that separated them. It is highly doubtful that he would have sat down to dinner with them. He could have no fellowship with them, for they were not his brethren (see below).

Paul asserts that these teachers are *troubling* the Galatian believers. The Greek term ταράσσω *(tarasso)* means to shake violently back and forth. While the Christians themselves most probably did not sense this shaking, their very foundations were being torn apart. It is rare that Christians can be moved from the faith when they *know* what is coming and what is happening to them. There are many instances where believers have withstood incredible persecution without denying their faith in Jesus Christ. Yet if they can be fooled and tricked into abandoning the faith, they can be defeated.

and wanting to distort the gospel of Christ: Paul teaches that these troublemakers have a personal desire (they "want" or "desire" to do what they do, θέλοντες) to change or pervert the gospel of Christ. He does not allow any suggestion that they are truly seeking to do the will of God and have simply strayed from the truth. Rather, they specifically (and maliciously) desire to distort or change (μεταστρέψαι) the gospel. These are not brethren who are misguided; in fact, in 2:4 Paul will call those with whom he had had an earlier contact ψευδαδέλφοι *(pseudadelphoi)* "false brethren." They are not believers; they are not Christians. Instead, they have as the desire of their hearts to *change the gospel of Christ.*

What does this mean? The term translated "change" is *metastrepsai.* This word most probably means not only "to change one thing to something else" but to change something into its opposite. If this is so, then Paul is alleging that the teaching of those who were troubling the believers is not simply something that is far enough out of line with the truth to be disqualified, but that it is diametrically opposed to the truth. It is not a slight imperfection, but a radical change, a complete twisting of reality. That the gospel of the Judaizers in Galatia is opposite the truth of the gospel of Jesus Christ is brought out clearly in 2:21.

"The gospel of Christ" is a phrase that appears frequently in Paul's letters. It is used in Romans 15:19; 1 Corinthians 9:12; 2 Corinthians 2:12; 9:13; Philippians 1:27; and 1 Thessalonians 3:2. Some of the other descriptions of the gospel given by Paul include "the gospel of God" (Romans 1:1; 15:16; 1 Thessalonians 2:8–9), "the gospel of the grace of God" (Acts 20:24), "the gospel of His Son" (Romans 1:9), "the gospel of the glory of Christ" (2 Corinthians 4:4), "the gospel of your salvation" (Ephesians 1:13), "the gospel of peace" (Ephesians 6:15), "the gospel of our

Lord Jesus" (2 Thessalonians 1:8), "the gospel of the glory of the blessed God" (1 Timothy 1:11), and frequently simply "my gospel" (2 Timothy 2:8).

Christ is the subject of the gospel—His work is the substance. The gospel does not exist separately from Christ, or Christ from the gospel. The term itself simply means "good news," but for Paul and all the Christian writers of the New Testament it came to have a concrete, technical meaning, referring to the finished and completed action of salvation in the person of Jesus Christ. As Paul summed it up in 1 Corinthians 15, the gospel is the death, burial, and resurrection of Jesus Christ. That this work of God in Christ is absolutely free, absolutely disconnected from any concept of merit on the part of man, will be demonstrated later in this letter.

1:8

> But even if we or an angel from heaven should preach a gospel contrary to the one we preached to you, let him be condemned to hell!

Alternate:

> But, even if we, or an angel from heaven, were to preach to you [a gospel] other than that which we preached to you, let him be anathema. (Author)

NA[27] Text:

ἀλλὰ καὶ ἐὰν ἡμεῖς ἢ ἄγγελος ἐξ οὐρανοῦ εὐαγγελίζηται ὑμῖν παρ' ὃ εὐηγγελισάμεθα ὑμῖν, ἀνάθεμα ἔστω.

But even if we or an angel from heaven: Here Paul introduces one of two sentences that make up verses 8 and 9. This sentence is a "third-class conditional" sentence, giving a highly improbable (yet possible) situation. Paul is basically saying, "But even if we, or an angel from heaven, were to do this . . ." It is a hypothetical situation.

should preach a gospel . . . to you: The verbal term εὐαγγελίζω *(euaggelizo)*, which literally means "to preach/proclaim good news," normally demands that the noun "gospel" be supplied, as it has been here.

contrary to the one we preached: The translation of the Greek preposition παρα *(para)* is somewhat of a compromise. The word itself can admit one of two different meanings when used with an accusative (as it is here). First, "beyond" or "more than" in the sense of preaching a gospel that goes beyond or contains more than the message they have already received. Second, "against," as in "contrary to." This would result in this message being "other than" in the sense of being contrary to the gospel. J. B. Lightfoot commented,

> The context is the best guide to the meaning of the preposition. St. Paul is here asserting the oneness, the integrity of his gospel. It will not brook any rival. It will not suffer any foreign admixture. The idea of "contrariety" therefore is alien to the general bearing of the passage, though independently of the context the preposition might well have this meaning.[2]

Actually, both meanings can be seen in the term, and both fit here—we need not make a dogmatic decision between the nuances of *para.* The reason is evident: Paul has already asserted that there is no gospel other than the one true message of Christ. All others are not *really* gospels at all. He has insisted that the Galatian teachers are wishing *to change the gospel of Christ.* And how have they done this? The rest of the letter will demonstrate that they have *added the works of man* to the free grace of God. Therefore, they have not only gone "beyond" the truth (and hence into error), but the resultant message is contrary to the truth as well. Both possible meanings of *para* can be seen to fit with Paul's intention.

which we preached to you: The tense indicates that Paul is referring to a point in the past where the gospel message was delivered to the Galatian people. There has been no change in Paul's teaching, nor could there ever be. The gospel of Christ is unchanging and unchangeable.

---

[2]Ibid., 77.

let him be condemned to hell: Literally this is, "let him be anathema." Paul places this in the imperative. *Anathema* finds its origin in the Hebrew term חֵרֶם *(cherem),* which means "devoted to destruction" (Joshua 7:1). When Achan took what was "under the ban" from Jericho, God's wrath was kindled against the children of Israel, and Achan paid with his life (and the lives of his family as well). That which was *cherem* was devoted to destruction, and hence hateful to God. The term then refers to the very curse of God, bringing His wrath. Paul went so far as to say that he could wish to be "accursed from Christ" if this would bring about the salvation of the Jewish people (Romans 9:3, though the form of the grammar indicates that this is not a possibility).

Those who would preach a gospel other than the gospel of Christ, Paul says, are under the curse of God. This displeasure is not merely that of a man, or a human censure of such an activity—Paul here speaks of the very wrath of the Almighty. Why? Why such an incredibly strong statement? Surely Paul knew what kind of reaction this statement would receive when it was read in each of the churches in Galatia! The teachers who were present might stand up indignantly and walk out or begin to shout and yell, protesting their innocence. Yet despite the obvious problems this statement could cause, Paul forensically placed these teachers under the anathema of God. Why?

The gospel of Christ is also called the gospel of God. It is God's way of bringing salvation to men. God the Son has come in human flesh to give His life as "a ransom for many." The gospel is the "power of God unto salvation." For reasons only God knows, He has chosen to bring men into the proper relationship with himself through the gospel, and by no other means!

In the gospel the love of God is seen, as well as His justice, His power, and His mercy. Therefore, it is not something to be treated lightly or with disrespect. Without question God is far more concerned with the purity of the gospel than He was with the touching of the ark of the covenant, yet when Uzzah broke God's law and touched the ark, God struck him dead (1 Chronicles 13:7–10). The same is to be said concerning Aaron's sons, for when they offered "strange fire" upon the altar in disobedience to God's revealed way of worship (Leviticus 10:1–3), God struck them dead on the spot. If God is so concerned with proper worship, will He not be even more concerned with the truth of the gospel of His Son?

To preach another gospel is to blaspheme God, who has revealed himself in Jesus Christ. To preach another gospel is to call God a liar and His testimony to His Son untrue. To preach another gospel is to deprive God of the glory that is His in His sovereign, free, and unconditional salvation of the elect.

But beyond even this, to preach another gospel is to show the greatest hatred for those to whom you deliver this message of death. Why? Only the true gospel saves; only the gospel of Christ is the power of God. A false gospel cannot save; it cannot redeem. To ensnare someone in a false gospel is to commit eternal murder. Ironically, many today preach a false gospel simply out of a desire not to "offend" anyone. They water down the strong teaching of God's wrath or man's sinfulness out of a concern (so they say) to "be at peace" with people, to "not drive them away." Do they not know that by so doing they are condemning the very people they claim to wish to save? God's truth does not need man's additions—God is well aware of the fact that man is offended by His claims to sovereignty and rulership. It will be no excuse at the judgment day to say "I just didn't want to offend." "You have offended Me" will come the answer, "and what do you think is more important?"

1:9

> As we have said before, and now I say again, if any one is preaching to you a gospel contrary to what you received, let him be condemned to hell!

Alternate:

> As we said before I say now again, if anyone is preaching [a gospel] other than that which you received, let him be anathema. (Author)

NA*[27] *Text:

ὡς προειρήκαμεν καὶ ἄρτι πάλιν λέγω· εἴ τις ὑμᾶς εὐαγγελίζεται παρ' ὃ ⸀παρελάβετε, ἀνάθεμα ἔστω.

| ⸀ ελαβετε 𝔓[51] ¦ ευηγγελισαμεθα υμιν Ψ

As we have said before, and now I say again: Commentators are split over whether this phrase refers to the immediately preceding verse, or whether it refers instead to the time of Paul's previous ministry among the churches of Galatia. Either could be correct, and neither would materially affect the meaning. This second sentence differs from the preceding verse in that rather than presenting a hypothetical case, here Paul gives a direct command.

if any one is preaching to you a gospel contrary to what you received: Here Paul presents a first-class conditional sentence, meaning that the condition (someone preaching another gospel) is fulfilled—this is actually taking place. It pictures the current condition in the churches of Galatia. He directly states that the gospel of these other teachers is other than that which he himself preached to them. Note as well that in verse 8 he speaks of the gospel that was preached by him and his colleagues to the Galatians; here he specifically asserts that they had *received* that gospel.

let him be condemned to hell: As he has just indicated that he is speaking of the teachers there in the churches, here he emphatically places them under the same curse of God as above. Surely there could be no turning back after this kind of statement.

1:10–12

> Am I now trying to gain the approval of people or of God? Or am I trying to please people? If I were still trying to please people, I would not be a slave of Christ. Now I want you to know, brothers and sisters, that the gospel I preached is not of human origin. For I did not receive it or learn it from any human source; instead I received it by a revelation of Jesus Christ.

Alternate:

> For am I now persuading men or God? Or am I seeking to please men? If I were yet pleasing men, I would not be a

servant of Christ. For I make known to you, brethren, that the gospel which was proclaimed by me is not according to man. For neither did I receive it from men, nor was I taught it; but [I received it] by a revelation of Jesus Christ. (Author)

NA*[27] *Text:
Ἄρτι γὰρ ἀνθρώπους πείθω ἢ τὸν θεόν; ἢ ζητῶ ἀνθρώποις ἀρέσκειν; εἰ ἔτι ἀνθρώποις ἤρεσκον, Χριστοῦ δοῦλος οὐκ ἂν ἤμην. Γνωρίζω γὰρ ὑμῖν, ἀδελφοί, τὸ εὐαγγέλιον τὸ εὐαγγελισθὲν ὑπ' ἐμοῦ ὅτι οὐκ ἔστιν κατὰ ἄνθρωπον· οὐδὲ γὰρ ἐγὼ παρὰ ἀνθρώπου παρέλαβον αὐτὸ οὔτε ἐδιδάχθην ἀλλὰ δι' ἀποκαλύψεως Ἰησοῦ Χριστοῦ.

Immediately upon completing this very strong beginning, Paul seemingly steps back and says, "OK, now given that, am I seeking to persuade men or God? Am I seeking to please men by saying these things?" The Greek term πείθω *(peithō)*, translated here "gain the approval of," is capable of numerous meanings. Here it probably refers to an attempt to conciliate, to win one's favor. The thought is, "In light of what I just said, am I still to be accused of attempting to win the favor of men? Or am I not clearly seeking to please God?" The following question, "or am I seeking to please people?" follows this line of thought and indicates that Paul knows of charges made against him by his enemies in Galatia. "Paul vacillates from one view to another," they charge, "at one time saying this, at another that, all just to please whoever might be listening." But the words of verses 6–9 hardly fit into such a scheme. Being a man-pleaser is something that Paul denies.

If I were still trying to please people, I would not be a slave of Christ: Here Paul presses yet a third kind of conditional sentence into service, the second-class conditional, where the condition is assumed to be unfulfilled. Therefore, Paul says that *if* he were a man-pleaser, then he would not be a servant of Christ. But that is just what he denies. Why does Paul use the term "still"? It is not to be thought that this is an admission that Paul as a Christian ever had been a man-pleaser; rather, it would seem that he is using the term in the sense of "after all I've been through, am I yet to be considered a man-pleaser?"

Now I want you to know, brothers and sisters: Paul addresses the true brethren, the believers, possibly in distinction to the false brethren, the false teachers. He seems to wish to separate the believers from these teachers in their own minds so that they can properly evaluate what these men are teaching.

that the gospel I preached is not of human origin: The gospel message that Paul himself had proclaimed to the Galatian believers was not humanly derived; that is, it did not find its origin in human thought or contemplation. Why is this important? Again, seemingly the teachers in Galatia were alleging that Paul's supposedly inconsistent behavior was perfectly in line with their accusation that his teaching was derived from human authorities, possibly from the other apostles.

For I did not receive it or learn it from any human source: He amplifies his denial of a human origin for his gospel by denying first that he received the gospel from men. The term translated "receive" is the same term that is used in 1 Corinthians 15:3, where Paul says that he *did receive* the gospel message and had passed it on to the Corinthians. Not only this, but the term frequently refers to the reception of something that is passed down, such as a teaching or a tradition.

So is Paul here contradicting himself? Is he doing just what it is alleged by the Galatian teachers that he always does, vacillating from one position to another? The answer seems to lie in the fact that in 1 Corinthians 15 Paul is speaking of the common *kerygma*, the common elements of the gospel, primarily the death, burial, and resurrection of Christ. In this passage, however, he is speaking of the entire content of the gospel, including (as we will see) the concepts of justification by faith, etc. The origin of his teaching regarding the law, circumcision, faith, and justification, is not from men but from Jesus Christ himself.

To better understand what Paul is denying in this passage, we need to note the adversative statement: *instead I received it by a revelation of Jesus Christ.* What Paul is disavowing is that the origin of his gospel message was simply human, as if he were getting a secondhand version that could not be trusted. Rather, he claims, he received his gospel (and, it seems to be inherent in his comments, his authority to proclaim it) directly from Jesus Christ.

The phrase "a revelation of Jesus Christ" may refer either to (1) a revelation given *by* Jesus Christ (a subjective genitive construction) or (2) a revelation *of* Jesus Christ (an objective genitive construction, wherein Jesus Christ would be the object of the revelation). If Paul is here referring to his Damascus-road incident (which seems quite likely, though he may be referring to certain incidents similar to his experiences recorded in 2 Corinthians 12:2–4), then the latter would be the most logical understanding, for in that vision of Christ Paul had a revelation of *who* Jesus Christ was, *of* Jesus Christ. Just as the other apostles were witnesses of the resurrected Jesus Christ, so too was Paul. His encounter with the Lord Jesus was very important to him—important to his divine call as an apostle, important to the divine nature of his gospel presentation.

Paul has now laid the groundwork for the apologetic defense of free justification he will present in chapters 2 and 3 of Galatians. No one can possibly take lightly the teaching he will now present.

CHAPTER 16

Paul Confronts Peter on the Gospel

SYNOPSIS:

The encounter between Paul and Peter at Antioch places the doctrine of justification by faith squarely in the center of the life of the church. In recording this incident and providing the background to it, the apostle reveals vitally important elements of the doctrine and how Christians of all ages should view it as definitional to the truth of the gospel. It ends with a full and firm proclamation of justification by grace through faith without human works of merit.

RESOURCES:

See chapter 15, page 254.

MAIN PASSAGE:

2:1 Then after fourteen years I went up to Jerusalem again
with Barnabas, taking Titus along too. **2:2** I went there because of

a revelation and presented to them the gospel that I preach among the Gentiles. But I did so only in a private meeting with the influential people, to make sure that I was not running or had not run in vain. **2:3** Yet not even Titus, who was with me, was compelled to be circumcised, although he was a Greek. **2:4** Now this matter arose because of the false brothers with false pretenses who slipped in unnoticed to spy out our freedom that we have in Christ Jesus, to make us slaves. **2:5** But we did not surrender to them even for a moment, so that the truth of the gospel would remain with you.

Regarding the doctrine of justification, this chapter is one of the most vital in the New Testament, for it gives us instruction regarding the attitude we are to have toward the gospel as a whole and justification in particular, *and how we are to stand for the truth of this doctrine.* It puts legs on the discussion, showing how it is vital in the context of everyday Christian living and integral to the life of the church itself. It moves the concept from the abstract to the concrete and shows the personal cost that must be paid by those who place the proper value upon the truth of the gospel.

The first few verses of the chapter are not directly related to justification. However, we must understand the background so as to have the proper context to understand both Paul's commitment to the truth of the gospel and how this truth played out in the incident in Antioch.

"Then after fourteen years" most probably should be dated from the point of his conversion rather than from the first visit to Jerusalem. This, however, introduces us to the major issue in this passage: exactly which visit to Jerusalem is this? He mentions taking Barnabas and Titus along with him, and in Acts we never meet Titus at all, while Barnabas accompanies Paul on two trips up to Jerusalem—the "famine relief effort" of approximately A.D. 44 (Acts 11:27–30; 12:25) and the great Jerusalem Council of Acts 15.

Which of these two visits fits with Galatians 2? As usual, scholars line up on both sides of the issue. John Calvin as well as F. F. Bruce and others opt for the first visit, that of Acts 11:30, for some of the following reasons: (1) Paul's argument would be seriously compromised if he omitted a visit to Jerusalem, since he is arguing for the non-manmade nature and authority of his gospel; (2) This couldn't be the meeting of Acts 15, for immediately thereafter Peter is at Antioch going against what he just pronounced earlier; (3) Acts 15 was an open, public council, while in Galatians 2 this is done in private; (4) This visit in Galatians 2 was "according to revelation," while the visit of Acts 15 was at the command of the church. The prophecy of Agabus in Acts 11:28 may provide a basis for Paul's usage of the term "revelation." There are other matters that are urged in favor of the Acts 11:30 visit being the same as this in Galatians 2.

On the other hand, there are many arguments in favor of the Galatians 2–Acts 15 identification: (1) The theme of Galatians 2 is the same as Acts 15, while Acts 11:30 is a famine-relief effort, not a theological roundtable; (2) In Acts 11 it is Barnabas who leads; in Galatians 2 and Acts 15 it is Paul; (3) If Galatians 2 and Acts 11:30 are the same visit, then there was no need for the Acts 15 meeting, since the issue had already been resolved; (4) In Acts 11:30 Barnabas and Saul only meet "elders," not the "apostles," as they do in Acts 15; (5) The chronological difficulties of making Galatians 2 and Acts 11:30 the same visit are supposed to be insurmountable, for as we know from the text of Acts itself, Herod dies right around the time of this visit, which takes place in A.D. 44. We also know from secular sources that famines gripped Judea at this time, peaking in A.D. 46–48. Now, if this visit takes place fourteen years after the first visit, which would be at least three and probably more like five years after Paul's conversion, then we have nineteen years to account for; going back from approximately A.D. 44 nineteen years puts us prior to the ministry of Christ! Those who defend the Acts 11 identification, however, do not date the fourteen years from the first visit to Jerusalem, but from Saul's conversion, and they would date the Acts 11 visit as being closer to the actual famine itself, sometime around A.D. 46.

And so the arguments go—those defending the earlier visit place the fourteen years of 2:1 from Paul's conversion, and the date of the Acts 11 visit in A.D. 46, making Paul's conversion date A.D. 32, very shortly after the ministry of Christ. Personally, I find answering the objections to the Acts 11 identification easier than answering the objections to the Acts 15 theory. The main reason I feel this way is that putting the Acts 15 meeting into Galatians 2 results in an incredible act of hypocrisy by Peter and Barnabas as well. There is also the fact that we have to assert that there was a private meeting prior to the public discussion that decided the same matter.

2:2

> I went there because of a revelation and presented to them the gospel that I preach among the Gentiles. But I did so only in a private meeting with the influential people, to make sure that I was not running or had not run in vain.

Alternate:

> Now I went up according to a revelation, and I related to them the gospel which I am preaching among the Gentiles, but privately to those who were "of reputation," lest I was running, or had run, in vain. (Author)

NA[27] Text:
ἀνέβην δὲ κατὰ ἀποκάλυψιν· καὶ ἀνεθέμην αὐτοῖς τὸ εὐαγγέλιον ὃ κηρύσσω ἐν τοῖς ἔθνεσιν, κατ' ἰδίαν δὲ τοῖς δοκοῦσιν, μή πως εἰς κενὸν τρέχω ἢ ἔδραμον.

I went there because of a revelation: This may refer to Agabus's prophecy in Acts 11:27–28. If one takes the Acts 15 position, this would simply refer to God's direction in sending Paul and Barnabas to Jerusalem, which could properly be understood to have functioned through the intermediation of the church itself.

and presented to them the gospel that I preach among the Gentiles is present tense, continuous action. What he related to the Jerusalem leaders was the exact same message he was preaching as he wrote this letter.

But I did so only in a private meeting with the influential people: I personally rendered the phrase "but privately to those who were 'of reputation.' " I have enclosed the phrase "of reputation" in quotes throughout my personal translation simply because it seems that Paul is using a term that comes from the enemy camp, so to speak. It is quite possible that the Judaizers in Galatia were claiming as their authority those men in Jerusalem who were "of repute" in the leadership of the church over against poor little Paul, the manmade apostle, as they claimed. Paul will point out that these "men of repute" (and the term itself, though it sounds derisive, should not be taken as such, other than with reference to those false teachers who would use the term to cloak their heresy) added nothing to him, taught him nothing, but instead offered him the right hand of fellowship and recognized the validity of his teaching and apostleship.

to make sure that I was not running or had not run in vain: This seems, at first blush, to be utterly out of character for the book and to be an incredibly damaging admission of that which Paul has denied from the very start—that his message was dependent upon human authority and approval. However, Paul shows no sign of having made such an admission, so to take it in this way is obviously a mistake. William Hendriksen commented,

> If, while Paul was preaching the gospel of justification by faith, without the works of the law, the other apostles, though in principle agreeing with him, would have been "soft" in their attitude toward those who seriously questioned the rightness of his convictions and of his preaching, the cause of mission work among the Gentiles would have been seriously undermined. The effectiveness of that which Paul had been doing in the past and was still doing would have been decisively weakened.[1]

The key term seems to be "run." Paul is not speaking of the authority of his gospel here—that was settled in chapter 1. Rather, he is now talking about his ministry among the Gentiles. If the Jerusalem body did not agree with his methodology, the result would be disastrous for the church—a true Jewish/Gentile split

[1]Hendriksen, *Galatians,* 76. See also Ronald Y. K. Fung, *The Epistle to the Galatians* (Eerdmans, 1988), 89–90.

could occur, which would be devastating for the future of the fledgling faith. Paul is here showing his unity with the Jerusalem leaders. He does not barge into the room and demand an immediate stamp of approval upon his ministry without first sharing with them what he has been doing and saying, and seeking to understand their concerns as well. This whole first section of Galatians 2 will speak primarily to the fact that Paul and the Jerusalem leaders agreed on the nature of the gospel of grace over against the concept of works-righteousness that was being preached in Galatia.

2:3

> Yet not even Titus, who was with me, was compelled to be circumcised, although he was a Greek.

NA*[27] *Text:
ἀλλ᾽ οὐδὲ Τίτος ὁ σὺν ἐμοί, Ἕλλην ὤν, ἠναγκάσθη περιτμηθῆναι·

Yet not even Titus, who was with me, was compelled to be circumcised, although he was a Greek: Here, in the midst of the very leadership of the Jerusalem church, is a pure Gentile, Titus. To show how united the leadership was in this regard, Paul mentions that, unlike his Judaizing enemies in Galatia, the leaders did not compel Titus to be circumcised! But the question did seem to come up, and we might speculate Paul wanted it to come up, which was why he brought Titus in the first place, sort of as a "test case."

2:4

> Now this matter arose because of the false brothers with false pretenses who slipped in unnoticed to spy out our freedom that we have in Christ Jesus, to make us slaves.

NA*[27] *Text:
διὰ δὲ τοὺς παρεισάκτους ψευδαδέλφους, οἵτινες παρεισῆλθον κατασκοπῆσαι τὴν ἐλευθερίαν ἡμῶν ἣν ἔχομεν ἐν Χριστῷ Ἰησοῦ, ἵνα ἡμᾶς καταδουλώσουσιν, . . .

Now this matter arose because of the false brothers with false pretenses: The passage is difficult to translate, as the term rendered "with false pretenses" (παρεισάκτους) literally means "to sneak in," resulting in the rather awkward "the sneaking in false brethren." Be that as it may, those who oppose Paul's gospel of free grace he here identifies clearly as false brethren (ψευδαδέλφους). The only meaning of the term that makes any sense at all is the surface meaning—these men were not Christians! They professed to be Christians but were in fact nonbelievers and, more, were enemies of the gospel! They were *in the church,* may well have held positions of leadership in the church, and would, from an external viewpoint, defy recognition as apostates outside of a doctrinal litmus test.

The use of this term by Paul is not an emotional overreaction based upon personal differences with the Judaizers (as is so often assumed by liberal exegetes today). It is instead the firmly held conclusion of the single man chosen by a sovereign God as His instrument, through which God revealed more about the church and the gospel of justification in Scripture than any other single individual after the resurrection of the Lord Jesus.

who slipped in unnoticed to spy out our freedom that we have in Christ Jesus, to make us slaves: These false brethren are said to have slipped into the fellowship. The term speaks of craftiness and deception, a consistent thought in Paul's description of these men. They entered the Christian congregation for a specific purpose, to spy out the freedom that was theirs in Christ Jesus. And why would they be interested in this freedom? Because it was their desire, as it seems to be the desire of most religious leaders who reject the gospel, to place the Christians in bondage. This bondage would be the same bondage that Israel experienced when they attempted to come to God through legalism rather than by faith—it is a bondage from which there is no escape outside of Christ. Since these men in Jerusalem were obviously doing the same things as the Judaizers in Galatia (might they be the same men, who upon being rebuffed at Jerusalem, went out on their own kind of mission to the Gentiles?), the description of their desires and intentions given by Paul here would be equally applicable in Galatia.

2:5

> But we did not surrender to them even for a moment, so that the truth of the gospel would remain with you.

NA[27] Text:
οἷς οὐδὲ πρὸς ὥραν εἴξαμεν τῇ ὑποταγῇ, ἵνα ἡ ἀλήθεια τοῦ εὐαγγελίου διαμείνῃ πρὸς ὑμᾶς.

But we did not surrender to them even for a moment: Paul is quick to assert that there was never a time when the issue was in doubt. These men sought their submission—submission to the laws and ordinances of human religion. The Christian apostles would have none of it and stood against their efforts.

This was in order that *the truth of the gospel* (ἡ ἀλήθεια τοῦ εὐαγγελίου) *would remain with you.* Here is Paul's reason for his strong stand against the Judaizers—the truth of the gospel. The gospel cannot be mixed with less-than-pure strains of religious teaching and still be called the gospel. If the leaders had been willing to compromise, to sit down in ecumenical dialogue with these men, the truth of the gospel would have been lost, and all that would have been left would be yet another human religion, powerless to save, powerless to deliver men from their sin and their guilt. Paul and the others had the right focus—the truth of the gospel is the number one priority for the Christian church. Why? Because without it, the church has nothing to say—she is utterly powerless, for the gospel is the "power of God unto salvation." It could not even be said that the church loves God if the church does not care about the truth of His message of salvation in Christ Jesus! The church is not fulfilling her purpose when she is no longer concerned about the truth of the gospel.

2:6–10 (SUMMARY)

In this section Paul continues the defense of his position by noting the interaction between himself and Peter, and the fact that those who were "of repute" added nothing to him or his gospel. There is then the recognition of the work of God in setting Peter aside and gifting him for work among the Jews, just as God gifted Paul for the task of bringing the gospel of grace to the Gentiles.[2] The unity that existed, *and continues to exist*, among the leaders of the church is emphasized when Paul speaks of the right hand of fellowship that was offered to him.

2:11–21

> **2:11** But when Cephas came to Antioch, I opposed him to his
> face, because he had clearly done wrong. **2:12** For until certain
> people came from James, he had been eating with the Gentiles. But when they arrived, he stopped doing this and separated himself because he was afraid of those who belonged to
> the circumcision party. **2:13** And the rest of the Jews also
> joined with him in this hypocrisy, so that even Barnabas was
> led astray with them by their hypocrisy. **2:14** But when I saw
> that they were not behaving consistently with the truth of the gospel, I said to Cephas in front of them all, "If you, although you are a Jew, live like a Gentile and not like a Jew, how can you try to force the Gentiles to live like Jews?"
>
> **2:15** We are Jews by birth and not Gentile sinners; **2:16** yet
> we know that no one is justified by the works of the law but by the faithfulness of Jesus Christ. And we have come to believe in Christ Jesus, so that we may be justified by the faithfulness of Christ and not by the works of the law, because by the works
> of the law no one will be justified. **2:17** But if while seeking to
> be justified in Christ, we ourselves have also been found to be sinners, is Christ then one who encourages sin? Absolutely
> not! **2:18** But if I build up again those things I once destroyed,
> I demonstrate that I am one who breaks God's law. **2:19** For
> through the law I died to the law so that I may live to God.
> **2:20** I have been crucified with Christ; and it is no longer I
> who live, but Christ lives in me. So the life I now live in the body, I live because of the faithfulness of the Son of God, who

[2]A strange idea if, in fact, Peter was considered the head of the church and the first pope. The segregation of fields of ministry shows the equality of the apostles and their recognition of the gifting of God for various works of ministry.

loved me and gave himself for me. **2:21** I do not set aside God's grace, because if righteousness could come through the law, then Christ died for nothing!

2:11

NA*[27] *Text:

⸀Ὅτε δὲ ἦλθεν ⸀Κηφᾶς εἰς Ἀντιόχειαν, κατὰ πρόσωπον αὐτῷ ἀντέστην, ὅτι κατεγνωσμένος ἦν.

| ⸀ Πετρος D F G 𝔐 it vg^{mss} sy^{h}; Ambst ¦ *txt* ℵ A B C H P Ψ 0278. 33. 81. 104. 365. 629. 1175. 1241^{s}. 1739. 1881 *pc* vg sy^{hmg}

But when Cephas came to Antioch: Peter's[3] visit to this mainly Gentile city results in a crisis for the recently decided unity in the leadership of the church on the issue of the Gentiles. While Peter has before given the right hand of fellowship to Paul and Barnabas, he does not find it possible to maintain his convictions in the face of religious peer pressure.

I opposed him to his face: Paul did not simply seek out a more opportune time to discuss the issue with Peter. In verse 14 we are told that Paul confronts Peter in a public situation, before all the members of the church, Jew and Gentile, including, we would imagine, the "certain ones from James" as well. Paul realized that the issues at hand were too important to allow even the smallest delay in dealing with them.

because he had clearly done wrong: or literally, "for he was to be condemned" (κατεγνωσμένος): Paul makes it clear that Peter's action was totally out of harmony with the principles of the gospel, resulting in his condemnation. Peter was guilty of compromise, and Paul knew that such was a dangerous precedent to set.

2:12

For until certain people came from James, he had been eating with the Gentiles. But when they arrived, he stopped doing

---

[3]The literal rendering is Cephas. Much has been written on why Paul would refer to Peter by his Aramaic name. So striking is the usage that, as the textual variant indicates, a majority of later manuscripts change it to Peter.

> this and separated himself because he was afraid of those who belonged to the circumcision party.

NA*[27] *Text:

πρὸ τοῦ γὰρ ἐλθεῖν τινας ἀπὸ Ἰακώβου μετὰ τῶν ἐθνῶν συνήσθιεν· ὅτε δὲ ἦλθον, ὑπέστελλεν καὶ ἀφώριζεν ἑαυτόν φοβούμενος τοὺς ἐκ περιτομῆς.

For until certain people came from James: Peter had obviously been at Antioch long enough to establish a pattern of behavior that would be interrupted by the arrival of these men from Jerusalem.

he had been eating with the Gentiles: At least Peter started in the right direction, following in line with the previously made decisions between himself, James, Paul, and Barnabas. He jettisoned the Jewish traditions regarding eating with Gentiles and showed the proper idea of unity in the body of Christ between Jew and Gentile.

But when they arrived, he stopped doing this and separated himself because he was afraid of those who belonged to the circumcision party: Seemingly these ones "from James" did not agree with the decisions reached in Jerusalem, or possibly they did not even know about them, as the discussion had been held in private. Whatever the case, we get a glimpse here of the Jerusalem church not living in harmony with the teachings of Christ, or even the precedent set by Peter himself in going to the house of Cornelius in Acts 10. It is obvious that these men from Jerusalem were not willing to eat together with Gentiles, and Peter knew this as well. (Did Peter, while in Jerusalem, eat with Gentiles? Seemingly not.) These men were "of the circumcision," meaning (in Paul's vocabulary) that he did not really differentiate between these men and those he was at that time fighting in Galatia—both viewed circumcision as a part of the necessary ordinances of Christian faith.

2:13

> And the rest of the Jews also joined with him in this hypocrisy, so that even Barnabas was led astray with them by their hypocrisy.

NA[27] Text:
καὶ συνυπεκρίθησαν αὐτῷ καὶ οἱ λοιποὶ Ἰουδαῖοι, ὥστε καὶ Βαρναβᾶς συναπήχθη αὐτῶν τῇ ὑποκρίσει.

Here indeed is a look at the strength of religious tradition. The Jewish members of the congregation at Antioch are so deeply influenced by the actions of Peter and those of the circumcision that they too withdraw fellowship from the Gentile believers. The meaning of this action is perfectly clear: it finds its basis in the idea that unless one is circumcised, one is not as much of a Christian as those who have undergone this religious rite. The ground at the foot of the cross is no longer level—religious rites and actions are now relevant to one's standing with God.

Those within the body of Christ now begin to discriminate against those who have not gone through the same actions as they themselves. And, shock of shocks, even Barnabas, the man who first took the feared Saul to the apostles, the very son of encouragement himself (Acts 4:36), reverts to being Jewish, denying the basis of his previous actions and doing anything but encouraging the Gentile believers. But we must remember that these men were Jews, and what one is taught in childhood will often be carried through the rest of life, even when further knowledge and understanding force us to recognize the shortcomings and limitations of that early teaching. There is no excuse for this hypocrisy; but it certainly says much to us about how we should be very sensitive to the possibility that we are deeply influenced by our own traditions as well.

2:14

> But when I saw that they were not behaving consistently with the truth of the gospel, I said to Cephas in front of them all, "If you, although you are a Jew, live like a Gentile and not like a Jew, how can you try to force the Gentiles to live like Jews?"

NA[27] Text:
ἀλλ᾽ ὅτε εἶδον ὅτι οὐκ ὀρθοποδοῦσιν πρὸς τὴν ἀλήθειαν τοῦ εὐαγγελίου, εἶπον τῷ Κηφᾷ ἔμπροσθεν πάντων· Εἰ σὺ Ἰουδαῖος

ὑπάρχων ἐθνικῶς καὶ οὐχὶ Ἰουδαϊκῶς ζῇς, πῶς τὰ ἔθνη ἀναγκάζεις Ἰουδαΐζειν;

But when I saw that they were not behaving consistently with the truth of the gospel: It is very doubtful that Peter or Barnabas openly repudiated what had been decided at the Jerusalem meeting. They did not make a written retraction of their theological teachings. If asked, they probably would have affirmed their orthodoxy. But their actions spoke louder than their words. By withdrawing from eating with the Gentiles, they were introducing distinctions into the body of Christ and were giving circumcision a place in determining a person's relationship with God.

Therefore, they were not "walking straight" (ὀρθοποδοῦσιν) according to the truth of the gospel. The Greek term refers to walking straight in accordance with a rule, and goes also to the consistency of the walk. The person who is walking straight is one who is not wavering or stumbling. Peter and Barnbas's actions denied the gospel. Their path deviated from the truth, and the inevitable result of this decision is to follow the path of error.

I said to Cephas in front of them all: One can almost see Paul placing himself right in front of the "kosher line" at dinnertime, making sure all were present, then in a loud voice (so that everyone could hear, of course), "If you, being a Jew . . ." One can also imagine that Peter was probably not too happy about either Paul's choice of timing or the circumstances. But Paul took the action he did simply because the issue was so momentous, so important.

If you, although you are a Jew, live like a Gentile: This was probably most painful for Peter, especially because the men from James could hear all of this. Paul is going to key on Peter's Jewishness in making his point of justification by faith alone in the following verses. Here he asks a rhetorical question, pointing out Peter's past pattern of not living strictly according to the rules of Judaism, which would include his eating together with Gentiles. Paul asks why Peter, who is a Jew but who does not seem to feel (as shown by his past actions) that living like a Jew is something that must be done, would insist that Gentiles should be compelled to live like Jews, observing the very same traditions and restrictions that he himself had ignored. No answer is forthcoming from Peter (we would doubt that Peter had much of a reply, as Paul's words are perfectly in line with Peter's own teachings as found elsewhere, especially after his encounter with Cornelius).

2:15

> We are Jews by birth and not Gentile sinners.

NA[27] Text:
Ἡμεῖς φύσει Ἰουδαῖοι καὶ οὐκ ἐξ ἐθνῶν ἁμαρτωλοί·

We are Jews by birth and not Gentile sinners: The terminology used by Paul is strictly Jewish; that is, the Jews would view those who were outside of the covenant, who did not have Torah, as ἁμαρτωλοί, *harmartoloi,* "sinners." While to modern ears this sounds downright insulting, it is simply a fact that this is how the Jew viewed the Gentile—a sinner in virtue of his parentage and separation from the law and covenant. Paul uses the Jewish terminology for a purpose; he will key on this term in verses 17–18.

2:16

> . . . yet we know that no one is justified by the works of the law but by the faithfulness of Jesus Christ. And we have come to believe in Christ Jesus, so that we may be justified by the faithfulness of Christ and not by the works of the law, because by the works of the law no one will be justified.

NA[27] Text:
εἰδότες δὲ ὅτι οὐ δικαιοῦται ἄνθρωπος ἐξ ἔργων νόμου ἐὰν μὴ διὰ πίστεως Ἰησοῦ Χριστοῦ, καὶ ἡμεῖς εἰς Χριστὸν Ἰησοῦν ἐπιστεύσαμεν, ἵνα δικαιωθῶμεν ἐκ πίστεως Χριστοῦ καὶ οὐκ ἐξ ἔργων νόμου, ὅτι ἐξ ἔργων νόμου οὐ δικαιωθήσεται πᾶσα σάρξ.

yet we know that no one is justified by the works of the law but by the faithfulness of Jesus Christ: Paul makes this assertion as something that must be understood. It is stated as a common belief between himself and Peter: they both know that a man is not justified by works of law—the only way of justification is by faith in Christ Jesus. But as major battles throughout the history of the Christian faith have been waged over just this statement, it would be best to take a few moments to delve a little deeper into what is here asserted.

We have already examined the meaning of the Greek family δικαιόω, δικαιοσύνη, δίκαιος (*dikaiō, dikaisune, dikaios*). Paul insists that a right relationship with God cannot come about by "works of law." What are these works of law? Is Paul limiting himself solely to the Mosaic law? Fung very rightly observes:

> By "the law" here Paul has in view not its ceremonial aspect only, but the law in its entirety; but while it is true that Paul does not anywhere explicitly distinguish between the ceremonial law and the moral law, an implicit distinction is clearly suggested in 1 Cor. 7:19 by the contrast between "circumcision" (which is part of God's law) and the keeping of God's commands, thus separating "the ethical from the ceremonial—the permanent from the temporal."[4]

Certainly in this context the Mosaic law (as seen in its sign of circumcision) is foremost in Paul's mind. But we should not limit this concept so closely so as to leave the door open to some other kind of legalistic system resulting in righteousness. If God's holy Torah could not bring a person righteousness, no other system will do so either. Paul insists that the law is simply incapable of bringing about righteousness—it was never designed to make someone righteous; it was designed to reveal God's holy nature and will. He will expand on this in chapter 3.

The Greek construction of the first phrase of verse 16 emphasizes that justification is not by works; in fact, it is only by faith in Christ Jesus. The exclusivity of justification by faith is clearly presented by the construction ἐὰν μὴ *(ean me)*. This is the only way of justification—faith in Christ. There should be no ambiguity concerning his meaning here. He is not saying that faith in Christ is *one* way, or a *better* way, nor is he saying that works of law are an

[4]Fung, *The Epistle to the Galatians*, 114.

acceptable avenue as long as one believes.

> ἐὰν μὴ is properly exceptive, not adversative . . . , but it may introduce an exception to the preceding statement taken as a whole or to the principal part of it—in this case to οὐ δικαιοῦται ἄνθρωπος ἐξ ἔργων νόμου or to οὐ δικαιοῦται ἄνθρωπος alone. The latter alternative is clearly to be chosen here, since the former would yield the thought that a man can be justified by works of law if this be accompanied by faith, a thought never expressed by the apostle and wholly at variance with his doctrine as unambiguously expressed in several passages. See, *e.g.*, the latter part of this verse and 3:10–14, where faith and works of law are set in sharp antithesis with one another. But since the word "except" in English is always understood to introduce an exception to the whole of what precedes, it is necessary to resort to the paraphrastic translation "but only."[5]

Likewise,

> *The antithesis* which Paul poses between "by doing what the law demands" and "through faith in Christ Jesus" is expressed in the absolute terms of a simple "not . . . but" (AV, RSV, NASB, NIV). The over-literal translation of the RV ("a man is not justified by the works of the law, save through faith in Christ Jesus") is misleading in that it might be taken to imply that faith in Christ is the means by which conformity to law, inadequate in itself, is made effective for salvation, whereas the expression rendered "save" *(ean me)* probably introduces an exception only to "a man is not justified" not to the entire clause, "a man is not justified by works of the law." By adding the word "only" before "through faith in Christ Jesus" (so also RV mg.; cf. RSV at Rom. 11:20) the NEB rightly stresses faith as the *exclusive* means of justification and faithfully reflects Paul's emphasis on "the total incapacity of man for any kind of self-justification. In justification the sinner . . . stands there with his hands entirely empty."[6]

[5]Burton, 121.

[6]Fung, 115. The final quoted sentence is from Hans Küng, *Justification*, 238, as cited by Fung.

J. Louis Martyn also notes the meaning of ἐὰν μὴ and says, "On the contrary, as regards salvation, observance of the Law and the faith of Christ constitute a genuine antinomy."[7]

The importance of this construction in Paul's strong words to Peter should not be overlooked. The opening phrases of Galatians 2:16 proclaim *sola fide* as clearly as it could possibly be pronounced. ἐὰν μὴ means that faith in Christ Jesus[8] is the *only* means of justification, the *sole* means. What is this if not *sola fide*? Further, the fact that these words, taken in context, truly do not allow for the "justified by works of law as long as you believe in Jesus" position is very relevant to the modern "justified by good deeds done in a state of grace" teaching of the Church of Rome.

And we have come to believe in Christ Jesus: Isn't this something of a redundancy? No, for Paul is still playing on his and Peter's Jewishness. Though he and Peter are Jews, even they had to believe in Christ for justification, just like any "Gentile sinner!" This is Paul's point, which he will emphasize in verses 17 and 18—the Jew must stand on the very same ground as the Gentile when it comes to faith in Christ. He must abandon any and all pretended advantage from his lineage as a Jew and become like a Gentile sinner.

so that we may be justified by the faithfulness of Christ and not by the works of the law: The NET takes πίστεως Χριστοῦ as a subjective genitive.[9] The more traditional translation, "in order that we

---

[7]Martyn, 251.

[8]My position is that these genitives are objective, based more upon Pauline usage and meaning than upon specific grammatical issues, especially in this passage. See John Murray, *Romans*, 368–72, and the next note for NET's translation.

[9]The NET provides the following translational note: Though traditionally translated "faith in Jesus Christ," an increasing number of New Testament scholars are arguing that πίστις Χριστοῦ (*pistis Christou*) and similar phrases in Paul (Romans 3:22, 26; Galatians 2:16, 20; 3:22; Philippians 3:9) involve a *subjective genitive* and mean "Christ's faith" or "Christ's faithfulness" (cf., e.g., G. Howard, "The 'Faith of Christ,'" *ExpTim* 85 (1974) 212–15; R. B. Hays, *The Faith of Jesus Christ: An Investigation of the Narrative Substructure of Galatians 3:1–4:11* (SBLDS 56; Chico: Scholars, 1983); M. D. Hooker, "Πίστις Χριστοῦ," NTS 35 (1989) 321–42. Noteworthy among the arguments for the subjective genitive view is that when πίστις takes a personal genitive it is almost never an objective genitive (cf. Matthew 9:2, 22, 29; Mark 2:5; 5:34; 10:52; Luke 5:20; 7:50; 8:25, 48; 17:19; 18:42; 22:32; Romans 1:8, 12; 3:3; 4:5, 12, 16; 1 Corinthians 2:5; 15:14, 17; 2 Corinthians 10:15; Philippians 2:17; Colossians 1:4; 2:5; 1 Thessalonians 1:8; 3:2, 5, 10; 2 Thessalonians 1:3; Titus 1:1; Philemon 6; 1 Peter 1:9, 21; 2 Peter 1:5). On the phrase translated the *faithfulness of Christ* Wallace, who notes that the grammar is not decisive, nevertheless suggests that "the faith/faithfulness of Christ is not a denial of faith in Christ as a Pauline concept (for the idea is expressed in many of the same contexts, only with the verb πιστεύω rather than the noun),

might be justified by faith in Christ and not by works of law" seems preferable, especially in this context. A clear antithesis is presented between faith in Christ and works of law. Faith in Christ, then, cannot admit of any concept of merit on the part of the one believing—it is an abandonment of all pretended self-righteousness and an admission of utter helplessness in saving oneself or in bringing about one's own righteousness by good works. The one seeking to be justified by good works cannot, in Paul's thinking, be exercising true faith in Christ, for true faith in Christ holds solely and completely to Him as the source of salvation. Paul will say pretty much the same thing in Galatians 5:4.

because by the works of the law no one will be justified: The statement that works of law are utterly and completely useless to bring about the justification of anyone is here presented with the strong phrase "no one," or literally, "no flesh" (σάρξ). The Gentile is not going to be justified by law, and the Jew as well will find himself under God's wrath if he holds to his supposed righteousness gained from works of law. This is true of anyone who adds works of merit to faith in Christ Jesus.

Galatians 2:16 stands with the greatest passages in Romans as the charter of the gospel of free grace, the basis of *sola fide* and *Soli Deo Gloria.* Paul's opening salvo in response to Peter's hypocrisy is no radical departure from the teachings of Christ but is the common belief of the apostles, the heart of the message entrusted by the Lord to His church. Paul is not introducing a new teaching to Peter: he is reminding Peter of what he already knows and of what *should be* guiding his behavior. That Peter has no rebuttal shows that he is well aware of the common faith that is his with Paul. If we walk the path of the apostles today, we must, like them, hold as our common belief this firm, unwavering proclamation: We are justified *only* by faith in Jesus Christ and *never* by the righteous works we do in accordance with even the highest expression of God's moral will, His law.

---

but implies that the object of faith is a worthy object, for he himself is faithful" (*Exegetical Syntax,* 116). Though Paul elsewhere teaches justification by faith, this presupposes that the object of our faith is reliable and worthy of such faith.

2:17–19

> But if while seeking to be justified in Christ, we ourselves have also been found to be sinners, is Christ then one who encourages sin? Absolutely not! But if I build up again those things I once destroyed, I demonstrate that I am one who breaks God's law. For through the law I died to the law so that I may live to God.

NA[27] Text:

εἰ δὲ ζητοῦντες δικαιωθῆναι ἐν Χριστῷ εὑρέθημεν καὶ αὐτοὶ ἁμαρτωλοί, ἆρα Χριστὸς ἁμαρτίας διάκονος; μὴ γένοιτο. εἰ γὰρ ἃ κατέλυσα ταῦτα πάλιν οἰκοδομῶ, παραβάτην ἐμαυτὸν συνιστάνω. ἐγὼ γὰρ διὰ νόμου νόμῳ ἀπέθανον, ἵνα θεῷ ζήσω. Χριστῷ συνεσταύρωμαι·

These verses have given rise to many divergent interpretations, but the simplest seems to be this: by seeking to be justified solely by faith in Christ, the Jew has been forced to step down onto the same level as the "Gentile sinner" (ἁμαρτωλοί). So the question that might be asked by the Jew goes along the lines, "If this is what Christ does, that is, if His work results in the destruction of the law as a supposed source of righteousness, then doesn't this mean that Jesus becomes a 'minister of sin' in the sense that He forces us all into the same category of sinners, transgressors of the law?" Paul's answer is very quick, "Absolutely not!" Christ is not a minister of sin simply because the whole basis of the Jewish idea is found to be in error. How so?

Paul says, "But if I build up again those things I once destroyed, I demonstrate that I am one who breaks God's law." In other words, if the Jew is to go back to the law that he has destroyed as a source of righteousness (which was the erroneous assumption made in the first place), then he is, by going back to it, proving himself a transgressor for ever having left it! There is no way to wed law and grace; one will either go totally with faith in Christ or one will go with the law—there is no turning back, is Paul's point.

For through the law I died to the law so that I may live to God: Here is Paul's testimony, but it is also the testimony of every Christian down through the ages. How has he died to the law? In Christ Jesus. The righteous judgment of the law fell upon Christ in the Christian's place. This is what it means to "die to the law through the law." But once a person is dead, the law can no longer condemn him—the punishment has been exacted, and the law has nothing more to say. So, Paul asserts, his death to the law with Christ results in his ability to live "to God." The law is no longer that for which he lives, but God is the One for which he lives.

2:20

> I have been crucified with Christ; and it is no longer I who live, but Christ lives in me. So the life I now live in the body, I live because of the faithfulness of the Son of God, who loved me and gave himself for me.

NA[27] Text:
ζῶ δὲ οὐκέτι ἐγώ, ζῇ δὲ ἐν ἐμοὶ Χριστός· ὃ δὲ νῦν ζῶ ἐν σαρκί, ἐν πίστει ζῶ τῇ τοῦ ⸀υἱοῦ τοῦ θεοῦ⸁ τοῦ ἀγαπήσαντός με καὶ παραδόντος ἑαυτὸν ὑπὲρ ἐμοῦ.

| ⸀ θεου και Χριστου 𝔓[46] B D* F G (b) MVict ¦ *txt* ℵ A C D[1] Ψ 0278. 33. 1739. 1881. 𝔐 lat sy co

I have been crucified with Christ: Surely this is one of the most incredible statements in all of holy Writ. This is one of Paul's central themes of theology—the union of God's people with Jesus Christ. And this is the logical outcome of his emphasis upon being "in Christ" or "in Him": His death becomes the death of His people as well. Paul can say that he has been crucified together with Christ—Paul knows the historical fact of the death of Christ was personally relevant to himself. The new life that is his in Christ was made possible simply because he had truly and really died with Christ on the cross of Calvary.

Some feel that since Paul (and just about every other believer) was not physically present at Calvary that this somehow means that the reality of our death with Christ is lessened. But the greatest reality is God's reality; our limited perception is hardly to be taken as superior to God's eternal one. The fact that the Scriptures teach us we have been chosen in Christ Jesus before the foundation of the earth is the final arbiter of what is real and what is not. The believer was just as surely united with Christ on the cross as John was standing at the foot of the cross that dark day; in fact, though John was physically present, in God's reality he was also crucified with Christ, so closely is our Substitute identified with us in His sacrificial death.

This concept of dying with Christ is an integral part of Paul's whole concept of what it means to be "in Christ." Elsewhere he proclaims that we were made alive together with Christ as well (Ephesians 2:5) and seated with Him in the heavenly places. Of course, unlike some modern liberals who end up denying the importance of the actual historical Jesus and His death upon the cross, Paul never confuses the believer and Christ, even though he asserts the closest relationship between Christ, our Head, and each individual believer as part of the body of Christ. The believer has been crucified together with Christ; the believer does not become Christ, and Christ is still crucified. For Paul, without the historical events of the death, burial, and resurrection of Jesus Christ, there would be no redemption at all. God did indeed join us to Christ before we even existed, but our redemption was worked out in time, in history, on the hill called Golgotha.

and it is no longer I who live, but Christ lives in me: Our old selves have been crucified, and our life is now Christ.

So the life I now live in the body, I live because of the faithfulness of the Son of God: Again the NET takes the subjective view of the phrase πίστει τοῦ υἱοῦ τοῦ θεοῦ, over the more traditional, "faith *in* the Son of God." Our life is Christ, our all is Christ, and our life is a life of faith in the Son of God.[10] While we still live on in the flesh, and in so doing seek to glorify our Lord Jesus, ours is a different kind of fleshly life in that we have the life of Christ within us. Ours is a supernatural existence, one that is not limited simply to the natural. The lost man does not have this life, for he

---

[10]As the NET notes, a number of important witnesses (cited in the textual variant data given above) contain a reference to the deity of Christ here, referring to Christ as God.

has not died with Christ, and the life he has is still the same old fleshly life without Christ.

who loved me and gave himself for me: Here is a description of the Lord Jesus Christ in very specific language. Jesus has a special and unique love for His people. How does this passage indicate this? The participles translated "loved" (ἀγαπήσαντός) and "gave Himself" (παραδόντος) are both aorist participles; that is, they can function so as to indicate a point of action in time. Paul's consistent usage of the aorist to describe the love of Christ for His people may point to that one moment in time when He did indeed "love" His people by "giving Himself up" in their place. I believe Paul is referring to Christ's voluntary sacrifice of himself in this passage, and that therefore this "love" spoken of here would be a specific love of the elect, a love that is limited solely and completely to the people of God.

Paul uses the personal pronoun "me" in this passage (ἀγαπήσαντός με and παραδόντος ἑαυτὸν ὑπὲρ ἐμοῦ), and this is a confession that can be made by every single child of God—Christ loved me and delivered himself up in my place! What a tremendous truth! The life I live, this life of faith in Christ, is a life that is mine by virtue of my Lord, the one who loved me and proved His love by dying in my place, thereby accomplishing my redemption, my salvation.

Note as well that Christ delivered himself up in my place. That is, this is a voluntary action on Christ's part on behalf of His people. The same reflexive pronoun, *heauton* (ἑαυτὸν), is used of Christ's voluntary humiliation in Philippians 2:7. (Note the use of the preposition *huper* [ὑπὲρ] in this passage, a common way of indicating the substitutionary aspect of the death of Christ.)

2:21

> I do not set aside God's grace, because if righteousness could come through the law, then Christ died for nothing!

NA[27] Text:
οὐκ ἀθετῶ τὴν χάριν τοῦ θεοῦ· εἰ γὰρ διὰ νόμου δικαιοσύνη, ἄρα Χριστὸς δωρεὰν ἀπέθανεν.

Here is a ringing challenge to any and all who would attempt to add works of law to the gospel of free grace in Christ Jesus. For Paul, the actions of Peter were representing the same kinds of concepts being preached by the Judaizers in Galatia—Peter was saying, by his actions, that the Gentiles were lacking a righteousness that came by law (via circumcision). Paul throws at this concept a devastating truth: if righteousness comes by law, then why did Christ need to die? There is no need for the death of the Perfect Substitute if it is possible for man to gain a righteous standing with God through the means of the law. So, Paul asserts, the concept of works-righteousness or justification coming by obedience to laws and ordinances does two things: (1) it "sets aside" or "nullifies" (ἀθετῶ) the grace of God, and (2) it makes the sacrifice of Jesus Christ meaningless and needless (δωρεὰν). These are strong words, but they must be understood.

Paul's concept of grace is clearly seen here. He is stating the same truth that is expressed in Romans 11:6, "If it is by grace, it is no longer by works, otherwise grace is no longer grace." The concept of grace in Paul's teaching is mutually exclusive to the concept of meritorious works of law. It is obviously an either/or situation for Paul—it is black and white. Either one is made righteous by works of law, or one is made righteous by God's grace. One cannot possibly be made righteous by a mixture of works of law and grace! To attempt, then, to hold on to both the grace of God and works-righteousness is to nullify or set aside the grace of God or, as Paul will assert in Galatians 5:4, to "fall away from grace."

Also, if there were a means of righteousness in the law, then there would be no need for the death of Christ. But if the law cannot bring about righteousness, then the death of Christ is necessary and indeed the only and exclusive way of justification. The death of Christ, then, cannot admit any addition to it—either the death of Christ makes righteousness a reality or it does not. One cannot say that it simply makes righteousness a possibility that is dependent upon some other action of man—even if we limit man's "addition" to nothing more than faith!

CHAPTER 17

Grace, Faith, and Law

SYNOPSIS:

In this section we will focus only on the passages directly referring to justification. In this chapter Paul discusses the relationship of law and faith and also shows the priority of faith as the instrument of justification *to the exclusion of the mixture of works of merit.*

RESOURCES:

See notes from chapter 15, page 254.

MAIN PASSAGE:

3:1 You foolish Galatians! Who has bewitched you? Before your eyes Jesus Christ was vividly portrayed as crucified! **3:2** The only thing I want to learn from you is this: Did you receive the Spirit by doing the works of the law or by believing what you heard? **3:3** Are you so foolish? Although you began with the Spirit, are you now trying to finish by human effort? **3:4** Have you suffered so many things for nothing?—if indeed it was for nothing. **3:5** Does God then give you the Spirit and work miracles among you by your doing the works of the law or by your believing what you heard?

3:6 Just as Abraham "*believed God, and it was credited to him as righteousness,*" **3:7** so then, understand that those who believe are the sons of Abraham. **3:8** And the scripture, foreseeing that God would justify the Gentiles by faith, proclaimed the gospel to Abraham ahead of time, saying, "*All the nations will be blessed in you.*" **3:9** So then those who believe are blessed along with Abraham the believer.

3:10 For all who rely on doing the works of the law are under a curse, for it is written, "*Cursed is everyone who does not keep on doing everything written in the book of the law.*" **3:11** Now it is clear no one is justified before God by the law, because "*the righteous one will live by faith.*" **3:12** But the law is not based on faith, but "*the one who does* the works of the law *will live by them.*" **3:13** Christ redeemed us from the curse of the law by becoming a curse for us (because it is written, "*Cursed is everyone who hangs on a tree*") **3:14** in order that in Christ Jesus the blessing of Abraham would come to the Gentiles, so that we could receive the promise of the Spirit by faith. . . .

3:23 Now before faith came we were held in custody under the law, kept as prisoners until the coming faith would be revealed. **3:24** Thus the law had become our guardian until Christ, so that we could be declared righteous by faith. **3:25** But now that faith has come, we are no longer under a guardian.

3:1–5

NA[27] Text:

Ὦ ἀνόητοι Γαλάται, τίς ὑμᾶς ἐβάσκανεν, οἷς κατ' ὀφθαλμοὺς Ἰησοῦς Χριστὸς προεγράφη ἐσταυρωμένος; τοῦτο μόνον θέλω μαθεῖν ἀφ' ὑμῶν· ἐξ ἔργων νόμου τὸ πνεῦμα ἐλάβετε ἢ ἐξ ἀκοῆς πίστεως; οὕτως ἀνόητοί ἐστε, ἐναρξάμενοι πνεύματι νῦν σαρκὶ ἐπιτελεῖσθε; τοσαῦτα ἐπάθετε εἰκῇ; εἴ γε καὶ εἰκῇ. ὁ οὖν ἐπιχορηγῶν ὑμῖν τὸ πνεῦμα καὶ ἐνεργῶν δυνάμεις ἐν ὑμῖν, ἐξ ἔργων νόμου ἢ ἐξ ἀκοῆς πίστεως;

| ⸆ τη αληθεια μη πειθεσθαι C D² Ψ 0278. 33ᶜ. 1881 𝔐 vgᶜˡ syʰ; Hierᵐˢˢ ¦ *txt* ℵ A B D* F G 6. 33*. 81. 630. 1739 *pc* lat syᵖ co

You foolish Galatians! The whole idea of being justified by works of law rather than relying upon the grace of God causes the apostle to break out in an expression of wonderment.

Who has bewitched you?[1] *Before your eyes Jesus Christ was vividly portrayed as crucified!* Paul asks the identity of these who have cast a spell over the minds of the Galatian Christians, resulting in their inability to see the only logical outcome of the crucifixion of Christ—the completion of the law and the resultant necessity of faith alone in opposition to works of law. The death of Christ, Paul has just asserted, is made of no effect when people believe that righteousness can come from law. So if these believers had heard the message of Jesus Christ publicly proclaimed, and if they had responded in faith, why are they then following a different path than the one they originally set out on?

The only thing I want to learn from you is this: Did you receive the Spirit by doing the works of the law or by believing what you heard? Like a parent scolding a child, saying "just tell me this one thing . . ." so here Paul asks the wayward Galatians an obvious question. They had received the Holy Spirit of God—how did they do so? Was it their obedience to works of law that brought the Spirit into their lives? Did they obey a number of ordinances, and this resulted in their reception of the Spirit? No, of course not. Instead, they received the Spirit when they heard with faith. The Greek parallels ἔργων νόμου ("works of law") with ἀκοῆς πίστεως ("hearing of faith"). The construction can convey some of the following ideas: works that originate in law and hearing that originates with faith; legalistic works and faithful hearing. The idea is a contrast between works that are legalistic in nature and hearing that is intimately connected with faith and is, in fact, dependent upon faith for its very existence.

The reception of the Spirit was a sign, in Paul's theology, of

[1]The modern translations differ from the *Majority Text* and the KJV/NKJV based upon the *Textus Receptus* in not containing the parallel corruption, τῇ ἀληθείᾳ μὴ πείθεσθαι, taken from Galatians 5:7, probably due to simple scribal assimilation (i.e., the scribe was accustomed to the phraseology found in 5:7 and inserted the phrase out of familiarity with the other passage).

the redeemed (Ephesians 1:13–14). Therefore, since the presence of the Spirit in a person's life was evidence of his justification and redemption, then Paul asks a logical question: How did the Galatians receive the Spirit, by works of righteousness or by hearing of faith? And since the answer to this question was all too obvious, the only logical conclusion was that any teaching that said righteousness came about only *after* certain rites or rituals must be false on its face. So it remains today—anyone who adds "requirements" to the gospel such as sacraments, baptism, various forms of obedience, etc., falls into the same error that Paul here attacks. Everything in the Christian life, including such proper acts of obedience as baptism or the doing of good works as Paul taught elsewhere (Ephesians 2:10), follows *after* justification and is a result of the believer being in right relationship to God.

Paul's exasperation at the foolishness of the Galatians is evident in his words throughout the entire epistle, but is nowhere more clearly evident than in this passage. Incredulity fills his voice as he asks yet another rhetorical question. Why should anyone who recognizes the role of the Spirit in bringing about the Christian life think that after beginning by the Spirit they could possibly be perfected (or completed) by the flesh? The Christian life is begun by the Spirit, continued by the Spirit, completed by the Spirit. "The flesh profits nothing," Jesus taught, and Paul would wholeheartedly agree, especially here in reference to justification.

Have you suffered so many things for nothing?—if indeed it was for nothing: Paul's words should be closely examined. For him, it was quite possible that the willingness of the Galatians to accept such a false teaching, and to be duped into a works-salvation system, was indicative of a false faith—a mere profession of belief rather than the real Spirit-created article. The suffering that would have been theirs would have been due to their profession of faith in Christ. Yet we see here clearly that men can profess faith in Christ, and even suffer for His name, yet the possibility remains that they are not truly Christians, not truly believers. Great sincerity, deep devotion—both are wonderful things, but neither takes the place of the purity of the gospel. If one does not have the gospel, if one still holds to some kind of works-righteousness, then one is lost no matter how profusely one might confess the name of Christ.

Does God then give you the Spirit and work miracles among you by your doing the works of the law or by your believing what you heard? Is God's work limited by man's actions? Is the mighty Spirit of God dependent upon acts of human righteousness? Paul asserts that He is not, while all those who say that man must do this or that to gain justification are, by so teaching, limiting the work of God to the actions of men.

3:6–9

> Just as Abraham "*believed God, and it was credited to him as righteousness,*" so then, understand that those who believe are the sons of Abraham. And the scripture, foreseeing that God would justify the Gentiles by faith, proclaimed the gospel to Abraham ahead of time, saying, "*All the nations will be blessed in you.*" So then those who believe are blessed along with Abraham the believer.

NA[27] Text:

Καθὼς Ἀβραὰμ *ἐπίστευσεν τῷ θεῷ, καὶ ἐλογίσθη αὐτῷ εἰς δικαιοσύνην·* γινώσκετε ἄρα ὅτι οἱ ἐκ πίστεως, οὗτοι υἱοί εἰσιν Ἀβραάμ. προϊδοῦσα δὲ ἡ γραφὴ ὅτι ἐκ πίστεως δικαιοῖ τὰ ἔθνη ὁ θεὸς, προευηγγελίσατο τῷ Ἀβραὰμ ὅτι ἐνευλογηθήσονται ἐν σοὶ πάντα τὰ ἔθνη· ὥστε οἱ ἐκ πίστεως εὐλογοῦνται σὺν τῷ πιστῷ Ἀβραάμ.

Paul here presents what seems to have been his favorite example of justification by faith—the story of Abraham. One should, of course, cross-reference his comments here with the fuller discussion provided in Romans chapter 4.

Just as Abraham "believed God": A quick perusal of Genesis 15 reveals that Abraham, while certainly believing or accepting the promises of God relative to God's blessing of him and his becoming a great nation and inheriting the land, went beyond simply the acceptance of a nationalistic promise. Abraham believed *God.* He accepted the promises of God and showed by so doing that he believed God to be *trustworthy.* Abraham did not simply believe *promises*, but he believed *God*. The object of Abraham's saving faith was Yahweh, God himself.

"*and it was credited to him as righteousness*": On the basis of his faith, God reckoned Abraham as righteous (Genesis 15:6). We saw earlier that the Hebrew term צְדָקָה *(zedekah)* found in Genesis 15:6 and translated as "righteousness" contains the legal aspect of meaning that is clearly seen in the New Testament usage as well. That is, it is used to speak of a person being judicially declared to be in proper relationship to the law rather than speaking of any moral character or change within the individual.

We should note as well the term "reckoned" (חָשַׁב) corresponding to Paul's term "imputed" (λογίζομαι). In this context it refers to the giving of something without basis in the one so receiving; that is, it fits nicely with Paul's concept of grace as well as his doctrine of justification by faith (there is nothing in faith that inherently would merit justification).

so then, understand that those who believe are the sons of Abraham: The NET rightly understands the Greek verb γινώσκετε (*ginōskete*) as an imperative, "understand." Paul is insisting that they realize, on the basis of the text itself, that those who wish to be called the "sons of Abraham" are those who follow in the footsteps of faithful Abraham (see below, verse 9). "Those who believe" (literally, "those who are of faith") are clearly contrasted in Paul's thinking against those who are "of works." Faith versus works continues to be the underlying theme.

And the scripture, foreseeing that God would justify[2] *the Gentiles by faith:* It is Paul's firm conviction that what he is preaching is the message of the Old Testament Scriptures. He asserts that the Scriptures themselves foresaw (and therefore in a sense prophesied) that God would be about the business *of justifying the Gentiles by faith.* Again, the contrast is over against justification by works of law. Note as well Paul's view that comes out here: the Scriptures, strictly speaking, did not even exist at the time of God's promise to Abraham. Yet for Paul, the words of Scripture are so much the

---

[2]While δικαιοῖ is present tense, (hence, "does justify"), modern translations render it "would justify" due to προϊδοῦσα and προευηγγελίσατο, both of which move the temporal context into the past, looking "forward" to the present.

words of God that God's statements to Abraham, recorded in Scripture, can be personified as the Scriptures speaking (cf. Romans 9:17).

So then those who believe are blessed along with Abraham the believer: Paul's enemies in Galatia, the Judaizers, thought that "union" with Abraham was connected with a physical act—circumcision. But Paul shows that to be blessed together with Abraham is to exercise the same kind of *faith* he did. The attitude of one's heart toward God is what matters, not one's religious pedigree. The Jews did not understand this, for they felt that being the physical offspring of Abraham was sufficient.

3:10–14

> For all who rely on doing the works of the law are under a curse, for it is written, "*Cursed is everyone who does not keep on doing everything written in the book of the law.*" Now it is clear no one is justified before God by the law, because "*the righteous one will live by faith.*" But the law is not based on faith, but "*the one who does* the works of the law *will live by them.*" Christ redeemed us from the curse of the law by becoming a curse for us (because it is written, "*Cursed is everyone who hangs on a tree*") in order that in Christ Jesus the blessing of Abraham would come to the Gentiles, so that we could receive the promise of the Spirit by faith.

NA*[27] *Text:

Ὅσοι γὰρ ἐξ ἔργων νόμου εἰσίν, ὑπὸ κατάραν εἰσίν· γέγραπται γὰρ ὅτι *ἐπικατάρατος πᾶς ὃς οὐκ ἐμμένει πᾶσιν τοῖς γεγραμμένοις ἐν τῷ βιβλίῳ τοῦ νόμου τοῦ ποιῆσαι αὐτά.* ὅτι δὲ ἐν νόμῳ οὐδεὶς δικαιοῦται παρὰ τῷ θεῷ δῆλον, ὅτι *ὁ δίκαιος ἐκ πίστεως ζήσεται·* ὁ δὲ νόμος οὐκ ἔστιν ἐκ πίστεως, ἀλλ' *ὁ ποιήσας αὐτὰ ζήσεται ἐν αὐτοῖς.* Χριστὸς ἡμᾶς ἐξηγόρασεν ἐκ τῆς κατάρας τοῦ νόμου γενόμενος ὑπὲρ ἡμῶν κατάρα, ὅτι γέγραπται, *ἐπικατάρατος πᾶς ὁ κρεμάμενος ἐπὶ ξύλου,* ἵνα εἰς τὰ ἔθνη ἡ εὐλογία τοῦ Ἀβραὰμ γένηται ἐν Χριστῷ Ἰησοῦ, ἵνα τὴν ἐπαγγελίαν τοῦ πνεύματος λάβωμεν διὰ τῆς πίστεως.

For all who rely on doing the works of the law are under a curse: Paul here refers to those who would seek God's favor by the means of works of law (over against faith in the promises of God). Why does he allege that all such men are under a curse? Because of Deuteronomy 27:26: "Cursed is the one who will not pledge himself to keep the words of this law and do them" (LXX).

Without directly stating it, the counterpart to this citation could be found in such passages as Ecclesiastes 7:20, "There is not a righteous man on earth who continually does good and who never sins." If one is to seek righteousness in the law, then one must meet the law's exacting standards: perfection and nothing less. Since it is understood that no man has done "all which has been written in the book of the law," then it follows naturally that all men who follow this path are under the curse pronounced in Deuteronomy 27:26. This is the negative scriptural proof. The positive is given in the next verse.

Now it is clear no one is justified before God by the law, because "the righteous one will live by faith": Paul asserts that the Old Testament revelation not only made it clear that righteousness on the basis of law-keeping was not the way of salvation, but that it also maintained that faith in God *was* the way to follow. Even today, many Christians do not seem to recognize that the law was always secondary to God's grace. The law was given to Israel as a part of His gracious covenant with them, coming *after* the promise, not before, and never superseding God's grace in dealing with the people of Israel. When the law is seen as part of God's gracious dealings with Israel, it is seen to function exactly as Paul describes it later in this chapter: as God's means of showing us His perfect will, so that we can see clearly our own sin and need of the Savior, Christ Jesus.

Because of this, Paul asserts, it is *clear* that no man is made righteous (justified) by the law. Yet if it is so clear, why did so many in the past, and why do so many today, teach that we are justified by works of law? Many factors combine to answer that question, but by and large the answer lies in man's sin and prideful rebellion against God. The way of faith is the way of humble dependence—there is no place for pride, arrogance, or boasting.

Rather than accept God's way, man most often goes his own.

Note as well that no man is justified *before God* by law. There is a sense of justification as used by James (2:19–24) that takes place before men that is based upon works—that is, the vindication of our faith as true faith is based upon our actions before men. But James is not speaking of the justification of sinners in the sight of the holy God as Paul is here.

But the law is not based on faith, but "the one who does the works of the law will live by them": I understand Paul's meaning here to be a contrast between the attitude of faith toward God and the concept of human action and merit that is part of the Jewish understanding of the law. One does not simply *believe* in the law, but one *does* the precepts and commandments of the law. Paul has just asserted that the just shall live by faith, and he quickly points out that the faith here spoken of is not doing the commandments of the law but believing in the promises of God. So the Judaizers would be incorrect to say that being circumcised is the same as having faith toward God. The faith of which Paul speaks is not based upon observance of law but upon the acceptance of the promises of God. This again shows us the true nature of saving faith and the stark contrast between this divine faith and any hybrid version that attempts to join human merit or action.

Christ redeemed us from the curse of the law by becoming a curse for us: Here Paul proclaims the means by which men can be redeemed or delivered from the curse of the law that he has just (implicitly) declared to be upon all men. Christ has delivered us from this curse by acting as our substitute. He has been made a curse in our place, on our behalf. Paul then quotes from Deuteronomy 21:23 as evidence of this, "Cursed is everyone who hangs on a tree." The means of the death of the Messiah, crucifixion, is seen as a sign of the curse of God upon Him, and this, Paul asserts, as the perfect substitute for God's people. He who deserved no curse becomes a curse and in so doing provides redemption from the curse that was rightfully ours for not doing "all that is written in the book of the law." He who did do all that was written in the law takes the place of those who did not. As Peter puts it, "Because Christ also suffered once for sins, *the just for the unjust,* to bring you to God, by being put to death in the flesh but by being made alive in the spirit" (1 Peter 3:18).

The purpose of this substitution is then presented: *in order that in Christ Jesus the blessing of Abraham would come to the Gentiles.* The curse is upon all men, Jew and Gentile alike, and the death of Christ makes it possible for the blessing that was given to Abraham to be given to all, including the Gentiles, for by the death of Christ the power of the curse is broken. Because the Gentiles too can be redeemed, *we could receive the promise of the Spirit by faith.* The Spirit is not given on the basis of works of law but rather, as Paul had said earlier in this chapter in the section of rhetorical questions, by the "hearing of faith." Therefore, the Spirit is made available to men upon the basis of faith, not works, and is therefore available to all who are of the faith of Abraham even if they are not of Jewish blood.

3:23–25

> Now before faith came we were held in custody under the law, kept as prisoners until the coming faith would be revealed. Thus the law had become our guardian until Christ, so that we could be declared righteous by faith. But now that faith has come, we are no longer under a guardian.

NA*[27] *Text:

Πρὸ τοῦ δὲ ἐλθεῖν τὴν πίστιν ὑπὸ νόμον ἐφρουρούμεθα συγκλειόμενοι εἰς τὴν μέλλουσαν πίστιν ἀποκαλυφθῆναι, ὥστε ὁ νόμος παιδαγωγὸς ἡμῶν ⸀γέγονεν εἰς Χριστόν, ἵνα ἐκ πίστεως δικαιωθῶμεν· ἐλθούσης δὲ τῆς πίστεως οὐκέτι ὑπὸ παιδαγωγόν ἐσμεν.

| ⸀ εγενετο 𝔓46 B; Cl[pt]

Now before faith came we were held in custody under the law, kept as prisoners until the coming faith would be revealed: The law functioned as the boundary that confined the Jewish people under its tutelage. But this was a temporary, merciful thing—it was in view of the coming faith, that is, faith in Christ Jesus. Paul then provides one of the clearest explanations of the function of the law. He writes, "Thus the law had become our guardian until Christ." The law is a παιδαγωγὸς (pedagogue), a servant charged with the care and direction of a child. The term does not really refer to a teacher in the proper sense, and "schoolmaster" might give us the wrong impression. "Tutor" might be a little more accurate. Be that as it may, the law does not point to itself, it points to Christ. It does so now, and it has always been designed to do this. The law is *Christocentric*, or as Paul would put it in his later letter to the Romans, "For Christ is the end [Greek, τέλος, *telos*, "end, goal"] of the law [for] righteousness to all who believe" (Romans 10:4).

To attempt to understand law apart from Christ is to attempt to understand a calculator without mathematics—it is simply impossible. A calculator is for doing math; the law is to point us to Christ. The teachers in Galatia were attempting to make the law something it was never intended to be—that is, the vehicle of justification. God had intended, from eternity past, to justify men in Jesus Christ and in Him alone. The law is a vital part of His plan, most certainly, but to understand it the way the Judaizers did (or, indeed, as so many do today) is to miss its true significance and purpose.

We note in passing that there is a textual variant in this verse. 𝔓[46] and B *(Vaticanus)* read "the law *became*," while the rest of the manuscript tradition has "the law *has become*." The difference is between an aorist and a perfect. The vast majority of the tradition has the perfect tense, "has become," which would indicate that the law *remains* in this role—it continues to point us to Christ. This could be interpreted as saying that the law will always function in this way—directing sinners unto Christ—or it could also mean that the law continues to function in this way in the life of the believer. The next phrase would favor the first interpretation.

so that we could be declared righteous by faith: The law directs away from itself *to* Christ. There is no life-giving aspect to the law. While promises for the obedient ones are found in the law, there is no remedy for those who fall, outside of sacrifice. And since the "blood of bulls and goats can never take away sin" (Hebrews

10:4), we must be pointed to the perfect and complete sacrifice, the sacrifice of Christ. This is what cleanses from sin, and we exercise faith in the all-sufficiency of the Savior, Jesus Christ. Note again the passive instrumental aspect of faith regarding justification.

But now that faith has come, we are no longer under a guardian: Paul's use of "faith" in this passage runs from one extreme to another; that is, we are justified by faith, yet now we see the "coming" of faith, that is, *the* faith, the body of Christian truth, seen primarily in the coming of Christ himself, the object of faith. Faith has "come" in that Christ has come, and this has changed the situation for God's people. They are no longer under a tutor, for the reality has arrived. The goal of the law has now been made manifest.

CHAPTER 18

Fallen From Grace

SYNOPSIS:

In these verses the apostle Paul shows us the true *gravity* and vital importance of the gospel by using some of the strongest language in all of Scripture. Further, as Galatians 5:4 is often urged against the perfection of the work of Christ in saving His people, its true nature in its native context should be examined.

RESOURCES:

See notes from chapter 15, page 254.

MAIN PASSAGE:

5:1 For freedom Christ has set us free. Stand firm, then, and do not be subject again to the yoke of slavery.

5:2 Listen! I, Paul, tell you that if you let yourselves be circumcised, Christ will be of no benefit to you at all! **5:3** And I testify again to every man who lets himself be circumcised that he is obligated to obey the whole law. **5:4** You who are trying to be declared righteous by the law have been alienated from Christ; you have fallen away from grace. **5:5** For through the Spirit, by faith, we wait expectantly for the hope of righteousness. **5:6** For in Christ Jesus neither circumcision nor uncircumcision carries any weight—the only thing that matters is faith working through love.

5:7 You were running well; who prevented you from obeying the truth? **5:8** This persuasion does not come from the one who calls you! **5:9** A little yeast makes the whole batch of dough rise! **5:10** I am confident in the Lord that you will accept no other view. But the one who is confusing you will pay the penalty, whoever he may be. **5:11** Now, brothers and sisters, if I am still preaching circumcision, why am I still being persecuted? In that case the offense of the cross has been removed. **5:12** I wish those agitators would go so far as to castrate themselves!

5:1–6

NA[27] Text:

Τῇ ἐλευθερίᾳ ἡμᾶς Χριστὸς ἠλευθέρωσεν· στήκετε οὖν καὶ μὴ πάλιν ζυγῷ δουλείας ἐνέχεσθε. Ἴδε ἐγὼ Παῦλος λέγω ὑμῖν ὅτι ἐὰν περιτέμνησθε, Χριστὸς ὑμᾶς οὐδὲν ὠφελήσει. μαρτύρομαι δὲ πάλιν παντὶ ἀνθρώπῳ περιτεμνομένῳ ὅτι ὀφειλέτης ἐστὶν ὅλον τὸν νόμον ποιῆσαι. κατηργήθητε ἀπὸ Χριστοῦ, οἵτινες ἐν νόμῳ δικαιοῦσθε, τῆς χάριτος ἐξεπέσατε. ἡμεῖς γὰρ πνεύματι ἐκ πίστεως ἐλπίδα δικαιοσύνης ἀπεκδεχόμεθα. ἐν γὰρ Χριστῷ Ἰησοῦ οὔτε περιτομή τι ἰσχύει οὔτε ἀκροβυστία ἀλλὰ πίστις δι᾽ ἀγάπης ἐνεργουμένη.

5:1

Paul begins now another strong series of statements on the subject of the freedom of grace over against the concept of justification by obedience to laws and ordinances. Note the translation that places exclamation points at the end of many of the statements. These are strong denunciations of false teachings that are plaguing the churches of Galatia. This section will end with a statement by the apostle that is, quite possibly, the strongest we have from his pen (5:12). Paul is deadly serious in what he has to say.

Paul asserts that Christ set us free—free from the bondage of sin, free from the bondage of law that would direct us to do things in attempts to gain God's favor. He has, throughout the letter, presented the contrast between saving faith and works, between grace and law. When we keep in mind his audience, and the purpose of his writing, we will not lose our balance and reject the truth that Christians are to honor the law and to do good works.

We will see, though, that the law and good works cannot add to the work of Christ, and we will see that we cannot ever think that doing any of the law's commands is meritorious in God's sight, nor will we ever think that Christ's work as Savior is dependent upon our works or actions. Christ has set us free from that kind of thinking. We are free men, yet the drag of our sin causes us to go back to the "weak and beggarly" ways of the world (4:9 NKJV). Like the children of Israel, we desire to be in bondage in Egypt again. But Paul warns us in no uncertain terms that to seek justification outside of Christ and Him alone is to be enslaved to a yoke of slavery once more. Christ will not allow His Saviorhood to be shared by anyone!

Listen! I, Paul, tell you that if you let yourselves be circumcised, Christ will be of no benefit to you at all! Paul clearly signals the coming of a strong statement regarding truth and asserts that he, the apostle of Jesus Christ, is now informing any and all who would seek to undergo circumcision as an addition to the work of Christ (as previously discussed, 2:21), as a necessary step to justification, that they have a choice to make. They must either choose Christ or the law. They cannot join the two. If they undergo circumcision, Christ will be of no benefit to them. They will, by doing so, be demonstrating a fundamental misunderstanding of the nature of the gospel, of the very work of Jesus Christ. Paul informs anyone who will listen that Christ must be the Savior alone, or He will not be Savior at all.

The import of these words must be properly understood. As has been repeatedly demonstrated throughout the epistle, Paul does not believe that Christ can be a mere addition to our way of salvation. Indeed, Christ will suffer nothing to be added to His work as Savior. All or nothing. Christ or human merit. There can be no mixture, no compromise. The same could be said of the many false teachings that have developed since then. The Church of Christ denomination seeks to add baptism to the work of Christ. Paul would say to them, "I, Paul, say to you that if you undergo baptism, thinking that it brings about your salvation, Christ will be of no benefit to you!" And he would say the same to the modern Roman Catholic as well.

And I testify again to every man who lets himself be circumcised that he is obligated to obey the whole law: Paul sees that the law is a whole. If you choose to follow the law in any way as the means to justification, then you must follow it completely. It is not just that Christ demands complete allegiance—the law does as well! If the Galatians undergo circumcision, they must place themselves once again fully under the tutelage of the law. They must seek their justification from that source (and Paul has already shown the futility of this, since the law was never intended to bring about justification but was intended to point us to the Savior, Christ Jesus) and that source alone! They cannot simply choose what portions of the law they will or will not accept. If they take the first step down that road, there is no turning back.

You who are trying to be declared righteous by the law have been alienated from Christ; you have fallen away from grace: Paul makes his meaning crystal clear in verse 4. It is amazing to note that this passage has been used by those who would deny the perseverance of the saints and who would assert that grace is a state from which one can fall. Paul is not talking about such a subject at all! He defines his audience: he is not talking to those who trust in Christ and Him completely for salvation. He is referring to those who would seek to be justified by law, to those who would be deceived into thinking that they can add to the work of Christ—those who would desire to mix grace and works. If a person thinks he knows Christ and yet knows so little of His Saviorhood as to attempt to add to His work, Paul has news for him: he is not in Christ at all! He is severed from Him, separated from Him, out of the sphere of God's grace in salvation.

We would be wrong to misinterpret Paul's words. He is not saying that these people once were united with Christ but now have been separated; he is not saying that they once were in grace but now are not. The language does not indicate this. It speaks of the fact that they, by their attitude, are separated from Christ, and they have fallen far away from the grace of God. Their misunderstanding of the gospel is a serious thing indeed.

I have often used the following illustration. If one were to encounter a famous athlete in a hotel and, not recognizing him for who he is, treat him rudely, one would be separating or alienating oneself from the realm of ever receiving season tickets from this person to the sport in which they excel. The offender would never have actually been in the realm of receiving a favor from the star in the first place, but by his actions he is ensuring he will never enter that realm either.

In the same way, the person who seeks justification through the law is severed from Christ, not in the sense of once having clung solely to Him for salvation (the very nature of saving faith as we have seen repeatedly already), but in engaging in an attitude and action that is utterly contrary to the kind of faith that brings union with Christ. Such a person is "fallen away from grace," not because he once dwelt in grace, but because he has chosen the exact opposite realm of grace, that of law-keeping.

Another vitally important truth comes from these words. The Judaizers in Galatia, as far as we can tell from Paul's words, were not saying that faith in Christ was not the first requirement of the gospel. In fact, as we saw in 3:1–2, they were! They said faith was vital. They preached faith in Jesus. But they then *added to this message.* How many "gospels" today fall into this very trap, and hence under the condemnation of Scripture!

These words should be on our lips often when speaking to those who insist upon adding religious ceremonies, human works, or man's merit to the gospel of Jesus Christ. Paul warned his readers with strong words, for this is an issue with eternal consequences. If we love as strongly as Paul loved, we will not hesitate to speak this truth, either. It may be out of step with our modern culture, but it is nonetheless in perfect line with the apostles and prophets of the Bible.

For through the Spirit, by faith, we wait expectantly for the hope of righteousness: Paul contrasts "we" with those who refuse to trust solely in Jesus Christ for salvation. "Christians, on the other hand," Paul says, "through the work of the Spirit, who is the source of faith, await eagerly and patiently the full revelation of the righteousness which indeed has been given to us by God's declaration now, but will, at the coming of Christ, be declared publicly and abroad." This makes it clear again that the audience in the preceding verses is, strictly speaking, limited to those who have refused the righteousness of Jesus Christ by faith. We await the hope of righteousness through the Spirit by faith, not by attempting to perform certain works that add to our justification.

The Spirit of God, Paul tells us, causes us to have the kind of faith that rests in the finished work of Christ. The Spirit never compels men to misunderstand the function of the law; the Spirit never leads us to attempt to add works of law to God's sovereign grace. Therefore, those who are attempting to add works to the gospel show that they are not being led by the Spirit. The fact that the work of the Spirit is in line with sound doctrine has been seen before in Galatians and is part of Paul's entire theology. He had already asked them if, having begun in the Spirit, they were now being made perfect by the flesh. It certainly is not the Spirit who would lead someone to act in this way!

For in Christ Jesus neither circumcision nor uncircumcision carries any weight—the only thing that matters is faith working through love: Here is a wonderful summary statement of Paul's thought at this point. He walks the perfect balance: circumcision, as far as the Christian is concerned, means nothing. It adds nothing to one's justification; it is not a part of one's salvation. Yet Paul also says that uncircumcision means nothing too. Neither the circumcised nor the uncircumcised has anything of which to boast. The condition of the man has no meaning relevant to eternal life and justification. What, then, does matter?

Faith working through love: This is the thing that matters. Faith, true faith that comes from the Holy Spirit of God, is a faith that works through love. It is no dead faith, no empty faith that is inactive—a kind of faith that does not result in good works, that does not bring about a concern for the glory of God. It is a living faith that works, but that work is only through love. The manner in which faith works is the manner of love—love for God as Creator, love for God as Redeemer, love for God as Lord and Master. This is what matters in the Christian life—not the physical condition of the believer relevant to this religious ceremony or that.

Paul is not here opening the door for the insertion of some concept of mixture of faith and works so that faith "working" can be understood as "faith joining itself with works" as a basis of justification. ἐνεργουμένη, translated "working," means "to be effective, active, operative." The emphasis is not upon ἐνεργουμένη but upon πίστις δι' ἀγάπης, for this provides the contrast to the circumcision/uncircumcision issue.

5:7–12

> You were running well; who prevented you from obeying the truth? This persuasion does not come from the one who calls you! A little yeast makes the whole batch of dough rise! I am confident in the Lord that you will accept no other view. But the one who is confusing you will pay the penalty, whoever he may be. Now, brothers and sisters, if I am still preaching circumcision, why am I still being persecuted? In that case the offense of the cross has been removed. I wish those agitators would go so far as to castrate themselves!

NA*[27] *Text:
Ἐτρέχετε καλῶς· τίς ὑμᾶς ἐνέκοψεν τῇ ἀληθείᾳ μὴ πείθεσθαι; ἡ πεισμονὴ οὐκ ἐκ τοῦ καλοῦντος ὑμᾶς. μικρὰ ζύμη ὅλον τὸ φύραμα ζυμοῖ. ἐγὼ πέποιθα εἰς ὑμᾶς ἐν κυρίῳ ὅτι οὐδὲν ἄλλο φρονήσετε· ὁ δὲ ταράσσων ὑμᾶς βαστάσει τὸ κρίμα, ὅστις ἐὰν ᾖ. Ἐγὼ δέ, ἀδελφοί, εἰ περιτομὴν ἔτι κηρύσσω, τί ἔτι διώκομαι; ἄρα κατήργηται τὸ σκάνδαλον τοῦ σταυροῦ. Ὄφελον καὶ ἀποκόψονται οἱ ἀναστατοῦντες ὑμᾶς.

You were running well; who prevented you from obeying the truth? What does this mean? They were running the race; they were pursuing the goal in the Christian life. They had begun the race well. But then the situation changed. It is almost as if they have run off the course so as to no longer be following the goal, here defined by Paul as truth. The Christian follows the path of truth, pursuing truth. And how did this happen? Someone, Paul says, quite literally "cut in" on them, causing them to veer off course. Someone hindered their ability to run straight along the path set before them. Obviously, Paul is referring to the false teachers in Galatia, again by using the third-person form of address. Paul simply refuses to address these teachers directly, for they are not truly a part of the church but instead are intent upon the distortion of the gospel.

This persuasion does not come from the one who calls you. The siren call of works-righteousness, the concept that is nearly universal in all the religions of men, does not come from the One who originally, in love, called the believers unto himself (τοῦ καλοῦντος ὑμᾶς). It is a foreign element—an alien presence in the relationship of the One who calls and those who were called. And that it is not simply a benign presence is clear from his next statement.

A little yeast makes the whole batch of dough rise: Literally, "a little leaven leavens the whole lump!" Just a little error, a little deviation from truth can't be that bad, can it? I mean, we don't want to appear to be nitpickers, do we?

But Paul points out that the gospel of Christ is pure. A little bit of leaven—just a small amount compared to the whole—affects the entirety of the lump. You can have a great doctrine of the Bible, a great doctrine of the nature of God, and a great doctrine of ethical living, but if you allow the means of salvation to be twisted, changed, corrupted, the entirety of your doctrine—everything—is affected thereby. Truth is a whole, not a collection of parts that are not connected to one another. A little leaven leavens the whole lump. Christians, then, should be people who are very concerned about the accurate preaching and proclamation of the Word of God in all things.

I am confident in the Lord that you will accept no other view. But the one who is confusing you will pay the penalty, whoever he may be: The NET's "confusing you" is a little paraphrastic; "troubling you" is more accurate. While the purposeful perversion of the gospel by Paul's enemies resulted in confusion on the Galatians' part, it was not their purpose to confuse but to pervert.

Paul expresses confidence that the Galatians will recognize the truth of his words and that they will not rebel against his correction. In so doing he proclaims the judgment that will certainly come upon the "one" who is troubling them. Possibly this refers to a single false teacher, possibly a charismatic type of leader, who was responsible for the problems among the Galatians. Or possibly this one is a "representative single" that is meant to refer to each of the false teachers. In either case, the false teacher is held responsible for hindering the Christians from following the truth. Such strong words should surely cause all who engage in the teaching ministry to be ever more zealous in seeking to accurately present the truth of the Word.

Now, brothers and sisters, if I am still preaching circumcision, why am I still being persecuted? In that case the offense of the cross has been removed: As we have seen before, Paul was under attack by the false teacher(s) at Galatia. Perhaps we see this again in the background, for possibly Paul is heading off an attack upon himself regarding his own consistency. Certainly Paul could have been attacked with regard to the circumcision of Timothy (Acts 16:3), and perhaps this is what is in the back of his mind. But Paul denies that he is inconsistent, at one time preaching circumcision, another denying it, depending on what is most convenient at the time. Instead, he points out the persecution he is receiving as evidence of the fact that if he was indeed a circumcision preacher, why would those preaching the circumcision afflict him as they were?

Further, the preaching of the cross (which he seemingly puts in direct contrast to the concept of circumcision and therefore works-righteousness) is done away with if one preaches circumcision. The Jews will not stumble at the scandal of the crucified Messiah if one neglects to present the fullness of the sufficiency of that act by the Messiah. Add human works to the work of the

Messiah and you do away with the scandal. The Messiah did not have to die if we can receive righteousness in any other way (Galatians 2:21).

How tremendously important this is to Paul can be seen in the words that follow—words that are quite possibly the strongest words in the New Testament. Paul expresses this thought: *I wish those agitators would go so far as to castrate themselves!* In case this translation seems too rough, my own translation would be, "Oh, that the ones troubling you would even make themselves eunuchs!" Various renderings have been given, and a few representative samples will make the thought clear: ". . . let them go on and castrate themselves!" (TEV); "Would that those disturbing you would go and castrate themselves" (TLB, mar.); "I wish they would go the whole way and emasculate themselves!" (NIV); "Tell those who are disturbing you I would like to see the knife slip" (JB); "I wish those who unsettle you would mutilate themselves!" (RSV).

The false teachers were very concerned with the circumcision of their converts. Paul seemingly says that since these false teachers are so interested in playing with knives, would that they would go all the way! There is definitely anger directed toward those who would enslave believers to a false system that denies the sufficiency of Christ.

CHAPTER 19

Paul's Summary of Salvation to the Ephesians

SYNOPSIS:

The term "justification" does not appear in the letter to the Ephesians, so one might reasonably question the inclusion of an exegesis of Ephesians 2:1–10 in a work focused upon justification itself. However, so many of the same concepts are repeated here, and so clearly does the passage speak to the central issues of sin, inability, grace, and the relationship between faith and works that a large hole would be left in the presentation were it not addressed, if only briefly. The main weight will be focused upon 2:5–10.

MAIN PASSAGE:

2:1 And although you were dead in your transgressions and sins, **2:2** in which you formerly lived according to this world's present path, according to the ruler of the kingdom of the air, the ruler of the spirit that is now energizing the sons of disobedience,

2:3 among whom all of us also formerly lived out our lives in the cravings of our flesh, indulging the desires of the flesh and the mind, and were by nature children of wrath even as the rest. . . .
2:4 But God, being rich in mercy, because of his great love with which he loved us, **2:5** even though we were dead in transgressions, made us alive together with Christ—by grace you are saved!—**2:6** and he raised us up with him and seated us with him in the heavenly realms in Christ Jesus, **2:7** to demonstrate in the coming ages the surpassing wealth of his grace in kindness toward us in Christ Jesus. **2:8** For by grace you are saved through faith, and this is not of yourselves, it is the gift of God; **2:9** it is not of works, so that no one can boast. **2:10** For we are his workmanship, having been created in Christ Jesus for good works that God prepared beforehand so we may do them.

2:1–3

This important section of Scripture was touched upon in the main presentation of the doctrine of justification and in particular the fact of man's sin. The main issue that is directly relevant to the doctrine of justification is the passage's witness to the *deadness* of man in sin, his *captivity* to the power of the Adversary, the *self-centeredness* of his sinful life, and that man is, until regeneration and the giving of the gift of faith, "by nature a child of wrath" even as the rest. Just as in Romans 1:18–3:18, Paul here gives the bad news prior to the good news, though of course on a more compressed spectrum than in Romans. Still the same point is in view: There can be no works-righteousness, no righteousness at all, outside of what God provides in the righteousness of Jesus Christ. As William Hendriksen has put it,

> No doubt he did this in order that the Ephesians, having been reminded at some length (verses 1–3) of the dreaded darkness of death in which they formerly walked, would rejoice all the more when at last (verse 4 ff.) they are told that all this is now past, since God, in his infinite mercy, love, and grace, had caused the light of life to dawn upon them (yes, upon "us"). The more men learn to see the dimensions of their utterly lost

condition the more they will also, by God's grace, appreciate their marvelous deliverance.[1]

2:4

But God, being rich in mercy, because of his great love with which he loved us . . .

NA[27] Text:
ὁ δὲ θεὸς πλούσιος ὢν ἐν ἐλέει, διὰ τὴν πολλὴν ἀγάπην αὐτοῦ ἣν ἠγάπησεν ἡμᾶς . . .

"But God" (ὁ δὲ θεὸς) has been described as one of the most precious phrases in Scripture, and rightly so. The first three verses close the door upon all systems of works-salvation, for spiritually dead slaves who are oblivious to their incapacity are hardly candidates for success in any works-righteousness system, no matter how much place is given to "grace" therein. The depth of the fall necessitates the glory of the remedy. Man has no mercy for himself or his fellow man, but God is "rich in mercy."

Mercy is what happens when grace meets sin. God's love is called "great." It is the source from which the inexhaustible mercy of God flows. God's love is not some indiscriminate feeling that overrides His justice and holiness. God's love is active, here expressed first as a substantive (ἀγάπην αὐτου) and then as a verbal phrase, "with which He loved us" (ἣν ἠγάπησεν ἡμᾶς). The aorist verb "he loved" could be a general statement of God's love as it is experienced in the lives of believers, or it is possible that the aorist points to a particular point at which God's love was ultimately expressed.

In light of the use of the aorist for Christ's love for His people in Galatians 2:20, both uses could be referring to the fullest expression in action of God's love: the cross of Christ. The presence of a direct object, "us," cannot be overlooked, for even in human affairs we do not say "I love" without expressing an object any more than we say "I believe" without expressing, or assuming in

[1]William Hendrikson, *Ephesians* (Baker, 1989), 111.

the immediate context, an object. God's love is expressed clearly and with the infallible result of the salvation of those who receive His mercy (Ephesians 1:4–6).

2:5

> . . . even though we were dead in transgressions, made us alive together with Christ—by grace you are saved!

NA[27] Text:
καὶ ὄντας ἡμᾶς νεκροὺς τοῖς παραπτώμασιν συνεζωοποίησεν τῷ Χριστῷ, — χάριτί ἐστε σεσῳσμένοι —

The stark contrast of true Christian conversion is expressed in the space of half a dozen words. We were dead in sin (that's the contribution of man: transgression, sin, death) and yet God, being rich in mercy (there is a play on words here, the participle of εἰμί being used to describe God's "being" rich in mercy and man's "being" dead in sin) makes us alive with Christ. The subject of the verb "He made alive" (συνεζωοποίησεν) is God. God raises from the dead, and He does so only in union with Christ. Clearly the idea of being "in Christ" and hence being crucified together with Him (Galatians 2:20) flows directly into the idea of being made alive with Him in His resurrection (2:6).

Paul joins the Ephesians as he speaks of the work of God in that he does not say "you" but "we." Hendriksen points to this and says,

> And it is high time that this be done. The great throbbing heart of this marvelous missionary, a heart so filled with compassion, can wait no longer. Here then finally, after all these modifiers and in connection with the repetition in verse 5 of the words of verse 1 . . . comes the main clause: the subject and the main verb: "God (verse 4) . . . made alive" (verse 5). However, for the reason already given, the apostle chooses to take his stand alongside of the Ephesians. He is convinced that his own state (and, in fact, the state of all the Jews who in former days were trusting in their own righteousness for salva-

> tion) was basically no better than that of the Gentiles, and also that the new-found joy is the same for all. So instead of saying, "And *you* he made alive," he says, "And *us* he made alive." Now if this be a case of syntactical inconsistency it is one of the most glorious cases on record![2]

Man is the object of this work of God. Better, *dead* men are. The impossibility of works-salvation, self-righteousness, or any other kind of contribution to the act of regeneration is plainly taught by the text. This is the basis for the arguments of the Reformers regarding *monergism*, the belief that there is *one energy*, one force, that brings the sinner from spiritual death to spiritual life.[3] Surely in this passage there is only one force active in bringing about salvation: God. He makes alive (συνεζωοποίησεν), He saves (σεσῳσμένοι, the passive pointing to God's action, not man's), He raises (2:6, συνήγειρεν), He seats (2:6, συνεκάθισεν), etc.

As surely as the passage is monergistic on the exegetical level, it is likewise antipluralistic. That is, all of these actions are done "with Christ," meaning in view of our union with Him. No person who is not "in Christ" is made alive, raised up, seated in heavenly places, etc. The idea of universalism, of many ways of salvation, is utterly foreign to the apostolic witness.

The NET reflects the fact that the last phrase, "by grace you are saved," is periphrastic in nature and sets it apart accordingly. This phrase, repeated in verse 8, is a three-word summary of the essence of the gospel. Grace is the means, the realm, the power by which salvation takes place. Grace is *all*, and grace is *enough.* And this salvation is not merely some provisional or temporary state. Paul uses a perfect passive participle along with a finite verb to express the fact that we *have been* and *continue to be* saved[4] by

---

[2]Ibid., 116–17.

[3]As opposed to the much more popular view, *synergism*, which proposes a mutual cooperation between the power of God and some kind of "power" of man.

[4]Some grammarians believe the force of the periphrastic, where the finite verb *strengthens* the ongoing element of the perfect participle, had weakened or passed from use by the time of the writing of the New Testament. Others believe this force remains evident in the New Testament. Given the context of its usage here, it is difficult to explain the effort to insert the paraphrastic if there is no inherent meaning being attached to it.

that grace. Saved by grace, kept by grace: such is without question the Pauline doctrine.

2:6

> . . . and he raised us up with him and seated us with him in the heavenly realms in Christ Jesus, . . .

NA*[27] *Text:
καὶ συνήγειρεν καὶ συνεκάθισεν ἐν τοῖς ἐπουρανίοις ἐν Χριστῷ Ἰησοῦ, . . .

All of Christian salvation takes place only *in Christ,* and in these words it is impossible to avoid noting the *certainty* of the success of His work. It is understandable why "He raised us up with Him" would be placed in the past, but "He seated us with Him" is likewise placed in the past. It would seem that from the perspective of this passage, the work of salvation, embodied in Christ, is as finished as the historical reality of Christ's death, burial, and resurrection into heaven itself. The union of God's elect (Ephesians 1:3–11) with their head, Jesus Christ, assures all the saints throughout the ages that the Son will always fulfill the will of the Father and that the will of the Father is that the Son lose none of those entrusted to Him (John 6:38–39).

2:7

> . . . to demonstrate in the coming ages the surpassing wealth of his grace in kindness toward us in Christ Jesus.

NA*[27] *Text:
. . . ἵνα ἐνδείξηται ἐν τοῖς αἰῶσιν τοῖς ἐπερχομένοις τὸ ὑπερβάλλον πλοῦτος τῆς χάριτος αὐτοῦ ἐν χρηστότητι ἐφ' ἡμᾶς ἐν Χριστῷ Ἰησοῦ.

The seventh verse fills out the reason for the work of God in Christ in glorifying the elect (Romans 8:30). There is a demonstration, a showing, of the "surpassing wealth" (or riches) of

God's grace in the salvation of His people. This demonstration of the fullness of God's grace as it has been expressed in His kindness toward us in Christ Jesus is parallel to the words of Ephesians 1:5–6, "He did this by predestining us to adoption as his sons through Jesus Christ, according to the pleasure of his will—to the praise of the glory of his grace that he has freely bestowed on us in his dearly loved Son." God is glorified in the redemption of sinners, both now in time as well as in eternity itself.

The issue of the *demonstration* of the glory and grace of God has been lost, by and large, in much of modern evangelical theology, let alone practice. When Yahweh destroyed the land of Egypt by plague, He did so to demonstrate His power and His might. When He redeems His people, He does so to show "in the ages to come" the surpassing riches of His grace as they have been lavished in kindness upon a completely and utterly undeserving people.

2:8–9

> For by grace you are saved through faith, and this is not of yourselves, it is the gift of God; it is not of works, so that no one can boast.

NA*[27] *Text:
Τῇ γὰρ χάριτί ἐστε σεσῳσμένοι διὰ πίστεως· καὶ τοῦτο οὐκ ἐξ ὑμῶν, θεοῦ τὸ δῶρον· οὐκ ἐξ ἔργων, ἵνα μή τις καυχήσηται.

This passage has been considered one of the key summary statements of the gospel of Jesus Christ in all of Scripture, and rightly so, for it is intended to function as such. It is in the context of soteriology; it is not apocalyptic or parabolic in its language. The words used are understandable, its grammar fully translatable. There truly is no reason to place it in the "difficult to understand" or "obtuse passages" category. What it says it says plainly and clearly. And yet it is so forceful, so utterly devastating to the pride of man that clings tenaciously to a claim of some portion of the glory in salvation, that it is often dismissed and ignored.

The first phrase was seen in verse 5, "by grace you have been saved." Here this grand teaching is filled out by the addition of "through faith," which had not appeared in its presentation earlier. Verses 8 and 9 could be charted out, in essence, in the following fashion:

> Saved by grace through faith
> that [the preceding clause] does not come from men
> that comes from God as a gift
>   a gift that is free and not earned
> all of this so that no man may boast
> (but so that God's glory may be seen: v. 7)

Of course, great dispute has arisen over what Paul means by saying "and *that* not of yourselves." The most natural reading of the passage is to see the neuter demonstrative, *touto* (τοῦτο) as referring to the entirety of the preceding clause.[5] This would mean that all the elements of the work of salvation by grace through faith are not human in origin. The key objection is that this would make faith a gift as well, a fact borne out, however, by many other passages in Paul and the New Testament in general. But it would be utterly inconsistent with what Paul is saying to insert, right in the middle of all these divine actions, both before and after verse 9, the idea of a human act of faith that determines whether all those divine actions can actually take place! Besides this, the "role" of man, if such is a proper term, appears in verse 10, where the new believer is said to be the workmanship of God, ordained *unto* good works, as we will see below. So to insert a human (as opposed to divine) action in the form of some kind of autonomous act of faith in the midst of the apostle's description of the work of God in salvation does not make any sense.

A. T. Robertson, the renowned American Greek scholar, specifically denied any connection between *touto* and "faith" on the basis of the difference in genders in his *Word Pictures in the New Testament.* His comments, however, are derived more from theol-

---

[5]τοῦτο often takes a conceptual antecedent, as in 1 Thessalonians 3:3.

ogy than grammar, as has been pointed out.[6]

Another possible understanding of the neuter demonstrative *touto,* though rarely discussed, is to take it as an adverbial, meaning "and at that, especially not of your own works. . . ." But the previous understanding seems more in line with the thrust of Paul's teaching.

Just as justification is by faith, so the only avenue Paul presents of salvation is by grace through faith. Salvation does not find its origin in believers; it is a gracious gift, that which is freely given. In Romans 3:24 Paul taught we are justified *freely*; here salvation as a whole is a *gift.*

Paul denies any role to works in verse 9, following very clearly the outlines of his presentation in Romans and Galatians, including the assertion that boasting of any sort must be excluded. This goes directly to the idea of accomplishment and merit, something unknown in the apostle's soteriology. As John Calvin commented:

---

[6]As William Hendrikson observed:

> *That offered by A. T. Robertson.* Commenting on this passage in his *Word Pictures in the New Testament,* Vol. IV, p. 525, he states, "Grace is God's part, faith ours." He adds that since in the original the demonstrative "this" (and *this* not of yourselves) is neuter and does not correspond with the gender of the word "faith," which is feminine, it does not refer to the latter "but to the act of being saved by grace conditioned on faith on our part." Even more clearly in Gram. N.T., p. 704, he states categorically, "In Eph. 2:8 . . . there is no reference to διὰ πίστεως [through faith] in τοῦτο [this], but rather to the idea of salvation in the clause before."
>
> Without any hesitancy I answer, Robertson, to whom the entire world of New Testament scholarship is heavily indebted, does not express himself felicitously in this instance. This is true first because in a context in which the apostle places such tremendous stress on the fact that from start to finish man owes his salvation to God, to him alone, it would have been very strange, indeed, for him to say, "Grace is God's part, faith ours." True though it be that both the responsibility of believing and also its activity are ours, for God does not believe for us, nevertheless, in the present context (verses 5–10) one rather expects emphasis on the fact that both in its initiation and in its continuation faith is entirely dependent on God, and so is our complete salvation. Also, Robertson, a grammarian famous in his field, knew that in the original the demonstrative (*this*), though neuter, by no means always corresponds in gender with its antecedent. That he knew this is shown by the fact that on the indicated page of his Grammar (p. 704) he points out that "in general" the demonstrative "agrees with its substantive in gender and number." When he says "in general," he must mean, "*not always* but most of the time." Hence, he should have considered more seriously the possibility that, in view of the context, the exception to the rule, an exception by no means rare, applies here. He should have made allowance for it. Finally, he should have justified the departure from the rule that unless there is a compelling reason to do otherwise the antecedent should be looked for in the immediate vicinity of the pronoun or adjective that refers to it.

Ought we not then to be silent about free-will, and good intentions, and fancied preparations, and merits, and satisfactions? There is none of these which does not claim a share of praise in the salvation of men; so that the praise of grace would not, as Paul shews, remain undiminished. When, on the part of man, the act of receiving salvation is made to consist in faith alone, all other means, on which men are accustomed to rely, are discarded. Faith, then, brings a man empty to God, that he may be filled with the blessings of Christ. And so he adds, not of yourselves; that claiming nothing for themselves, they may acknowledge God alone as the author of their salvation. . . . This passage affords an easy refutation of the idle cavil by which Papists attempt to evade the argument, that we are justified without works. Paul, they tell us, is speaking about ceremonies. But the present question is not confined to one class of works. Nothing can be more clear than this. The whole righteousness of man, which consists in works,—nay, the whole man, and everything that he can call his own, is set aside. We must attend to the contrast between God and Man, between grace and works. Why should God be contrasted with man, if the controversy related to nothing more than ceremonies?

Papists themselves are compelled to own that Paul ascribes to the grace of God the whole glory of our salvation, but endeavor to do away with this admission by another contrivance. This mode of expression, they tell us, is employed, because God bestows the first grace. It is really foolish to imagine that they can succeed in this way, since Paul excludes man and his utmost ability,—not only from the commencement, but throughout,—from the whole work of obtaining salvation.

But it is still more absurd to overlook the apostle's inference, lest any man should boast. Some room must always remain for man's boasting, so long as, independently of grace, merits are of any avail. Paul's doctrine is overthrown, unless the whole praise is rendered to God alone and to his mercy. And here we must advert to a very common error in the interpretation of this passage. Many persons restrict the word gift to faith alone. But Paul is only repeating in other words the former sentiment. His meaning is, not that faith is the gift of

> God, but that salvation is given to us by God, or, that we obtain it by the gift of God.[7]

2:10

> For we are his workmanship, having been created in Christ Jesus for good works that God prepared beforehand so we may do them.

NA[27] Text:
αὐτοῦ γάρ ἐσμεν ποίημα, κτισθέντες ἐν Χριστῷ Ἰησοῦ ἐπὶ ἔργοις ἀγαθοῖς οἷς προητοίμασεν ὁ θεὸς, ἵνα ἐν αὐτοῖς περιπατήσωμεν.

No believer in Christ can ever boast for the simple reason that we are the workmanship of Another. We have not formed ourselves but are instead the glorious work of God the Father in Christ Jesus. Just as Paul referred to believers as "pots" in Romans 9:21–23, so here he refers to Christians as created by God. This refers, in context, to their state *as believers.* A Christian is such solely because of the activity of God who has brought him into the state of salvation. More clear monergism.

But as in every other passage, this activity of the Father is solely *in Christ.* The salvific work of the Father in "creating" the redeemed is strictly limited to creation in Christ Jesus.

Special attention should be given to the phrase "for good works" (ἐπὶ ἔργοις ἀγαθοῖς). This provides the end to which Christians are "created" in Christ. Christians are not created *by* good works, but *for* good works. This single consideration provides the balanced understanding of grace, faith, and good works in the Christian life.

It is the inherent tendency of man to reverse the order, making his actions the grounds upon which God is then "enabled" to save. But this is *not* the divine order. God saves by grace. God forms or creates believers and He does so for a purpose: that they might perform good works. Indeed, so much is this the goal of

---

[7]John Calvin, *Commentary on the Epistle to the Ephesians* in *The Comprehensive John Calvin Collection* (Ages Digital Library, 1998).

His work in their lives that Paul says these good works are foreordained, "prepared beforehand" so that we might do them (literally, "walk in them," i.e., as a habit or way of life).

The good works do not form Christians or in any way provide a basis of boasting (καύχησις), for Paul clearly denied this earlier. The proper order is salvation solely by God's grace to His glory alone, resulting in a changed life that is marked by doing good works as a matter of course. The renewed heart/nature does good works with the natural ease that the old nature lived in sin and rebellion. But the order cannot be reversed, for to do so is to undercut the entire message of grace.

CHAPTER 20

James Attacks Empty Faith

SYNOPSIS:

The entire purpose of James 2:14–26 can be summarized by the words "show me." It is the apostle's intention to call Christians to the very same living faith that Paul speaks of in Ephesians 2:10. This exhortation of Christians is not addressing how the ungodly are declared righteous before God, but how that declaration is shown outwardly in the Christian life. As such it is a penetrating and convicting call to godly living that is perfectly consistent with Paul's doctrine of God as the gracious Justifier of His elect people.

RESOURCES:

James Adamson, "The Epistle of James" in *The New International Commentary on the New Testament* (Eerdmans, 1976).

Peter Davids, "The Epistle of James" in *The New International Greek Testament Commentary* (Eerdmans, 1982).

Ronald Y. K. Fung, "Justification in the Epistle of James" in *Right With God: Justification in the Bible and the World*, D. A. Carson, ed., (World Evangelical Fellowship, 1992).

Zane Hodges, *The Epistle of James* (Grace Evangelical Society, 1994).

Luke Timothy Johnson, *The Letter of James: A New Translation with Introduction and Commentary* (Doubleday, 1995).

Ralph Martin, "James" in the *Word Biblical Commentary* (Word, 1988).

Joseph Mayor, *The Epistle of James* (Kregel, 1990).

Douglas Moo, "The Epistle of James" in the *Pillar New Testament Commentary* (Eerdmans, 2000);

———,"The Letter of James" in the *Tyndale New Testament Commentaries* (Eerdmans, 1985).

MAIN PASSAGE:

2:14 What good is it, my brothers and sisters, if someone claims to have faith but does not have works? Can this kind of faith save him? **2:15** If a brother or sister is poorly clothed and lacks daily food, **2:16** and one of you says to them, "Go in peace, keep warm and eat well," but you do not give them what the body needs, what good is it? **2:17** So also faith, if it does not have works, is dead being by itself.

2:18 But someone will say, "You have faith and I have works." Show me your faith without works and I will show faith by my works. **2:19** You believe that God is one; well and good. Even the demons believe that—and tremble with fear.

2:20 But would you like evidence, you empty person, that faith without works is useless? **2:21** Was not Abraham our father justified by works when he offered Isaac his son on the altar? **2:22** You see that his faith was working together with his works and his faith was perfected by works. **2:23** And the scripture was fulfilled that says, "*Now Abraham believed God and it was counted to him for righteousness,*" and *he was called God's friend.* **2:24** You see that a person is justified by works and not by faith alone. **2:25** And similarly, was not Rahab the prostitute also justified by works when she welcomed the messengers and sent them out by another way? **2:26**

For just as the body without the spirit is dead, so also faith without works is dead.

Work on this passage since the Reformation has been deeply influenced by the polemic citation of the text by both sides in the debate over justification. The breakdown in believing exegesis has likewise led to the constant discussion of whether James was, in fact, contradicting, or even warring against, Paul or the "Pauline faction" in the primitive church. As with all previous passages, we will exegete the text on the basis of faith in the text as θεόπνευστος γραφή, starting with the conviction that the same Holy Spirit who spoke through Paul spoke through the words of James as well.

The primary passage does not introduce any disjunction in the argument James is presenting. It flows without any radical break from the preceding section (2:1–13), and the same audience is addressed in 2:1; 2:14; and 3:1, showing the continuity of discourse (Ἀδελφοί μου, "my brothers"). What is vital to note is that the nature of the polemic does not change, either: James is still exhorting Christians to live in light of their profession of faith "in our glorious Lord Jesus Christ" (2:1). This is vital, for the context of 2:14–26 must be fully integrated into the exegesis. The meaning of such terms as "faith," "works," and "justify" cannot be ascertained outside of the context in which James uses them.

James 2:14–26 forms a single argument: verse 26 could be quoted immediately after verse 14 and the meaning would remain intact. Hence, a single point needs to be ascertained from the section. Once the primary thrust of the author is determined, other issues can then be addressed, but often this is not accomplished in the comments offered on the passage. The cohesiveness of the section likewise highlights the necessity of allowing the head verse (14) its proper place in determining the meaning of the rest of the passage. James defines the kind of faith he is decrying in his opening statement, and he concludes with the same kind of dead faith at the end of the section. While true faith is noted (by contrast) in the section, the point is the same all the way through: deedless faith is not saving faith. To miss this point is to ignore the forest while staring at a single tree.

In similar fashion the literary genre of James is unmistakable and important to a proper understanding of his message. Most commentaries draw the parallels between James and various popular forms of wisdom and morality literature.[1] Surely there are a number of works, Jewish and otherwise, that provide striking similarities to James's strong exhortation of moral behavior. Comparisons to Matthew's rendition of the Sermon on the Mount as well as to the *Didache* have been drawn, and properly so,[2] for James fits in the same kind of moral teaching/wisdom type of literary genre.

Likewise 2:14–26 is the negative application of the positive command of a preceding section of James, specifically 1:22–26. There James exhorts his brothers and sisters in Christ to live out the gospel so as not to deceive themselves. Notice his words:

> **1:22** But be sure you live out the message and do not merely listen to it and so deceive yourselves. **1:23** For if someone merely listens to the message and does not live it out, he is like someone who gazes at his natural face in a mirror. **1:24** For he gazes at himself and then goes out and immediately forgets what sort of person he was. **1:25** But the one who peers into the perfect law of liberty and sticks with it, and does not become a forgetful listener but one who lives it out—he will be blessed in what he does. **1:26** If someone thinks he is religious and does not control his tongue but deceives his heart, his religion is futile.

The positive-form parallels to 2:14–26 are striking and must be acknowledged: living out the message (literally, "doing" the word) is contrasted with merely hearing it and doing nothing more (the reverse parallel to saying one believes and yet has no works). In both the situation is clearly unnatural: looking in a mirror and then walking away and forgetting what you saw is as problematic positively as claiming to have faith and having no deeds is negatively. James condemns an abnormality in both passages: in

[1]Peter Davids, *The Epistle of James* in *The New International Greek Testament Commentary*, (1982), 22–57.

[2]Ralph Martin, *James* in the *Word Biblical Commentary* (Word, 1988), lxxv–lxxvii.

1:22–24 we see the abnormality of the forgetful hearer, and in 2:14–26 the abnormality of the faith-claimer who has no evidence to back up his profession.

Thus, 2:14–26 should be seen as an elaboration, a sermon illustration in the negative, pursuing the same goal of exhortation of godly living found both before and after its appearance in the epistle. The same "abnormality" theme appears only a few sentences later, in 3:9–11, where James addresses the inherent contradiction in a mouth that both blesses and curses. "These things should not be so" James says in 3:10. In the same way, anyone *claiming* faith should not be left without the first bit of evidence to show the *reality* of that faith.

In the course of the exegesis major points that impact the entire passage will be noted (such as the use of the translation "deeds" over against "works"). The key issues arise within the first paragraph, such as the nature of faith, what kind of "works" are under discussion, etc.

2:14

> What good is it, my brothers and sisters, if someone claims to have faith but does not have works? Can this kind of faith save him?

Alternates:

> What good is it, my brothers, if a man claims to have faith but has no deeds? Can such faith save him? (NIV)

> What use is it, my brothers, if someone says he has faith but does not have deeds? Is the faith able to save him? (Luke Timothy Johnson, *The Letter of James*, 236)

NA*[27] *Text:

Τί τὸ ὄφελος, ἀδελφοί μου, ἐὰν πίστιν ⸉λέγῃ τις⸊ ἔχειν ἔργα δὲ μὴ ἔχῃ; μὴ δύναται ἡ πίστις σῶσαι αὐτόν;

| ⸉ *2 1* A C *pc* ¦ λεγεις 049

The text of the verse presents no difficult variants, and its translation is not questioned in the main. However, one significantly important syntactical issue must be addressed, that being the translation of the last phrase and in particular the presence of the definite article ἡ before the word πίστις *(faith)*. As this is the opening statement of James's thesis for 2:14–26, we need to take special care in our understanding of what he intends to communicate.

What good is it, my brothers: literally, "what benefit or gain" is there? The phrase is repeated in 2:16, and the question is rhetorical. There is no benefit or substance to the claim being made, any more so than there is in 16. The NET takes the plural masculine as a generic plural for the entire Christian congregation ("brothers and sisters"), recognizing that the words of James apply equally to men and women.

if someone claims to have faith but does not have works? Literally the text reads, "says" rather than "claims," but the NET translation is very accurate, retaining the infinitival form "to have." James presents a hypothetical question: Is there any benefit or use in the *claim* of a person to be in possession (ἔχειν) of faith (πίστιν, placed first in the clause for emphasis) when he is *not* in possession of ἔργα, *deeds*? Two immediate issues confront us:

First, the subjunctive λέγῃ *(says, claims)* will be expanded upon by James throughout the section. It is plainly his intention to contrast the mere *claim* existing only in the realm of words with the true possession of real faith that is demonstrated by something more than mere speaking. Hence the accuracy of the NET's "claims," for this carries more forcefully in English the idea of *empty profession* than merely "says." This translation will be seen to fully fit James's application in the next two verses.

Next, what is the correct translation of ἔργα? Obviously both "deeds" and "works" fit the original meaning. Johnson comments, "The translation of *erga* as 'deeds' attempts to represent more accurately the point as well as to avoid precipitous or inaccurate comparisons with Paul."[3]

A person seeking to equate Paul's context with James's context will object to such a translation. Paul's normative use of ἔργα is

---

[3]Luke Timothy Johnson, *The Letter of James* (Doubleday, 1995), 237.

actually perfectly in line with that of James. Paul often speaks of deeds done in righteousness that flow from a changed heart. Indeed, Paul teaches that we are saved by grace through faith *unto* good works (Ephesians 2:8–10). He insists that it is God's purpose that we should "walk in" or "live in" doing good works (ἔργοις ἀγαθοῖς).

Yet we also know Paul says that "no one is declared righteous before him by works of the law" (Romans 3:20) and that "God credits righteousness apart from works" (Romans 4:6 NASB). So it is primarily in Paul that we see the same Greek term being used in more than one sense. Since the confusion generated by this passage is due to the errant assertion that James is addressing the same context that Paul addresses in his decrying of "works," choosing, with Johnson and the NIV, to use the term "deeds" makes perfect sense, and the wisdom of the translation will be borne out throughout the exegesis of the text.

has no deeds: We should not assume that this means the person is morally neutral. No one is. Instead, this person *has no actions by which to demonstrate the existence of the reality of the claimed faith.* He has nothing in the realm of the demonstrable that is consistent with the Christian claim, "I believe."

Can this kind of faith save him? The phrase begins with μή, indicating the expected answer is negative: "No, that kind of faith cannot save." Here the issue of the translation of ἡ πίστις comes into play. The KJV and NKJV render the phrase without reference to the definite article: "Can faith save him?" The *Textus Receptus*, however, reads identically to the *NA*[27] in having the article before πίστις. Most translations recognize this as the anaphoric use of the article, pointing back to the previous appearance of the same term (i.e., to the faith that has no works). Hence the NASB reads "that faith"; the NIV "such faith"; the NET, "this kind of faith"; ASV, "that faith"; NLT, "that kind of faith," etc. Yet some, including the NRSV, leave the article untranslated.

Daniel B. Wallace lists this as an example of the anaphoric use of the article. He commented on this passage after rendering it "this kind of faith":

> The author introduces his topic: faith without works. He then

> follows it with a question, asking whether this kind of faith is able to save. The use of the article both points back to a certain kind of faith as defined by the author and is used to particularize an abstract noun.
>
> Against the vast bulk of commentators, Hodges argues that the article is not anaphoric, since otherwise the articular πίστις in the following verses would also have to refer back to such a workless faith. He translates the text simply as "Faith cannot save him, can it?" Although it may be true that the article with πίστις in vv 17, 18, 20, 22, and 26 is anaphoric, the antecedent needs to be examined in its own immediate context. In particular, the author examines two kinds of faith in 2:14–26, defining a non-working faith as a non-saving faith and a productive faith as one that saves. Both James and Paul would agree, I believe, with the statement: "Faith alone saves, but the faith that saves is not alone."[4]

The passage makes a firm statement: a faith that exists only in words (one that is "claimed") but has no evidence of its existence in actions (deeds) is a faith that cannot save. It is non-salvific, or lacks the ability to save. As such, the question can profitably be asked, "Does it follow that a faith that exists both in word and in deed can, in fact, save?" The answer would seem to be yes. It can and does in James's understanding of the gospel. It should be remembered that the Protestant doctrine of *sola fide* has *never* meant "faith in isolation" but instead "faith alone without the addition of human works of merit." James is not addressing such a concept of faith here: his assertion is that "this kind" of words-only, deedless faith simply cannot save.

2:15–16

> If a brother or sister is poorly clothed and lacks daily food, and one of you says to them, "Go in peace, keep warm and eat well," but you do not give them what the body needs, what good is it?

[4]Daniel B. Wallace, *Greek Grammar Beyond the Basics—Exegetical Syntax of the New Testament* (Galaxie Software, 1999), 219.

NA*[27] *Text:
ἐὰν ἀδελφὸς ἢ ἀδελφὴ γυμνοὶ ὑπάρχωσιν καὶ λειπόμενοι τῆς ἐφημέρου τροφῆς εἴπῃ δέ τις αὐτοῖς ἐξ ὑμῶν· ὑπάγετε ἐν εἰρήνῃ, θερμαίνεσθε καὶ χορτάζεσθε, μὴ δῶτε δὲ αὐτοῖς τὰ ἐπιτήδεια τοῦ σώματος, τί τὸ ὄφελος;

James provides an illustration that fills out the strong assertion ending verse 14. The repetition of τί τὸ ὄφελος; ("What use is it?") at the end of 16 shows that 14–16 are one unit. His example is simple, yet it casts great light upon his thesis. A brother or sister is in simple need of food and clothing. "One of you" (τις ἐξ ὑμῶν) makes the application *very* personal and *very* direct. Again the words uttered have no corresponding reality in actions. The wishing of peace and fulfillment is an empty line of words unless it is backed up by action, for the words are action words.

Be warmed! Be filled! These are words that require action to be meaningful. Yet no actions are undertaken, and hence the words carry no meaning. The same inconsistency exists here between saying "be filled" without providing bread that exists between a mouth that blesses at one moment and curses at the next. This is the inconsistency, the abnormality, that James decries. The speaking of the words is said by James to be useless, just as saying "I believe" without having any corresponding evidence of the reality of faith is useless. There is a direct parallel in 1 John 2:4–6, where we read,

> The one who says "I have come to know God" and yet does not keep his commandments is a liar, and the truth is not in such a person. But whoever obeys his word, truly in this person the love of God has been perfected. By this we know that we are in him. The one who says he resides in God ought himself to walk just as Jesus walked.

"The one who says" here in 1 John (ὁ λέγων) is parallel to the πίστιν λέγῃ of 2:14 and the εἴπῃ δέ τις αὐτοῖς of 2:16. There is a fundamental inconsistency between the profession of knowledge of God and a lifestyle of rebellion: John uses the plain term "liar" to describe this false confession. James might well call the claim of faith that has no proof of its existence a lie as well.

2:17

So also faith, if it does not have works, is dead being by itself.

Alternates:

So also faith, if it does not have deeds, is by itself dead. (Johnson).

So with faith; if it does not lead to action, it is in itself a lifeless thing. (NEB)

NA[27] Text:

οὕτως καὶ ἡ πίστις, ἐὰν μὴ ἔχῃ ἔργα, νεκρά ἐστιν καθ' ἑαυτήν.

James then connects his illustration directly back to his original thrust and provides his first summary point (using οὕτως): a faith that is alone, solitary, unsubstantiated, is dead. Translations differ as to whether the final phrase is best understood as "faith by itself is dead" or if it is "*that kind* of faith is dead by itself" i.e., in its very essence. The first could be called a tautology that would amount to a strong emphasis by James upon the "aloneness" of this dead faith. The other viewpoint would emphasize the fact that a workless faith is, by nature, dead or lifeless. There really isn't all that major a difference in the final interpretation of the verse no matter how one understands the relationship of καθ' ἑαυτήν to the rest of the sentence. In either case, James here expands upon the earlier use of τί τὸ ὄφελος ("what use is it?") and now makes the blanket statement that the kind of faith he has denounced from verse 14 is dead, lifeless, and therefore useless to bring about salvation.

Obviously, the reverse of this assertion would be that faith that does possess deeds would be a living faith that, we would then assume, can save. Saving faith, by nature, will ἔχῃ ἔργα, possess deeds. Dead faith, by nature, is useless due to the fact that it lacks *a constituent part of saving faith,* that being evidence of its existence in the form of deeds. Already one conclusion can be drawn: The contrast in this passage is not between *faith* and *works* but between *dead faith* and *living faith.*

2:18

> But someone will say, "You have faith and I have works." Show me your faith without works and I will show faith by my works.

Alternate:

> But someone may *well* say, "You have faith and I have works; show me your faith without the works, and I will show you my faith by my works." (NASB)

NA[27] Text:

Ἀλλ᾽ ἐρεῖ τις, σὺ πίστιν ἔχεις, κἀγὼ ἔργα ἔχω· δεῖξόν μοι τὴν πίστιν σου ⸀χωρὶς τῶν ἔργων, κἀγώ σοι δείξω ἐκ τῶν ἔργων μου τὴν πίστιν⸆.

| ⸀εκ 𝔓[54vid] 𝔐; Cass ¦ *txt* ℵ A B C P Ψ 33. 69. 81. 614. 1241. 1505. 1739 *al* latt sy co
| ⸆μου 𝔓[74] A p[vid]𝔐 vg sy ¦ *txt* ℵ B C Ψ 33. 81. 323. 614. 630. 1241. 1505. 1739 *al* ff

Commentators are united in one thing regarding James 2:18: it is a very difficult text, mainly because of the problem it presents in interpreting the punctuation of the passage. As one can see from a quick glance at the most popular translations, there are a number of possible interpretations. Some make the entire verse one quotation (NASB), while others stop the quotation after the third clause, κἀγὼ ἔργα ἔχω (NET). Aside from these two possibilities, another that has much to commend it would break the text down as follows:[5]

> But someone will say, "Do you have faith?" And I *will say,* "I have works. Show me *your faith* apart from your works, and I by my works will show you my faith."

[5]See the discussion in Ronald Fung, *Justification in the Epistle of James* in D. A. Carson, *Right with God* (1992), 148–51.

This then flows into verse 19, "*You believe* that God is one. . . ." Each possibility has arguments to commend it, and each can be understood logically. But a key issue is the fact that it would seem the introductory phrase "But someone will say" should introduce the words of an objector, an opponent. Unless we understand the initial words of this interlocutor as a question, we are forced to attempt to understand the statement in one of two ways. First, if we take only the second and third clauses as the quotation, we have the words of a person who is not so much an objector to James as one who is promulgating some theory that separates faith from works, as if works by themselves could avail. But this hardly fits with the flow of the text or the purpose of James. Second, if we take the entire verse as a single quotation, it makes perfect sense only if we view the person saying these words as *agreeing* with James's thesis rather than being an *objector.* The final sentence ("show me your faith without the works, and I will show you my faith by my works") is surely the conviction and position of James. So some theorize this is a supporter of James's position. However, this conclusion seems highly unlikely.

The third possibility, while fitting the context better, requires two possibly objectionable assumptions: that the phrase σὺ πίστιν ἔχεις is actually a question (which is syntactically quite possible) and that the phrase κἀγὼ ἔργα ἔχω will allow the translation, "And I *will say* 'I have works,' " supplying the verbal idea of *will say* or *will respond.* There is some warrant for supplying the phrase (Acts 9:5, 10; 25:22) in recording conversations, which has some parallel here. The result fits perfectly, though, with the context: the imaginary objector, responding to James's emphasis upon deeds, asks if James has faith at all. James, rejecting the abnormality already seen (faith that cannot prove its existence by actions), responds by saying that he possesses evidence, works, and that he can demonstrate the existence of his *real* faith by those very works. The objector cannot demonstrate the existence of faith without the corresponding actions.

In any of the three possibilities, the final sentence is fully understandable and in fact key to the rest of the pericope. James uses the term δεῖξόν, from δείκνυμι, a word that refers to demonstrating something to someone else, proving, giving evidence of, showing, revealing. James challenges the questioner, and thus all professing believers, to prove and demonstrate the reality of their faith. The use of such a term is vital, for it carries in its very meaning the idea of external and personal demonstration. This is clearly its meaning in the only other use in James, in 3:13:

> Which of you is wise and understanding? By his good conduct he should show (δειξάτω, aorist imperative of δείκνυμι) his works done in the gentleness that wisdom brings.

Only once in thirty-three uses in the New Testament is the term used in a way that does not include a direct, personal object of the demonstration being made (1 Timothy 6:15). The challenge James is making to the person claiming to have faith must be understood. James calls for demonstration that is (1) personal, and (2) observable. In 2:18 this challenge is in the form of an argument: James well knows his opponent cannot demonstrate the existence of his faith without external, observable actions. It is an argument based upon the impossibility of the fulfillment of the challenge. "Show me" is the challenge: it is placed squarely within the human realm. It involves providing observable evidence within the realm of human knowledge. Therefore, it must involve *external* demonstration, not merely the claim of the existence of an *internal* reality (faith). That this provides the immediate context of 2:20–24 is key to understanding the rest of the pericope. Any attempted exegesis that ignores the challenge to personally and outwardly demonstrate (δείκνυμι) the existence of the inward quality of faith will, of necessity, misinterpret the entire passage.

In contrast to the futility of attempting to demonstrate faith *sans* deeds, James is confident that a true faith can prove its existence by deeds. James uses δείξω, the future form, to express this confidence that true, saving faith has the capacity to provide external, personal demonstration. Further, we should note the contrast between χωρίς ("without" deeds) and ἐκ ("by" or literally "from" deeds). The first speaks of attempting to make a demonstration without any basis (without deeds); the other speaks of proving the existence of faith *from* deeds, or by *means of* deeds. Deeds are a tool, an instrument whereby the existence of something that is unseen by nature (faith) can be proven to exist.

2:19

> You believe that God is one; well and good. Even the demons believe that—and tremble with fear.

NA*[27] *Text

σὺ πιστεύεις ὅτι ⸀εἷς ἐστιν ὁ θεός⸌, καλῶς ποιεῖς· καὶ τὰ δαιμόνια πιστεύουσιν καὶ φρισσουσιν.

|⸀ *3 4 1 2* (K* *om l*) 𝔐 ¦ *4 1 2* 69 *al* ¦ *2 4* Ψ ¦ *1 4 2* B 614. 630. 1505. 1852 *al* ¦ *1 3 4 2* C 33[vid]. 81. 1243 *pc* ¦ unus deus ff ¦ *1 2 4* 945. 1241. 1739. 2298 ¦ *txt* 𝔓[74] ℵ A 2464 *pc*

James's use of direct address in verse 19 suggests that the final understanding of the punctuation variants in verse 18 is correct, for the flow is then uninterrupted. The same "me" who is being challenged to show or demonstrate the reality of his claimed faith is addressed directly in verse 19. But here James adds an important element: the person claiming faith is orthodox. That is, over against the common polytheism of the day, this person confesses something closely akin to the *Shema* of Deuteronomy 6:4. There we have the phraseology ἄκουε Ἰσραήλ κύριος ὁ θεὸς ἡμῶν κύριος εἷς ἐστιν in the LXX, which likewise explains the first of the textual variants noted above (later scribes seemingly harmonizing the phrase with the LXX word order).

But we also have 1 Corinthians 8:6, εἷς θεὸς, which might lie behind the reading of B (the fourth listed variant). Translations differ as to whether the issue is "there is one God" or "God is one," yet in either case James's point is clear: the same person who is claiming faith is not heretical in his view of the Godhead. He is not a pagan. Instead, he embraces part of the very heart of Jewish and Christian confession: monotheism, the fact that there is only one true God.

From this we can gather a vital element of James's polemic: the confession of dead, empty faith that he is attacking, which he plainly says cannot bring salvation, is not to be condemned for its error as to orthodoxy, but is condemned for its abnormality in lacking deeds as evidence of its vitality. That is, a dead faith can speak the right words without being a true and living faith. Dead orthodoxy is just as much a danger in James's thinking as living heresy is for Paul. Both extremes have constantly plagued the church throughout history.

James warns those who rest in the orthodoxy of their confession that such a faith is no more salvific than the orthodox recognition of the truth that there is only one God that even the demons possess. Their "orthodox faith" results only in their trembling in fear at the recognition of the God who will eventually judge and destroy them. The term James uses is graphic: φρίσσουσιν refers to the involuntary shaking and trembling that comes over someone when faced with overwhelming fear or awe. The recognition of the existence of the one true God is only a source of terror.

James says the confession is "well and good," for surely it is not his intention to say that heretical, false confessions accompanied by "good deeds" would be salvific. But it is the anomaly, the abnormality, of such an orthodox confession existing without the corresponding deeds that calls forth his wrath and, in fact, as one can sense, his sarcasm. Surely it is the attitude of the Pharisees one sees here, where full orthodoxy exists in doctrine, with glaring inconsistency in the realm of action. If demons are "orthodox" in their theology, obviously that alone cannot suffice, for saving faith is both orthodox and alive.

2:20

> But would you like evidence, you empty person, that faith without works is useless?

Alternates:

> But are you willing to recognize, you foolish fellow, that faith without works is useless? (NASB)

> You foolish man, do you want evidence that faith without deeds is useless? (NIV)

NA^{27} Text:

Θέλεις δὲ γνῶναι, ὦ ἄνθρωπε κενέ, ὅτι ἡ πίστις χωρὶς τῶν ἔργων ⸀ ἀργή ἐστιν;

| ⸀ κενη 𝔓^{74}ff ¦ νεκρα ℵ A C^{2} P Ψ 33 𝔐 t vg^{cl} sy bo ¦ *txt* B C* 323. 945. 1739 *pc* vg$^{st.ww}$ sa

Verse 20 opens with terminology common in moral treatises and diatribes. The phrase θέλεις δὲ γνῶναι is literally "do you wish to know," but a more dynamic meaning is "do you desire evidence" or "don't you understand" or "do you need to be convinced?" "Foolish man" is literally "empty man," a man without understanding or insight. Certainly this strong language flows from the previous verses and the refutation of this objector's failed attempt to promote or establish a faith that is, by nature, deedless. The "deedless faith" proponent is a person lacking knowledge, wisdom, and insight, and is, as far as Christian wisdom is concerned, foolish. James offers to provide evidence to the foolish man that deedless faith is useless, and he then does so in verses 21–25, using the examples of Abraham and Rahab.

James uses a play on words that is missed by some texts. The *Majority Text* reads νεκρά, "dead," and therefore the KJV and NKJV, following the TR, give this reading. 𝔓^{74} gives the unusual reading κενή, "empty," seemingly playing on κενέ in "empty man." But the scribe familiar with the language would know that ἀργή is a contraction of ἀ+ἐργη, literally, "not-work," "no-work," so that "faith without works does no work," a play on words. By extension the word can be "barren," "untilled," "without fruit." Deedless faith, being an anomaly by nature, is unproductive. It cannot, and will not, produce the fruit of *true* faith, that being salvation.

Verse 20, then, is an introduction to the illustrations that will follow. James offers evidence of his thesis: deedless faith is not salvific. This verse follows inexorably on the heels of 14–19 in spirit and in topic, so that the deedless faith of 2:20 is the same "said" or "spoken" faith of 2:14. This provides the overriding interpretive statement for the illustrations that follow: each, in James's mind, proves the truth of his argument. Faith that exists only in the realm of words (deedless faith) is useless. Therefore, ἀργή (20) τί τὸ ὄφελος (14) νεκρά καθ' ἑαυτήν (17).

We should note, with Johnson, the difference in the concern of James and that of Paul in Romans and Galatians:

> James is not asserting *anything* about the value of deeds "apart from" faith. It is precisely the disjunction that he challenges. Above all, there is no reason to read this statement as a response to such Pauline passages as Rom 3:28 . . . , because that contrast is simply not at issue here. Rather, James' contrast is between mere faith as belief and faith as a full response to God.[6]

2:21

> Was not Abraham our father justified by works when he offered Isaac his son on the altar?

Alternates:

> Was not our father Abraham shown to be righteous on the basis of deeds when he offered his son Isaac on the altar? (Luke Timothy Johnson, *The Letter of James,* 236)

> Was not our ancestor Abraham considered righteous for what he did when he offered his son Isaac on the altar? (NIV)

NA[27] Text:
Ἀβραὰμ ὁ πατὴρ ἡμῶν οὐκ ἐξ ἔργων ἐδικαιώθη ἀνενέγκας Ἰσαὰκ τὸν υἱὸν αὐτοῦ ἐπὶ τὸ θυσιαστήριον;

The first example James offers comes from the life of Abraham. It is the centrality of Abraham in Jewish national existence that causes James to refer to him, not an attempted counterargument against a Pauline doctrine. But the immediate question

[6]Johnson, 242.

asked of the text in the vast majority of instances, that of the relationship to Paul, is so common, so prevalent, that the fact that these words *continue* the preceding context and argument is often lost. Indeed, polemicists who need to find in this passage a foundation for some kind of synergistic works-salvation system insist that James's use of the identical term for "justified" (δικαιόω) and the identical phrase for "by works" (ἐξ ἔργων, see, for example, Romans 3:20; 4:2; Galatians 2:16) proves beyond question that we must read James's use of these terms in the *same context* that Paul uses in Romans and Galatians.

But we have already seen that James is arguing against a use of the word "faith" (a deedless, dead, empty, useless faith that exists only in the realm of words and not of action) that is *not* paralleled in the Pauline passages that speak of how one is justified. Second, Paul speaks of justification "before God" (παρὰ τῷ θεῷ, Galatians 3:11) or "in His sight" (ἐνώπιον αὐτοῦ, Romans 3:20), while the context of James is δεῖξόν μοι, "show me."

The assertion that the verbal parallels override the immediate contexts must be rejected, for it has no basis. James's use must be allowed to stand on its own. As a result, the translation of ἐδικαιώθη as "shown to be righteous" or "considered righteous" (NIV) flows not from a precommitment to a theological perspective but from the context itself. Luke Timothy Johnson defends his translation of ἐδικαιώθη as "shown to be righteous":

> The hardest term to translate here is *dikaioun*, primarily because of its frequent use by Paul in contexts opposing righteousness by faith and "works of the law" . . . and the complex use of the verb and its cognates in the OT (e.g., LXX Gen 38:26; Exod 23:7; Deut 25:1; Pss 50:6; 81:3; 142:2; Sir 1:22). The precise meaning in each case must be determined by context, not some general theological concept. Given the previous statement demanding the *demonstration* of faith, the translation here as "shown to be righteous" seems appropriate (see Hort, 63, "appear righteous in God's sight," and Marty, 104, "God sanctions his righteousness").... It is in this light that the present translation renders the Greek as "shown to be righteous," (2:21, 24), for the entire line of argument here has

involved *demonstration*: "show me your faith apart from deeds, and by my deeds I will show you my faith (2:18)."[7]

These considerations are more than sufficient to establish James's use in 2:21–24. And to the immediate objection, "James cannot be talking about a *demonstration* of faith by deeds, for in the offering of Isaac only God saw the act," the response is obvious: not only does this ignore Isaac, who *surely* observed this, but it also ignores every person who has read Genesis since then, who sees in Abraham the exemplar of faith. Surely no one would argue that this was not part of God's plan in bringing this event about in the first place.

Even God's own words point to this *demonstration* of faith in the act of obedience, for surely what else could God mean when He says, "Do not stretch out your hand against the lad, and do nothing to him; *for now I know* that you fear God, since you have not withheld your son, your only son, from Me" (Genesis 22:12 NASB, emphasis mine) than that Abraham has *given evidence* of the faith he possessed decades earlier in Genesis 15:6? Surely God knew of the reality of the faith that was Abraham's when He declared Abraham righteous. But it is the *demonstration* of that faith in Abraham's *actions* that draws James's attention and application. As Johnson observes, "James sees the offering of Isaac as the *demonstration* of this faith rather than its replacement."[8] This is exactly the point that is brought out clearly in verses 22–23 with the citation of Genesis 15:6 and the discussion of the *perfection* of faith.

2:22

> You see that his faith was working together with his works and his faith was perfected by works.

Alternate:

> You see that his faith and his actions were working together, and his faith was made complete by what he did. (NIV)

---

[7]Ibid., 242, 248.
[8]Ibid., 243.

NA*[27] *Text:

βλέπεις ὅτι ἡ πίστις ⸀συνήργει τοῖς ἔργοις αὐτοῦ καὶ ἐκ τῶν ἔργων ⸆ ἡ πίστις ἐτελειώθη . . .

| ⸀συνεργει ℵ* A 33. 630 *pc* ff vg^mss ¦ *txt* ℵ^c B C P Ψ 049. 1739 𝔐 vg sy co | ⸆ αυτου 614. 630. 1505. 1852 *al* vg^ms

Ironically, James says "you *see* that . . . ," showing the *demonstrative* element he is pushing into the forefront. The verb is singular, addressed to the interlocutor of the preceding verses. James wishes his hearers to *see* something from the example of Abraham's obedience to God in the offering of Isaac. We are to *see* Abraham's deeds "working together with," alongside of, faith. Dead faith, we have been told, is ἀργή, "without work," but living faith (as seen in Abraham, the father of all those who believe, Romans 4:16), by nature *works together with* deeds. Here the abnormality seen in previous verses is not present: the harmony of living faith and faithful deeds is summed up in the verb συνήργει. This is something James desires his readers to *see*: the necessary, definitional synergism that exists between living faith and the deeds that flow therefrom.

By these kinds of deeds (not faithless deeds, but deeds that accompany living faith) James says faith is "perfected" or "brought to completion." The subject of both clauses of 2:22 is faith: faith works together with deeds; faith is completed by deeds. In no situation are deeds seen as salvific in and of themselves, and in both clauses it would be absurd to think of Abraham's faith as being the same kind of empty, actionless faith James has been decrying.

Because this is so, we must be careful not to think that James is saying that it is the *addition* of works to faith that is in view in the second clause: the idea that saving faith can exist without deeds is the very thing James is denying. The "perfection" of faith by the deeds is not to be seen as the raising of one incomplete thing to completion by the addition of something *foreign* to faith. It is not James's assertion that works are an *addition* to faith. It would be absurd to think that James believed Abraham had a deedless faith from Genesis 15 to Genesis 22, for that would be to grant to his imaginary objectors the very thing they were claiming for themselves! "Oh, I can't show you my faith right now, but I will, eventually." No, faith, if it is truly faith, will be a living faith, one that συνήργει, *works together with* deeds. Abraham's offering of Isaac did not change the nature of his faith relationship with God: it showed that relationship, begun decades earlier, was real, living, vital, and demonstrable. The perfection of the faith by the deeds did not change the faith, but showed that it was real faith, not just said, but actual; a matter of the heart, not just the mind.

2:23

> And the scripture was fulfilled that says, "*Now Abraham believed God and it was counted to him for righteousness,*" and *he was called God's friend.*

NA^{27} Text:

καὶ ἐπληρώθη ἡ γραφὴ ἡ λέγουσα, *ἐπίστευσεν δὲ Ἀβραὰμ τῷ θεῷ, καὶ ἐλογίσθη αὐτῷ εἰς δικαιοσύνην* καὶ ⸀φίλος θεοῦ ἐκλήθη.

| ⸀δουλος 429. 614. 630. 1505. 1852. *al* sy^{h}

James connects the demonstration of faith in the offering of Isaac upon the altar with the *fulfillment* of Genesis 15:6. How so? Again, his consistency is striking: Abraham's confession of faith is recorded in Genesis 15:6. God justified Abraham upon the exercise of that faith. The reality of the faith Abraham had, upon which he was justified, is demonstrated in the offering of Isaac. Hence, Genesis 15:6 is fulfilled in that act not through the addition of something to faith as the means of justification, but by the demonstration that Abraham truly *did* believe in Genesis 15. This is the only meaning that can be attached to ἐπληρώθη that fits with the context. The passage is not strictly prophetic, so the regular meaning of "fulfill" would not apply here. Instead, continuing with the theme of "real faith works," the fulfillment of the faith of Abraham is seen in the actions that flowed from the faith.

Much discussion exists as to why James includes the additional phrase, "and he was called God's friend." There is no direct quotation wherein this particular phrase is used. The LXX of Daniel (which differs substantially from the Hebrew Masoretic text) does use the word φίλος of Abraham, and in other places Abraham is said to be loved of God (2 Chronicles 20:7, where the NASB translates אֹהַבְךָ as "friend," and the LXX translates it as ἠγαπημένῳ, "beloved," likewise in Isaiah 41:8). What is James's purpose here? Is Abraham called the friend of God because he believed in God (15:6), or because he offered Isaac, or both? What does it mean to be God's friend?

There are a number of possibilities, but two stand out. First, the phrase may just reflect the Jewish view of Abraham as a special representative of God, beloved of God. He was a friend of God because of His faith in Yahweh. This, then, would be a contrast with James's second illustration, that of Rahab. Abraham, the friend of God, showed his faith by his deeds. Rahab, a harlot, showed her faith by her deeds. Hence, whether one is a godly man or a sinful woman, it does not matter: real faith will show itself in deeds of faith.

The second possibility is that Abraham, having received the righteousness of God by faith, is called the friend of God in the sense that he is in right relationship to God. This friendship, then, would parallel Paul's teaching that the justified person has εἰρήνη with God, true peace, שָׁלוֹם, *shalom* (Romans 5:1). Since his was a true and living faith, demonstrated by the existence of deeds of faith, his friendship with God was real.

2:24

> You see that a person is justified by works and not by faith alone.

Alternates:

> You see that a person is shown to be righteous on the basis of deeds and not on the basis of faith only. (Johnson)

> You see that a person is justified by what he does and not by faith alone. (NIV)

NA*[27] *Text:
ὁρᾶτε ὅτι ἐξ ἔργων δικαιοῦται ἄνθρωπος καὶ οὐκ ἐκ πίστεως μόνον.

Most translations take ὁρᾶτε as an indicative, "you see." But in light of the use of βλέπεις in verse 22, the phrase may be stronger, with ὁρᾶτε taking the imperative, "So realize that . . ." The term is plural, so James has moved from rebutting the specific objector he was focusing on earlier and now gives a general statement to the audience in general.

If this passage were found in a context that is soteriologically prescriptive (i.e., how to be saved), it would be a direct, unquestionable contradiction of Paul's teaching. The similarity in language immediately causes even the careful interpreter to leap from the context and interpret the words in light of Pauline theology. But if we can resist the temptation for just a moment, the meaning of the words is clear.

ὁρᾶτε ὅτι introduces the conclusion of the first illustration, drawn from Abraham. And what is to be drawn from Abraham's actions? That he was shown to be righteous by what he did in offering Isaac. An alone faith cannot demonstrate righteousness. In this context the phrase πίστεως μόνον, "faith alone," refers back to deedless faith, for James has made it plain that living faith cannot, by definition, be separated from deeds of faith. So when James says "not by faith alone," he is saying "not by that anomalous, abnormal, words-only claim of faith that I have already demonstrated to be dead, useless, and empty." Johnson rightly observes,

> The use of the adverb *monon* ("only") corresponds exactly to that in 1:22, where it involved the contrast between "hearing only" and "doing the word." . . . Here, the contrast has been between "faith only" and "doing the faith." The *monon* is also equivalent to the *pistis kath' heauten* in 2:17.[9]

It might be argued that Abraham was justified not by his faith in Genesis 15, but by his works in Genesis 22. Yet this is not at all

[9]Ibid., 245.

a part of the argument of James; it must be read into the text. This would involve the assertion that Abraham had *false* faith in the decades between Genesis 15 and 22, as well as the *implicit assumption* that living faith (which surely Abraham had) is insufficient to justify. But James has not addressed that issue in this pericope: he remains focused on his goal, the demonstration that faith, if it is truly faith, never exists in a state where it does not accomplish the very purpose for which God gives it to His elect people. Or as Paul put it so well, "having been created in Christ Jesus for good works that God prepared beforehand so we may do them" (Ephesians 2:10). A belief in the *insufficiency of living faith* to justify finds no ground here: the only faith that is said to be non-salvific is dead faith, not living faith. The distinction has been drawn since 2:14, and it must be allowed to stand in 2:24 as well.

2:25

> And similarly, was not Rahab the prostitute also justified by works when she welcomed the messengers and sent them out by another way?

NA[27] Text:
ὁμοίως δὲ καὶ Ῥαὰβ ἡ πόρνη οὐκ ἐξ ἔργων ἐδικαιώθη ὑποδεξαμένη τοὺς ἀγγέλους καὶ ἑτέρᾳ ὁδῷ ἐκβαλοῦσα;

The second illustration James offers, linking the two together with the term ὁμοίως, continues the same thought in brief. The focus is upon Rahab's *actions* in welcoming and sending out the messengers of Israel. The *evidentiary* nature of this justification is again clearly seen: no one would argue God justifies prostitutes on the basis of hiding spies. Instead, the faith she had come to possess in the God of Israel manifested itself in her willingness to act in accordance with her confession found in these words: "the Lord your God, He is God in heaven above and on earth beneath" (Joshua 2:11 NASB).

2:26

> For just as the body without the spirit is dead, so also faith without works is dead.

NA*[27] *Text:
ὥσπερ γὰρ τὸ σῶμα χωρὶς πνεύματος νεκρόν ἐστιν, οὕτως καὶ ἡ πίστις χωρὶς ἔργων νεκρά ἐστιν.

The apostle concludes the entire section by repeating the initial assertion found in 2:14: Deedless faith is a dead, useless thing. But in his conclusion he gives one of the clearest examples of the central theme that has appeared throughout the pericope: A body without a spirit is *abnormal.* A spirit without a body is as well. In biblical thinking, man is body and spirit, one whole. The separation of the two is unnatural. Resurrection is intended to restore man as a whole, single unit. This is part and parcel of Christian thinking concerning man.[10]

By pointing to the body-spirit combination and by stating the obvious truth that a body without a spirit is dead, James is explaining the definitional union of faith and deeds that must exist when speaking of living, true faith. Faith, saving faith, is vital faith, and such a faith will not be a deedless, words-only entity. The words-only faith that many loudly claim is, to James, no different than a lifeless body, a mannequin propped up for looks but of no use to anyone.

Yet the positive aspect of this assertion must be recognized as well. The body and spirit form a single unit—man. While distinguishable, they are not separable in the sense that the result of such a separation is not properly called "a human being." As this is true, the same must be said of faith and works. By definition, they form a single whole, as we have seen in Paul. Divine faith, the gift of God given to the elect, is a unitary whole in that the fiduciary element never exists separately from and to the exclusion of the changed nature of the one to whom faith is given. Saving faith, which by nature includes the lifestyle that results from the redeemed being made a new creation in Christ, is a living thing and therefore must be seen as salvific by James.

So what of James and Paul? Both say the same thing. When the

---

[10]Another possibility that is directly in line with the context is to understand *πνεύμα* as "breath"; hence, the point is that every living body "breathes" naturally, and when breathing stops, there is no life.

context of each is allowed to stand and attention is given (often against the polemic desires brought to the text) to the purpose and goal of the author, the heart-stirring consistency of Holy Scripture, even when penned by men in different circumstances and with different concerns, comes to the fore. When Paul and James both address Christian behavior and Christian life, they speak as one: in fact, the normative use of "deeds" in Paul is the exact same as that found in James. It is the *unwarranted* transference of James's context into that of Paul that has resulted in problems down through history.

When we allow James to speak for himself, in his own context, and allow him to define his own terms (rather than forcing the specific meanings defined by Paul in arguing for justification by grace through faith), his intentions and purposes are clear. The biblical truth is truly beyond controversy: Living faith (1) can demonstrate its existence and is consistent with godly living and (2) is sufficient unto salvation in contrast to dead faith, which is not.

CHAPTER 21

Exegesis of Important Passages Not Yet Covered

MAIN PASSAGE: 2 CORINTHIANS 5:17–21

5:17 So then, if anyone is in Christ, he is a new creation; what is old has passed away, see, what is new has come! **5:18** And all these things are from God who reconciled us to himself through Christ, and who has given us the ministry of reconciliation. **5:19** In other words, in Christ God was reconciling the world to himself, not counting people's trespasses against them, and he has given us the message of reconciliation. **5:20** Therefore we are ambassadors for Christ, as though God were making His plea through us. We plead with you on Christ's behalf, "Be reconciled to God!" **5:21** God made the one who did not know sin to be sin for us, so that in him we would become the righteousness of God.

The relevance of this passage comes from the appearance of δικαιοσύνη θεοῦ ("righteousness of God") in verse 21. The brevity of verse 21 seems to indicate it is a summary statement, one well known to the expected audience in Corinth. Its importance is heightened by a number of other considerations, including the close connection of καταλλαγή/καταλλάσσω ("reconciliation"/"to be reconciled") in the immediate context, and also the direct assertion that the *purpose* of Christ's "being made sin" is so that we might be made the righteousness of God in Him. Important as well is the parallel of μὴ λογίσηται/ἁμαρτίαν in Romans 4:8 and here in 5:19, μὴ λογιζόμενος/παραπτώματα, the non-imputation of sin. As such it provides a vital complement to the fuller passages we have already examined.

5:17

> So then, if anyone is in Christ, he is a new creation; what is old has passed away, see, what is new has come!

NA[27] Text:
ὥστε εἴ τις ἐν Χριστῷ, καινὴ κτίσις· τὰ ἀρχαῖα παρῆλθεν, ἰδοὺ γέγονεν ⸀καινά·

| ⸀ τα παντα κ. 6. 33. 81. 614. 630. 1241. 1505. 1881 *pm* a b vg^{cl}; (Ambst) ¦ κ. τα π. D^{2} K L P Ψ 104. 326. 945. 2464 *pm* sy^{h} ¦ *txt* 𝔓^{46} ℵ B C D* F G 048. 0243. 365. 629. 1175. 1739. *l* 249 *pc* vgst co; Cl

This passage is surely one of the most precious in all of Scripture, one which many of the saints have put to memory, and for good reason. Prior to this passage Paul has been explaining the relationship of the death of Christ to the life of the Christian. Using strong substitutionary terminology, Paul speaks of the union that exists between Christ and His people, and the one who has died with Christ yet lives (echoing Galatians 2:20) is described negatively as one who does not live "to himself" but instead lives "for him who died for them and was raised" (5:15). This is a tremendous picture of true Christian living: the focus of the Christian is "Christ-life" not "self-life." This Christ-centeredness is the background of "a new creation" here in 5:17.

The first truth spoken is that all who are in Christ, "whosoever," experience this "new creation." To be in Christ is to be a new creation. There is no such thing as a person who is in union with Christ who is not a new creation. The two are coextensive, the one descriptive of the *effect* of the other. While some interpreters have taken καινὴ κτίσις ("new creation") in an exhortational sense ("let him be a new creature"), this is not Paul's thrust. Paul is describing the effect of God's work in Christ, and the words that follow, "what is old has passed away, see, what is new has come" are stating a fact, not a hope.

The meaning of "new" is filled out by the following phrase, for the term can also mean "unpolluted" as well. But it is indeed the sense of newness of life in Christ that is in Paul's mind. The "new creation" harkens back to Old Testament promises such as:

> For look, I am ready to create
> new heavens and a new earth!
> The former ones will not be remembered;
> no one will think about them anymore. (Isaiah 65:17)

But it also points forward to eschatological fulfillments:

> And the one seated on the throne said: "Look! I am making all things new!" Then he said to me, "Write it down, because these words are reliable and true" (Revelation 21:5).

Here in Paul's words, however, the reality is *now.* To be in Christ is to be a new creation, to have passed out of death into life. Resurrection life is, in some wonderful and fascinating way, "new." We have not been given new life so as to merely go back to our old ways of living. There is a fundamental change for the person who has been born again and now experiences Christ's life being lived within.

This change is described as "the old things" or "former things" having "passed away." This is a past action. In the same way, "new things have come" sees this transition into the Christian life as a past event with present effects. Many are familiar with the reading of the King James/*New King James* (based upon the *Textus Receptus*), "all things have become new." As the textual data listed above shows, the shorter reading has the support of 𝔓[46] (major and very early papyri manuscript of the Pauline corpus), א

(Aleph, *Codex Sinaiticus*), and B *(Codex Vaticanus)*, as well as numerous other witnesses.

This passage is fully representative of Paul's insistence that soteriology and Christian living are aspects of one whole. To be in Christ is to experience καινότητι ζωῆς ("newness of life," Romans 6:4) and καινότητι πνεύματος ("newness of the Spirit," Romans 7:6). It is the Father's will that all who are in Christ will experience His life as a new creation.

5:18

> And all these things are from God who reconciled us to himself through Christ, and who has given us the ministry of reconciliation.

NA[27] Text:
τὰ δὲ πάντα ἐκ τοῦ θεοῦ τοῦ καταλλάξαντος ἡμᾶς ἑαυτῷ διὰ Χριστοῦ καὶ δόντος ἡμῖν τὴν διακονίαν τῆς καταλλαγῆς. . .

Paul's theocentricism finds strong expression when he affirms that "all these things are from God," that is, being in Christ, the newness of life, the new creation—salvation is a divine work from first to last. There is never any room for human boasting (1 Corinthians 1:30–31). While Paul will speak of us as "fellow workers with God" in preaching the gospel in 6:1, never does the apostle view His chief and most glorious work, the redemption of His people, as a cooperative effort.

The divine nature of salvation is likewise the theme of Paul's description of God as the One "who reconciled us to himself through Christ." Reconciliation is a divine work. God the Father takes the initiative in reconciling sinful men to himself. The participle καταλλάξαντος has God as its subject and the redeemed ("us") as its object. But even more God reconciled us *unto himself.* As sinners, our relationship with the Holy God was severed. The very heart of grace is that the offended Majesty is the one who reconciles wretched sinners to himself! He does not merely make a way of reconciliation *available*, but He actually, actively, and powerfully *reconciles.*

Yet as the holy God He could not bring about reconciliation without dealing with the *reason* for the disruption in relationship: sin. So this reconciliation takes place by one specific means, which again flows from the initiative of the Father: "through Christ." Jesus constantly taught that He was sent by the Father, and while Jesus voluntarily made himself of no reputation (Philippians 2:6), the Scriptures represent Him as the "sent" One. Here Paul only mentions Christ as the means: in 5:19 and 21 the exact nature of Christ's provision of the grounds of reconciliation will be laid out.

The message of what the Father has done in Christ is likened to a "ministry" (διακονίαν) wherein we are privileged to proclaim to others that the God who is justly wrathful over sin is found to be gracious in and through the work of Jesus Christ. The next verse restates this thought (the NET uses "in other words" to introduce verse 19) as "he has given us the message of reconciliation." While there is an immediate and special application to the apostles, all who proclaim the gospel as ambassadors for Christ (5:20) are likewise entrusted with this message.

5:19

> In other words, in Christ God was reconciling the world to himself, not counting people's trespasses against them, and he has given us the message of reconciliation.

NA[27] Text:
ὡς ὅτι θεὸς ἦν ἐν Χριστῷ κόσμον καταλλάσσων ἑαυτῷ, μὴ λογιζόμενος αὐτοῖς τὰ παραπτώματα αὐτῶν καὶ θέμενος ἐν ἡμῖν τὸν λόγον τῆς καταλλαγῆς.

The NET takes 5:19 as an expansion and restatement of 5:18, and this is surely the best understanding. Therefore, "in Christ God was reconciling the world to himself" would be the expansion or explanation of "God who reconciled us to himself through Christ." While some have seen references to the Incarnation, etc., in the phrase "in Christ" (ἐν Χριστῷ), there is no reason to take this as anything other than another way of stating διὰ Χριστοῦ ("by Christ," 5:18). God was *by means of Christ's sacrificial death* reconciling the world to himself.[1] In both phrases the repetition of ἑαυτῷ further strengthens the identification of 5:19 as a parallel explanation of 5:18. This is a reconciliation *to himself.* God is the reconciler.[2]

In the next phrase we meet both an explanation of the *how* of the reconciliation as well as a passage we have seen before in our discussion of the non-imputation of sin. How can the holy God heal the rupture of sin? The assertion is literally "not imputing to them their trespasses." The extent of "them" and "their" is limited by what has come before: these are those who are "in Christ" (5:17), a "new creation" (5:17), who have been reconciled to God (5:18). The NET rendering is somewhat unclear, "not counting people's trespasses against them," when there is no generic word "people's" in the text. μὴ λογιζόμενος αὐτοῖς is literally "not imputing to them." Imputation is specific and personal, not general, since "trespasses" is likewise a more specific rather than generic term for sin (Paul uses the more generic term in 5:21).

God reconciles men and women to Christ by not imputing their trespasses to them. Well, how can this be? A person who commits a sin by all rights must be held accountable for that sin. The guilt and punishment of the sin must be borne by the one who committed it, *or by a substitute.* And it is just here that the answer to the problem of sin is given: God's justice does demand that the penalty of sin be paid, the guilt and judgment borne. But if the sins of those in Christ are not imputed to them, then to whom are they imputed? They are borne by Christ (1 Peter 2:24). This is the direct assertion of 5:21 and the implication of 5:19. It is the work God the Father did by means of Jesus Christ that

[1]The frequent use of this passage by modalists to attempt to promote the idea that this presents their idea of Christ as two persons (God the Father and the Son as merely the human nature) removes it completely from its context and purpose.

[2]But a further item to note from the parallel explanation motif is that the parallel of ἡμᾶς ("us") in 5:18 is the anarthrous use of κόσμον (world) in 5:19. Charles Hodge wrote, "By *the world* (κόσμος, without the article) is meant *man, mankind.* The reference or statement is perfectly indefinite; it merely indicates the class of beings toward whom God was manifesting himself as propitious. In the same sense our Lord is called the Saviour of the world, or, the Saviour of men, Jesus Salvator Hominum. (Charles Hodge, *A Commentary on 1 & 2 Corinthians* in the *Geneva Commentary Series* [Banner of Truth, 1983], 520–21). Further, the use of "them" and "their trespasses" regarding the non-imputation of sin would refer to only those who, as Paul taught in Romans 4:8, receive the blessedness of the imputation of righteousness apart from works (Romans 4:6), those who are "in Christ," a "new creation."

makes it possible for any man or woman to be freed from the debt of sin, to experience the non-imputation of their trespasses. The technical term "non-imputation" may not thrill the soul at first glance, but anyone who truly understands what it means that one's sins are imputed *to another* and not to himself can find in this term the most joyous truth of the good news itself.

The NET's rendering "he has given us the message of reconciliation" translates καὶ θέμενος ἐν ἡμῖν τὸν λόγον τῆς καταλλαγῆς, literally, "and has placed within us/among us the word of reconciliation." It is possible to understand this as to refer to a placement of the message of reconciliation in the hearts of believers, but in light of the next verse, it is probably best to take the traditional understanding in the sense of "committed to us" this message. The "us" could be understood as the apostles as a group, and, by extension, those who function as "ambassadors" in the next verse, those who proclaim the message of Christ.

5:20

> Therefore we are ambassadors for Christ, as though God were making His plea through us. We plead with you on Christ's behalf, "Be reconciled to God!"

NA[27] Text:
ὑπὲρ Χριστοῦ οὖν πρεσβεύομεν ὡς τοῦ θεοῦ παρακαλοῦντος δι' ἡμῶν· δεόμεθα ὑπὲρ Χριστοῦ, καταλλάγητε τῷ θεῷ.

Since the message of reconciliation, the message of the cross, has been entrusted to the church, and it is the message itself that is powerful to save (Romans 1:16–17), those who proclaim that message speak with divine authority as πρεσβεύομεν, "ambassadors" or "representatives." There are a number of important points that flow from this statement.

First, the authority of the preacher comes from the message preached. Fidelity to the λόγον τῆς καταλλαγῆς ("word" or "message" of reconciliation) guarantees that the authority of the preaching is *God's* authority, for Paul says that it is "as though God were making His plea through us." So frequently it is asked,

"Does God speak today?" Paul's answer is, "Yes, He surely does—when the gospel is preached, God is speaking that message of reconciliation, and He will do so until the last of His elect is gathered in!" Hence, the nature of the gospel itself *precludes the need for further revelation* in the sense of fulfilling the desire for a "continuing revelation." The gospel meets the needs of God's people in all places and at all times.

It would likewise follow from this that there is only one "word" of reconciliation in which God "speaks" and "makes His plea." That is, *God does not speak in false gospels.* God has freely chosen to limit His "plea" to only the proclamation of the gospel, and nothing else.

What does it mean that God is "making his plea"? The Greek term παρακαλέω *(parakaleō)* can have as gentle a meaning as "urge" or "request" through the slightly stronger "console" all the way to "invite" and "summon." There are two opposite contextual clues as to which direction we should see this term going: first, the "ambassador" was an official representative, vested with the authority of the one who sent him. And second, when the message is given, it is "We beg [δεόμεθα, "implore"] you on behalf of Christ. . . ." This would be a strong term of exhortation, showing a sincere desire.

So how are we to understand these words? Most often they are taken as a general evangelistic statement, yet Paul is addressing the Corinthians as believers in this passage. And within only two sentences he will write,

> Now because we are fellow workers, we also urge you not to receive the grace of God in vain. For he says, "*I heard you at the acceptable time, and in the day of salvation I helped you.*" See, now is *the acceptable time*; see, now is *the day of salvation!* We do not give anyone an occasion for taking an offense in anything, so that no fault may be found with our ministry. (2 Corinthians 6:1–3)

So attuned are most evangelical ears to a very limited and specific use of the word "salvation" that this use may cause confusion. In many churches salvation and evangelism are all outward and never inward. Yet it is the duty of ministers to exhort all hearers to be reconciled to God, both in an initial sense as well as in the continuous sense of living the Christian life and embracing daily the promises of God. Just as we would not dream of telling someone to love God once (but not for the rest of one's life), or to believe only once, but not daily, so too it is the regular exhortation of the ministers of the gospel in the church that we must all live in the light of forgiveness, reconciliation, and grace. As Charles Hodge noted,

> *Be ye reconciled unto God*; this does not mean, "Reconcile yourselves unto God." The word, καταλλάγητε, is passive. *Be ye reconciled,* that is, embrace the offer of reconciliation. The reconciliation is effected by the death of Christ. God is now propitious. He can now be just, and yet justify the ungodly. All we have to do is not to refuse the offered love of God. Calvin remarks that his exhortation is not directed exclusively to the unconverted. The believer needs daily, and is allowed whenever he needs, to avail himself of the offer of peace with God through Jesus Christ. It is not the doctrine of the Scriptures that the merits of Christ avail only for the forgiveness of sins committed before conversion, while for post-baptismal sins, as they are called, there is no satisfaction but in the penances of the offender. Christ ever lives to make intercession for us, and for every short-coming and renewed offence there is offered to the penitent believer, renewed application of that blood which cleanses from all sin.[3]

Christians need to hear about, understand, and dwell upon the means by which they have been "accepted in the Beloved One." They need to know the promise is ever new, always theirs, forever valid.

5:21

> God made the one who did not know sin to be sin for us, so that in him we would become the righteousness of God.

---

[3]Ibid., 523.

NA[27] Text:
τὸν μὴ γνόντα ἁμαρτίαν ὑπὲρ ἡμῶν ἁμαρτίαν ἐποίησεν, ἵνα ἡμεῖς γενώμεθα δικαιοσύνη θεοῦ ἐν αὐτῷ.

The offered reconciliation is based upon a divine act. While the NET inserts the word "God," the Greek is simply "He made." The referent is the Father. The Father undertook this action. But what did He do?

He made to be sin "the One not knowing sin." The innocent One, the pure One, Christ. Here the Father acts with reference to the Son, who did not know sin. Surely the Messiah, who had faced the insane hatred of the Pharisees, knew what sin was. Surely He who had said to the woman caught in adultery, "Go and sin no more" *knew* the nature, character, and extent of sin. In fact, it could be rightly said that the Son of God *knew* sin better than anyone else, as He alone became incarnate, lived as the sinless and pure Messiah in the midst of sinners, touched them, ministered to them, loved them. So, obviously this is not the sense of "know" that Paul is using here. Instead, he speaks of the kind of knowledge of sin that we *as sinners* possess. We "know" sin because we *experience* it. So the main thrust is that the Son was not a sinner. He was, as is the testimony of all of Scripture, the pure, spotless, blameless Lamb of God (Hebrews 4:15; 1 Peter 2:22; 1 John 3:5).

This pure One was "made sin" (ἁμαρτία). Simple words cannot express the depth of such a divine mystery. Obviously the meaning is not that Jesus committed sin, nor that His perfect holiness was stripped from Him. The key to understanding "made" (ἐποίησεν) is seen by hearing the entire sentence: He is made sin *so that* "we would become the righteousness of God." Hodge put it well:

> He was made sin, we are made "righteousness." The only sense in which we are made the righteousness of God is that we are in Christ regarded and treated as righteous, and therefore the sense in which he was made sin, is that he was regarded and treated as a sinner. His being made sin is consistent with his being in himself free from sin; and our being

> made righteous is consistent with our being in ourselves ungodly. In other words, our sins were imputed to Christ, and his righteousness is imputed to us.[4]

This is surely the proper meaning in light of the use of λογιζόμενος ("imputing") in verse 19. Christ is "made" sin in His role as the all-sufficient sacrifice for sin via the imputation of the sins of His people to Him. He then bears, as the divine substitute, their sin in His body, "becoming" sin on their behalf, taking the punishment due to those transgressions. He bears what is not personally His by nature (our sins) so that we might bear what is not personally ours by nature: the righteousness of God. Every word is filled with deep meaning.

Salvation flows from the fountainhead of the Father's mercy. This action begins with the divine initiative. God is the one who accomplishes salvation through the work of Christ.

Christ's sacrifice has a distinct purpose, and given that God does not fail in His purposes, we can conclude it has a specific effect: His death results in men and women being made the righteousness of God. That is, the death of Christ is said to have a specific purpose that is fulfilled in the justification of sinners. This falls directly in line with the apostle's teaching in Romans 8:30: "And those God predestined, he also called; and those he called, he also justified; and those he justified, he also glorified." Christ's work *never* fails.

Substitutionary atonement is the means by which justification is secured. Christ is made sin "for us," ὑπὲρ ἡμῶν, a term of substitution.[5] There is no *biblical* doctrine of atonement that does not see this central aspect of substitution. Many of the errors in soteriology that one can find in church history can be traced directly to a shallow, unbiblical view of atonement, one that did not recognize this vital aspect of penal and personal substitution on the part of the Lord Jesus Christ.

The righteousness of God is the possession of those who are "in Him." Union with Christ is not an ancillary concept, one that

[4]Ibid., 524–25.

[5]See the in-depth discussion by Daniel B. Wallace of this aspect of the Greek preposition ὑπὲρ in *Greek Grammar Beyond the Basics*, 383–89.

may or may not be realized in the life of those who are justified. All who are in Christ are justified; all who are justified are in Christ. To be in Christ one must possess God-given righteousness, and all who are in Him cannot fail but to receive that very gift.

So we can see that the Protestant doctrine of double imputation is indeed biblical in nature and that this truth is tied directly to the substitutionary nature of the atoning death of Christ. Substitution and imputation are inextricably linked. Therefore, when it is said that our sins are imputed to Christ, this is nothing more than to say that Christ took our place substitutionarily. This touches on the very heart of the gospel, the means by which any believer stands clothed in the righteousness of Christ.

MAIN PASSAGE: TITUS 3:4–7: THE TRINITY REDEEMS

3:4 But "when the kindness of God our Savior appeared and
his love for mankind appeared, **3:5** He saved us not by works of
righteousness that we have done but on the basis of his mercy,
through the washing of the new birth and the renewing of the
Holy Spirit, **3:6** whom he poured out on us in full measure
through Jesus Christ our Savior. **3:7** And so, since we have been
justified by his grace, we become heirs with the confident expectation of eternal life."

The relevance of this key passage is also easily recognized. Most of the key soteriological terms used by Paul appear in this singular section, such as ἔργων, δικαιοσύνη, ἔλεος, χάριτι, and ἐλπίδα. This passage functions as a summary statement, somewhat like a miniature confession of faith, in Paul's epistle to Titus. Since it picks up so much of Paul's doctrine of salvation, it is important to our purpose of establishing the biblical basis of justification by faith.

It is also important for the fact that all three divine Persons—Father, Son, and Holy Spirit—are presented in their salvific work. The *NA*[27] text places these four verses in poetic form. Some scholars describe this section as hymnic or liturgical, while others deny it should be treated in this manner.[6] These verses comprise

[6]Gordon Fee, *1 and 2 Timothy, Titus* in *The New International Biblical Commentary* (Hendrickson, 1988), 203.

a single sentence, and it ends with Paul's assertion in verse 8 that "This saying is trustworthy," referring to the "saying" of 4–7. So if this section is not hymnic, it is close to being an early creedal summary, at least of Paul's teaching. One is tempted to think that it is a summary that Paul taught to Titus and Timothy and others to whom he passed on his teaching and doctrine.

God's kindness appeared in the person of Jesus Christ in history and for each individual believer when the gospel came with life-transforming power into their own experience. The rendering "love for mankind" comes from φιλανθρωπία. The NIV simply translates the word as "love," while the NRSV has "loving kindness." It seems better to take the two terms as a group, "the kindness and love of God" (NIV) and "the goodness and loving kindness of God" (NRSV).

God is "God our Savior," a term used of both the Father and the Son (Titus 2:13) in this epistle (a usage that is reminiscent of Paul's ease in exchanging "Spirit of Christ" and "Spirit of God"). Christ is the very embodiment of the love of God, the Incarnation the irrefutable proof that God is loving and merciful.

3:5

> He saved us not by works of righteousness that we have done but on the basis of his mercy, through the washing of the new birth and the renewing of the Holy Spirit . . .

NA[27] Text:

οὐκ ἐξ ἔργων τῶν ἐν δικαιοσύνῃ ἃ ἐποιήσαμεν ἡμεῖς ἀλλὰ κατὰ τὸ αὐτοῦ ἔλεος ἔσωσεν ἡμᾶς διὰ λουτροῦ παλιγγενεσίας καὶ ἀνακαινώσεως πνεύματος ἁγίου . . .

The first item that strikes the mind is the use of the aorist regarding the work of salvation. "He saved us" is past tense, looking back upon the work of God. Next, the subject of the verb is God. He did the saving. "Us" is the direct object of the verb.

Also striking from the Greek text is the fact that Paul places the phrase "not by works which we did in righteousness" at the beginning, giving it prominence. "He saved us" comes well into the verse. He rushes to deny any ground for salvation outside of the mercy of God, most specifically, "works done in righteousness." In point of fact, he denies the possibility of a mixture by positing the two as opposites: the use of ἀλλα *(alla)* introduces a strong contrast, "not by this, *but instead* by this." Since the text has God doing the action of saving, the denial of the role of human actions, *even though done in "righteousness,"* is remarkable.

The conjunction of ἐποιήσαμεν with ἔσωσεν (aorist with aorist) would lead us to understand that the basis of God's action of saving is not found in the actions of men, even those actions done "in righteousness." God's mercy is predicated as the contrasting ground. God's mercy and man's works of righteousness are polar opposites, just as we have already seen in Romans 4:4–5. This also casts light on the issue of "merit" in "earning" a reward in Romans 4:4. Even works done in righteousness are to be rejected as a ground when they will in any way impinge upon the singular glory of the mercy of God as the *sole* foundation from which the work of salvation arises. The fact that Paul also includes "which *we* have done" completes the divine/human contrast. Christian salvation is, from first to last, a divine activity, a divine work, all to His praise.

While Paul uses ἐξ ἔργων in the first phrase ("*from* works"), he uses κατὰ τὸ αὐτοῦ ἔλεος ("*because of* His mercy") in the second. "His" is placed in a position of prominence to continue the force of the strong contrast between the human and the divine.

Mercy is made the basis of the action of saving, just as Paul has elsewhere made love and grace the ground (Ephesians 2:4ff). Mercy, love, and grace comprise a word cluster that communicates the graciousness of God as Savior. Mercy, like grace (Romans 11:6), is focused upon the disposition of the merciful one, not upon anything in the recipient. Divine mercy is free. The verbal form of "mercy" (which has no strict parallel in English) is used by Paul in Romans 9:15, "I will *mercy* whoever I mercy," with the meaning being, "I will mercy whoever *I freely choose* to mercy." George Knight summarizes what we have seen in 3:5 thus far:

> The concept of salvation presented here is, therefore, grand in its perspective and inclusive in its accomplishment. The perspective is that God enters into history with his gracious attitude to act for us, transforming us now and making us heirs for an eternity with him. The accomplishment is that we are delivered from past bondage to sin, made here and now a new and transformed people who are indwelt by God's Holy Spirit, thus already declared justified at the bar of God's judgment, and finally made heirs of future eternal life.[7]

Up to this point the flow of the text is direct and clear. And in reality, it continues that way. But at this point the traditions of men greatly impact the way in which the rest of the text is heard by many. Leaving aside the historical baggage that comes with this text, let's see how simply the meaning is conveyed by continuing with the context as we have already established it.

As soon as the work of God in saving His people is presented, Paul provides the *means* by which this work has been accomplished in their lives: "through the washing of the new birth and the renewing of the Holy Spirit." The NET takes λουτροῦ παλιγγενεσίας as "the washing of the new birth" rather than the more traditional translation, "washing of regeneration." There are a number of issues that bear examination, but a few major points should suffice for our purposes here.

First, what is the meaning of "washing of regeneration"? Paul uses the term "washing" (λουτρόν) only one other time, Ephesians 5:26, here in context:

> **5:25** Husbands, love your wives just as Christ loved the church and gave himself for her **5:26** to sanctify her by cleansing her with the washing of the water by the word **5:27** so that he may present the church to himself as glorious—not having a stain or wrinkle, or any such blemish, but holy and blameless.

Another form of the word, ἀπολύομαι, is used in Acts 22:16 and 1 Corinthians 6:11. In both Titus 3:5 and Ephesians 5:26 the cleansing is clearly spiritual in nature, lacking any direct physical

---

[7]George Knight III, *The Pastoral Epistles* in *The New International Greek Testament Commentary* (Eerdmans, 1992), 341.

component. If we are to take λουτροῦ παλιγγενεσίας as a unit, this would likewise point to the spiritual nature of this "washing," as "regeneration" (rebirth, new beginning, new genesis) is plainly in reference to the newness of life in Christ (2 Corinthians 5:17) wrought by the Holy Spirit, and this position is further supported by the rest of the phrase, "the renewing of the Holy Spirit." Given that the immediate context includes the assertion of the divine nature of salvation and that it is God who saves *apart from* human actions done in righteousness, it follows that the most natural interpretation of the phrase is that, just as in John 3:5 (the probable origin of this Pauline teaching in the words of Christ), the promise of Ezekiel 36:25–27 is in view:

> **36:25** I will sprinkle pure water over you and you will be clean from all your uncleanness; I will purify you from all your idols. **36:26** I will give you a new heart, and I will put a new spirit within you; I will remove the heart of stone from your body and give you a heart of flesh. **36:27** I will put my spirit within you, and I will make you walk in my statutes and keep my ordinances, and you will do them.

This is the promise of the new birth, as Jesus explained it to Nicodemus, and as Paul now explains it as the work of God in saving His people, accomplished by the applicatory work of the Spirit. Removing a "heart of stone" and giving a "heart of flesh" is surely a work rightly styled a "new beginning, renewal." And so the work of regeneration and renewal that makes salvation the present reality in the believer is just as fully divine and God-centered as all that has come before. Here Paul is describing the *means* by which He has saved.

There is much discussion concerning exactly how the four nouns (all genitives) in the chain are to be related to one another. The most basic way would be to speak of the "washing of regeneration" as one group and the "renewing of [or "by"] the Holy Spirit" as the second. But this would create two "actions." Instead, both here and in John 3:5, one work is in view, and it is accomplished *en toto* by the Spirit. That is, in John 3:5, being born "of water and the Spirit" does not refer to two separate events, and here in Titus 3:5 "washing of regeneration" and "renewal" are *both* works accomplished by the work of the third person of the Trinity. The death of Christ provides the basis upon which forgiveness and cleansing can be accomplished: the Spirit then applies that work in the individual life of the believer in the washing of regeneration, the creation of a new creature in Christ, who is likewise renewed. Knight's insightful exegesis concludes:

> Therefore, in Tit. 3:5 Paul considers this inner transformation from two different perspectives in a manner analogous to Ezk. 36:25–27 and 1 Cor. 6:11. He arranges the four genitive nouns chiastically with the most distinguishable terms first and last and with the terms for the result, the transformation, in the center. The first pair of genitives focuses on the need for cleansing from past sin: "washing" and a word that speaks of that washing as an inner transformation, a "new beginning." . . . The second pair focuses on the new life received and to be lived: The "Holy Spirit," the giver and sustainer of the new life, must do his work *within* Christians and so is joined to a word that speaks of such a new life as an inner transformation, "renewal."[8]

This God-centered proclamation of the work of the Spirit in applying the salvation won by Christ flows directly from the text, yet due to the impact of tradition upon the thinking of so many, a completely foreign concept is normally read into the passage. Instead of seeing "washing" as a necessary action of the Spirit in applying the redemption of Christ, the human action of baptism is inserted into the divine work as if this was the very means of the application of the work of God in Christ. Despite the popularity of such a view, the text provides no reason to leap from the idea of God mercifully saving to the idea that He does so through the means of the "sacrament of baptism." And what is more, the context immediately flows onward in its God-centered course, leaving no hint of the insertion of a human action that becomes the physical channel through which a divine act is accomplished. In fact,

[8]Ibid., 343–44.

the summary statement of verse 7 further militates against inserting baptism into the passage, as we will see.

3:6

> . . . whom he poured out on us in full measure through Jesus Christ our Savior.

NA[27] Text:
. . . οὗ ἐξέχεεν ἐφ' ἡμᾶς πλουσίως διὰ Ἰησοῦ Χριστοῦ τοῦ σωτῆρος ἡμῶν.

Here the Holy Spirit is said to be poured out upon believers "in full measure." There is no limitation in the Spirit's presence, as if His activity could be divided and subdivided. The Spirit, who renews in verse 5, is "poured out" upon believers (but only through Jesus Christ our Savior). The use of such a term, "poured," within only six words of λουτρόν, would be highly unusual *if* it was Paul's intention to switch, midsentence, from the work of the Spirit to a physical act, and then move back to the Spirit's work in the lives of believers. If the "washing" of verse 5 is baptism, are we to believe that the "pouring" of the Spirit is likewise somehow to be connected with the same concept?

There is somewhat of a reciprocity indicated by the prepositions in Paul's presentation: God saves on the basis of His mercy, and he does so "through" (διὰ) the work of the Spirit in regeneration and renewal, and the Spirit is poured out on believers "through" (διὰ) Jesus Christ our Savior. One cannot help but see the progression:

God our Savior (the Father)
His love appears (the incarnation of the Son)
Redemption applied by the Spirit
The Spirit poured out through Jesus Christ
Christ is called "our Savior," the same term used of the Father initially.

Truly redemption is a Triune activity, all to the honor and glory of Father, Son, and Spirit!

3:7

And so, since we have been justified by his grace, we become heirs with the confident expectation of eternal life.

NA*[27] *Text:

ἵνα δικαιωθέντες τῇ ἐκείνου χάριτι κληρονόμοι γενηθῶμεν κατ᾽ ἐλπίδα ζωῆς αἰωνίου.

The NET takes verse 7, which is the conclusion of a single sentence, and sets it off as its own sentence, making it a summary statement to the preceding verses. Many other translations use "so that, having been justified" as their connective. In either case, we find in this passage a clear parallel to Romans 5:1, which we likewise already saw functions as a summary and transition statement. Both use the aorist participle, δικαιωθέντες. Here Paul and his audience can look back upon their justification (just as in Romans 5:1).

In Romans 5:1 we are said to have been justified "by faith," and here it is "by His grace." Paul is not teaching two different methods of justification. He uses δικαιωθέντες three times: Romans 5:1 (justified by faith), 5:9 (justified by Christ's blood), and here (justified by grace). Faith, the blood of Christ, and grace are not three differing grounds of justification, and when the fact that the faith that saves is a gift from God is recognized, we can see that Paul is perfectly consistent. In each instance, we are justified on the basis of something that is divinely perfect in nature and utterly outside anything that could be called human merit.

The phrase δικαιωθέντες τῇ ἐκείνου χάριτι ("having been justified by His grace") is vital. That justification is accomplished on the basis of *grace* (paralleling "mercy" in 3:5) is important in further establishing the truth of the main assertion we have already made regarding Paul's use of this term: it is a gracious act on the part of God that is by nature free and outside the control of man. Grace is not merely a helping power, but is instead the very power of God accomplishing what man not only does not deserve, but de-merits. Grace admits of no mixture of man's works (Romans 11:6), no human merit, nothing that could demand a response on God's part as God "mercies" whom He will (Romans 9:15); God "graces" freely and outside of the control of man. The Christian who looks back upon his or her justification can *never* say "that act took place due to the cooperation of God's grace and my actions" any more than they can say "I was justified by the blood of Christ *plus* these actions done in righteousness" (or "a state of grace").

The NET renders this entire phrase in a very confident manner, expressing the conditional sentence in a strong and positive fashion. The reader should remember that the conclusion, "we become heirs with the confident expectation of eternal life," flows from the divine act of justification by grace. *Since* we have been justified by His grace, *as a result* we become heirs with confident expectation of eternal life. *Only* the justified, and *all* of the justified, have this promise of being heirs, and *only* these can have the true hope of eternal life.

BIBLIOGRAPHY

Adamson, James. "The Epistle of James." In *The New International Commentary on the New Testament.* Grand Rapids: Eerdmans, 1976.

Bainton, Roland. *Here I Stand.* Nashville: Abingdon Press, 1978.

Bauer, Walter. *A Greek-English Lexicon of the New Testament and Other Early Christian Literature.* 3rd ed. Edited and revised by Frederick William Danker. Chicago: University of Chicago Press, 2000.

Beckwith, Roger. *The Old Testament Canon of the New Testament Church.* Grand Rapids: Eerdmans, 1985.

Berkhof, Louis. *Systematic Theology.* Grand Rapids: Eerdmans, 1982.

Boice, James Montgomery. "Galatians." In *The Expositor's Bible Commentary.* Grand Rapids: Zondervan, 1976.

Bruce, F.F. "Commentary on Galatians." In *New International Greek Testament Commentary.* Grand Rapids: Eerdmans, 1982.

Buchanan, James. *The Doctrine of Justification.* Carlisle, Pa.: Banner of Truth Trust, 1984.

Burton, Ernest D. "A Critical and Exegetical Commentary on the Epistle to the Galatians." In *The International Critical Commentary.* Edinburgh: T&T Clark, 1988.

Calvin, John. "Commentary on Galatians," *The Comprehensive John Calvin Collection* (CD-ROM), Ages Digital Library, Rio, WI, 1999, 3:6.

———. "Commentary on the Epistle to the Ephesians," *The Comprehensive John Calvin Collection* (CD-ROM), Ages Digital Library, Rio, WI, 1999.

———. *Institutes of the Christian Religion* (CD-ROM), Ages Digital Library, Rio, WI, 1999.

———. "Sermons on Galatians," *The Comprehensive John Calvin Collection* (CD-ROM), Ages Digital Library, Rio, WI, 1999, Sermon 3.

Cranfield, C.E.B. *Romans, A Shorter Commentary.* Grand Rapids: Eerdmans, 1985.

———. "Romans." In *The International Critical Commentary.* Edinburgh: T&T Clark, 1980.

Davids, Peter. "The Epistle of James." In *The New International Greek Testament Commentary.* Grand Rapids: Eerdmans, 1982.

Dunn, James D.G. "Romans 1–8." In *The Word Biblical Commentary.* Waco, Tex.: Word, 1988.

Edwards, Jonathan. *Justification by Faith Alone.* Morgan, Pa.: Soli Deo Gloria, 2000.

Fee, Gordon. *1 and 2 Timothy, Titus.* New International Biblical Commentary, vol. 13. Peabody, Mass.: Hendrickson, 1988.

Fitzmyer, Joseph A. "Romans." In *The Anchor Bible.* Garden City: Doubleday, 1992.

Fung, Ronald Y. K. "Justification in the Epistle of James." In *Right With God: Justification in the Bible and the World,* edited by D.A. Carson. Grand Rapids: World Evangelical Fellowship, 1992.

———. "The Epistle to the Galatians." In *The New International Commentary on the New Testament.* Grand Rapids: Eerdmans, 1988.

Harrison, Everett F. "Romans." In *The Expositor's Bible Commentary.*

Grand Rapids: Zondervan, 1976.

Hendriksen, William. "1 & 2 Timothy & Titus." *Exposition of Thessalonians, the Pastorals, and Hebrews.* Grand Rapids: Baker Book House, 1989.

———. "Ephesians." *Exposition of Galatians, Ephesians, Philippians, Colossians, and Philemon.* Grand Rapids: Baker Book House, 1989.

———. *Exposition of Galatians.* Grand Rapids: Baker Book House, 1968.

———. "Galatians." *Exposition of Galatians, Ephesians, Philippians, Colossians, and Philemon.* Grand Rapids: Baker Book House, 1989.

Hillerbrand, Hans. *The Reformation.* Grand Rapids: Baker Book House, 1987.

Hodge, Charles. *A Commentary on 1&2 Corinthians.* In *Geneva Commentary Series.* Carlisle, Pa.: Banner of Truth, 1983.

———. *Commentary on the Epistle to the Romans.* Grand Rapids: Eerdmans, 1983.

———. *Systematic Theology.* Grand Rapids: Eerdmans, 1986.

Hodges, Zane. *The Epistle of James.* Irving, Tex.: Grace Evangelical Society, 1994.

The Jerome Biblical Commentary. Raymond E. Brown, Joseph A. Fitzmyer, and Roland E. Murphy, eds. Englewood Cliffs, NJ: Prentice-Hall, 1968.

Johnson, Luke Timothy. *The Letter of James: A New Translation with Introduction and* . Garden City: Doubleday, 1995.

Knight III, George. "The Pastoral Epistles." In *The New International Greek Testament Commentary.* Grand Rapids: Eerdmans, 1992.

Lightfoot, J.B. *The Epistle of St. Paul to the Galatians.* Peabody, Mass: Hendrickson, 1981.

Longenecker, Richard N. "Galatians." In *Word Biblical Commentary.* Waco, Tex.: Word, 1990.

Luther, Martin. *Commentary on Romans.* Grand Rapids: Kregel Publications, 1985.

———. *Commentary on Galatians.* Grand Rapids: Kregel Publications, 1979.

MacArthur, John. "Galatians." In *The MacArthur New Testament Commentary*. Chicago: Moody Press, 1987.

———. "Romans 1–8." In *The MacArthur New Testament Commentary*. Chicago: Moody Press, 1991.

Martin, Ralph. "James." In *Word Biblical Commentary*. Nashville: Word, 1988.

Martyn, J. Louis. "Galatians: A New Translation with Introduction and Commentary." In *The Anchor Bible*. Garden City: Doubleday, 1997.

Mayor, Joseph. *The Epistle of James*. Grand Rapids: Kregel Publications, 1990.

McGrath, Alistair. *Iustitia Dei: A History of the Christian Doctrine of Justification*. New York: Cambridge University Press, 1998.

Metzger, Bruce. *A Textual Commentary on the Greek New Testament*. New York: United Bible Societies, 1975.

Moo, Douglas. "The Epistle of James." In *Pillar New Testament Commentary*. Grand Rapids: Eerdmans, 2000.

———. "The Epistle to the Romans." *The New International Commentary on the New Testament*. Grand Rapids: Eerdmans, 1996.

———. "The Letter of James." In *Tyndale New Testament Commentaries*. Grand Rapids: Eerdmans, 1985.

Morris, Leon. *Galatians: Paul's Charter of Christian Freedom*. Downers Grove, Ill.: InterVarsity Press, 1996.

———. *New Testament Theology*. Grand Rapids: Zondervan, 1986.

———. *The Apostolic Preaching of the Cross*. pp.208–210. Grand Rapids: Eerdmans, 1983.

———. *The Epistle to the Romans*. Grand Rapids: Eerdmans, 1988.

Moulton, James Hope and George Milligan. *The Vocabulary of the Greek Testament*. Grand Rapids: Eerdmans, 1930.

Murray, John. *The Epistle to the Romans*. Grand Rapids: Eerdmans, 1997.

———. *Redemption Accomplished and Applied*. p.117. Grand Rapids: Eerdmans, 1955.

Nicoll, W. Robertson. "Romans." In *The Expositor's Greek Testament*. Grand Rapids: Eerdmans, 1983.

Reymond, Robert. *A New Systematic Theology of the Christian Faith*. Nashville: Thomas Nelson, 1998.

Robertson, A.T. *Word Pictures in the New Testament.* Vol. IV. Grand Rapids: Baker Book House, n.d.

Sanday, William and Arthur Headlam. "A Critical and Exegetical Commentary on the Epistle to the Romans." In *The International Critical Commentary.* Edinburgh: T&T Clark, 1980.

Schreiner, Thomas R. "Romans." In *Baker Exegetical Commentary on the New Testament.* Grand Rapids: Baker Book House, 1998.

Sproul, R.C. *The Holiness of God.* Wheaton, Ill.: Tyndale, 1986.

Trench, Richard C. *Synonyms of the New Testament.* Grand Rapids: Eerdmans, 1983.

Wallace, Daniel. *Greek Grammar Beyond the Basics.* Grand Rapids: Zondervan, 1996.

Warfield, Benjamin Breckenridge. "The Biblical Doctrine of Faith." In *The Works of Benjamin B. Warfield.* Vol. II. Grand Rapids: Baker Book House, 1981. p.504.

Subject Index

J

K

L

M

N

O

P

R

T

U

V

W

Y

Scripture Index

Thank you for selecting a book from
BETHANY HOUSE PUBLISHERS

Bethany House Publishers is a ministry of Bethany Fellowship International, an interdenominational, nonprofit organization committed to spreading the Good News of Jesus Christ around the world through evangelism, church planting, literature distribution, and care for those in need. Missionary training is offered through Bethany College of Missions.

Bethany Fellowship International is a member of the National Association of Evangelicals and subscribes to its statement of faith. If you would like further information, please contact:

Bethany Fellowship International
6820 Auto Club Road
Minneapolis, MN 55438 USA